Dharma Rain

DHARMA RAIN

*

Sources of Buddhist Environmentalism

—————— *Edited by* ——————

STEPHANIE KAZA *and* KENNETH KRAFT

SHAMBHALA

Boston & London

2000

Shambhala Publications, Inc.
Horticultural Hall
300 Massachusetts Avenue
Boston, MA 02115
www.shambhala.com

9   8   7   6   5   4   3   2

Printed in the United States of America

⊗ This edition is printed on acid-free paper that meets the American National
Standards Institute z39.48 Standard.

Distributed in the United States by Random House, Inc., and in Canada by
Random House of Canada Ltd

Library of Congress Cataloging-in-Publication Data

Dharma rain: sources of Buddhist environmentalism/edited by
Stephanie Kaza and Kenneth Kraft.
p.   cm.
ISBN 1-57062-475-5 (pbk.)
1. Human ecology—Religious aspects—Buddhism.   2. Nature—
Religious aspects—Buddhism.   3. Environmental responsibility.
4. Environmental ethics.   5. Buddhist ethics.   6. Buddhism—Social
aspects.   I. Kaza, Stephanie, 1947–   II. Kraft, Kenneth, 1949–   .
BQ4570.E23D49   2000   99-34712
294.3'378362—dc21   CIP

CONTENTS

✿

✿

❋

❋

❊

PART SEVEN: PASSAGES FOR CEREMONIES AND DAILY PRACTICE

EDITORS' NOTE

THE SELECTIONS AND TRANSLATIONS in this anthology originate from numerous cultures, languages, and periods. As a result,
the reader will notice differences in stylistic conventions such as capital-
ization and the romanization of Chinese. Diacritical marks on all non-
English words have been removed.

Dharma Rain

INTRODUCTION

✳

THE SCALE OF THE ENVIRONMENTAL CRISIS now goes beyond any individual's capacity to imagine it. Local losses touch every corner—a beloved tree taken down, a swimming hole polluted, the town woods cleared for a mall. Checkerboard patterns carve up mountain slopes, dead fish float on poisoned lakes, neighborhoods give way to urban sprawl. As the damage deepens, the suffering spreads. People around the world struggle for access to clean water and safe food. Some fear that even the global systems of air and ocean circulation are gyrating out of balance. Who can accurately assess the gravity of this unprecedented situation? Governments have yet to demonstrate the intention, much less the ability, to address these multidimensional problems. Religious traditions have been caught similarly unprepared.

At the turn of the millennium, Buddhism and other world religions are being asked to come forward with relevant teachings and take a stand against global ecological destruction. Leading environmentalists have made it clear that the dilemmas we face cannot be solved solely by technological, political, or economic means. Spiritual traditions will also have a critical role in collaborative efforts to stem the tide of devastation.

This book is in part a response to that challenge. The title *Dharma Rain* alludes to the *Lotus Sutra*, where the Dharma—the true nature of reality, taught by Shakyamuni Buddha—is compared to a beneficent rain that nourishes all beings. In a time when the very health of the planet is threatened, such cool and refreshing waters may still serve as an elixir of possibility.

Buddhist environmentalism draws from both old and new sources. Rooted in Buddhist heritage, it is a distinctively modern movement and path of practice. Gathered here for the first time are classic Buddhist texts, modern commentaries, resources for ecologically oriented spiritual practice, and guidelines for action. Respected teachers, front-line activists, and concerned scholars explore the many dimensions of Buddhism's encounter with environmentalism. The selections offer a diversity of Asian and Western voices representing the three main streams of Buddhism—Theravada, Mahayana, and Vajrayana.

From the tropics of South and Southeast Asia, to the temperate zones of China and Japan, to the snowy mountain passes of the Himalayas, Buddhism has evolved in a wide range of ecological contexts. Over the course of this history, teachings about nature and human-nature relations have varied considerably. The earliest texts contain admonitions to treat plants, animals, and water with respect. They emphasize the principle of nonharming, or *ahimsa*, as the cardinal ethical precept. Centuries later, Mahayana traditions developed the ideal of the bodhisattva—one dedicated to enlightenment who vows to relieve the suffering of all beings. Several schools of Buddhism, in East Asia especially, refined an understanding of nature as relational, each phenomenon dependent on a multitude of causes and conditions.

Throughout these diverse cultural and natural settings, Buddhism consistently holds that liberation from suffering is achieved through awareness. In traditional terms, the aspiration to enlightenment is a crucial first step. Deep realization of the Buddha Way requires sustained effort, moment by moment, day after day. For many of the works presented here, awakening remains the primary focus. Others explore the elements and teachings of the natural world, but with little or no emphasis on human responsibilities toward nature.

Nonetheless, contemporary Buddhists are raising new questions relevant to today's world. What does it mean to practice during a time of environmental crisis? What are the spiritual and moral dimensions of the ecocrisis? Different ways of answering these questions appear in the following pages. Today, liberation from suffering through awareness may have new meanings beyond individual transformation. Engaged spiritual practice can evolve into political actions that call for structural change. It is possible to imagine "enlightened" institutions or even "enlightened" social systems. How might the practice of liberation find expression in an ecological context? The affinities between spiritual awakening and ecological awakening are just beginning to be explored.

In recent decades, Buddhists around the world have responded creatively to environmental problems. The Dalai Lama, the exiled religious and secular leader of Tibet, proposes to turn Tibet into an ecological preserve. In Thailand, monks ritually ordain trees to save threatened forests. In North America, the roots of Buddhist environmentalism can be traced to the 1950s when Gary Snyder, Zen student and poet, began to make connections between Buddhist training and ecological activism. Members of the Beat generation and the sixties counterculture continued to explore those links, asserting that spiritual vision and moral leadership were necessary to halt planetwide ecological destruction. In the 1970s the environmental movement swelled, and Buddhist centers put down firm roots in the United States. In places these developments intersected: groups such as Green Gulch Zen Center outside San Francisco set up organic farms and gardens. The Buddhist Peace Fellowship, founded in 1978, gave prominence to environmental concerns on its activist agenda.

By the 1980s Buddhist leaders were explicitly addressing the ecocrisis and incorporating ecological awareness in their teaching. The Vietnamese peace activist and Zen monk Thich Nhat Hanh spoke of "interbeing" using ecological examples. Zen teacher Robert Aitken in Hawaii examined the Buddhist precepts from an environmental perspective. Joanna Macy creatively synthesized elements of Buddhism and deep ecology, challenging colleagues and students to take their insights into direct action.

In 1990 Middlebury College in Vermont hosted a conference on Spirit and Nature where the Dalai Lama stressed his commitment to protection of the environment. At the 1993 World Parliament of Religions in Chicago, when Buddhists gathered with Hindus, Muslims, pagans, Jews, Jains, and Christians from all over the world, a top agenda item was the role of religion in responding to the environmental crisis. Parallel interest in the academic community culminated in ten major Religion and Ecology conferences at Harvard University, with the intention of defining a new academic field. The first of these conferences, convened in 1996, inaugurated the field of Buddhism and ecology. At the start of a new century, we stand at a remarkable vantage point, drawing widely from the plenitude of Buddhist traditions as we prepare to respond to the unprecedented challenges ahead.

❊

Dharma Rain is divided into seven sections. Each section stands independently yet reflects the concerns and ideas developed throughout the book.

Part One, "Teachings from Buddhist Traditions," introduces sutras (scriptures) and other religious works from India, China, Japan, and Tibet. The passages are organized around three themes: reverence for life, nature as teacher or refuge, and the nature of nature. The diversity of cultural contexts and genres is immediately apparent, as these are samples from an immense body of literature. One early text is a demanding guide for monks choosing the path of solitary forest practice. Selections from the *Jataka* tales depict the Buddha as selflessly compassionate in his former lives. Shantideva, an eighth-century Indian monk, expounds the bodhisattva vow to save all beings. Chinese poet Han-shan proclaims the contemplative virtues of living close to nature. Several authors attest to the vast dimensions of interdependence—as direct experience and cardinal concept. Nearly a third of this section consists of poetry, often the preferred medium for expressing religious truths and nature's beauty.

Part Two, "Contemporary Interpretations of the Teachings," presents twentieth-century Buddhist thinkers who are addressing the ecocrisis and reexamining Buddhist tradition in light of that crisis. Classic doctrines become avenues to fresh understanding; time-tested teachings find new forms of expression. Gary Snyder investigates "mountains walking," an ancient Zen expression of nonduality, and plunges deep into the logging culture of the Pacific Northwest. Thich Nhat Hanh outlines the interpenetrating dimensions of interbeing. Joanna Macy commends an approach to Buddhist practice that is "focused less on the annihilation of the self than on the experience of extension into and through other beings, in wider and wider circles." In an era when scientists contest definitions of life at the molecular level, William LaFleur revives the longstanding debate within Buddhism on whether or not plants are sentient beings. Collectively, these reinterpretations demonstrate that contemporary Buddhism is in the midst of a historic shift toward deeper engagement with the world.

Part Three, "Buddhism in the World," takes a hard look at the environmental realities facing Buddhist (and formerly Buddhist) countries today. From the deforestation of teak forests in Thailand to uranium mining in Tibet, ecosystems in Buddhist Asia are in serious trouble. Thailand's leading Buddhist activist, Sulak Sivaraksa, offers a sharp critique of Western approaches to economic development. Prayudh Payutto addresses the three poisons of greed, hate, and delusion that drive "the religion of the market." Wildlife photographer Galen Rowell exposes the rapid ecological deterioration of Tibet since the Chinese invasion. Tree-ordination ceremonies, ecology walks, and grassroots protests highlight the need for new avenues of engagement and religious practice. As the Dalai Lama and others attest, urgent action on behalf of the environment is needed not only in Asia but also throughout the world.

Part Four, "Environmental Activism as Buddhist Practice," considers the challenges of integrating ecological awareness, spiritual development, and political activism. From tree-sitters in ancient redwoods to citizens tracking nuclear-waste shipments, people in many walks of life are exploring new paths of engaged spirituality. How can Buddhism support these well-intentioned actions? And how can such actions become extensions of spiritual practice?

In the first essays, teachers representing a number of Buddhist lineages show how nonharming, compassion, service, and self-restraint belong at the center of any engagement. Philip Kapleau and Chögyam Trungpa attest that even in the midst of adversity and pressure, Buddhist methods of mindful attention and nondualistic perception help to strengthen spiritual insight. Authors Joanna Macy and Christopher Titmuss, addressing the dangers of despair and burnout, urge a view born of long-term practice. Since many ecological problems will not be solved in our lifetimes, commitment must be sustained more by equanimity than anxiety. In the second group of readings, activists for forest defense, animal rights, and responsible nuclear-waste management tell of their efforts to carry the bodhisattva vow into the field, defending sentient beings with compassion.

Part Five, "Home Practice, Wild Practice," focuses on practice with nature, represented both by encounters in the wild and by daily life at home. Contemporary Buddhists describe experiments in backpacking retreats, bush practice, and mall walking. They find that meditation practice can inform ecological awareness, affording a deepened sense of the earth that goes beyond scientific or economic views. For writers Peter Matthiessen and Patrick McMahon, insight is linked to the experience of seeking solace in wilderness. Zen practitioner Wendy Johnson brings Buddhist environmentalism down to earth in her organic garden, meeting the challenges of pests, rot, and seed protection. As global pressures for food and water increase, choosing what to eat involves myriad ethical decisions. Gary Snyder and other writers explore the complexities of food choices in light of the first precept's injunction: cause no unnecessary harm.

Part Six, "Challenges in Buddhist Thought and Action," takes up some of the intellectual and practical problems of developing an environmental Buddhism. Some people regard Buddhism as the most "green" of the major world religions. Yet this favorable view overlooks internal philosophical conflicts and significant gaps between theory and practice. William Ophuls evaluates Buddhist politics and economics for alternatives to resource-exploiting capitalism. Rita Gross offers a potentially controversial analysis of population and consumption issues. Bill Devall and Robert Aitken challenge the capacity of socially engaged Buddhism to deal with structural systemic violence toward the earth. How can insight be translated into compassionate action? Do Buddhist principles support liberation for institutions as well as individuals? What are the moral implications, the "eco-karma," of actions that affect the environment? This section pushes Buddhist environmentalism toward self-critique, deepening the complexity of the conversation.

Part Seven, "Passages for Ceremonies and Daily Practice," presents guided meditations, ecologically oriented adaptations of traditional verses, and other resources for individual and group practice. As Buddhism meets environmentalism in Asia and the West, forms of practice are steadily evolving. In the last ten years, Earth Day celebrations, solstice and equinox rites, and grief rituals for environmental losses have become part of the ceremonial landscape in American Buddhist culture. Original verses by Thich Nhat Hanh and Robert Aitken encourage mindful awareness of ecological processes in everyday activity. Gary Snyder's "Smokey the Bear Sutra" fuses ancient and modern paradigms of protection on behalf of the world's ecosystems. As increasing numbers of people address the environmental crisis, the need for new practice forms will undoubtedly grow. This collection from diverse sources, the first of its kind, points to the emergence of an entirely new genre of ecospiritual material.

*

The Dharma rain of Buddhism has nourished many watersheds and bioregions since the Buddha first walked the earth 2,500 years ago. As a new century opens, the goals of liberation from suffering and freedom through awakening are as valid as ever; now they must be actualized in new lands and contexts. Buddhism is not the only or necessarily the best path for dealing with the environmental crisis. Politics, community organizing, and moral leadership from all religious traditions will be required to resist the forces causing planetwide ecological devastation. In conjunction with these efforts, committed practitioners of nonharming can serve as inspiration for others who are trying to move away from destructive practices. If Buddhist ideas continue to gain favor in Western culture, they have the potential to influence decision-makers of diverse persuasions. Informed by a Buddhist perspective, academics, public-policy analysts, and poets may bring fresh insights to once-intractable problems. There are many roles for those who speak for the earth with compassion and wisdom.

It has been said that every generation has its great work. For the generations of today, caring for the environment may be that fateful task. As the fires of greed and ignorance continue to rage across the landscape, our descendants will face the enormous challenge of reshaping human-nature relations. *Dharma Rain* is dedicated especially to young people, who will carry these ideas and practices into the future. May this book, and the efforts of everyone who contributed to it, help coming generations bring fresh life and promise to the earth and all beings.

PART ONE

✳

TEACHINGS *from* BUDDHIST TRADITIONS

The rain falls everywhere,
coming down on all four sides.
Its flow and saturation are measureless,
reaching to every area of the earth,
to the ravines and valleys of the mountains and streams,
to the remote and secluded places where grow
plants, bushes, medicinal herbs,
trees large and small,
a hundred grains, rice seedlings,
sugar cane, grape vines.
The rain moistens them all;
none fails to receive its full share.

—*Lotus Sutra*

INTRODUCTION

❊

THE IDEAS AND PRACTICES HANDED DOWN by Shakyamuni Buddha and his followers contain teachings of profound relevance for those who care for the earth. From the earliest stories of the Buddha's previous lives to the finely honed koans of Zen, many Dharma texts offer wise guidance for living in right relation with nature. The classic passages in this section are a small sample from an immense body of writing that spans 2,500 years of history and dozens of cultures.

The initial selections demonstrate reverence for life, often expressed in terms of nonharming or nonviolence (*ahimsa*). The first Buddhist precept, "Do not kill," is at the same time an ethical standard, an intrinsic worldview, and a disposition to be cultivated. In "Dwelling in the Forest," the Buddha advises solitary monks to live in a way that is attentive to the other beings of the forest. A fifth-century Indian monk, Buddhagosa, uses the story of a wounded tree-spirit to establish the precept not to harm plants and trees. Another early text, again in the words of the Buddha, advocates an attitude of friendliness even toward poisonous snakes, who may then be friendly in return.

Two *Jataka* tales, from a popular genre with pre-Buddhist origins, depict the Buddha-to-be in his previous lives. In one, a lowly clump of grass saves a tree from a carpenter's axe; in the other, a rabbit sacrifices himself as food for a poor traveler, throwing his body onto a fire "as joyfully as a bird drops into a bed of lotuses." In manifesting their compassion, both the grass and the rabbit are on their way to becoming Buddha.

In the Theravada tradition of Buddhism, a devotee practices self-restraint and consideration for others; in the Mahayana tradition, followers aspire to liberate all beings from suffering. The following selections reveal that on the subject of compassion the two streams have much in common. In the *Metta Sutta*, recited by Theravada monks and lay adherents alike, the source of loving-kindness is a boundless heart: "Even as a mother protects with her life her child, her only child, so with a boundless heart should one cherish all living beings." A selection from an influential Mahayana text, the *Hua-yen Sutra*, extends the domain of compassion to all manner of beings, even those "without thoughts or form."

A bodhisattva is one who aspires to enlightenment for the sake of others. This ideal achieves full expression in the spiritually impassioned poetry of the eighth-century monk Shantideva, who vows to "always support the life of all the boundless creatures." Dedicating himself completely to the path of compassion, Shantideva takes upon himself the burdens of others' suffering. The revered Tibetan master Milarepa uses Dharma teachings, sung in poetic verses, to pacify a violent hunter and his ferocious dog. This account infers that the natural world responds in some mysterious way to human intention and morality.

The historical Buddha lived and taught in the company of nature and experienced his great awakening under a large fig tree. In the second set of selections, nature shines forth as teacher, companion, and source of refuge. For Buddhists throughout Asia, the natural world not only expresses truth directly, it also points metaphorically to the richness and generosity of Dharma teachings. The *Lotus Sutra* figuratively describes the Buddha's teachings as rain. Just as rain falls everywhere, the Buddha looks upon all things "as being universally equal." Yet in the midst of this equality, people vary in their spiritual capacities. Just as plants of varying sizes receive moisture as needed, the Buddha offers teachings to serve the needs of his listeners.

The *Hua-yen Sutra* asks: If the truth is one, how can there be so many different teachings in so many languages? Again, answers are found in metaphors from nature: one ocean that travels in myriad waves, one wind that blows everywhere, one sun that shines in all directions. Mahakashyapa, a principal disciple of the Buddha, extols the pleasures of practice amid nature, surpassed only by the joy of true insight. Across a span of many centuries and cultures, the Chinese poet Han-shan withdraws to Cold Mountain and finds nothing lacking:

As for me, I delight in the everyday Way,
Among mist-wrapped vines and rocky caves.

Here in the wilderness I am completely free,
With my friends, the white clouds, idling forever.

For three Japanese haiku poets, nature is at once intimately familiar and infinitely mysterious. Although these writers may not formally qualify as Buddhist poets, their work is steeped in Buddhist perceptions of nature.

But what exactly is the meaning of nature for Buddhists? The answer is complex, for there is neither a single Buddhist philosophy of nature nor a universally shared experience of nature. The third set of selections, "The Nature of Nature," begins with the Buddhist teaching of interdependence: all phenomena depend on all other phenomena for their existence. As an aid to understanding this central concept, the Chinese scholar-monk Tu-shun envisions the radiant Net of Indra, in which multifaceted jewels reflect one another ad infinitum. Eighth-century Chinese Ch'an (Zen) master Shih-t'ou marvels at the perfect interlocking of essence and particularity, "as a lid fits its box." Myoe, a thirteenth-century Japanese monk who liked to meditate in trees, writes an unusual "Letter to the Island" in which personal declarations of fondness are interspersed with Buddhist teachings.

The final two selections are by the early Japanese Zen masters Dogen (1200–1253) and Daito (1282–1337), who founded lineages that remain influential today. For both masters, the reality of nature is synonymous with the nature of reality. In the realm of nonduality, mountains and human beings are not separate. Dogen points to this dimension when he declares, "Green mountains are always walking." For Daito, a surprise rainshower becomes a fresh experience of oneness with the moment: "I'll just use the rain as my raincoat."

These explorations of the Buddhist canon are merely a beginning. Many sutras, commentaries, and other seminal works have yet to be reviewed for their potential environmental significance. Whatever the future of an ecologically oriented Buddhism, the process of identifying and assessing historical roots will surely continue. The works presented here suggest that those roots have the strength to support many more seasons of growth.

REVERENCE FOR LIFE

✳

Dwelling in the Forest

MAHARATNAKUTA SUTRA

THEN MAHAKASHYAPA asked the Buddha, "World-Honored One, some monks declare themselves to be forest-dwelling monks. World-Honored One, how should a monk act to be called a forest-dwelling monk? How should a monk act to be called a food-begging monk? How should a monk act to be called one who wears a garment of cast-off rags? How should a monk act to be called one who dwells under a tree? How should a monk act to be called one who wanders in a graveyard? How should a monk act to be called one who lives in the open air?"

The Buddha replied to Kashyapa, "A forest-dwelling monk must delight in a secluded forest and live in it. Kashyapa, a secluded place is a place where there are no loud noises and no deer, tigers, wolves, flying birds, robbers, cowherds, or shepherds. Such a place is suitable for a *sramana*'s Dharma practice. Therefore, such a monk should devote himself to Dharma practice in a secluded place.

"A monk should think of eight things if he wishes to live in a secluded place. What are the eight?

To renounce the body;
to renounce life;
to relinquish material possessions;

The *Maharatnakuta Sutra* is composed of forty-nine Mahayana sutras. The text was collated and rendered in Chinese by the sixth-century monk Bodhiruchi. Translation by Garma C. C. Chang.

to leave all beloved places;
to die on a mountain, like a deer;
to perform the deeds of a forest-dweller when in a secluded place;
to live by the Dharma; and
not to abide in afflictions.

Kashyapa, a monk who wishes to live in a secluded forest should contemplate these eight things, and then he should go to a secluded place.

"Kashyapa, after a forest-dwelling monk arrives at a secluded place, he should follow the Dharma of a forest-dweller and perform eight deeds to show kindness for all sentient beings. What are the eight?

To benefit sentient beings;
to gladden sentient beings;
not to hate sentient beings;
to be straightforward;
not to discriminate among sentient beings;
to be compliant with sentient beings;
to contemplate all dharmas; and
to be as pure as space.

Kashyapa, a forest-dwelling monk should perform these eight deeds to show kindness for all sentient beings.

"Kashyapa, when a forest-dwelling monk arrives at a secluded place, he should think, 'I have come to this remote place alone, with no companion. No one teaches or rebukes me, whether I practice virtue or nonvirtue.' He should think further, 'However, there are gods, dragons, ghosts, spirits, and Buddhas, the World-Honored Ones, who know that I apply my mind entirely to devotion. They can be my witnesses. Now I am here to practice what a forest-dweller should. If I bear malice, I shall not be free and at ease. Now I am in this remote place all alone; I associate closely with no one and have nothing to call my own. I should now beware of feelings of desire, hatred, annoyance, and so forth. I should not be like those who are fond of crowds or attached to villages. If I am, I shall be deceiving the gods, dragons, ghosts, and spirits; and the Buddhas will not like to see me. If I now follow the right practice of a forest-dweller, the gods, dragons, ghosts, and spirits will not upbraid me, and the Buddhas will be glad to see me.'

"Kashyapa, when a forest-dwelling monk lives in a secluded place, he should practice the right actions of a forest-dweller:

> to persist, with all his heart, in keeping the precepts leading to liberation;
>
> to maintain well the precepts of every category, and purify his own deeds, words, and thoughts;
>
> not to practice flattery or fraud;
>
> to earn his livelihood in a proper way;
>
> to keep his mind inclined to *dhyanas*;
>
> to memorize the Dharma he has heard;
>
> to cultivate right thought diligently;
>
> to move toward passionless, quiescent, and cessative nirvana;
>
> to be afraid of *samsara*;
>
> to regard the five aggregates as enemies, the four elements as poisonous snakes, and the six senses as uninhabited villages;
>
> to be adept in devising skillful means;
>
> to contemplate the twelve links of dependent origination in order to part with the views of eternalism and nihilism;
>
> to contemplate the emptiness of a sentient being, of a self, of a personal identity, and of a life;
>
> to understand that the dharmas are devoid of signs, and to practice signlessness;
>
> to decrease his actions gradually and to practice nonaction;
>
> to fear the activities of the three realms;
>
> always to practice the Dharma diligently, as if to save his head from being burned;
>
> always to strive with vigor and never regress;
>
> to contemplate the reality of the body, thinking and contemplating so as to know the origin of suffering, to sever the cause of suffering, to realize the cessation of suffering, and to cultivate assiduously the path leading to the cessation of suffering;
>
> to practice kindness;
>
> to abide securely in the four mindfulnesses;

to avoid unwholesome dharmas and enter the door to wholesome
   dharmas;
to establish himself in the four right efforts;
to master the four bases of miraculous powers;
to protect the five good roots and to have a command of the five
   powers;
to be awakened to the seven factors of enlightenment;
to practice the eightfold noble path industriously;
to develop *dhyana* and *samadhi*; and
to discriminate all the forms of dharmas by virtue of wisdom.

"Kashyapa, a forest-dwelling monk adorns himself with such doctrines. Having adorned himself in this way, he should live in a mountain
grove, and diligently cultivate the various practices even in the early and
late parts of the night without sleeping then. He should always be eager
to attain the supramundane Dharma.

"Kashyapa, a forest-dwelling monk should constantly cultivate the
path wherever he is; he should not decorate his body with fine clothes; he
should gather withered grass to cushion his seat; he should not take things
from resident or visiting monks. In a secluded place, a forest-dwelling
monk should, in order to practice the noble path, be content with any
garment which can cover his body.

"Kashyapa, if a forest-dwelling monk goes to a city or a village to
beg for food, he should think, 'I have come to this city or village from my
secluded place in order to beg for food; my mind should be neither depressed nor elated, whether I obtain food or not. Indeed, if I am not given
food, I should be content and regard it as the karmic retribution for deeds
in my previous lives, and from now on I should cultivate virtuous deeds
industriously.' Furthermore, he should remember that even the Tathagata
did not always acquire food when he begged for it.

"A forest-dwelling monk should adorn himself with the Dharma before he begs for food in a city or a village, and should go to beg only after
he has done so. How does he adorn himself with the Dharma? He should
not be contaminated with or attached to the sight of pleasant forms, nor
be angry at the sight of unpleasant forms, and likewise with pleasant or
unpleasant sounds, odors, tastes, textures, and dharmas. He should pro-

tect his sense organs from being attracted, and should gaze no farther than several feet ahead. He should control his mind well and keep in mind the Dharma he has contemplated. He should practice begging for food without defiling his mind with food. He should beg for food from door to door without feeling attachment to a place where he is given food or feeling aversion toward a place where he is not. If he obtains nothing after begging at ten or more houses, he should not be worried, and should think, 'These elders and brahmins do not give me food for many reasons. They have never even thought of me, not to speak of giving me food.' Kashyapa, a forest-dwelling monk will not be afraid when begging for food if he can think in this way.

"Kashyapa, if a forest-dwelling monk sees men, women, boys, girls, or animals when begging for food, he should have kindness and compassion toward them and think, 'I strive with vigor so that I can make the vow that sentient beings who see me and those who give me food will all be reborn in heaven.'

"Kashyapa, after a forest-dwelling monk obtains food, whether it is coarse or of high quality, he should look for poor people in the city or village and share half the food with them. If he does not see any poor people, he should think, 'I [mentally] give the best of the food I obtain to the sentient beings whom I do not see with my eyes. I am the donor and they are the recipients.'

"Kashyapa, a forest-dwelling monk should return to his secluded dwelling-place with the food given to him and wash his hands and feet. According to the pure rules of deportment for a *sramana*, he should arrange a seat with grass he has gathered, sit cross-legged on the seat, and eat without attachment, pride, hatred, or distraction. When he is about to eat, he should think, 'In my body, there are eighty thousand worms which will be secure and happy when they obtain the food I eat. Now I attract these worms to my following with food; but when I attain supreme enlightenment, I shall attract them to my following with the Dharma.'

"Kashyapa, when a forest-dwelling monk does not have enough to eat, he should think, 'Now that my body is light, I can cultivate patience, purify evils, and have less excrement and urine. My mind is light when my body is light. Therefore, I can sleep little and have no desire.' He should think in this way.

"Kashyapa, if a forest-dwelling monk is given much food, he should gladly put a handful of it on a clean rock, thinking, 'I give this to the birds and beasts that can eat it. I am the donor and they are the recipients.'

"Kashyapa, after eating, a forest-dwelling monk should wash and dry his bowl and rinse his hands and mouth. He should put away his patched robe and walk near his secluded place, pondering the forms of dharmas.

"Kashyapa, a forest-dwelling monk who is still an ordinary man and has not yet achieved the fruit of a *sramana* may be approached at times by tigers or wolves as he cultivates the practices of a forest-dweller. When he sees these beasts, he should not fear them, but should think, 'Since I came to this secluded place, I have relinquished my body and life; therefore, instead of being afraid, I should cultivate kindness and rid myself of all evils and fears. If tigers or wolves kill me and eat my flesh, I should think that I am greatly benefited, for I shall get rid of my fragile body and gain a stable one. I have no food to give to the tigers or wolves, but they will be comfortable and happy after they eat my flesh.' Kashyapa, a forest-dwelling monk should relinquish his body and life in this way when he follows the right practice of a forest-dweller.

"Kashyapa, when a forest-dwelling monk follows the right practice of a forest-dweller, nonhumans may come to his place in either beautiful or ugly forms. Toward such nonhumans, he should generate neither love nor hate.

"Kashyapa, if the gods who have met the Buddha come to the place of a forest-dwelling monk and bring up many questions, the monk should explain to them as best he can the doctrines which he has studied. If he cannot give an answer to a difficult question which a god puts to him, he should not become arrogant, but should say, 'I have not learned much, but do not despise me. From now on I shall cultivate and study the Buddha-Dharma more diligently, so that one day I may be thoroughly conversant with the Buddha-Dharma and able to answer all questions.' He should also urge the gods to preach, saying, 'Please explain the Dharma to me. I shall hear and accept it.' He should also say gratefully, 'May you not refuse my request!'

"Moreover, Kashyapa, a forest-dwelling monk who follows the right practice of a forest-dweller should cultivate well the thoughts of a forest-dweller: 'Just as grass, trees, tiles, and stones have no inner master, self, or owner, so it is with the body. There is no self, no life, no personal identity, no sentient being, no contention. The body arises from the combination of conditions. If I contemplate it well, I shall sever all wrong views.' A forest-dwelling monk should always think of the doctrine of emptiness, signlessness, and nonaction.

"Kashyapa, when a forest-dwelling monk follows the right practice of a forest-dweller, he will find that fruits, herbs, grass, and trees arise from the combination of conditions and cease with their dispersion. These external things have no master, no 'I' or 'mine,' and no contention; they arise naturally and cease naturally, yet there is no entity that arises or ceases. Kashyapa, just as grass, trees, tiles, and stones have no self, master, or owner, so it is with the body. There is no self, no life, no personal identity, no sentient being, no contention. All dharmas arise from the combination of conditions and cease with their dispersion. In reality, no dharma arises or ceases.

"Kashyapa, a forest-dwelling monk should cultivate this doctrine when he stays in a secluded place. Kashyapa, a forest-dwelling monk who practices this doctrine will achieve the fruit of a *sramana* quickly if he follows the Sravaka-vehicle. If he is hindered from achieving the fruit of a *sramana* in this life, he will without fail end all his defilements after seeing one buddha, or two, or at most three. If he follows the bodhisattva-vehicle, he will obtain in this life the realization of the nonarising of dharmas and the Dharma of nonobstruction, see future buddhas without fail, and attain supreme enlightenment quickly."

When this discourse on the forest-dwelling monk was spoken, five hundred monks eliminated all their defilements and achieved liberation.

A Tree-Spirit Joins the Assembly of Monks

BUDDHAGHOSA

After the Teacher had given permission to the congregation of monks to lodge outside the walls of the monastery . . . a certain monk decided to build himself a lodging, and seeing a tree that suited him, began to cut it down. Thereupon a certain spirit who had been reborn in that tree, and who had an infant child, appeared before the monk, carrying her child on her hip, and begged him not to cut down the tree, saying, "Master, do not cut down my home." But the monk said, "I shall not be able to find another tree like this," and paid no further attention to what she said.

The tree-spirit thought to herself, "If he but look upon this child, he will desist," and placed the child on a branch of the tree. The monk, however, had already swung his axe, was unable to check the force of his upraised axe, and cut off the arm of the child. Furious with anger, the tree-spirit raised both her hands and exclaimed, "I will strike him dead!" In an instant, however, the thought came to her, "This monk is a righteous man; if I kill him, I shall go to hell. Moreover, if other tree-spirits see monks cutting down their own trees, they will say to themselves, 'Such and such a tree-spirit killed a monk under such circumstances,' and will follow my example and kill other monks. Besides, this monk has a master; I will therefore content myself with reporting this matter to his master."

Lowering her upraised hands, she went weeping to the Teacher, and having saluted him, stood on one side. Said the Teacher, "What is the matter, tree-spirit?" The tree-spirit replied, "Reverend sir, your disciple did this and that to me. I was sorely tempted to kill him, but I thought this and that, refrained from killing him, and came here." So saying, she

Buddhaghosa, an Indian monk of the early fifth century, wrote *The Path to Purification* and commented extensively on the early Buddhist canon. These works became the mainstream of Theravada teachings. Translation by Eugene W. Burlingame.

told him the story in all its details. When the Teacher heard her story, he said to her, "Well done, well done, spirit! You have done well in holding in, like a swift-speeding chariot, your anger when it was thus aroused." So saying, he pronounced the following stanza:

> Whoever controls his anger like a swift-speeding chariot, when it is aroused,
> Him I call a charioteer; other folk are merely holders of reins.

At the conclusion of the lesson, the tree-spirit was established in the fruit of conversion. The assembled company also profited by it.

But even after the tree-spirit had obtained the fruit of conversion, she stood weeping. The Teacher asked her, "What is the matter, tree-spirit?" "Reverend sir," she replied, "my home has been destroyed; what am I to do now?" Said the Teacher, "Enough, tree-spirit, be not disturbed; I will give you a place of abode." With these words he pointed out near the Perfumed Chamber at Jetavana a certain tree from which a tree-spirit had departed on the preceding day and said, "In such and such a place is a tree which stands by itself; enter therein." Accordingly the tree-spirit entered into that tree. Thenceforth, because the tree-spirit had received her place of abode as a gift from the Buddha, although spirits of great power approached that tree, they were unable to shake it. The Teacher took this occasion to lay down and enjoin upon the monks observance of the precept regarding the injuring of plants and trees.

Love for Animals

CULLAVAGGA

Now at that time a certain priest had been killed by the bite of a snake, and when they announced the matter to the Blessed One, he said:

"Surely now, O priests, that priest never suffused the four royal families of the snakes with his friendliness. For if that priest had suffused the four royal families of the snakes with his friendliness, that priest would not have been killed by the bite of a snake. And what are the four royal families of the snakes? The Virupakkhas are a royal family of snakes; the Erapathas are a royal family of snakes; the Chabyaputtas are a royal family of snakes; the Kanhagotamakas are a royal family of snakes. Surely now, that priest did not suffuse the four royal families of the snakes with his friendliness. For surely, if that priest had suffused the four royal families of the snakes with his friendliness, that priest would not have been killed by the bite of a snake. I enjoin, O priests, that you suffuse these four royal families of the snakes with your friendliness; and that you sing a song of defense for your protection and safeguard. In this manner shall you sing:

Virupakkhas, I love them all,
The Erapathas, too, I love,
Chabyaputtas, I love them too,
And all Kanhagotamakas.

Creatures without feet have my love,
And likewise those that have two feet,
And those that have four feet I love,
And those, too, that have many feet.

Cullavagga is one section of the *Vinaya*, which records the regulations that govern the communal life of Buddhist monks and nuns. The texts that comprise the *Vinaya* were written in the first to fourth centuries CE. Translation by the Pali Text Society.

May those without feet harm me not,
And those with two feet cause no hurt;
May those with four feet harm me not,
Nor those who many feet possess.

Let creatures all, all things that live,
All beings of whatever kind,
See nothing that will bode them ill!
May no evil come to them!

Infinite is the Buddha, infinite the Dharma, infinite the Sangha. Finite are creeping things: snakes, scorpions, centipedes, spiders, lizards, and mice. I have now made my protection, and sung my song of defense. Let all living beings retreat! I revere the Blessed One and the seven Supreme Buddhas!

The Wishing Tree and The Noble Hare

JATAKA TALES

THE WISHING TREE

Once, during the Buddha's earthly sojourn, there was a merchant who was friendly with a poor man and, though his friends tried to break the friendship, said that friendship did not depend on equality or inequality of external things. To show his trust, he left his affairs in the hands of the poor friend when he went away, and they prospered.

The Buddha told him:

Jatakas are moral tales of the Buddha's heroic self-cultivation during his former lives. Inspired by pre-Buddhist narrative traditions, the stories depict Gautama's 357 past lives as a human being, 123 rebirths as an animal, and 66 incarnations as a god. Translation by Ethel Beswick.

A friend rightly called is never inferior.
The standard measure for friendship is the ability to befriend.

Then he told the following story.

Once the life that was to become the Buddha was born as the spirit that lived in a clump of kusa grass growing in the king's park. Nearby was a wishing tree whose trunk was straight and tall, with many spreading branches. The king's own seat was near the tree, for he was very fond of it. Between the spirit of the wishing tree and the spirit of the lowly kusa grass grew up a great friendship.

One day it was noticed that the pillar which supported the king's house was weak, and another had to be found to replace it. The carpenters therefore searched for a tree trunk straight enough and tall enough and strong enough for the purpose. At last they came to the wishing tree and found what they needed. Knowing that the king was very fond of the tree, they dared not cut it down before telling him. But when he heard that it was perfect for the new pillar, he said that even though he was fond of it, it must be cut down.

The carpenters then took sacrifices to the tree and let it know that they were coming to cut it down on the next day.

When the wishing tree spirit heard this, it burst into tears, and its friends in the forest came to ask what was the matter. But though they were full of sympathy, they could do nothing to help.

That night the kusa grass spirit called to see the tree spirit and heard the news and determined to save his friend.

Changing himself into a chameleon, he went to the tree before the men came, and got into the roots. Then he worked his way up to the branches, making the tree look full of holes. When he had finished he rested on a branch, his head moving from side to side.

In the morning the men came to saw the tree down, but before beginning the leader struck the trunk with his hand. Of course, it sounded as if it was rotten! Turning away, he blamed them for not looking more carefully the day before, and they went to look for another tree.

All the tree spirits sang the praises of the kusa grass spirit, for they said that they had not known how to help their friend even though they were stronger than the kusa grass. And the wishing tree spirit sang:

Let great and small and equals, all,
Do each their best, if harm befall,
And help a friend in evil plight,
As I was helped by the kusa sprite.

The Master identified the birth: Ananda was the tree spirit and "I myself the kusa grass spirit."

THE NOBLE HARE

Once the Buddha and his brotherhood were welcomed and fed by a landowner for many days. At the end, the Buddha told this old legend to show that it was a tradition of the wise men to sacrifice even themselves to beggars.

Once the life that was to become the Buddha took form as a hare and made his home in a forest near a stream of fresh water, so clean and clear that it looked as blue as lapis lazuli. The grass nearby was green and tender and soft to the touch of the feet of the animals who lived there. The trees were full of flowers and fruit. It was such a verdant spot, and the jungle around it was so pleasant with creeping plants and trees, that men had also begun to live there.

The hare, though strong, was gentle. He was also wise, and in time the other animals who lived in this part of the forest began to look up to him as though he were their king. Three of them became his special friends—a monkey, a jackal, and an otter—and every evening they sat together and talked of many things. Gradually their character began to change and many bad habits were dropped, including the habit of stealing, and they became friendly toward all the other animals.

One evening as they sat together, and the moon, nearly full, was shining very brightly in the dark midnight sky, the hare told his friends that by its appearance he could tell that the following day would be a holy day. He told them it was, therefore, a good thing if they all arranged not to eat anything that day but to give whatever food they found to anyone who asked for it. Quite cheerfully they agreed to do so.

In the morning the monkey went to the mountain nearby, gathered some ripe mango fruits, and took them back to his home. There he put them aside and sat waiting to see if anyone would come for them. And he thought to himself that if no one came he would have a good meal the next day.

The jackal found a lizard and a pot of milk-curds outside a hut, and asking aloud if they belonged to anyone and not receiving any answer, took the cord attached to the pot of curds and placed it round his neck, picked up the lizard and went home. Then, like the monkey, he sat and wondered if anyone would ask for them. He thought, too, that if no one wanted them he would have a good meal the next day.

The otter found some fish in the sand by the river where they had been placed by a fisherman. He asked aloud if they belonged to anyone; receiving no reply, he took them home. Then he sat and waited, and thought of the good meal he would have the next day if no one wanted them.

The hare started out to get his food, which was grass. Suddenly he realized that men did not eat grass, and therefore he had nothing to offer. After worrying for a little while, he remembered that men ate flesh. All the flesh he had to offer was his own body, and he decided, with joy in his heart, that he would offer his body to anyone who asked for food.

The force of this great vow was felt by the whole earth. The mountains shook with joy, the oceans stirred to their depths, the air seemed full of music and the sky full of glorious colors. Lightning flashed and thunder rolled gently, making a very pleasing sound. Flowers fell around him, and the wind in tribute blew the pollen over him.

Sakka, lord of the Devas, heard the vow and thought he would put it to the test. So, at noon, he went to the forest, making himself look like a poor lonely traveler, and cried out that he had lost his caravan and was hungry and tired. He begged for help.

When he came near the monkey, he called again for help. The monkey immediately offered him the mango fruit, but he refused it, saying if he needed it he would come again later on. Hearing his cry, the otter offered his fish, but it was also refused. The jackal offered the lizard and the pot of curds but they, too, were refused, the traveler saying he would come again if he needed them.

When he came to the hare, the hare immediately offered his own body as food. Then a problem arose: how could a man kill someone who had been kind to him? Such a thing was not possible.

In consternation the hare pondered.

While he thought, Sakka caused a charcoal fire to appear behind him, with golden flames and without smoke. As soon as the hare saw it he rushed toward it. Shaking his body three times and calling to any little insect that might be in his fur to come out, he jumped into the middle of the flames as joyfully as a bird drops into a bed of lotuses.

The flames did not feel hot to him, but cool and refreshing, and Sakka, with his jeweled hands soft and white like the petals of the lotus, lifted him up and took him to heaven. There he told the heavenly beings of this wonderful sacrifice, and to commemorate it for all time he caused an image of the hare to appear on his palace, Vaigravanta, and another on Sudharma, the Hall of the Devas. And with the juice he obtained from a mountain, he drew, for all men to see, the figure of the hare on the face of the moon. There it will remain until the end of the great period of time in which we live, as a reminder of the sacrifice of the hare.*

This is one of the great marvels of our age.

The Buddha identified the birth: Moggallana was the jackal, Ananda the otter, Sariputta the monkey. "I myself was the hare."

---

*In many parts of Asia, people see the image of a hare in the moon, just as westerners see "the man in the moon."

Loving-kindness

METTA SUTTA

This is what should be done
By those who are skilled in goodness,
And who know the path of peace:
Let them be able and upright,
Straightforward and gentle in speech,
Humble and not conceited,
Contented and easily satisfied,
Unburdened with duties and frugal in their ways,
Peaceful and calm, wise and skillful,
Not proud and demanding in nature.
Let them not do the slightest thing
That the wise would later reprove.
Wishing: in gladness and in safety,
May all beings be at ease.
Whatever living beings there may be,
Whether they are weak or strong, omitting none,
The great or the mighty, medium, short or small,
The seen and the unseen,
Those living near and far away,
Those born and to-be-born—
May all beings be at ease!
Let none deceive another,
Or despise any being in any state.
Let none through anger or ill-will
Wish harm upon another.
Even as a mother protects with her life
Her child, her only child,

The *Metta Sutta* is part of the *Suttanipata*, which contains some of the oldest texts of the Buddhist canon. This passage is a locus classicus for the term *metta*, loving-kindness. Translation by members of the Amaravati Monastery.

So with a boundless heart
Should one cherish all living beings,
Radiating kindness over the entire world,
Spreading upward to the skies,
And downward to the depths,
Outward and unbounded.
Freed from hatred and ill-will,
Whether standing or walking, seated or lying down,
Free from drowsiness,
One should sustain this recollection.
This is said to be the sublime abiding.
By not holding to fixed views,
The pure-hearted one, having clarity of vision,
Being freed from all sense desires,
Is not born again into this world.

How Bodhisattvas Serve Sentient Beings

HUA-YEN SUTRA

O NOBLE-MINDED PEOPLE, in what manner should one accommodate and serve sentient beings? To do so, one should think:

Throughout the realm-of-dharma and the realm-of-space, in the ocean-like cosmoses in the ten directions, there are infinite kinds of sentient beings; some are born of eggs; some are born of the womb, of wetness, or of metamorphosis. . . . Some live by earth, some by water, fire, wind, space, trees, or flowers. . . . O countless are their kinds, and infinite are their forms, shapes, bodies, faces, longevities, races, names, disposi-

---

The *Hua-yen* (*Flower Ornament*) *Sutra* is a vast and prominent Mahayana scripture. Its teachings form the basis of Hua-yen, a principal school of Buddhism in China. The first comprehensive Chinese version was completed in 420 CE. Translation by Garma C. C. Chang.

tions, views, knowledge, desires, inclinations, manners, costumes, and diets. They abide in numerous kinds of dwellings: in towns, villages, cities, and palaces. They comprise the devas, the *naga*s, the eight-groups, men, non-men, the beings without feet, the beings with two, four, or many feet; some are with form, some are without form, some with or without thoughts, or neither with nor without thoughts. To all these infinite kinds of beings, I will render my service, and accommodate them in whatever way is beneficial to them. I will provide them with all they need and serve them as though serving my parents, teachers, or even arhats and Tathagatas, all equally without discrimination. To the sick, I will be a good physician; to those who have lost their way, I will show them the right path; to the wanderers in darkness, I will light the light; and to the poor and needy, I will show the treasury.

It is in these ways that a Bodhisattva should benefit all sentient beings without discrimination. Why? Because, if a Bodhisattva accommodates sentient beings as such, he is then making sincere offerings to all Buddhas. If he respects and serves sentient beings, he is paying respect and giving service to all Tathagatas. If he makes sentient beings happy, he is making all Tathagatas happy. Why? Because the essence of Buddhahood consists in great compassion. Because of sentient beings, a great compassion is aroused; because of the great compassion, the thought-of-enlightenment is aroused; because of the thought-of-enlightenment, supreme Buddhahood is achieved. This is like unto a great tree in the wilderness of a desert; if its roots are well watered, it will flourish in full foliage, blossom, and bear plentiful fruit. So it is also with the great Tree-of-Bodhi . . . all sentient beings are its roots, and all the Bodhisattvas and Tathagatas are its flowers and fruits. If a Bodhisattva applies the water of compassion to help sentient beings, the Bodhi-tree will bear the fruit of Tathagata's wisdom. Why is this so? Because if a Bodhisattva can benefit man with the water of compassion, he will most assuredly attain the supreme enlightenment. Therefore, Bodhi belongs to sentient beings; without them no Bodhisattva can achieve the supreme Buddhahood.

O noble-minded people, if you can help all sentient beings equally without discrimination, you will then consummate the full and perfect compassion, with which, if you accommodate sentient beings, you can then make all Tathagatas happy and satisfied. In this manner a Bodhisattva should accommodate and embrace all sentient beings. This compassionate embracing will not cease till the realm-of-space is ended, the realm-of-beings is ended, the karmas, sorrows, and passion-desires are ended, thought succeeding thought without interruption, with bodily, oral, and mental deeds without weariness.

Again, O noble-minded person, how should one turn over one's merits to all? To do so, one should think:

All the merits I have acquired from the commencement of paying homage to the serving of all sentient beings, I will turn over to each and every living being throughout the entire Dharmadhatu in the infinite realm-of-space. By the power of my merits, I wish them to be always happy and free from all ills and sorrows; I wish all their evil plans to fail, and all their virtuous undertakings to succeed. Let all the doors that lead to evil and misery be closed, and let the broad paths that lead to heaven and Nirvana be open! Let me take upon myself the burdens and sufferings of all sentient beings, lest they suffer the heavy afflictions of retribution. In this manner, I will continue to turn over my merits to all until the realm-of-space is exhausted, the sphere-of-beings is ended, and the karmas, sorrows, and passion-desires of beings are ended, thought following upon thought without interruption, with bodily, oral, and mental deeds without weariness.

The Bodhisattva Path

SHANTIDEVA

May I be the doctor and the medicine,
And may I be the nurse
For all sick beings in the world
Until everyone is healed.

May a rain of food and drink descend
To clear away the pain of thirst and hunger,
And during the eon of famine
May I myself change into food and drink.

May I become an inexhaustible treasure
For those who are poor and destitute.
May I turn into all things they could need,
And may these be placed close beside them.

Without any sense of loss or attachment,
I shall give up my body and enjoyments
As well as all my virtues of the three times
For the sake of benefitting all.

By giving up all, sorrow is transcended,
And my mind will realize the sorrowless state.
It is best that I now give everything to all beings
In the same way as I shall at death.

✳

Shantideva, a revered monk, scholar, and poet, lived in India in the eighth century. *A Guide to the Bodhisattva's Way of Life*, the source of these verses, is a classic evocation of the bodhisattva path. Translation by Stephen Batchelor.

May I be a protector for those without one,
A guide for all travelers on the way.
May I be a bridge, a boat and a ship
For all who wish to cross the water.

May I be an island for those who seek refuge
And a lamp for those desiring light.
May I be a bed for all who wish to rest
And a slave for all who want a slave.

May I be a wishing jewel, a magic vase,
Powerful mantras and great medicine.
May I become a wish-fulfilling tree
And a cow of plenty for the world.

Just like space
And the great elements such as earth,
May I always support the life
Of all the boundless creatures.

And until they pass away from pain,
May I also be the source of life
For all the realms of varied beings
That reach unto the ends of space.

The Hunter and the Deer

MILAREPA

HAVING DIRECTED HIS DISCIPLE to remain at different hermitages for their devotions, Jetsun Milarepa went to a secluded place at Nyi Shang Gur Da Mountain on the border between Nepal and Tibet. The upper slopes were very rugged, cloudy, foggy, and continuously deluged with rain. To the right of the mountain towered a precipitous hill where one could always hear the cries of wild animals and watch vultures hovering above. To its left stood a hill clothed with soft, luxuriant meadows, where deer and antelopes played. Below there was a luxurious forest with all kinds of trees and flowers and within which lived many monkeys, peacocks, turkeys, and other beautiful birds. The monkeys amused themselves by swinging and leaping among the trees, the birds darted here and there with a great display of wing, while warblers chirped and sang. In front of the hermitage flowed a stream, fed by melting snow and filled with rocks and boulders. A fresh, clear, bubbling sound could always be heard as one passed by.

This hermitage was called Ghadaya. It was a very quiet and delightful place with every favorable condition for devotees. And so it was here that Jetsun Milarepa indulged in the River-Flow Samadhi, while all the benevolent local deities rendered him services and oblations.

One day, Milarepa heard a dog barking in the distance; after that a great noise arose. He thought, "Hitherto, this place has been very favorable for meditation. Is some disturbance on the way?" So he left the cave, came to a huge rock, and sat upon it absorbed in the Compassion of Nondiscrimination. Before long, a black, many-spotted deer ran up, badly frightened. Seeing this, an unbearable compassion arose within the Jetsun. He thought, "It is because of the evil karma this deer has acquired

---

Milarepa (1040–1123), cofounder of the Kagyupa school of Tibetan Buddhism, spent years meditating alone in high Himalayan caves. *The Hundred Thousand Songs of Milarepa*, the source of this passage, is a classic of Tibetan literature. Translation by Garma C. C. Chang.

in the past that he was born in such a pitiable form. Though he has not committed any sinful deeds in this life, he must still undergo great suffering. What a pity! I shall preach to him the Dharma of Mahayana, and lead him to eternal bliss." Thinking thus, he sang to the deer:

> I bow down at the feet of Marpa;
> Pray, relieve the sufferings of all beings!
>
> Listen to me, you deer with sharp antlers!
> Because you want to escape
> From something in the outer world,
> You have no chance to free yourself
> From inner blindness and delusions.
>
> With no regret or sadness,
> Forget your mind and outer body—
> The time has come for you
> To renounce all blindness and delusion.
>
> The ripening karma is fearful and compelling,
> But how can you escape from it
> By fleeing with your delusory body?
>
> If escape is what you want,
> Hide within mind-essence;
> If you want to run away,
> Flee to the place of enlightenment.
> There is no other place of safe refuge.
>
> Uprooting all confusion and from your mind,
> Stay with me here in rest and quiet.
> At this very moment the fear of death is full upon you;
> You are thinking, "Safety lies on the far side of the hill;
> If I stay here I shall be caught!"
> This fear and hope is why you wander in Samsara.
>
> I shall now teach you the six yogas of Naropa,
> And set you to practicing the Mahamudra.

Thus he sang in a tuneful voice like that of the god Brahma. Had there been anyone to hear, he could not have helped feeling charmed and delighted.

Affected by the Jetsun's compassion, the deer was relieved from its painful fear of capture. With tears streaming from its eyes, it came near to Milarepa, licked his clothes, and then lay down at his left side. He thought, "This deer must be hunted by a ferocious dog, the one whose barking I heard just now."

As Milarepa was wondering what kind of a dog it could be, a red dog with a black tail and a collar round her neck ran toward him. She was a hunting dog—such a savage and fearful creature that her tongue was hanging out like a blazing ribbon, while the sharp claws on her feet could rend any prey, and her threatening growl was like thunder. Milarepa thought, "It must be this dog that has been chasing the deer. She is indeed ferocious. Full of anger, she regards whatever she sees as her enemy. It would be good if I could calm her and quench her hatred." Great pity for the dog rose in him, and he sang with great compassion:

> I bow down at the feet of Marpa;
> I pray for you, pacify the hate of all beings.
>
> Oh you dog with a wolf's face,
> Listen to this song of Milarepa!
>
> Whatever you see, you deem it to be your foe;
> Your heart is full of hatred and ill thoughts.
> Because of your bad karma, you were born a dog,
> Ever suffering from hunger, and agonized by passion.
>
> If you do not try to catch the Self-mind within,
> What good is it to catch prey outside?
> The time has come for you to capture your Self-mind;
> Now is the time to renounce your fury,
> And with me sit here restfully.
>
> Your mind is full of greed and anger,
> Thinking, "If I go that way, I shall lose him,

But I will catch him if I go forward on this side."
This hope and fear is why you wander in Samsara!

I shall now teach you the six yogas of Naropa,
And set you to practicing the Mahamudra.

Hearing this song of Dharma, sung in a heavenly voice and with immense compassion, the dog was greatly moved, and her fury subsided. She then made signs to the Jetsun by whining, wagging her tail, and licking his clothes. Then she put her muzzle under her two front paws and prostrated herself before him. Tears fell from her eyes, and she lay down peacefully with the deer.

Milarepa thought, "There must be a sinful person who is following these two animals. He will probably be here any moment." Before long, a man appeared looking very proud and violent; from under his lashes his eyes glared fiercely, his hair was knotted on the top of his head, and his long sleeves flapped from side to side as he ran toward the Jetsun. In one hand he held a bow and arrow, and in the other a long lasso for catching game. As he dashed up, one could hear his breath coming in suffocating gasps and see streams of sweat pouring down his face and almost choking him to death. When he saw the Jetsun with the dog and deer lying beside him, like a mother with her sons, he thought, "Are the deer and my dog both bewitched by this yogi?" He then cried angrily to Milarepa, "You fat, greasy repas and yogis! I see you here, there, and everywhere! High in the mountain snows you come to kill game; low on lake shores you come to hook fish; on the plains you visit towns to trade in dogs and fight with people. It does not matter if one or two like you die. You may have the power of keeping my dog and my deer, but now see whether your clothes can also keep out my arrow." So saying, the hunter drew his long bow, aimed at Milarepa, and shot. But the arrow went high and missed. The Jetsun thought, "If even ignorant animals understand my preaching, he should be able to understand it too, for after all he is a man."

So he said: "You need not hurry to shoot me, as you will have plenty of time to do so later. Take your time, and listen to my song." Whereupon, in a tuneful voice like that of the god Brahma, the Jetsun sang to the hunter, whose name was Chirawa Gwunbo Dorje:

I pray to all accomplished beings;
I pray you to extinguish the five poisonous defilements.

You man with a human body but a demon's face,
Listen to me. Listen to the song of Milarepa!

Men say the human body is most precious, like a gem;
There is nothing that is precious about you.
You sinful man with a demon's look,
Though you desire the pleasures of this life,
Because of your sins, you will never gain them.
But if you renounce desires within,
You will win the Great Accomplishment.

It is difficult to conquer oneself
While vanquishing the outer world;
Conquer now your own Self-mind.
To slay this deer will never please you,
But if you kill the five poisons within,
All your wishes will be fulfilled.

If one tries to vanquish foes in the outer world,
They increase in greater measure.
If one conquers the Self-mind within,
All one's foes soon disappear.

Do not spend your life committing sinful deeds;
It is good for you to practice holy Dharma.
I shall now teach you the six yogas of Naropa,
And set you to practicing the Mahamudra.

While the Jetsun was singing this, the hunter waited and listened. He thought, "There is nothing to prove that what this yogi has just said is true. Usually, a deer is very frightened, and my dog very wild and savage. Today, however, they lie peacefully together, one on his left and the other on his right, like a mother with her sons. Hitherto I have never missed a shot during my winter hunting in the snow mountains, but today I could not hit him. He must be a black magician, or a very great and unusual Lama. I will find out how he lives."

Thinking thus, the hunter entered the cave, where he found nothing but some inedible herbs; seeing such evidence of austerity, a great faith suddenly arose within him. He said, "Revered Lama, who is your Guru, and what teachings do you practice? Where did you come from? Who is your companion, and what do you own? If I am acceptable to you, I should like to be your servant; also I will offer you the life of this deer."

Milarepa replied, "I shall tell you of my companion, from whence I come, and how I live. If you can follow my way of life, you may come with me." And he sang to Chirawa Gwunbo Dorje:

The Lamas Tilopa, Naropa, and Marpa—
These three are my Gurus;
If you they satisfy,
You may come with me.

The Guru, the Yidham, and the Dakini—
To these three Mila pays his homage;
If you they satisfy,
You may come with me.

The Buddha, the Dharma, and the Sangha—
These three are Mila's refuge;
If you they satisfy,
You may come with me.

The view, the practice, and the action—
These three are the dharmas Mila practices;
If you can absorb these teachings,
You may come with me.

The snow, the rocks, and the clay mountains—
These three are where Mila meditates;
If you they satisfy,
You may come with me.

The deer, the argali, and the antelope—
These three are Mila's herd;
If you they satisfy,
You may come with me.

The lynx, the wild dog, and the wolf—
These three are Mila's watchdogs;
If you they satisfy,
You may come with me.

The grouse, the vulture, and the singing Jolmo—
These three are Mila's flock;
If you they satisfy,
You may come with me.

The sun, the moon, and the stars—
These three are Mila's pictures;
If you they satisfy,
You may come with me.

The gods, the ghosts, and the sages—
These three are Mila's neighbors;
If you they satisfy,
You may come with me.

The hyena, the ape, and the monkey—
These three are Mila's playmates;
If you they satisfy,
You may come with me.

Bliss, illumination, and non-thought—
These three are my companions;
If you they satisfy,
You may come with me.

Porridge, roots, and nettles—
These three are Mila's food;
If you they satisfy,
You may come with me.

Water from snow, and spring, and brook—
These three are Mila's drink;
If you they satisfy,
You may come with me.

The *nadi*s, breaths, and *bindu*s—
These three are Mila's clothing:
If you they satisfy,
You may come with me.

The hunter thought, "His words, thoughts, and actions are truly consistent." The uttermost faith thus arose within him. He shed many tears and bowed down at Mila's feet, crying, "Oh precious Jetsun! I now offer you my deer, my dog, my bow and arrows, and my lasso. I and my dog have committed many sins. I pray you to free my dog, Red Lightning Lady, thus delivering her to the higher realms; and I pray you to bring this black deer to the Path of Great Happiness. I pray you grant me, the hunter Chirawa Gwunbo Dorje, the teaching of the Dharma and lead me to the Path of Liberation."

NATURE AS TEACHER OR REFUGE

❉

Dharma Rain

LOTUS SUTRA

A T THAT TIME THE WORLD-HONORED ONE spoke in verse form, saying:

The Dharma King, destroyer of being,
when he appears in the world
accords with the desires of living beings,
preaching the Law in a variety of ways.
The Thus Come One, worthy of honor and reverence,
is profound and far-reaching in wisdom.
For long he remained silent regarding the essential,
in no hurry to speak of it at once.
If those who are wise hear of it
they can believe and understand it,
but those without wisdom will have doubts and regrets
and for all time will remain in error.
For this reason,
he adjusts to the person's power when preaching,

The *Lotus Sutra* (*Sutra of the Lotus of the Wonderful Dharma*), a widely influential Mahayana scripture, expounds seminal Buddhist teachings. Probably composed in the early third century CE, it is best known in a Chinese version produced in 406. Translation by Burton Watson.

taking advantage of various causes
and enabling the person to gain a correct view.
You should understand
that it is like a great cloud
that rises up in the world
and covers it all over.
This beneficent cloud is laden with moisture;
the lightning gleams and flashes,
and the sound of thunder reverberates afar,
causing the multitude to rejoice.
The sun's rays are veiled and hidden,
a clear coolness comes over the land;
masses of darkness descend and spread—
you can almost touch them.
The rain falls everywhere,
coming down on all four sides.
Its flow and saturation are measureless,
reaching to every area of the earth,
to the ravines and valleys of the mountains and streams,
to the remote and secluded places where grow
plants, bushes, medicinal herbs,
trees large and small,
a hundred grains, rice seedlings,
sugar cane, grape vines.
The rain moistens them all,
none fails to receive its full share.
The parched ground is everywhere watered,
herbs and trees alike grow lush.
What falls from the cloud
is water of a single flavor,
but the plants and trees, thickets and groves,
each accept the moisture that is appropriate to its portion.
All the various trees,
whether superior, middling, or inferior,
take what is fitting for large or small,
and each is enabled to sprout and grow.

Root, stem, limb, leaf,
the glow and hue of flower and fruit—
one rain extends to them
and all are able to become fresh and glossy.
Whether their allotment
of substance, form, and nature is large or small,
the moistening they receive is one,
but each grows and flourishes in its own way.
The Buddha is like this
when he appears in the world,
comparable to a great cloud
that covers all things everywhere.
Having appeared in the world,
for the sake of living beings
he makes distinctions in expounding
the truth regarding phenomena.
The great sage, the World-Honored One,
to heavenly and human beings,
in the midst of all beings,
pronounces these words:
I am the Thus Come One,
most honored of two-legged beings.
I appear in the world
like a great cloud
that showers moisture upon
all the dry and withered living beings,
so that all are able to escape suffering,
gain the joy of peace and security,
the joys of this world
and the joy of nirvana.
All you heavenly and human beings of this assembly,
listen carefully and with one mind!
All of you should gather around
and observe the one of unexcelled honor.
I am the World-Honored One,
none can rival me.

In order to bring peace and security to living beings
I have appeared in the world
and for the sake of this great assembly
I preach the sweet dew of the pure Law.
This Law is of a single flavor,
that of emancipation, nirvana.
With a single wonderful sound
I expound and unfold its meaning;
constantly for the sake of the Great Vehicle
I create causes and conditions.
I look upon all things
as being universally equal,
I have no mind to favor this or that,
to love one or hate another.
I am without greed or attachment
and without limitation or hindrance.
At all times, for all things
I preach the Law equally;
as I would for a single person,
that same way I do for numerous persons.
Constantly I expound and preach the Law,
never have I done anything else,
coming, going, sitting, standing,
never to the end growing weary or disheartened.
I bring fullness and satisfaction to the world,
like a rain that spreads its moisture everywhere.
Eminent and lowly, superior and inferior,
observers of precepts, violators of precepts,
those fully endowed with proper demeanor,
those not fully endowed,
those of correct views, of erroneous views,
of keen capacity, of dull capacity—
I cause the Dharma rain to rain on all equally,
never lax or neglectful.
When all the various living beings
hear my Law,

they receive it according to their power,
dwelling in their different environments.
Some inhabit the realm of human and heavenly beings,
of wheel-turning sage kings,
Shakra, Brahma and the other kings—
these are the inferior medicinal herbs.
Some understand the Law of no outflows,
are able to attain nirvana,
to acquire the six transcendental powers
and gain in particular the three understandings,
or live alone in mountain forests,
constantly practicing meditation
and gaining the enlightenment of pratyekabuddhas—
these are the middling medicinal herbs.
Still others seek the place of the World-Honored One,
convinced that they can become Buddhas,
putting forth diligent effort and practicing meditation—
these are the superior medicinal herbs.
Again there are sons of the Buddha
who devote their minds solely to the Buddha way,
constantly practicing mercy and compassion,
knowing that they themselves will attain Buddhahood,
certain of it and never doubting—
these I call the small trees.
Those who abide in peace in their transcendental powers,
turning the wheel of non-regression,
saving innumerable millions
of hundreds of thousands of living beings—
bodhisattvas such as these
I call the large trees.
The equality of the Buddha's preaching
is like a rain of a single flavor,
but depending upon the nature of the living being,
the way in which it is received is not uniform,
just as the various plants and trees
each receive the moisture in a different manner.

The Buddha employs this parable
As an expedient means to open up and reveal the matter,
using various kinds of words and phrases
and expounding the single Law,
but in terms of the Buddha wisdom
this is no more than one drop of the ocean.
I rain down the Dharma rain,
filling the whole world,
and this single-flavored Dharma
is practiced by each according to the individual's power.
It is like those thickets and groves,
medicinal herbs and trees
which, according to whether they are large or small,
bit by bit grow lush and beautiful.
The Law of the Buddhas
is constantly of a single flavor,
causing the many worlds
to attain full satisfaction everywhere;
by practicing gradually and stage by stage,
all beings can gain the fruits of the way.

One Truth, Countless Teachings

HUA-YEN SUTRA

THEN MANJUSHRI ASKED CHIEF OF THE VIRTUOUS, "Since that which the Buddhas realize is but one truth, how is it that they expound countless teachings, manifest countless lands, edify countless beings, speak in countless languages, appear in countless bodies, know countless minds, demonstrate countless mystic powers, are able to shake countless worlds, display countless extraordinary adornments, reveal boundless different realms of objects, whereas in the essential nature of things these different characteristics cannot be found at all?" Chief of the Virtuous answered in verse:

> The meaning of what you ask
> Is deep and hard to fathom.
> The wise are able to know it,
> Always delighting in Buddha's virtues.
>
> Just as the nature of earth is one
> While beings each live separately,
> And the earth has no thought of oneness or difference,
> So is the truth of all Buddhas.
>
> Just as the nature of fire is one,
> While able to burn all things
> And the flames make no distinction,
> So is the truth of all Buddhas.
>
> Just as the ocean is one
> With millions of different waves,

The *Hua-yen* (*Flower Ornament*) *Sutra* is a vast and prominent Mahayana scripture. Its teachings form the basis of Hua-yen, a principal school of Buddhism in China. The first comprehensive Chinese version was completed in 420 CE. Translation by Thomas Cleary.

Yet the water is no different:
So is the truth of all Buddhas.

And as the nature of wind is one
While able to blow on all things,
And wind has no thought of oneness or difference:
So is the truth of all Buddhas.

Also like great thunderheads
Raining all over the earth,
The raindrops make no distinctions:
So is the truth of all Buddhas.

Just as the element earth, while one,
Can produce various sprouts,
Yet it's not that the earth is diverse:
So is the truth of all Buddhas.

Just as the sun without clouds overcast
Shines throughout the ten directions,
Its light beams having no difference:
So is the truth of all Buddhas.

And just as the moon in the sky
Is seen by all in the world
Yet the moon doesn't go to them:
So is the truth of all Buddhas.

Just as the king of the gods
Appears throughout the universe
Yet his body has no change:
So is the truth of all Buddhas.

Then Manjushri asked the bodhisattva Chief in Vision, "Buddhas as fields of blessings are one and the same to all—how is it that when sentient beings give alms to them, the resulting rewards are not the same—various forms, various families, various faculties, various property, various masters, various followers, various official positions, various virtuous qualities, various kinds of knowledge—and yet the Buddhas are impartial toward them, not thinking of them as different?" Chief in Vision answered in verse:

> Just as the earth is one
> Yet produces sprouts according to the seeds
> Without partiality toward any of them,
> So is the Buddhas' field of blessings.

> And just as water is uniform
> Yet differs in shape according to the vessel,
> So is the Buddhas' field of blessings:
> It differs only due to beings' minds.

> And just as a skilled magician
> Can make people happy,
> So can the Buddhas' field of blessings
> Cause sentient beings joy.

> As a king with wealth and knowledge
> Can bring gladness to the masses,
> So can the Buddhas' field of blessings
> Bring peace and happiness to all.

> Like a clear mirror
> Reflecting images according to the forms,
> So from the Buddhas' field of blessings
> Rewards are obtained according to one's heart.

> Like a panacea
> Which can cure all poisoning,
> So does the Buddhas' field of blessings
> Annihilate all afflictions.

> And just as when the sun comes up
> It illuminates the world,
> Thus does the Buddhas' field of blessings
> Clear away all darkness.

> Like the clear full moon
> Shining over the earth,

So is the Buddhas' field of blessings
Equal in all places.

Just as a great conflagration
Can burn up all things,
So does the Buddhas' field of blessings
Burn up all fabrication.

Just as a violent wind
Can cause the earth to tremble,
So does the Buddhas' field of blessings
Move all living beings.

At Home in the Mountains

MAHAKASHYAPA

Strung with garlands of flowering vines,
This patch of earth delights the mind;
The lovely calls of elephants sound—
These rocky crags do please me so!

The shimmering hue of darkening clouds,
Cool waters in pure streams flowing;
Enveloped by Indra's ladybugs—
These rocky crags do please me so!

Like the lofty peaks of looming clouds,
Like the most refined of palaces;
The lovely calls of tuskers sound—
These rocky crags do please me so!

Mahakashyapa, a principal disciple of the Buddha, was noted for his ascetic self-discipline. It is said that when the Buddha silently held up a flower, only Mahakashyapa smiled in comprehension. He was later recognized as the first Indian patriarch of Zen. Translation by Andrew Olendzki.

The lovely ground is rained upon,
The hills are full of holy seers;
Resounding with the cry of peacocks—
These rocky crags do please me so!

Being clothed in flaxen flowers,
As the sky is covered in clouds;
Strewn with flocks of various birds—
These rocky crags do please me so!

Not occupied by village folk,
But visited by herds of deer;
Strewn with flocks of various birds—
These rocky crags do please me so!

With clear waters and broad boulders,
Holding troops of monkey and deer;
Covered with moist carpets of moss—
These rocky crags do please me so!

But there is not so much contentment
For me in the five-fold music,
As in truly seeing Dharma
With a well-concentrated mind.

Cold Mountain Poems

HAN-SHAN

1

I climb the road to Cold Mountain,
The road to Cold Mountain that never ends.
The valleys are long and strewn with stones;
The streams broad and banked with thick grass.
Moss is slippery, though no rain has fallen;
Pines sigh, but it isn't the wind.
Who can break from the snares of the world
And sit with me among the white clouds?

2

As for me, I delight in the everyday Way,
Among mist-wrapped vines and rocky caves.
Here in the wilderness I am completely free,
With my friends, the white clouds, idling forever.
There are roads, but they do not reach the world;
Since I am mindless, who can rouse my thoughts?
On a bed of stone I sit, alone in the night,
While the round moon climbs up Cold Mountain.

3

If you sit in silence and never speak,
What stories will you leave for the young people to tell?
If you live shut away in a forest thicket,
How can the sun of wisdom shine out?
No dried-up carcass can be the guardian of the Way.

Han-shan, a poet and Buddhist layman, lived in China during the late eighth
or early ninth century. After withdrawing to Cold Mountain (Han-shan), he
is said to have scrawled his poems on cliffs and trees. Translation by Burton
Watson.

Wind and frost bring sickness and early death.
Plow with a clay ox in a field of stone
And you will never see the harvest day!

4

Yesterday I saw the trees by the river's edge,
Wrecked and broken beyond belief,
Only two or three trunks left standing,
Scarred by blades of a thousand axes.
Frost strips the yellowing leaves,
River waves pluck at withered roots.
This is the way the living must fare.
Why curse at Heaven and Earth?

5

Living in the mountains, mind ill at ease,
All I do is grieve at the passing years.
At great labor I gathered the herbs of long life,
But has all my striving made me an immortal?
Broad is my garden and wrapped now in clouds,
But the woods are bright and the moon is full.
What am I doing here? Why don't I go home?
I am bound by the spell of the cinnamon trees!

6

Here is a tree older than the forest itself;
The years of its life defy reckoning.
Its roots have seen the upheavals of hill and valley,
Its leaves have known the changes of wind and frost.
The world laughs at its shoddy exterior
And cares nothing for the fine grain of the wood inside.
Stripped free of flesh and hide,
All that remains is the core of truth.

Haiku in the Rain

BASHO, BUSON, SHIKI

A lightning flash—
the sound of water drops
falling through bamboo
> —*Buson*

❊

Sweet springtime showers
and no words can express
how sad it all is
> —*Buson*

❊

Rain falls on the grass,
filling the ruts left by
the festival cart
> —*Buson*

❊

The thunderstorm breaks up,
one tree lit by setting sun,
a cicada cry
> —*Shiki*

❊

Basho (1644–1694), widely regarded as Japan's finest poet, elevated haiku to new levels of expression. Buson (1716–1783) was a noted painter as well as a haiku master. Shiki (1867–1902) was a skilled practitioner of *tanka*, a thirty-one-syllable verse form. Translation by Sam Hamill.

The clouds come and go,
providing a rest for all
the moon viewers

—*Basho*

❋

The camellia tips,
the remains of last night's rain
splashing out

—*Buson*

THE NATURE OF NATURE

❊

The Jewel Net of Indra

Tu-shun

QUESTION: Things being thus, what about knowledge?

ANSWER: Knowledge accords with things, being in one and the same realm, made by conditions, tacitly conjoining, without rejecting anything, suddenly appearing, yet not without before and after. Therefore the sutra says, "The sphere of the universal eye, the pure body, I now will expound; let people listen carefully." By way of explanation, the "universal eye" is the union of knowledge and reality, all at once revealing many things. This makes it clear that reality is known to the knowledge of the universal eye only and is not the sphere of any other knowledge. The "sphere" means things. This illustrates how the many things interpenetrate like the realm of Indra's net of jewels—multiplied and remultiplied ad infinitum. The pure body illustrates how all things, as mentioned before, simultaneously enter each other. Ends and beginnings, being collectively formed by conditional origination, are impossible to trace to a basis—the seeing mind has nothing to rest on.

Now the celestial jewel net of Kanishka, or Indra, Emperor of Gods, is called the net of Indra. This imperial net is made all of jewels: because the jewels are clear, they reflect each other's images, appearing in each

---

Tu-shun (557–640), a specialist in the *Hua-yen Sutra*, became the first patriarch of the Hua-yen school of Chinese Buddhism. He is remembered as a monk with exceptional healing abilities who lived close to the peasants. Translation by Thomas Cleary.

other's reflections upon reflections, ad infinitum, all appearing at once in one jewel, and in each one it is so—ultimately there is no going or coming.

Now for the moment let us turn to the southwest direction and pick a jewel and check it. This jewel can show the reflections of all the jewels all at once—and just as this is so of this jewel, so it is of every other jewel: the reflection is multiplied and remultiplied over and over endlessly. These infinitely multiplying jewel reflections are all in one jewel and show clearly—the others do not hinder this. If you sit in one jewel, then you are sitting in all the jewels in every direction, multiplied over and over. Why? Because in one jewel there are all the jewels. If there is one jewel in all the jewels, then you are sitting in all the jewels too. And the reverse applies to the totality if you follow the same reasoning. Since in one jewel you go into all the jewels without leaving this one jewel, so in all jewels you enter one jewel without leaving this one jewel.

QUESTION: If you say that one enters all the jewels in one jewel without ever leaving this one jewel, how is it possible to enter all the jewels?

ANSWER: It is precisely by not leaving this one jewel that you can enter all the jewels. If you left this one jewel to enter all the jewels, you couldn't enter all the jewels. Why? Because outside this jewel there are no separate jewels.

QUESTION: If there are no jewels outside this one jewel, then this net is made of one jewel. How can you say then that it's made of many jewels tied together?

ANSWER: It is precisely because there is only one jewel that many can be joined to form a net. Why? Because this one jewel alone forms the net—that is, if you take away this jewel there will be no net.

QUESTION: If there is only one jewel, how can you speak of tying it into a net?

ANSWER: Tying many jewels to form a net is itself just one jewel. Why? "One" is the aspect of totality, containing the many in its formation. Since all would not exist if there were not one, this net is therefore made by one jewel. The all entering the one can be known by thinking about it in this way.

QUESTION: Although the jewel in the southwest contains all the jewels in the ten directions completely, without remainder, there are jewels in every direction. How can you say then that the net is made of just one jewel?

ANSWER: All the jewels in the ten directions are in totality the one jewel of the southwest. Why? The jewel in the southwest *is* all the jewels of the ten directions. If you don't believe that one jewel in the southwest is all the jewels in the ten directions, just put a dot on the jewel in the southwest. When one jewel is dotted, there are dots on all the jewels in all directions. Since there are dots on all the jewels in the ten directions, we know that all the jewels are one jewel. If anyone says that all the jewels in the ten directions are not one jewel in the southwest, could it be that one person simultaneously put dots on all the jewels in the ten directions? Even allowing the universal dotting of all the jewels in the ten directions, they are just one jewel. Since it is thus, using this one as beginning, the same is so when taking others first—multiplied over and over boundlessly, each dot is the same. It is obscure and hard to fathom: when one is complete, all is done. Such a subtle metaphor is applied to things to help us think about them, but things are not so; a simile is the same as not a simile—they resemble each other in a way, so we use it to speak of. What does this mean? These jewels only have their reflected images containing and entering each other—their substances are separate. Things are not like this, because their whole substance merges completely. The book on natural origination in the *Hua-yen Sutra* says, "In order to benefit sentient beings and make them all understand, nonsimiles are used to illustrate real truth. Such a subtle teaching as this is hard to hear even in immeasurable eons; only those with perseverance and wisdom can hear of the matrix of the issue of thusness." The sutra says, "Nonsimiles are used as similes. Those who practice should think of this in accord with the similes."

> Vairocana Buddha's past practices
> Made oceans of Buddha-fields all pure.

Immeasurable, innumerable, boundless,
He freely permeates all places.
The reality-body of the Buddha is inconceivable;
Formless, signless, without comparison,
It manifests material forms for the sake of beings.
In the ten directions they receive its teaching,
Nowhere not manifest.
In the atoms of all Buddha-fields
Vairocana manifests self-subsistent power,
Promising the thundering sound of the ocean of Buddhahood
To tame all the species of sentient beings.

The Coincidence of Opposites

SHIH-T'OU

The mind of the great sage of India
 was intimately conveyed from west to east.
Though people may be sharp-witted or dull.
 there's no north and south in the Way.
The deep spring sparkles in the pure light,
 its branches streaming through the darkness.
Grasping at phenomena is the source of delusion;
 uniting with the absolute falls short of awakening.
All of the senses, all the things sensed—
 they interact without interaction.
Interacting, they permeate one another.
 yet each remains in its own place.

Shih-t'ou (700–790) is one of the great figures of early Chinese Zen (Ch'an). According to tradition, he built himself a small hut on a large flat rock, and thereby acquired the nickname Stone-head (Shih-t'ou). Translation by Nelson Foster.

By nature, forms differ in shape and appearance.
  By nature, sounds bring pleasure or pain.
In darkness, the fine and mediocre accord;
  brightness makes clear and murky distinct.
Each element comes back to its own nature
  just as a child finds its own mother.
Fire is hot, the wind blows,
  water is wet and earth solid,
eyes see forms, ears hear sounds,
  noses smell, tongues tell salty from sour—
so it is with everything everywhere.
  The root puts forth each separate shoot.
Both root and shoot go back to the fundamental fact.
  Exalted and lowly is just a matter of words.
In the very midst of light, there's darkness;
  don't meet another in the darkness.
In the very midst of darkness, there's light;
  don't observe another in the light.
Light and darkness complement each other,
  like stepping forward and stepping back.
Each of the myriad things has its particular virtue
  inevitably expressed in its use and station.
Phenomena accord with the fundamental as a lid fits its box;
  the fundamental meets phenomena like arrows in midair.
Hearing these words, understand the fundamental;
  don't cook up principles from your own ideas.
If you overlook the Way right before your eyes,
  how will you know the path beneath your feet?
Advancing has nothing to do with near and far,
  yet delusion creates obstacles high and wide.
Students of the mystery, I humbly urge you,
  don't waste a moment, night or day!

Letter to the Island

MYOE

DEAR MR. ISLAND:

How have you been since the last time I saw you? After I returned from visiting you, I have neither received any message from you, nor have I sent any greetings to you.

I think about your physical form as something tied to the world of desire, a kind of concrete manifestation, an object visible to the eye, a condition perceivable by the faculty of sight, and a substance composed of earth, air, fire, and water that can be experienced as color, smell, taste, and touch. Since the nature of physical form is identical to wisdom, there is nothing that is not enlightened. Since the nature of wisdom is identical to the underlying principle of the universe, there is no place it does not reach. The underlying principle of the universe is identical to the absolute truth, and the absolute truth is identical to the ultimate body of the Buddha. According to the rule by which no distinctions can be made between things, the underlying principle of the universe is identical to the world of ordinary beings and thus cannot be distinguished from it. Therefore, even though we speak of inanimate objects, we must not think of them as being separated from living beings.

It is certainly true that the physical substance of a country is but one of the ten bodies of the Buddha. There is nothing apart from the marvelous body of the radiant Buddha. To speak of the teaching of nondifferentiation and perfect interfusion of the six characteristics of all things—their general conditions, specific details, differences, similarities, formation, and disintegration—is to say that your physical form as an island consists of the land of this nation, which is one part of the body of the Buddha. In terms of the characteristic that things differ, we can speak of you also as the other nine bodies of the Buddha: the bodies of living beings, the

---

Myoe (1173–1232), a monk of the Japanese Shingon sect, spent most of his life at Kozanji temple in the mountains outside Kyoto. He endorsed Hua-yen (Kegon) teachings and advocated a return to strict observance of the precepts. Translation by George J. Tanabe, Jr.

body of karmic retribution, the bodies of those who listen to the teachings, the bodies of those who are self-enlightened, the bodies of bodhisattvas, the bodies of buddhas, the body of the truth, the body of wisdom, and the body of emptiness. Your own substance as an island is the substance of these ten bodies of the Buddha, and since these ten bodies are all fused together, they exist in a state of perfect union. This is the epitome of Indra's net, and goes beyond explanation because it far transcends the boundaries of conscious knowledge.

Therefore, in the context of the enlightenment of the ten buddhas in the Kegon sect, the underlying principles of you as an island can be thought of as the nondifferentiation between the karmic determinations of who we are and where we live, the identical existence of the one and the many, Indra's net that intertwines all things, the inexhaustibility of everything, the universality of the world of truth, the perfect interfusion that cannot be explained, and the complete endowment of the ten bodies of the Buddha in all things. Why do we need to seek anything other than your physical form as an island since it is the body of the radiant Buddha?

Even as I speak to you in this way, tears fill my eyes. Though so much time has passed since I saw you so long ago, I can never forget the memory of how much fun I had playing on your island shores. I am filled with a great longing for you in my heart, and I take no delight in passing time without having the time to see you.

And then there is the large cherry tree that I remember so fondly. There are times when I so want to send a letter to the tree to ask how it is doing, but I am afraid that people will say that I am crazy to send a letter to a tree that cannot speak. Though I think of doing it, I refrain in deference to the custom of this irrational world. But really, those who think that a letter to a tree is crazy are not our friends. We will keep company with the Sovereign Master of the Sea, who searched for Treasure Island, and will live on the great ocean, making crossings to islands. Our friend will be the Ocean Cloud Monk with whom we will play to our heart's delight. What more could we want?

Having visited you and carried out my religious practice as I wanted to, I am firmly convinced that you, more than some wonderful person, are truly an interesting and enjoyable friend. Having observed the ways of the world for some time now, I think it suitable that there were those in the past who followed the custom of digging a hole in the ground and speaking into it.

These are all ancient matters. These days no one does anything like this, but when we speak of it there is a certain yearning that we have for it. However, I now practice the precepts of a community of monks who are living in the realm of the one truth. We do not serve the interests of friends living on the outside; neither do we have a mind for embracing all living beings. All in all, however, I do not think that this sin is a sin at all.

At any rate, I should like to write to you again at a later time.

With deepest respect,
Koben

After this letter was written, the messenger asked, "To whom shall I deliver this letter?" Myoe replied, "Simply stand in the middle of Karma Island; shout in a loud voice, 'This is a letter from Myoe of Toganoo!' Leave the letter, and return."

Mountains and Waters Sutra

DOGEN

I

Mountains and waters right now are the actualization of the ancient buddha way. Each, abiding in its phenomenal expression, realizes completeness. Because mountains and waters have been active since before the Empty Eon, they are alive at this moment. Because they have been the self since before form arose they are emancipation-realization.

Dogen (1200–1253) founded the Soto sect of Japanese Zen. This treatise is from his principal work, *Treasury of the Eye of the True Dharma*, considered a crowning expression of Zen thought. Translation by Arnold Kotler and Kazuaki Tanahashi.

2

Because mountains are high and broad, the way of riding the clouds is always reached in the mountains; the inconceivable power of soaring in the wind comes freely from the mountains.

3

Priest Daokai of Mt. Furong said to the assembly, "The green mountains are always walking; a stone woman gives birth to a child at night."

Mountains do not lack the qualities of mountains. Therefore they always abide in ease and always walk. You should examine in detail this quality of the mountains' walking.

Mountains' walking is just like human walking. Accordingly, do not doubt mountains' walking even though it does not look the same as human walking. The buddha ancestors' words point to walking. This is fundamental understanding. You should penetrate these words.

4

Because green mountains walk, they are permanent. Although they walk more swiftly than the wind, someone in the mountains does not realize or understand it. "In the mountains" means the blossoming of the entire world. People outside the mountains do not realize or understand the mountains walking. Those without eyes to see mountains cannot realize, understand, see, or hear this as it is.

If you doubt mountains' walking, you do not know your own walking; it is not that you do not walk, but that you do not know or understand your own walking. Since you do know your own walking, you should fully know the green mountains' walking.

Green mountains are neither sentient nor insentient. You are neither sentient nor insentient. At this moment, you cannot doubt the green mountains' walking.

5

You should study the green mountains, using numerous worlds as your standards. You should clearly examine the green mountains' walking and your own walking. You should also examine walking backward and backward walking and investigate the fact that walking forward and backward has never stopped since the very moment before form arose, since the time of the King of the Empty Eon.

If walking stops, buddha ancestors do not appear. If walking ends, the buddha-dharma cannot reach the present. Walking forward does not cease; walking backward does not cease. Walking forward does not obstruct walking backward. Walking backward does not obstruct walking forward. This is called the mountains' flow and the flowing mountains.

6

Green mountains master walking and eastern mountains master traveling on water. Accordingly, these activities are a mountain's practice. Keeping its own form, without changing body and mind, a mountain always practices in every place.

Don't slander by saying that a green mountain cannot walk and an eastern mountain cannot travel on water. When your understanding is shallow, you doubt the phrase, "Green mountains are walking." When your learning is immature, you are shocked by the words "flowing mountains." Without fully understanding even the words "flowing water," you drown in small views and narrow understanding.

Yet the characteristics of mountains manifest their form and life-force. There is walking, there is flowing, and there is a moment when a mountain gives birth to a mountain child. Because mountains are buddha ancestors, buddha ancestors appear in this way.

Even if you see mountains as grass, trees, earth, rocks, or walls, do not take this seriously or worry about it; it is not complete realization. Even if there is a moment when you view mountains as the seven treasures shining, this is not returning to the source. Even if you understand mountains as the realm where all buddhas practice, this understanding is not something to be attached to. Even if you have the highest understanding of mountains as all buddhas' inconceivable qualities, the truth is not only this. These are conditioned views. This is not the understanding of buddha ancestors, but just looking through a bamboo tube at a corner of the sky.

Turning an object and turning the mind is rejected by the great sage. Explaining the mind and explaining true nature is not agreeable to buddha ancestors. Seeing into mind and seeing into true nature is the activity of people outside the way. Set words and phrases are not the words of liberation. There is something free from all of these understandings: "Green mountains are always walking," and "Eastern mountains travel on water." You should study this in detail.

7

"A stone woman gives birth to a child at night" means that the moment when a barren woman gives birth to a child is called "night."

There are male stones, female stones, and nonmale nonfemale stones. They are placed in the sky and in the earth and are called heavenly stones and earthly stones. These are explained in the ordinary world, but not many people actually know about it.

You should understand the meaning of giving birth to a child. At the moment of giving birth to a child, is the mother separate from the child? You should study not only that you become a mother when your child is born, but also that you become a child. This is the actualization of giving birth in practice-realization. You should study and investigate this thoroughly.

8

Great Master Kuangzhen of Yumen said, "Eastern mountains travel on water."

The reason these words were brought forth is that all mountains are eastern mountains, and all eastern mountains travel on water. Because of this, Nine Mountains, Mt. Sumeru, and other mountains appear and have practice-realization. These are called "eastern mountains." But could Yun-men penetrate the skin, flesh, bones, and marrow of the eastern mountains and their vital practice-realization?

9

Now in Great Song China there are careless fellows who form groups; they cannot be set straight by the few true masters. They say that the statement, "The eastern mountains travel on water," or Nanquan's story of a sickle, is illogical; what they mean is that any words having to do with logical thought are not buddha ancestors' Zen stories, and that only illogical stories are buddha ancestors' expressions. In this way they consider Huangbo's staff and Linji's shout as beyond logic and unconcerned with thought; they regard these as great enlightenments that precede the arising of form.

"Ancient masters used expedient phrases, which are beyond understanding, to slash entangled vines." People who say this have never seen a true master and they have no eye of understanding. They are immature, foolish fellows not even worth discussing. In China these last two or three hundred years, there have been many groups of bald-headed rascals. What a pity! The great road of buddha ancestors is crumbling. People who hold this view are not even as good as listeners of the Small Vehicles and are more foolish than those outside the way. They are neither lay people nor monks, neither human nor heavenly beings. They are more stupid than animals who learn the buddha way.

The illogical stories mentioned by you bald-headed fellows are only illogical for you, not for buddha ancestors. Even though you do not understand, you should not neglect studying the buddha ancestors' path of understanding. Even if it is beyond understanding in the end, your present understanding is off the mark.

I have personally seen and heard many people like this in Song China. How sad that they do not know about the phrases of logical thought, or penetrating logical thought in the phrases and stories! When I laughed at them in China, they had no response and remained silent. Their idea about illogical words is only a distorted view. Even if there is no teacher to show you the original truth, your belief in spontaneous enlightenment is heretical.

10

You should know that "eastern mountains traveling on water" is the bones and marrow of the buddha ancestors. All waters appear at the foot of the eastern mountains. Accordingly, all mountains ride on clouds and walk in the sky. Above all waters are all mountains. Walking beyond and walking within are both done on water. All mountains walk with their toes on all waters and splash there. Thus in walking there are seven paths vertical and eight paths horizontal. This is practice-realization.

11

Water is neither strong nor weak, neither wet nor dry, neither moving nor still, neither cold nor hot, neither existent nor nonexistent, neither deluded nor enlightened. When water solidifies, it is harder than a diamond. Who can crack it? When water melts, it is gentler than milk. Who can destroy it? Do not doubt that these are the characteristics water manifests. You should reflect on the moment when you see the water of the ten directions as the water of the ten directions. This is not just studying the moment when human and heavenly beings see water; this is studying the moment when water sees water. Because water has practice-realization of water, water speaks of water. This is a complete understanding. You should go forward and backward and leap beyond the vital path where other fathoms other.

12

All beings do not see mountains and waters in the same way. Some beings see water as a jeweled ornament, but they do not regard jeweled ornaments as water. What in the human realm corresponds to their water? We only see their jeweled ornaments as water.

Some beings see water as wondrous blossoms, but they do not use blossoms as water. Hungry ghosts see water as raging fire or pus and blood. Dragons see water as a palace or a pavilion. Some beings see water as the seven treasures or a wish-granting jewel. Some beings see water as a forest or a wall. Some see it as the dharma nature of pure liberation, the true human body, or as the form of body and essence of mind. Human beings see water as water. Water is seen as dead or alive depending on causes and conditions.

Thus the views of all beings are not the same. You should question this matter now. Are there many ways to see one thing, or is it a mistake to see many forms as one thing? You should pursue this beyond the limit of pursuit. Accordingly, endeavors in practice-realization of the way are not limited to one or two kinds. The ultimate realm has one thousand kinds and ten thousand ways.

When we think about the meaning of this, it seems that there is water for various beings but there is no original water—there is no water common to all types of beings. But water for these various kinds of beings does not depend on mind or body, does not arise from actions, does not depend on self or other. Water's freedom depends only on water.

Therefore, water is not just earth, water, fire, wind, space, or consciousness. Water is not blue, yellow, red, white, or black. Water is not forms, sounds, smells, tastes, touchables, or mind-objects. But water as earth, water, fire, wind, and space realizes itself.

For this reason, it is difficult to say who is creating this land and palace right now or how such things are being created. To say that the world is resting on the wheel of space or on the wheel of wind is not the truth of the self or the truth of others. Such a statement is based only on a small view. People speak this way because they think that it must be impossible to exist without having a place on which to rest.

13

Buddha said, "All things are ultimately liberated. There is nowhere that they abide."

You should know that even though all things are liberated and not tied to anything, they abide in their own phenomenal expression. However, when most human beings see water they only see that it flows unceasingly. This is a limited human view; there are actually many kinds of flowing. Water flows on the earth, in the sky, upward, and downward. It can flow around a single curve or into many bottomless abysses. When it rises it becomes clouds. When it descends it forms abysses.

14

Wenzi said, "The path of water is such that when it rises to the sky, it becomes raindrops; when it falls to the ground, it becomes rivers."

Even a secular person can speak this way. You who call yourselves

descendants of buddha ancestors should feel ashamed of being more ignorant than an ordinary person. The path of water is not noticed by water,
but is realized by water. It is not unnoticed by water, but is realized by
water.

"When it rises to the sky, it becomes raindrops" means that water
rises to the heavens and skies everywhere and forms raindrops. Raindrops
vary according to the different worlds. To say that there are places water
does not reach is the teaching of the listeners of the Small Vehicles or the
mistaken teaching of people outside the way. Water exists inside fire and
inside mind, thought, and ideas. Water also exists within the wisdom of
realizing buddha nature.

"When it falls to the ground, it becomes rivers" means that when
water reaches the ground it turns into rivers. The essence of the rivers
becomes wise people.

Now ordinary fools and mediocre people think that water is always
in rivers or oceans, but this is not so. Rivers and oceans exist in water.
Accordingly, even where there is not a river or an ocean, there is water.
It is just that when water falls down to the ground, it manifests the characteristics of rivers and oceans.

Also do not think that where water forms rivers or oceans there is
no world and there is no buddha land. Even in a drop of water innumerable buddha lands appear. Therefore it is not a question of whether there
is only water in the buddha land or a buddha land in water.

The existence of water is not concerned with past, future, present,
or the phenomenal water. Yet water is actualization of the fundamental
point. Where buddha ancestors reach, water never fails to appear. Because of this, buddha ancestors always take up water and make it their
body and mind, make it their thought.

15

In this way, the words "Water does not rise" are not found in scriptures
inside or outside of Buddhism. The path of water runs upward and downward and in all directions.

However, one Buddhist sutra does say, "Fire and air go upward,
earth and water go downward." This "upward" and "downward" require

examination. You should examine them from the Buddhist point of view. Although you use the word "downward" to describe the direction earth and water go, earth and water do not actually go downward. In the same way, the direction fire and air go is called "upward."

The phenomenal world does not actually exist in terms of up, down, or the cardinal directions. It is tentatively designated according to the directions in which the four great elements, five great elements, or six great elements go. The Heaven of No Thought should not be regarded as upward nor the Avichi Hell as downward. The Avichi Hell is the entire phenomenal world; the Heaven of No Thought is the entire phenomenal world.

16

Now when dragons and fish see water as a palace, it is just like human beings seeing a palace. They do not think it flows. If an outsider tells them, "What you see as a palace is running water," the dragons and fish will be astonished, just as we are when we hear the words, "Mountains flow." Nevertheless, there may be some dragons and fish who understand that the columns and pillars of palaces and pavilions are flowing water.

You should reflect and consider the meaning of this. If you do not learn to be free from your superficial views, you will not be free from the body and mind of an ordinary person. Then you will not understand the land of buddha ancestors, or even the land or the palace of ordinary people.

Now human beings well know as water what is in the ocean and what is in the river, but they do not know what dragons and fish see as water and use as water. Do not foolishly suppose that what we see as water is used as water by all other beings. You who study with buddhas should not be limited to human views when you are studying water. You should study how you view the water used by buddha ancestors. You should study whether there is water or no water in the house of buddha ancestors.

17

Mountains have been the abode of great sages from the limitless past to the limitless present. Wise people and sages all have mountains as their inner chamber, as their body and mind. Because of wise people and sages, mountains appear.

You may think that in mountains many wise people and great sages are assembled. But after entering the mountains, not a single person meets another. There is just the activity of the mountains. There is no trace of anyone having entered the mountains.

When you see mountains from the ordinary world, and when you meet mountains while in mountains, the mountains' head and eye are viewed quite differently. Your idea or view of mountains not flowing is not the same as the view of dragons and fish. Human and heavenly beings have attained a position concerning their own worlds which other beings either doubt or do not doubt.

You should not just remain bewildered and skeptical when you hear the words, "Mountains flow"; but together with buddha ancestors you should study these words. When you take one view you see mountains flowing, and when you take another view, mountains are not flowing. One time mountains are flowing, another time they are not flowing. If you do not fully understand this, you do not understand the true dharma wheel of the Tathagata.

An ancient buddha said, "If you do not wish to incur the cause for Unceasing Hell, do not slander the true dharma wheel of the Tathagata." You should carve these words on your skin, flesh, bones, and marrow; on your body, mind, and environs; on emptiness and on form. They are already carved on trees and rocks, on fields and villages.

18

Although mountains belong to the nation, mountains belong to people who love them. When mountains love their master, such a virtuous sage or wise person enters the mountains. Since mountains belong to the sages and wise people living there, trees and rocks become abundant and birds and animals are inspired. This is so because the sages and wise people extend their virtue.

You should know it as a fact that mountains are fond of wise people and sages. Many rulers have visited mountains to pay homage to wise people or to ask for instructions from great sages. These have been important events in the past and present. At such times these rulers treat the sages as teachers, disregarding the protocol of the usual world. The imperial power has no authority over the wise people in the mountains. Mountains are apart from the human world. At the time the Yellow Emperor visited Mt. Kongdong to pay homage to Guangcheng, he walked on his knees, touched his forehead to the ground, and asked for instruction.

When Shakyamuni Buddha left his father's palace and entered the mountains, his father the king did not resent the mountains, nor was he suspicious of those who taught the prince in the mountains. The twelve years of Shakyamuni Buddha's practice of the way were mostly spent in the mountains, and his attainment of the way occurred in the mountains. Thus even his father, a wheel-turning king, did not wield authority in the mountains.

You should know that mountains are not the realm of human beings nor the realm of heavenly beings. Do not view mountains from the scale of human thought. If you do not judge mountains' flowing by the human understanding of flowing, you will not doubt mountains' flowing and not-flowing.

19

On the other hand, from ancient times wise people and sages have often lived near water. When they live near water they catch fish, catch human beings, and catch the way. For long these have been genuine activities in water. Furthermore there is catching the self, catching catching, being caught by catching, and being caught by the way.

Priest Decheng abruptly left Mt. Yao and lived on the river. There he produced a successor, the wise sage of the Huating. Is this not catching a fish, catching a person, catching water, or catching the self? The disciple seeing Decheng is Decheng. Decheng guiding his disciple is his disciple.

20

It is not only that there is water in the world, but there is a world in water. It is not just in water. There is also a world of sentient beings in clouds. There is a world of sentient beings in the air. There is a world of sentient beings in fire. There is a world of sentient beings on earth. There is a world of sentient beings in the phenomenal world. There is a world of sentient beings in a blade of grass. There is a world of sentient beings in one staff.

Wherever there is a world of sentient beings, there is a world of buddha ancestors. You should thoroughly examine the meaning of this.

21

Therefore water is the true dragon's palace. It is not flowing downward. To consider water as only flowing is to slander water with the word "flowing." This would be the same as insisting that water does not flow.

Water is only the true thusness of water. Water is water's complete virtue; it is not flowing. When you investigate the flowing of a handful of water and the not-flowing of it, full mastery of all things is immediately present.

22

There are mountains hidden in treasures. There are mountains hidden in swamps. There are mountains hidden in the sky. There are mountains hidden in mountains. There are mountains hidden in hiddenness. This is complete understanding.

An ancient buddha said, "Mountains are mountains, waters are waters." These words do not mean mountains are mountains; they mean mountains are mountains.

Therefore investigate mountains thoroughly. When you investigate mountains thoroughly, this is the work of the mountains.

Such mountains and waters of themselves become wise persons and sages.

At the hour of the Rat, eighteenth day, tenth month, first year of Ninji [1240], this was taught to the assembly at Kannondori Kosho Horin Monastery.

Poetry of Daito
DAITO

No Dharmas

P'an-shan instructed, "There are no dharmas in the three realms; where can mind be sought?"

> Rain clears from distant peaks, dew glistens frostily.
> Moonlight glazes the front of my ivied hut among the pines.
> How can I tell you how I am, right now?
> A swollen brook gushes in the valley darkened by clouds.

Buddhas

Nan-ch'uan said, "I don't know anything about buddhas in the three worlds."

> If he had known buddhas exist
>   in the three worlds,
> suddenly no spring flowers,
> no full moon in the fall.

Shakyamuni's Great Awakening

One glance at the morning star, and the snow got even whiter.
The look in his eye chills hair and bones.
If earth itself hadn't experienced this instant,
Old Shakyamuni never would have appeared.

Daito (1282–1337), a Japanese Zen master of the Rinzai sect, cofounded a lineage that remains influential today. With the support of two emperors, he established Daitokuji monastery in Kyoto. Translation by Kenneth Kraft.

Here I Am

No form, no sound—
here I am;
white clouds fringing the peaks,
river cutting through the valley.

Rain

No umbrella, getting soaked,
I'll just use the rain as my raincoat.

PART TWO

❋

CONTEMPORARY
INTERPRETATIONS
of the
TEACHINGS

In our former lives, we were rocks, clouds, and trees. . . . This is not just Buddhist; it is scientific. We humans are a young species. We were plants, we were trees, and now we have become humans. We have to remember our past existences and be humble.

—*Thich Nhat Hanh*

INTRODUCTION

❋

B UDDHISM IS TAKING A NEW TURN in the hands of modern
practitioners, teachers, and scholars. The environmental crisis has
compelled those committed to a Buddhist path to reexamine the tradition
for sources of insight and guidance. Can Buddhism be helpful in understanding and transforming the current spiral of destruction? Can the
Buddha-Dharma bring clear-eyed wisdom and fresh hope to the urgent
task of living sustainably on this damaged earth?

Often, the answer seems to be yes. For Thich Nhat Hanh, ecological
principles reflect the cardinal Buddhist tenet of interdependence. Sulak
Sivaraksa applies the Four Noble Truths to the heightened tension of
suffering and desire in consumerist societies. The practice of nonharming, discussed by Lily de Silva, virtually mandates policies of kindness
toward plants and animals. Gary Snyder and John Daido Loori use the
teachings of mountains and rivers to demonstrate that nondualism radically changes the nature of human relationship to home, place, and activity. From tales of bodhisattvas making sacrifices for others, Rafe Martin
draws encouragement for engagement rather than withdrawal. "In this
turning of the wheel," writes Joanna Macy, "the spiritual goal is not escape from the world, but transformation of the world."

Fresh interpretations of material from other times and places always
carry the risk of misrepresentation. Inevitably, each person brings different perspectives and experiences to his or her reflections. Today's teachers and thinkers accordingly acknowledge that they are exploring new
territory rather than preaching final truths. Yet without this process of
translation, a living tradition becomes dead. Some would argue further
that unless the ancient teachings are reengaged in contemporary contexts,
their true depth cannot be fathomed.

Naturally, perplexities arise. Should plants be considered sentient beings or not? If yes, a Buddhist endorsement of the intrinsic value of trees could add spiritual weight to the growing forest-protection movement. Can animals be seen as aspiring bodhisattvas in nonhuman form? If so, the implications for factory farming and cosmetic testing are profound. What about the collective karma of colonizers who, in taking new lands, commit genocide of native peoples? A new type of moral reckoning may be necessary on many blood-spattered pieces of ground.

The Western world has inherited a view of nature as object, as background, as inferior to human activity. Plundering natural resources with little regard for the consequences, global industrial civilization has amassed a material fortune that is unprecedented and unsustainable. Buddhist teachings suggest another kind of prosperity, one that may be more sensitive to the heart's response to other living beings and more congruent with humanity's true place on earth.

The Sun My Heart

Thich Nhat Hanh

W HEN I FIRST LEFT VIETNAM, I had a dream in which I was a young boy, smiling and at ease, in my own land, surrounded by my own people, in a time of peace. There was a beautiful hillside, lush with trees and flowers, and on it was a little house. But each time I approached the hillside, obstacles prevented me from climbing it, and then I woke up.

The dream recurred many times. I continued to do my work and to practice mindfulness, trying to be in touch with the beautiful trees, people, flowers, and sunshine that surrounded me in Europe and North America. I looked deeply at these things, and I played under the trees with the children exactly as I had in Vietnam. After a year, the dream stopped. Seeds of acceptance and joy had been planted in me, and I began to look at Europe, America, and other countries in Asia as also my home. I realized that my home is the Earth. Whenever I felt homesick for Vietnam, I went outside into a backyard or a park, and found a place to practice breathing, walking, and smiling among the trees.

But some cities had very few trees, even then. I can imagine someday soon a city with no trees in it at all. Imagine a city that has only one tree left. People there are mentally disturbed, because they are so alienated from nature. Then one doctor in the city sees why people are getting sick, and he offers each person who comes to him this prescription: "You are sick because you are cut off from Mother Nature. Every morning, take a bus, go to the tree in the center of the city, and hug it for fifteen minutes. Look at the beautiful green tree and smell its fragrant bark."

After three months of practicing this, the patient will feel much better. But because many people suffer from the same malady and the doctor always gives the same prescription, after a short time, the line of people waiting their turn to embrace the tree gets to be very long, more than a mile, and people begin to get impatient. Fifteen minutes is now too long for each person to hug the tree, so the city council legislates a five-minute maximum. Then they have to shorten it to one minute, and then only a few seconds. Finally, there is no remedy at all for the sickness.

If we are not mindful, we might be in that situation soon. We have to remember that our body is not limited to what lies within the boundary of our skin. Our body is much more immense. We know that if our heart stops beating, the flow of our life will stop, but we do not take the time to notice the many things outside of our bodies that are equally essential for our survival. If the ozone layer around our Earth were to disappear for even an instant, we would die. If the sun were to stop shining, the flow of our life would stop. The sun is our second heart, our heart outside of our body. It gives all life on Earth the warmth necessary for existence. Plants live thanks to the sun. Their leaves absorb the sun's energy, along with carbon dioxide from the air, to produce food for the tree, the flower, the plankton. And thanks to plants, we and other animals can live. All of us—people, animals, plants, and minerals—"consume" the sun, directly and indirectly. We cannot begin to describe all the effects of the sun, that great heart outside of our body.

When we look at green vegetables, we should know that it is the sun that is green and not just the vegetables. The green color in the leaves of the vegetables is due to the presence of the sun. Without the sun, no living being could survive. Without sun, water, air, and soil, there would be no vegetables. The vegetables are the coming-together of many conditions near and far.

There is no phenomenon in the universe that does not intimately concern us, from a pebble resting at the bottom of the ocean, to the movement of a galaxy millions of light years away. Walt Whitman said, "I believe a blade of grass is no less than the journey-work of the stars . . ." These words are not philosophy. They come from the depths of his soul. He also said, "I am large, I contain multitudes."

This might be called a meditation on "interbeing endlessly interwoven." All phenomena are interdependent. When we think of a speck of dust, a flower, or a human being, our thinking cannot break loose from the idea of unity, of one, of calculation. We see a line drawn between one and many, one and not one. But if we truly realize the interdependent nature of the dust, the flower, and the human being, we see that unity cannot exist without diversity. Unity and diversity interpenetrate each other freely. Unity is diversity, and diversity is unity. This is the principle of interbeing.

If you are a mountain climber or someone who enjoys the country-side or the forest, you know that forests are our lungs outside of our bodies. Yet we have been acting in a way that has allowed millions of square miles of land to be deforested, and we have also destroyed the air, the rivers, and parts of the ozone layer. We are imprisoned in our small selves, thinking only of some comfortable conditions for this small self, while we destroy our large self. If we want to change the situation, we must begin by being our true selves. To be our true selves means we have to *be* the forest, the river, and the ozone layer. If we visualize ourselves as the forest, we will experience the hopes and fears of the trees. If we don't do this, the forests will die, and we will lose our chance for peace. When we understand that we inter-are with the trees, we will know that it is up to us to make an effort to keep the trees alive. In the last twenty years, our automobiles and factories have created acid rain that has destroyed so many trees. Because we inter-are with the trees, we know that if they do not live, we too will disappear very soon.

We humans think we are smart, but an orchid, for example, knows how to produce noble, symmetrical flowers, and a snail knows how to make a beautiful, well-proportioned shell. Compared with their knowl-edge, ours is not worth much at all. We should bow deeply before the orchid and the snail and join our palms reverently before the monarch butterfly and the magnolia tree. The feeling of respect for all species will help us recognize the noblest nature in ourselves.

An oak tree is an oak tree. That is all an oak tree needs to do. If an oak tree is less than an oak tree, we will all be in trouble. In our former lives, we were rocks, clouds, and trees. We have also been an oak tree. This is not just Buddhist; it is scientific. We humans are a young species. We were plants, we were trees, and now we have become humans. We have to remember our past existences and be humble. We can learn a lot from an oak tree.

All life is impermanent. We are all children of the Earth, and, at some time, she will take us back to herself again. We are continually arising from Mother Earth, being nurtured by her, and then returning to her. Like us, plants are born, live for a period of time, and then return to the Earth. When they decompose, they fertilize our gardens. Living vegetables and decomposing vegetables are part of the same reality. Without one, the other cannot be. After six months, compost becomes fresh vegetables again. Plants and the Earth rely on each other. Whether the Earth is fresh, beautiful, and green, or arid and parched depends on the plants.

It also depends on us. Our way of walking on the Earth has a great influence on animals and plants. We have killed so many animals and plants and destroyed their environments. Many are now extinct. In turn, our environment is now harming us. We are like sleepwalkers, not knowing what we are doing or where we are heading. Whether we can wake up or not depends on whether we can walk mindfully on our Mother Earth. The future of all life, including our own, depends on our mindful steps.

Birds' songs express joy, beauty, and purity, and evoke in us vitality and love. So many beings in the universe love us unconditionally. The trees, the water, and the air don't ask anything of us; they just love us. Even though we need this kind of love, we continue to destroy them. By destroying the animals, the air, and the trees, we are destroying ourselves. We must learn to practice unconditional love for all beings so that the animals, the air, the trees, and the minerals can continue to be themselves.

Our ecology should be a deep ecology—not only deep, but universal. There is pollution in our consciousness. Television, films, and newspapers are forms of pollution for us and our children. They sow seeds of violence and anxiety in us and pollute our consciousness, just as we destroy our environment by farming with chemicals, clear-cutting the trees, and polluting the water. We need to protect the ecology of the Earth and the ecology of the mind, or this kind of violence and recklessness will spill over into even more areas of life.

Our Earth, our green beautiful Earth, is in danger, and all of us know it. Yet we act as if our daily lives have nothing to do with the situation of the world. If the Earth were your body, you would be able to feel many areas where she is suffering. Many people are aware of the world's suffering, and their hearts are filled with compassion. They know what needs to be done, and they engage in political, social, and environmental work to try to change things. But after a period of intense involvement, they become discouraged, because they lack the strength needed to sustain a life of action. Real strength is not in power, money, or weapons, but in deep, inner peace.

If we change our daily lives—the way we think, speak, and act—we change the world. The best way to take care of the environment is to take care of the environmentalist.

Many Buddhist teachings help us understand our interconnectedness with our Mother, the Earth. One of the deepest is the *Diamond Sutra*, which is written in the form of a dialogue between the Buddha and his senior disciple, Subhuti. It begins with this question by Subhuti: "If daughters and sons of good families wish to give rise to the highest, most fulfilled, awakened mind, what should they rely on and what should they do to master their thinking?" This is the same as asking, "If I want to use my whole being to protect life, what methods and principles should I use?"

The Buddha answers, "We have to do our best to help every living being cross the ocean of suffering. But after all beings have arrived at the shore of liberation, no being at all has been carried to the other shore. If you are still caught up in the idea of a self, a person, a living being, or a life span, you are not an authentic bodhisattva." Self, person, living being, and life span are four notions that prevent us from seeing reality.

Life is one. We do not need to slice it into pieces and call this or that piece a "self." What we call a self is made only of nonself elements. When we look at a flower, for example, we may think that it is different from "nonflower" things. But when we look more deeply, we see that everything in the cosmos is in that flower. Without all of the nonflower elements—sunshine, clouds, earth, minerals, heat, rivers, and consciousness—a flower cannot be. That is why the Buddha teaches that the self does not exist. We have to discard all distinctions between self and nonself. How can anyone work to protect the environment without this insight?

The second notion that prevents us from seeing reality is the notion of a person, a human being. We usually discriminate between humans and nonhumans, thinking that we are more important than other species. But since we humans are made of nonhuman elements, to protect ourselves we have to protect all of the nonhuman elements. There is no other way. If you think, "God created man in His own image and He created other things for man to use," you are already making the discrimination that man is more important than other things. When we see that humans have no self, we see that to take care of the environment (the nonhuman elements) is to take care of humanity. The best way to take good care of men and women so that they can be truly healthy and happy is to take care of the environment.

I know ecologists who are not happy in their families. They work hard to improve the environment, partly to escape family life. If someone is not happy within himself, how can he help the environment? That is why the Buddha teaches that to protect the nonhuman elements is to protect humans, and to protect humans is to protect nonhuman elements.

The third notion we have to break through is the notion of a living being. We think that we living beings are different from inanimate objects, but according to the principle of interbeing, living beings are comprised of non-living-being elements. When we look into ourselves, we see minerals and all other non-living-being elements. Why discriminate against what we call inanimate? To protect living beings, we must protect the stones, the soil, and the oceans. Before the atomic bomb was dropped on Hiroshima, there were many beautiful stone benches in the parks. As the Japanese were rebuilding their city, they discovered that these stones were dead, so they carried them away and buried them. Then they brought in live stones. Do not think these things are not alive. Atoms are always moving. Electrons move at nearly the speed of light. According to the teaching of Buddhism, these atoms and stones are consciousness itself. That is why discrimination by living beings against nonliving beings should be discarded.

The last notion is that of a life span. We think that we have been alive since a certain point in time and that prior to that moment, our life did not exist. This distinction between life and nonlife is not correct. Life is made of death, and death is made of life. We have to accept death; it makes life possible. The cells in our body are dying every day, but we never think to organize funerals for them. The death of one cell allows for the birth of another. Life and death are two aspects of the same reality. We must learn to die peacefully so that others may live. This deep meditation brings forth nonfear, nonanger, and nondespair, the strengths we need for our work. With nonfear, even when we see that a problem is huge, we will not burn out. We will know how to make small, steady steps. If those who work to protect the environment contemplate these four notions, they will know how to be and how to act.

In another Buddhist text, the *Avatamsaka* (*"Adorning the Buddha with Flowers"*) *Sutra*, the Buddha further elaborates his insights concerning our "interpenetration" with our environment. Please meditate with me on the "Ten Penetrations":

The first is, "All worlds penetrate a single pore. A single pore penetrates all worlds." Look deeply at a flower. It may be tiny, but the sun, the clouds, and everything else in the cosmos penetrates it. Nuclear physicists say very much the same thing: one electron is made by all electrons; one electron is in all electrons.

The second penetration is, "All living beings penetrate one body. One body penetrates all living beings." When you kill a living being, you kill yourself and everyone else as well.

The third is, "Infinite time penetrates one second. One second penetrates infinite time." A *ksana* is the shortest period of time, actually much shorter than a second.

The fourth penetration is, "All Buddhist teachings penetrate one teaching. One teaching penetrates all Buddhist teachings." As a young monk, I had the opportunity to learn that Buddhism is made of non-Buddhist elements. So, whenever I study Christianity or Judaism, I find the Buddhist elements in them, and vice versa. I always respect non-Buddhist teachings. All Buddhist teachings penetrate one teaching, and one teaching penetrates all Buddhist teachings. We are free.

The fifth penetration is, "Innumerable spheres enter one sphere. One sphere enters innumerable spheres." A sphere is a geographical space. Innumerable spheres penetrate into one particular area, and one particular area enters into innumerable spheres. It means that when you destroy one area, you destroy every area. When you save one area, you save all areas. A student asked me, "Thây, there are so many urgent problems, what should I do?" I said, "Take one thing and do it very deeply and carefully, and you will be doing everything at the same time."

The sixth penetration is, "All sense organs penetrate one organ. One organ penetrates all sense organs"—eye, ear, nose, tongue, body, and mind. To take care of one means to take care of many. To take care of your eyes means to take care of the eyes of innumerable living beings.

The seventh penetration is, "All sense organs penetrate non-sense organs. Non-sense organs penetrate all sense organs." Not only do non-sense organs penetrate sense organs, they also penetrate non-sense organs. There is no discrimination. Sense organs are made of non-sense-organ elements. That is why they penetrate non-sense organs. This helps us remember the teaching of the *Diamond Sutra*.

The eighth penetration is, "One perception penetrates all perceptions. All perceptions penetrate one perception." If your perception is not accurate, it will influence all other perceptions in yourself and others. Suppose a bus driver has an incorrect perception. We know what may happen. One perception penetrates all perceptions.

The ninth penetration is, "Every sound penetrates one sound. One sound penetrates every sound." This is a very deep teaching. If we understand one sound or one word, we can understand all.

The tenth penetration is, "All times penetrate one time. One time penetrates all times—past, present, and future. In one second, you can find the past, present, and future." In the past, you can see the present and the future. In the present, you can find the past and future. In the future, you can find the past and present. They "inter-contain" each other. Space contains time, time contains space. In the teaching of interpenetration, one determines the other, the other determines this one. When we realize our nature of interbeing, we will stop blaming and killing, because we know that we inter-are.

Interpenetration is an important teaching, but it still suggests that things outside of one another penetrate into each other. Interbeing is a step forward. We are already inside, so we don't have to enter. In contemporary nuclear physics, people talk about implicit order and explicit order. In the explicit order, things exist outside of each other—the table outside of the flower, the sunshine outside of the cypress tree. In the implicit order, we see that they are inside each other—the sunshine inside the cypress tree. Interbeing is the implicit order. To practice mindfulness and to look deeply into the nature of things is to discover the true nature of interbeing. There we find peace and develop the strength to be in touch with everything. With this understanding, we can easily sustain the work of loving and caring for the Earth and for each other for a long time.

Early Buddhist Attitudes toward Nature

Lily de Silva

B UDDHISM STRICTLY LIMITS ITSELF to the delineation of a way of life designed to eradicate human suffering. The Buddha refused to answer questions which did not directly or indirectly bear on the central problem of human suffering and its ending. Environmental pollution is a problem of the modern age, unheard of and unsuspected during the time of the Buddha. Therefore it is difficult to find any specific discourse which deals with the topic we are interested in here. Nevertheless, as Buddhism is a full-fledged philosophy of life reflecting all aspects of experience, it is possible to find enough material in the Pali canon to delineate the Buddhist attitude towards nature.

The word *nature* means everything in the world which is not organized and constructed by man. The Pali equivalents which come closest to "nature" are *loka* and *yathabhuta*. The former is usually translated as "world," while the latter literally means "things as they really are." The words *dhammata* and *niyama* are used in the Pali canon to mean "natural way or way."

NATURE AS DYNAMIC

According to Buddhism, changeability is one of the perennial principles of nature. Everything changes in nature and nothing remains static.

This concept is expressed by the Pali term *anicca*. Everything formed is in a constant process of change (*sabbe sankhara anicca*).[1] The world is therefore defined as that which disintegrates (*lujjati ti loko*). The world is so called because it is dynamic and kinetic; it is constantly in a process of undergoing change.[2] In nature there are no static and stable "things"; there are only ever-changing, ever-moving processes. Rain is a good example to illustrate this point. Though we use a noun called "rain" which appears to denote a "thing," rain is nothing but the process of drops of water falling from the skies. Apart from this process, the activity of raining, there is no rain as such which could be expressed by a seemingly static nominal concept. The very elements of solidity (*pathavi*), liquidity (*apo*), heat (*tejo*), and mobility (*vayo*), recognized as the building material of nature, are all ever-changing phenomena. Even the most solid-looking mountains and the very earth that supports everything on it are not beyond this inexorable law of change. One sutta explains how the massive king of mountains—Mount Sumeru, which is rooted in the great ocean to a depth of 84,000 leagues and which rises above sea level to another great height of 84,000 leagues and which is the very classical symbol of stability and steadfastness—also gets destroyed by heat, without leaving even ashes, with the appearance of multiple suns.[3] Thus change is the very essence of nature.

MORALITY AND NATURE

The world passes through alternating cycles of evolution and dissolution, each of which endures for a long period of time. Though change is inherent in nature, Buddhism believes that natural processes are affected by the morals of man.

According to the *Agganna Sutta*,[4] which relates the Buddhist legend regarding the evolution of the world, the appearance of greed in the primordial beings who at that time were self-luminous, subsisting on joy and traversing in the skies, caused the gradual loss of their radiance, the ability to subsist on joy and move about in the sky. The moral degradation had effects on the external environment, too. At that time the entire earth was covered over by a very flavorsome fragrant substance similar to butter.

When beings started partaking of this substance with more and more greed, on the one hand their subtle bodies became coarser and coarser. On the other hand the flavorsome substance itself started gradually diminishing. With the solidification of bodies, differences of form appeared; some were beautiful while others were homely. Thereupon conceit manifested itself in those beings, and the beautiful ones started looking down upon the others. As a result of these moral blemishes, the delicious edible earth-substance completely disappeared. In its place there appeared edible mushrooms and later another kind of edible creeper. In the beings who subsisted on them successively, sex differentiation became manifest and the former method of spontaneous birth was replaced by sexual reproduction.

Self-growing rice appeared on earth, and through laziness to collect each meal man grew accustomed to hoarding food. As a result of this hoarding habit, the growth rate of food could not keep pace with the rate of demand. Therefore land had to be divided among families. After private ownership of land became the order of the day, those who were of a more greedy disposition started robbing from others' plots of land. When they were detected, they denied that they had stolen. Thus through greed, vices such as stealing and lying became manifest in society. To curb the wrongdoers and punish them, a king was elected by the people, and thus the original simple society became much more complex and complicated. It is said that this moral degeneration had adverse effects on nature. The richness of the earth diminished, and self-growing rice disappeared. Man had to till the land and cultivate rice for food. This rice grain was enveloped in chaff; it needed cleaning before consumption.

The point I wish to emphasize by citing this evolutionary legend is that Buddhism believes that though change is a factor inherent in nature, human moral deterioration accelerates the process of change and brings about changes which are adverse to human well-being and happiness.

The *Cakkavattisihanada Sutta* of the *Digha Nikaya* predicts the future course of events when human morals undergo further degeneration.[5] Gradually human health will deteriorate so much that life expectancy will diminish until at last the average human lifespan is reduced to ten years and marriageable age to five years. At that time all delicacies such as ghee, butter, honey, etc., will have disappeared from the earth; what is considered the poorest coarse food today will become a delicacy of that day. Thus Buddhism maintains that there is a close link between human morals and the natural resources available.

According to a discourse in the *Anguttara Nikaya*, when profligate lust, wanton greed, and wrong values grip the heart of man, and immorality becomes widespread in society, timely rain does not fall. When timely rain does not fall, crops get adversely affected with various kinds of pests and plant diseases. Through lack of nourishing food, the human mortality rate rises.[6]

Thus several suttas from the Pali canon show that early Buddhism believes there to be a close relationship between human morality and the natural environment. This idea has been systematized in the theory of the five natural laws *(panca niyamadhamma)* in the later commentaries.[7] According to this theory, in the cosmos there are five natural laws or forces at work, namely *utuniyama* (lit. "season-law"), *bijaniyama* (lit. "seed-law"), *cittaniyama*, *kammaniyama* and *dhammaniyama*. They can be translated as physical laws, biological laws, psychological laws, moral laws, and causal laws, respectively. While the first four laws operate within their respective spheres, the last-mentioned law of causality operates *within* each of them as well as *among* them.

This means that the physical environment of any given area conditions the growth and development of its biological component, i.e., flora and fauna. These in turn influence the thought pattern of the people interacting with them. Modes of thinking determine moral standards. The opposite process of interaction is also possible. The human morals influence not only the psychological makeup of the people but the biological and physical environment of the area as well. Thus the five laws demonstrate that people and nature are bound together in a reciprocal causal relationship with changes in one necessarily bringing about changes in the other.

The commentary on the *Cakkavattisihanada Sutta* goes on to explain the pattern of mutual interaction further.[8] When mankind is demoralized through greed, famine is the natural outcome; when moral degeneration is due to ignorance, epidemic is the inevitable result; when hatred is the demoralizing force, widespread violence is the ultimate outcome. If and when mankind realizes that large-scale devastation has taken place as a result of moral degeneration, a change of heart takes place among the few surviving human beings. With gradual moral regeneration, conditions improve through a long period of cause and effect, and people again start to enjoy gradually increasing prosperity and longer life. The world, including nature and mankind, stands or falls with the type of moral force at work. If immorality grips society, people and nature deteriorate; if morality reigns, the quality of human life and nature improves. Thus greed, hatred, and delusion produce pollution within and without. Generosity, compassion, and wisdom produce purity within and without. This is one reason the Buddha has pronounced that the world is led by the mind, *cittena niyati loko*.[9] Thus people and nature, according to the ideas expressed in early Buddhism, are interdependent.

HUMAN USE OF NATURAL RESOURCES

For survival, mankind has to depend on nature for food, clothing, shelter, medicine, and other requisites. . . . Buddhism tirelessly advocates the virtues of nongreed, nonhatred, and nondelusion in all human pursuits. Greed breeds sorrow and unhealthy consequences. Contentment (*santutthi*) is a much praised virtue in Buddhism.[10] The man leading a simple life with few wants easily satisfied is upheld and appreciated as an exemplary character.[11] Miserliness[12] and wastefulness[13] are equally deplored in Buddhism as two degenerate extremes. Wealth has only instrumental value; it is to be utilized for the satisfaction of human needs. Hoarding is a senseless antisocial habit comparable to the attitude of the dog in the manger. The vast hoarding of wealth in some countries and the methodical destruction of large quantities of agricultural produce to keep market prices from falling, while half the world is dying of hunger and starvation, is really a sad paradox of the present affluent age.

Buddhism commends frugality as a virtue in its own right. Once Ananda explained to King Udena the thrifty economic use of robes by the monks in the following order. When new robes are received, the old robes are used as coverlets, the old coverlets as mattress covers, the old mattress covers as rugs, the old rugs as dusters, and the old tattered dusters are kneaded with clay and used to repair cracked floors and walls.[14]

Thus nothing usable is wasted. Those who waste are derided as "wood-apple eaters."[15] A man shakes the branch of a wood-apple tree and all the fruits, ripe as well as unripe, fall. The man collects only what he wants and walks away, leaving the rest to rot. Such a wasteful attitude is deplored in Buddhism as not only antisocial but criminal. The excessive exploitation of nature today would certainly be condemned by Buddhism in the strongest possible terms.

Buddhism advocates a gentle, nonaggressive attitude toward nature. According to the *Sigalovada Sutta,* a householder should accumulate wealth as a bee collects pollen from a flower.[16] The bee harms neither the fragrance nor the beauty of the flower, but gathers pollen to turn it into sweet honey. Similarly, people are expected to make legitimate use of nature so that they can rise above nature and realize their innate spiritual potential.

ATTITUDES TOWARD ANIMAL AND PLANT LIFE

The well-known Five Precepts (*panca sila*) form the minimum code of ethics that every lay Buddhist is expected to adhere to. The first precept involves abstention from injury to life. It is explained as the casting aside of all forms of weapons, being conscientious about depriving a living being of life. In its positive sense, it means the cultivation of compassion and sympathy for all living beings.[17] The Buddhist layman is expected to abstain from trading in meat too.[18]

The Buddhist monk has to abide by an even stricter code of ethics than the layman. He has to abstain from practices which would involve even unintentional injury to living creatures. For instance, the Buddha promulgated the rule against going on a journey during the rainy season because of possible injury to worms and insects that come to the surface in wet weather.[19] The same concern for nonviolence prevents a monk from digging the ground.[20] Once a monk who was a potter prior to ordination built for himself a clay hut and set it on fire to give it a fine finish. The Buddha strongly objected to this as so many living creatures would have been burned in the process. The hut was broken down on the Buddha's instructions to prevent it from creating a bad precedent for later generations.[21] The scrupulous nonviolent attitude toward even the smallest living creatures prevents the monks from drinking unstrained water.[22] It is no doubt a sound hygienic habit, but what is noteworthy is the reason which prompts the practice, namely, sympathy for living creatures.

Buddhism also prescribes the practice of *metta*, "loving-kindness" toward all creatures of all quarters without restriction. The *Karaniyametta Sutta* enjoins the cultivation of loving-kindness toward all creatures, timid and steady, long and short, big and small, minute and great, visible and invisible, near and far, born and awaiting birth.[23] All quarters are to be suffused with this loving attitude. Just as one's own life is precious to oneself, so is the life of the other precious to himself. Therefore a reverential attitude must be cultivated toward all forms of life.

The *Nandivisala Jataka* illustrates how kindness should be shown to animals domesticated for human service.[24] Even a wild animal can be tamed with kind words. Parileyya was a wild elephant who attended on the Buddha when he spent time in the forest away from the monks.[25] The infuriated elephant Nalagiri was tamed by the Buddha with no other miraculous power than the power of loving-kindness.[26] People and animals can live and let live without fear of one another if only man cultivates sympathy and regards all life with compassion.

The understanding of kamma and rebirth prepares the Buddhist to adopt a sympathetic attitude toward animals. According to this belief, it is possible for human beings to be reborn in subhuman states among animals. The *Kukkuravatika Sutta* substantiates this view.[27] The Jatakas provide ample testimony to this view from commentarial literature. It is possible that our own close relatives have been reborn as animals. Therefore it is only right that we should treat animals with kindness and sympathy. The Buddhist notion of merit also engenders a gentle nonviolent attitude toward living creatures. It is said that if one throws dishwashing water into a pool where there are insects and living creatures, intending that they feed on the tiny particles of food thus washed away, one accumulates merit even by such trivial generosity.[28] According to the *Macchuddana Jataka*, the Bodhisattva threw his leftover food into a river in order to feed the fish, and by the power of that merit he was saved from an impending disaster.[29] Thus kindness to animals, be they big or small, is a source of merit—merit needed for human beings to improve their lot in the cycle of rebirths and to approach the final goal of Nibbana.

Buddhism expresses a gentle nonviolent attitude toward the vegetable kingdom as well. It is said that one should not even break the branch of a tree that has given one shelter.[30] Plants are so helpful to us in providing us with all necessities of life that we are expected not to adopt a callous attitude toward them. The more strict monastic rules prevent monks from injuring plant life.[31]

Prior to the rise of Buddhism, people regarded natural phenomena such as mountains, forests, groves, and trees with a sense of awe and reverence.[32] They considered them as the abode of powerful nonhuman beings who could assist human beings at times of need. Though Buddhism gave man a far superior Triple Refuge (*tisarana*) in the Buddha, Dhamma, and Sangha, these places continued to enjoy public patronage at a popular level, as the acceptance of terrestrial nonhuman beings such as *devatas*[33] and *yakkhas*[34] did not violate the belief system of Buddhism. Therefore, among the Buddhists there is a reverential attitude toward specially long-standing gigantic trees. They are called *vanaspati* in Pali, meaning "lords of the forests."[35] As huge trees such as the ironwood, the sala, and the fig are also recognized as the Bodhi trees of former Buddhas, the deferential attitude toward trees is further strengthened.[36] It is well known that *Ficus religiosa* is held as an object of great veneration in the Buddhist world today as the tree under which the Buddha attained enlightenment.

The construction of parks and pleasure groves for public use is considered a great meritorious deed.[37] Sakka, the lord of gods, is said to have reached this status as a result of social services such as the construction of parks, pleasure groves, ponds, wells, and roads.[38]

The open air, natural habitats, and forest trees have a special fascination for the Eastern mind as symbols of spiritual freedom. The home life is regarded as a fetter (*sambadha*) that keeps people in bondage and misery. Renunciation is like the open air (*abbhokasa*), nature unhampered by human activity.[39] The chief events in the life of the Buddha took place in the open air. He was born in a park at the foot of a tree in Kapilavatthu; he attained enlightenment in the open air at the foot of the Bodhi tree in Bodhgaya; he inaugurated his missionary activity in the open air in the deer park at Isipatana, and he attained Parinibbana too in the open air in the sala grove of the Mallas in Pava. The Buddha's constant advice to his disciples was to resort to natural habitats such as forest groves and glades. There, undisturbed by human activity, they could zealously engage themselves in meditation.[40]

ATTITUDES TOWARD POLLUTION

Environmental pollution has assumed such vast proportions today that people have been forced to recognize the presence of an ecological crisis. We can no longer turn a blind eye to the situation, as we are already threatened with new pollution-related diseases. Pollution to this extent was unheard of during the time of the Buddha. But there is sufficient evidence in the Pali canon to give us insight into the Buddhist attitude toward the pollution problem. Several Vinaya rules prohibit monks from polluting green grass and water with saliva, urine, and feces.[41] These were the common agents of pollution known during the Buddha's day, and rules were promulgated against causing such pollution. Cleanliness was highly commended by the Buddhists, both in the person and in the environment. They were much concerned about keeping water clean, be it in the river, pond, or well. These sources of water were for public use, and each individual had to use them with proper public-spirited caution so that others after him could use them with the same degree of cleanliness. Rules regarding the cleanliness of green grass were prompted by ethical and aesthetic considerations. Moreover, grass is food for most animals, and it is man's duty to refrain from polluting it by his activities.

Noise is today recognized as a serious personal and environmental pollutant troubling everyone to some extent. It causes deafness, stress, and irritation, breeds resentment, saps energy, and inevitably lowers efficiency.[42] The Buddha's attitude to noise is very clear from the Pali canon. He was critical of noise and did not hesitate to voice his stern disapproval whenever such an occasion arose.[43] Once he ordered a group of monks to leave the monastery for noisy behavior.[44] He enjoyed solitude and silence immensely and spoke in praise of silence, as it is most appropriate for mental culture. Noise is described as a thorn to one engaged in the first step of meditation,[45] but thereafter noise ceases to be a disturbance as the meditator passes beyond the possibility of being disturbed by sound.

The Buddha and his disciples reveled in the silent solitary natural habitats unencumbered by human activity. In choosing sites for monasteries, the presence of undisturbed silence was an important quality.[46] Silence invigorates those who are pure at heart and raises their efficiency for meditation. But silence overawes those who are impure with ignoble impulses of greed, hatred, and delusion. The *Bhayabherava Sutta* beautifully illustrates how even the rustle of leaves by a falling twig in the forest sends tremors through an impure heart.[47] . . .

As to the question of the Buddhist attitude to music, it is recorded that the Buddha spoke quite appreciatively of music on one occasion.[48] When Pancasikha the divine musician sang a song while playing the lute in front of the Buddha, the Buddha praised his musical ability, saying that the instrumental music blended well with his song. Again, the remark of an Arahat that the joy of seeing the real nature of things is far more exquisite than orchestral music[49] shows the recognition that music affords a certain amount of pleasure even if it is inferior to higher kinds of pleasure. But it is stressed that the ear is a powerful sensory channel through which man gets addicted to sense pleasures. Therefore, to dissuade monks from getting addicted to melodious sounds, the monastic discipline describes music as a lament.[50]

The psychological training of the monks is so advanced that they are expected to cultivate a taste not only for external silence, but for inner silence of speech, desire, and thought as well. The subvocal speech, the inner chatter that goes on constantly within us in our waking life, is expected to be silenced through meditation.[51] The sage who succeeds in quelling this inner speech completely is described as a *muni*, a silent one.[52] His inner silence is maintained even when he speaks! . . .

Even Buddhist laymen were reputed to have appreciated quietude and silence. Pancangika Thapati can be cited as a conspicuous example.[53] Once Mahanama the Sakyan complained to the Buddha that he was disturbed by the hustle of the busy city of Kapilavatthu. He explained that he experienced calm serenity when he visited the Buddha in the quiet salubrious surroundings of the monastery, and his peace of mind was disturbed when he went to the city.[54]

Though noise to the extent of being a pollutant causing health hazards was not known during the Buddha's day, we have adduced enough material from the Pali canon to illustrate the Buddha's attitude to the problem. Quietude is much appreciated as spiritually rewarding, while noise is condemned as a personal and social nuisance.

Nature as Beautiful

The Buddha and his disciples regarded natural beauty as a source of great joy and aesthetic satisfaction. The spiritually advanced monks who purged themselves of sensuous worldly pleasures responded to natural beauty with a detached sense of appreciation. The average poet looks at nature and derives inspiration mostly by the sentiments it evokes in his own heart; he becomes emotionally involved with nature. For instance, he may compare the sun's rays passing over the mountain tops to the blush on a sensitive face; he may see a tear in a dew drop, the lips of his beloved in a rose petal, etc. But the appreciation of the monk is quite different. He appreciates nature's beauty for its own sake and derives joy unsullied by sensuous associations and self-projected ideas. The simple spontaneous appreciation of nature's exquisite beauty is expressed by the Elder Mahakashyapa in the following words:[55]

Those upland glades delightful to the soul,
Where the Kaveri spreads its wildering wreaths,
Where sound the trumpet-calls of elephants:
Those are the hills wherein my soul delights.

Those rocky heights with hue of dark blue clouds
Where lies embossed many a shining lake
Of crystal-clear, cool waters, and whose slopes
The "herds of Indra" cover and bedeck:
Those are the hills wherein my soul delights.

Fair uplands rain-refreshed, and resonant
With crested creatures' cries antiphonal,
Lone heights where silent Rishis oft resort:
Those are the hills wherein my soul delights.

The poem of Kaludayi inviting the Buddha to visit Kapilavatthu contains a beautiful description of spring:[56]

Now crimson glow the trees, dear Lord, and cast
Their ancient foliage in quest of fruit,
Like crests of flame they shine irradiant
And rich in hope, great Hero, is the hour.

Verdure and blossom-time in every tree
Wherever we look delightful to the eye,
And every quarter breathing fragrant airs,
While petals falling, yearning comes fruit:
It is time, O Hero, that we set out hence.

The long poem of Talaputa is a fascinating soliloquy.[57] His religious aspirations are beautifully blended with a profound knowledge of the teachings of the Buddha against the background of a sylvan resort. Many more poems could be cited for spiritual appreciation of nature, but it is not necessary to burden the essay with any more quotations. Suffice it to know that the Buddha's followers, too, were sensitive to the beauties and harmony of nature and that their appreciation is colored by spontaneity, simplicity, and a nonsensuous spirituality. . . .

Buddhism teaches that mind is the forerunner of all things, mind is supreme. If one acts with an impure mind, i.e., a mind sullied with greed, hatred, and delusion, suffering is the inevitable result. If one acts with a pure mind, i.e., with the opposite qualities of contentment, compassion, and wisdom, happiness will follow like a shadow.[58] One has to understand that pollution in the environment happens when there is psychological pollution within oneself. If one wants a clean environment, one has to adopt a lifestyle that springs from a moral and spiritual dimension.

Buddhism offers a simple moderate lifestyle eschewing both extremes of self-deprivation and self-indulgence. Satisfaction of basic human necessities, reduction of wants to the minimum, frugality, and contentment are its important characteristics. . . . The Buddhist admonition is to utilize nature in the same way as a bee collects pollen from the flower, neither polluting its beauty nor depleting its fragrance. Just as the bee manufactures honey out of pollen, so people should be able to find happiness and fulfillment in life without harming the natural world in which they live.

NOTES

All Pali texts referred to are editions of the Pali Text Society, London. Abbreviations used are as follows:

A	*Anguttara Nikaya*	M	*Majjhima Nikaya*
D	*Digha Nikaya*	S	*Samyutta Nikaya*
Dh	*Dhammapada*	Sn	*Sutta-nipata*
Dh.A	*Dhammapada Attakatha*	Thag	*Theragatha*
J	*Jataka*	Vin	*Vinaya Pitaka*

1. A. IV, 100.
2. S. IV, 52.
3. A. IV, 100.
4. D. III, 80.
5. D. III, 71.
6. A. I, 160.
7. Atthasalini, 854.
8. Dh. A. III, 854.
9. S. I, 39.
10. Dh. v. 204.
11. A. IV, 2, 220, 229.
12. Dh. A. I, 20 ff.
13. Dh. A. III, 129 ff.
14. Vin. II, 291.
15. A. IV, 283.
16. D. III, 188.
17. D. I, 4.
18. A. III, 208.
19. Vin. I, 137.
20. Vin. IV, 125.
21. Vin. III, 42.
22. Vin. IV, 125.
23. Sn. vv. 143–152.
24. J. I, 191.
25. Dh. A. I, 58 ff.
26. Vin. II, 194 f.
27. M. I, 387 f.
28. A. I, 161.
29. J. II, 423.
30. Petavatthu II, 9, 3.
31. Vin. IV, 34.
32. Dh. v. 188.
33. S. I, 1–45.
34. S. I, 206–215.
35. S. IV, 302; Dh.A. I, 3.
36. D. II, 4.
37. S. I, 33.
38. J. I, 199 f.
39. D. I, 63.
40. M. I 118; S. IV, 373.
41. Vin. IV, 205–206.
42. Robert Arvill, *Man and Environment* (Penguin Books, 1978), p. 118.
43. A. III, 31.
44. M. I, 457.
45. A. V, 135.
46. A. V, 15.
47. M. I, 16–24.
48. D. II, 267.
49. Thag. v. 398.
50. A. I, 261.
51. S. IV, 217, 293.
52. Sn. vv. 207–221; A. I, 273.
53. M. II, 23.
54. S. V, 369.
55. Thag. vv. 1062–1071.
56. Thag. vv. 527–529.
57. Thag. vv. 1091–1145.
58. Dh. vv. 1, 2.

Thoughts on the Jatakas

RAFE MARTIN

THE JATAKA TALES (*jataka* simply means "birthlet"), or tales of the Buddha's earlier births, are the record, through countless life-times, of both the historical Buddha's and any ripening bodhisattva's compassionate and often heroic self-giving. Two major collections of such tales have come down to us. Five hundred fifty tales are retained in the classic Pali *Jataka* and another thirty-five, with some overlap from the *Jataka*, in the Sanskrit *Jatakamala* (or "Garland of Jatakas") of Aryashura. These written records are just a small portion of a much larger oral tradition of *avadana* ("noble deed" or "noble giving") literature which has largely vanished. The Jatakas themselves, in written, oral, and dramatic forms, have persisted through the centuries and have been immensely popular in all the traditional Buddhist countries. Indeed, many of the greatest Buddhist monuments of Asia are carved and painted with hundreds of scenes from the Jatakas.

The Pali *Jataka* contains many kinds and levels of tales from monkish moralizings and simple animal fables to moving and compassionate animal-birth stories and fragments of larger heroic epics. Each is accompanied by a verse, which is canonical. Tradition asserts that all these verses and tales were told by the Buddha himself as a way of explaining a particular life situation of concern to his monks and lay followers at that moment. Taking the current incident (traditionally titled "The Story of the Present"), he told a tale of one of his own earlier births ("The Story of the Past"), which revealed the karmic origins of the situation at hand. The *Jatakamala* is a more literary, devotional, and centrally Mahayana work. Its core is the bodhisattva ideal. In it, tales of compassion and self-sacrifice are given thematic preeminence.

In both collections, however, the Buddha is shown not as withdrawing from the world, but as acting with compassion and wisdom for the benefit of all living beings. These untold lifetimes of effort, caring, and self-sacrifice, then, underlay his six years of ardent formal meditation practice when, as the ex-Prince Siddhartha, he at last attained his long-sought goal of Buddhahood. Just prior to his final enlightenment, legend records that Mara, the tempter, appeared before the future Buddha and asked him if he was truly worthy of attaining so high a goal. In response, he touched the earth lightly with his right hand, asking the humble earth to witness for him. The earth replied, "He is worthy! There is not a single spot on this globe where, through countless lifetimes, he has not offered his own life for the welfare of others!" All those past lives to which the earth bore witness are the lives recorded in the Jatakas. They are the hidden foundation upon which the Buddha's great, historical attainment necessarily stands.

In the Jatakas we discover the essence of the Buddhist attitude brought to life—the attitude of universal compassion which Lama Govinda describes as "the spontaneous urge to help others flowing from the knowledge of inner oneness." Elsewhere he also says that:

> The way of the Buddha was not one of running away from the world, but of overcoming it through growing knowledge (*prajna*). through active love (*maitri*) toward one's fellow beings, through inner participation in the joys and sufferings of others (*karuna muditha*), and equanimity with regard to one's own weal and woe. This way was vividly illustrated by the innumerable forms of existence of the Buddha (up to his last as Gautama Shakyamuni), as told in the Jatakas.

In the Jatakas, we learn that, long ago, as a Deer King, the Buddha risked his own life to free all creatures from danger; as a monkey he saved an ungrateful hunter; as a lion he saved all the frightened beasts from their own fears; as a parrot he flew selflessly through flames to save all those trapped in a burning forest; as an elephant he offered his life so that starving men might live; as a king he offered his own flesh to save a dove; as a prince he gave his life so that a starving tigress and her cubs might live. The Jatakas, in short, dramatically express the actions, in the world, of one liberated from all self-concern. They demonstrate the natural workings of the bodhisattva mind and heart, and by so doing, turn all of existence into a vast field of spiritual effort in which no life form, no matter how seemingly insignificant, is outside the Path. All beings are revealed as potential buddhas and bodhisattvas. Microbe, sparrow, dog, monkey, horse, dolphin, man. Each at its own level can feel compassion for the suffering of others and act selflessly to ease the pain of all beings. At some moment in life, it seems, each is offered an opportunity and a choice. Besides revealing the character of the Buddha in his own Path to Buddhahood, the Jatakas simultaneously validate and give credence to our own natural feelings of compassion and our own spontaneous acts of selflessness. These tales ideally show us how to live in a suffering world, as well as offer us a noble and deeply spiritual vision of the nature of the universe.

The message of the Jatakas is especially poignant in our own time. As we grow increasingly aware of the depredations our own twentieth-century lifestyles make on the planet, as the plight of whales, mountain gorillas, wolves, and other endangered species, as well as the cruel treatment which cats, dogs, rabbits, monkeys, rats, and mice receive—often to little purpose—in our laboratories, becomes increasingly clear to us, the Jatakas can only stand out in even greater relief. Who knows, perhaps as the Jatakas suggest, among the very animals which we as a culture now maim, torment, slaughter, and devour are sensitive and aspiring beings, bodhisattvas, and future buddhas. The Jatakas, once taken to heart, transform our own sensibilities and imaginations. After entering the world of the Jatakas, it becomes impossible not to feel more deeply for animals. It also becomes harder to believe that they are simply "below us"—that they are here for our own enjoyment and use. The Jatakas help us sense that animals have their own lives, their own karma, tests, purposes, and aspirations. And, as often brief and painful as their lives may be, they are also graced with a purity and a clarity which we can only humbly respect, and perhaps even occasionally envy. The Jatakas validate our deepest feelings and keep alive for us today knowledge of the wisdom inherent in all life forms. To lose respect for other species and the fundamental wisdom they too embody is, after all, to weaken the first and most fundamental of the precepts—not to kill but to cherish all life. Was not the Buddha a hare? A quail? A monkey, a lion, deer, or ox? Who is to say that the dog guarding our porch or the cat twining around our legs is not a bodhisattva on the Path even now? Entering the market one sees live rabbits and chickens and turkeys for sale. And one wonders, "Why are they here?"

and is torn. "Should I buy them all? How can I save them?" For in the Jatakas one has seen that their inner life is the same as our own. One seeks to save them all, and they too, looking out at us with black or with golden shining eyes, yearn only to liberate us.

Let me tell you a classic Jataka tale:

The Hungry Tigress

Once, long, long ago, the Buddha came to life as a noble prince named Mahasattva, in a land where the country of Nepal exists today. One day, when he was grown, he went walking in a wild forest with his two older brothers. The sky seemed alight with flames.

Suddenly, they saw a tigress. The brothers turned to flee, but the tigress stumbled and fell. She was starving and desperate and her two cubs were starving, too. She eyed her cubs miserably and, in that dark glance, the prince sensed long months of hunger and pain. He saw too that unless she had food soon, she might even be driven to devour her own cubs. He was moved by compassion for the difficulty of their lives. "What, after all, is this life for?" he thought.

Stepping forward, he removed his outer garments and lay down before her. Tearing his skin with a stone, he let the starving tigress smell the blood. Mahasattva's brothers fled. Hungrily, the tigress devoured the prince's body and chewed the bones. She and her cubs lived on, and for many years the forest was filled with a golden light.

Centuries later, a mighty king raised a pillar of carved stone on this spot, and pilgrims still go there to make offerings even today.

Deeds of compassion live on forever.

In this powerful and mysterious story, deep compassion, that profound, spontaneous inner urge to help others, is clearly and unhesitatingly embodied. Does the story mean that we too, as Buddhists, should rush out and open our veins so that starving dogs and cats may live? Perhaps for someone in whom such a response arose unselfconsciously, with no need to imitate or prove a thing, that would be the Way. But for most of us, this Jataka and others like it imaginatively sustain our own vision of the real nature of things, and pose fundamental questions which can only be resolved, over time, through the daily realities of our own practice and lives. Jatakas like "The Hungry Tigress" acknowledge our interrelation with all living things. And they remind us that, at some point, we too must act on our own deepest intuitions and experiences.

Compassion, they seem to say, must ultimately express itself in action, must take form, if it is to be real. How one does this, of course, is up to each of us. There is no one "right" way. All sincere efforts will be equally to the point.

Working with others to create communities that liberate the best in all their members; working selflessly to bring an end to the hells of nuclear destruction; creating places and opportunities for practice and teaching; caring for the land itself and for the many species which share its bounty with us; exposing the pitiful plight of laboratory animals; working to nourish the hearts and imaginations of children lost in a land of soulless TV dreams—wherever one turns, the opportunities are present. The tigress is before our eyes.

Such activities are part of the cutting of firewood and the drawing of water for today's world. The modern world of engaged Buddhism, the traditional world of the Jatakas and of the bodhisattva path, and the confusing, fragmented world in which we daily live and work today are, after all, seamlessly connected and cannot be separated from one another by even so much as the thickness of a single whisker or hair.

Enlightenment for Plants and Trees

WILLIAM LAFLEUR

W<small>E HAVE SEEN IT PORTRAYED IN ART</small> so often that perhaps we do not notice it anymore: Shakyamuni Buddha, in attaining enlightenment, is seated under a tree. It is called the Bodhi tree or the tree of enlightenment; its name in Latin became *Ficus religiosa*. And in the history of Buddhism it is an extremely important tree, the stimulus and symbol for a lot of thinking about trees, plants, and nature in general. Some modern scholars have been slightly embarrassed by that tree, taking it to be the persistence in Buddhism of some kind of primitive tree cult, some unseemly vestige of animism. But, of course, it was not so at all. The Bodhi tree posed a question of critical importance: Just how and where does enlightenment take place? Is the tree merely an inert setting, something under which a man sat until one day something profound spread through his mind, the ganglia of his consciousness, and to the ends of his body? Or was it, rather, human's companion in Bodhi, that without which he could have no perfection?

The question touched off a long debate, especially in China and Japan, where Buddhists got quite absorbed in the logic and implications. Old texts from India said that the goal of Buddhism is the eventual enlightenment of "all sentient beings." But did this widen or narrow the vehicle? It was puzzling. There was an amplitude in the mention of "all" but then a restriction to "sentient beings." All agreed that animals were included in the "sentient" category, but the status of plants and trees was left in doubt. Chi-t'sang, a master of the Madhyamika in China, seems to have been the first to use the phrase "Buddhahood attained by plants and trees." Sentient or not, plants achieve enlightenment; he felt that the Mahayana logically would have to include the vegetable realm. Then, in the eighth century, Chan-jan, a thinker of the T'ien-t'ai school, dissolved the whole sentient/insentient distinction and, though pushed to it by Buddhist logic, became almost lyrical in his vision of what we might call *coenlightenment*. He wrote:

The man whose mind is rounded out to perfection knows full well that Truth is not cut in half and that things do not exist apart from the mind. In the great Assembly of the Lotus all are present—without divisions. Grass, trees, the soil on which these grow—all have the same kinds of atoms. Some are barely in motion while others make haste along the Path, but they will all in time reach the precious land of Nirvana. . . . Who can really maintain that things inanimate lack buddhahood?[1]

Of course, the impulse in the Mahayana is to be as copious as possible, to make the large vehicle ever larger. But this is not soft sentimentality; it is something required by logic and by the sharp skeptical reflex in the Buddhist mind. For there was little confidence in what usually passes for common sense; most Buddhists regarded common sense as nothing more than widely shared illusion. Chan-jan suggested that we have no *real* way of knowing what is sentient and what is not. Thus the common sense of society dictates the use of various degrees of mobility to judge and categorize the elements that comprise our world. It is true that some are "barely in motion" while others "make haste" but, as Chan-jan saw it, the sentient/insentient distinction had no ultimate validity. He relativized it: animals move faster than plants, and plants move faster than soil, and soil moves faster than mountains. But all move! Later Zen masters were to pick up the point, writing cryptically of mountains moving through many *kalpa*s of time and even of giving birth.

Was it just hyperbole? The pathetic fallacy pushed to pathetic conclusions? Or was it something else, a perspective by the eye of the mind coursing through many *kalpa*s, guessing by intuition or observation that the mountains have, in fact, already "walked" here and there in interaction with seas and glaciers? Useless distinctions were reduced to absurdity so that there might be an affirmation of the wholeness and complex interdependence of the world. Now even stone and dirt had to be included in buddhahood. In Japan, Saicho wrote of the enlightenment of rocks and Dogen composed "The Mountains and Rivers Sutra."[2]

It was quite a remarkable development; in these brief pages I can offer only its highlights.[3] It came both out of galloping Mahayana universalism and the logic of interdependence. How, when misery is rooted in egotism, could there be peace—real peace—which is exclusive, limited to my group or category of being? By definition *bodhi* would have to be shared by all *sattva*: every kind of being and phenomenon there is. Strictly speaking, delusion begins when man thinks he is separable from his world or his environment, when he wants only some kind of private "peace of mind."

The Buddhist philosophers had more to say. They thought not only about goals but also about practice. And they concluded that not even the art or science called meditation was limited to human beings. This too came out in discussion of the status of plants and was lucidly stated by a Japanese monk named Ryogen. He had been a major participant in a public debate precisely on this topic held under imperial auspices in 963 CE, and he wrote up his position in a pamphlet.

Ryogen noted that there had long been in Buddhism a classical sequence applied to man, a four-page process. First, the implanting of the seat of enlightenment in the mind and heart; second, sustained disciplines and meditation in one place; third, the flower of enlightenment appearing in man; and finally there was a tranquil passage into complete nirvana. Ryogen wondered about the simile that runs throughout this sequence and carried it back to its source. He saw, in fact, no better Buddhist yogis in the world than the plants and trees in his own garden: still, silent, serene beings disciplining themselves toward nirvana.

And why not? If it made sense to speak of human practitioners assuming a lotus posture and getting themselves rooted in a place of non-movement for a while, it made equally good sense to think of trees and plants as beings that are fixed where they are so that they can be expert practitioners of their own kind of zazen. If similes and analogies can be lifted out of the natural world so that humanity can be explained, why not explain nature in terms of humanity? The compliment ought to be returned. Metaphor, the language of poetry, is one of exchange . . . but it ought to be a *mutual*, reciprocal exchange. It is almost as if these Buddhists of long ago anticipated William Carlos Williams trying through metaphor to reconcile the people and the stones.[4]

The whole mood and mode of Mahayana philosophy was to use logic to chop up logic's penchant for chopping up the world into multiple, disparate, and easily lost pieces. And then, of course, the philosophy had to slip into poetry. To "know" or be "scientific" *must* involve more than merely making up a taxonomy and classifying things. Certain schools of Buddhists had become expert at that sort of endeavor, but it seemed to lead nowhere except to long lists. The old distinction between sentient and insentient had been one of those ways of dividing up the world. But something had been missing. Underneath all the kingdoms, the phyla, the families, the genera, and the species—or their more ancient equivalents—lies their commonality, the embracing rubric called *sattva*. Michael Foucault, in *The Order of Things*, states it well:

> *Taxinomia* also implies a certain continuum of things (a nondiscontinuity, a plenitude of being) and a certain power of the imagination that renders apparent what is not, but makes possible, by this very fact, the revelation of that continuity.[5]

This is what the Madhyamika, the Hua-yen, the T'ien-t'ai, and the Zen grasped so well and why with them the philosophy naturally went poetic. They moved with ease into Foucault's definition: The poet is he who, beneath the named, constantly expected differences, rediscovers the buried kinships between things, their scattered resemblances.[6] He has an eye and an ear for *sattva*.

But in some ways the poets were expressing these sentiments even before the philosophers had worked out the details. Sun Ch'o, a fourth-century Buddho-Taoist, wrote about his wandering on Mt. T'ien-t'ai:

The great Void, vast and unimpeded,
Stirs the latent actuality of the Self so,
Now melted, forming streams and brooks;
congealed, becoming hills or mounds.[7]

The poets often returned to sit under their trees, since now all trees had become Bodhi trees. And, of course, trees were most useful when kept whole. The Buddhists picked up something of the Taoist wisdom about the "utility of the useless" as culled from the Chuang Tzu. It too had dealt with trees:

Tzu-ch'i of Nan-po was wandering around the Hill of Shang when he saw a huge tree there, different from all the rest. A thousand teams of horses could have taken shelter under it and its shade would have covered them all. Tzu-ch'i said, "What tree is this? It must certainly have some extraordinary usefulness!" But, looking up, he saw that the small limbs were gnarled and twisted, unfit for beams or rafters, and looking down, he saw that the trunk was pitted and rotten and could not be used for coffins. He licked one of the leaves and it blistered his mouth and made it sore. He sniffed the odor and it was enough to make a man drunk for three days. "It turns out to be a completely unusable tree," said Tzu-ch'i, "and so it has been able to grow this big. Aha! It is this unusableness that the Holy Man makes use of!"[8]

To the Buddhists the tree in its natural state becomes a place for shade; if so, shade itself becomes for humanity a kind salvation within this world. Refreshed under a willow, the Japanese Buddhist monk Saigyo drifts off into ecstasy:

"Just a brief stop"
I said when stepping off the road
Into a willow's shade
Where a bubbling stream flows by . . .
As has time since my "brief stop" began.[9]

The buddhahood of plants and trees is commonly assumed and discussed in the classical Noh drama of Japan. There plants act and speak on stage and often show people the Way. Donald Shively notes that in Noh, "not only is the Buddha nature contained in all things, but human beings may be led to a conception of the truth of reality by the grasses and the trees."[10]

And Basho, the great haiku poet of the seventeenth century, took his name from a banana plant growing near his hut. He felt a deep affinity to the fragile, humble plant.[11]

In the twelfth century, Saigyo already had a certain modern sense of the gap between human greed and nature's beneficence. This rather

poignant poem, direct from his own experience, expresses Saigyo's observation of his own greed and the generosity of nature:

> Scaling the crags
> Where azalea bloom . . . not for plucking
> But for hanging on!
> The saving creature of this rugged
> Mountain face I'm climbing.[12]

It was not unlike the greed that William Carlos Williams blamed for
decimating Paterson, New Jersey, and perhaps our whole world in the
twentieth century.[13] The magnitude is, of course, very different; but being
oblivious to *sattva* is the root cause of the problem in all cases. Interdependence is more than a neat point of logic, it is something of critical
importance for both humanity and the world.

We don't know exactly how the dialectics of the monks got out from
behind the monastery walls and into the minds of the common people.
In part it was through poems, celebrations of nature easily memorized
and sung while walking mountain paths. In part it was also through a
renaming of the things of the world, providing of Buddha-names for
them. Sensitivity to *sattva* seems to have spread thus. We can detect this
from the writings of Lafcadio Hearn (1850–1904), whom Kenneth Rexroth calls "the first important American writer to live in Japan and to
commit his imagination and considerable literary powers to what he
found there."[14]

Hearn's interest was in the Buddhism of common people, and one
of the things he found—much to his delight—was a rich set of names for
things. Through Hearn's eyes and writing we can glimpse something of
an era when the multiple creatures of the world were still somewhat
wrapped in protective nomenclatures. It did not lead to prohibition
against use; but it did instill a sense of reverence and restraint.

Hearn recorded many of the names in use at the time. Rockmoss was
the fingernails of the Buddha. Swamp-cabbage was Bodhidharma's plant.
A certain type of oak was that of the Arhat. Grasshoppers were creatures
upon which the blessed dead rode back to town for their midsummer
visits with pleased relatives. The Japanese warbler was imagined to be

calling out "hok-ke-kyo," the title of the holy *Lotus Sutra*. Even the ham-mer-head shark was referred to as a priest of the Nembutsu chant because its T-shaped head resembled the mallet used to strike a gong during their prayers.[15] In reading this today one wishes to wrap or rewrap the whale in some kind of protective name. Could it not be called Serene Bodhi-sattva of the Sea?

New names alone, of course, don't accomplish much. They can be no more than part of an effort to recapture or create a widespread sensi-tivity to the domain of *sattva*. John Passmore has written a rather chilling account of the way animals were thought of and treated in the history of the West.[16] Some, such as John Chrysostom and Saint Francis, showed compassion, but this was unusual. For the most part animals were consid-ered void of reason and thus not worthy of consideration—an argument from the Stoics. A kind of nadir was reached by Descartes and Malebran-che who thought it "impossible . . . to be cruel to animals, since animals are incapable of feeling."

Passmore thinks this had a direct effect upon such things as the pop-ularity of public vivisections in the seventeenth century. Only in the last century and a half has the situation changed. Schopenhauer, influenced by Asian thought, was a key figure in this. Clearly, it has been necessary for the mind of Europe and America to develop some new sensitivities.

Passmore has an interesting and important final comment:

> So the history we have been tracing is at once discouraging, insofar as it took two thousand years for Westerners to agree that it is wrong to treat animals cruelly, and encouraging insofar as it sug-gests that human opinion on such matters can change with consid-erable rapidity.[17]

The point is not to portray a sharp dichotomy between East and West. Neither the human mind nor historical accuracy can tolerate that. But the past does offer materials and insights that may be of use in coping with a set of crises facing us today, in both the East and the West.

NOTES

1. Fung Yu-lan, *A History of Chinese Philosophy*, vol. 2 (Princeton, N.J.: Princeton University Press, 1953), 386.

2. See Carl William Bielefeldt, "Dogen's 'The Mountains and Rivers Sutra,' " M.A. Thesis, University of California, Berkeley.
3. For more detailed treatment see my "Saigyo and the Buddhist Value of Nature, Parts I and II," *History of Religions* (Chicago: University of Chicago Press), vol. 13, 2 and 3, 93–128 and 227–248.
4. William Carlos William, "A Sort of a Song," *Selected Poems* (New York: New Directions, 1949), 108.
5. Michael Foucault, *The Order of Things: An Archeology of the Human Sciences* (New York: Vintage Books, 1970), 72.
6. Ibid., 49.
7. Richard B. Mather, "The Mystical Ascent of the T'ien T'ai Mountains: Sun Ch'os Yu-T'ien-t'ai'shan Fu," *Monumenta Serica* 20 (1961):226–245, quotation from 237.
8. Burton Watson, trans., *Chuang Tzu: Basic Writings* (New York: Columbia University Press, 1964), 61.
9. William R. LaFleur, *Mirror for the Moon: Poems by Saigyo* (New York, New Directions, 1978).
10. Donald H. Shively, "Buddhahood for the Nonsentient: A Theme in No Plays," *Harvard Journal of Asiatic Studies*, vol. 20 (1957):135–161. Quotation from 143.
11. Donald H. Shively, "Basho—The Man and the Plant," *Harvard Journal of Asiatic Studies*, vol. 16 (1953):146–161, especially 153–154.
12. William R. LaFleur, *Mirror for the Moon*.
13. See Joel Conarroe, *William Carlos Williams' Paterson: Language and Landscape* (Philadelphia: University of Pennsylvania Press, 1970).
14. Kenneth Rexroth, introduction to *The Buddhist Writings of Lafcadio Hearn* (Santa Barbara: Ross-Erikson, 1977), xxxvi.
15. Lafcadio Hearn, "Buddhist Names of Plants and Animals," in Rexroth, *Lafcadio*, 202–213.
16. John Passmore, "The Treatment of Animals," *Journal of the History of Ideas*, vol. 36:2 (April–May 1975):195–218.
17. Ibid., 217, emphasis mine.

Buddhism with a Small b

SULAK SIVARAKSA

T HE FOUNDER OF BUDDHISM was an ordinary man. He lived in the sixth century BCE, as the prince of a small state in what is now Nepal. Deeply concerned about life, death, and suffering, he discovered a solution to these deepest of human problems. His insight was universal and radical. It addressed suffering as such, not just this or that sort of suffering. Neither the cause nor the cure of suffering were revealed to him. The Buddha simply discovered them, as others could have before or since. He was a doctor for the ills of humankind. Buddhist liberation, *nirvana*, requires neither the mastery of an arcane doctrine nor an elaborate regimen of asceticism. In fact, the Buddha condemned extreme austerity as well as intellectual learning that does not directly address the urgent questions of life and death. The Buddha advocated the middle path between the extremes of hedonism and asceticism. He promised immediate release, saying that there is no need to work one's way through a sequence of karmic stages to some remote level where release is feasible. Zen Buddhism is well known in the West for emphasizing that release may come directly and to anyone. The behavior and teachings of meditation masters in the Theravada tradition do not differ from those of Zen masters on this point.

The Buddha's original teaching remains a common fund for all branches of Buddhism, and it is expressed in the Four Noble Truths: Suffering; the Cause of Suffering, namely desire or craving; the Cessation of Suffering; and the Way to the Cessation of Suffering, namely the Eightfold Path—Right Understanding, Right Mindfulness, Right Speech, Right Action, Right Livelihood, Right Effort, Right Attention, and Right Concentration. It is not enough merely to attain an intellectual understanding of these propositions; one has to practice them to make them part of life. Having medicine in a bottle does no good; medicine must be swallowed in order to enter the bloodstream.

If we do not regard suffering as real and threatening, we are not taking the message of the Buddha seriously. According to the Buddha, even ordinary existence is filled with pain. The early Buddhists enumerated many kinds of suffering. We moderns try to ignore the sad, dark aspects of our lives by using external distractions like television, music, and our own busy-ness. We are busy all the time, always thinking or doing things, incessantly fleeing this basic experience of angst. When we look deeply at our inner lives, we cannot deny that there are many things that cause us to suffer. The Buddha said that we will never be at ease until we overcome this fundamental anxiety, and he offered us a way to do it.

We cannot avoid contact with suffering. To be a Buddhist, we must be willing to share the suffering of others. The Buddha taught that gain and loss, dignity and obscurity, praise and blame, happiness and pain are all worldly conditions. Most people seek positive experiences and try to avoid the negative at all costs, but those who practice the Buddha's teaching take both positive and negative as they come. They do not grasp after one or the other, and in this way they continuously test their inner spiritual strength in the midst of the world.

The first step in the teaching of the Buddha is awareness. Recognition of what is going on is enlightenment. Recognition of the fact of suffering is the first step towards its mitigation. The most difficult thing for someone who is sick or addicted is to acknowledge his or her illness. Only when this occurs can there be progress. The Buddha also pointed out that when we realize suffering is universal, we can relieve a certain amount of anxiety already. When an adolescent realizes that his sufferings are the sufferings of all young people, he is taking a significant step toward their mitigation. It is a question of perspective. One of the Buddha's celebrated cures was with a mother who was mad with grief over the death of her child. She asked the Buddha to restore her child to life, and he told her that all that was required was a small bit of mustard seed from a household that had not seen death. Of course she couldn't find such a home, but she did find that the condition she lamented was universal and that restoring her child to life would only postpone inevitable sadness. The Buddha changed nothing, but the mother saw the facts in a different way and was transformed. The Buddha found that the cause of suffering is ignorance, and that by extinguishing ignorance, suffering is extinguished.

To practice the teachings of the Buddha, one must practice mindfulness. One must look deeply into one's own body, feelings, mind, and the objects of mind. It may sound simple, but to sustain oneself in the practice, one generally needs a teacher and a community of fellow practitioners to remind and encourage one. "Good friend" (*kalyana mitta*) is the technical term to describe such a person. Of course, one's "good friends" need not call themselves Buddhists. Living masters of any faith who are selfless and compassionate can be "good friends." People of any faith or any age can help each other. Members of the sangha—the community of monks and nuns in Buddhist countries—must join us in our efforts, so that the sangha can become relevant again. The sangha can be a great resource for bringing openness, love, and selflessness to many people.

Many people in the West think that Buddhism is only a vehicle for deep meditation and personal transformation, not for social involvement. The great sociologist Max Weber once said of Buddhism:

> Salvation is an absolutely personal performance of the self-reliant individual. No one, and particularly no social community, can help him. The specific asocial character of genuine mysticism is here carried to its maximum.[1]

This misunderstanding has been repeated by scholars in the West, and even by reputable Indian scholars:

> The Arahat [enlightened noble disciple] rests satisfied with achieving his own private salvation; he is not necessarily and actively interested in the welfare of others. The ideal of the Arahat smacks of selfishness; there is even a lurking fear that the world would take hold of him if he tarried here too long.[2]

To speak of Buddhism in this way is to ignore the Buddha's doctrine of no-self, or interdependence. Buddhism is primarily a method of overcoming the limits or restrictions of the individual self. Buddhism is not concerned just with private destiny, but with the lives and consciousness of all beings. This inevitably entails a concern with social and political matters, and these receive a large share of attention in the teachings of the Buddha as they are recorded in the *Pali Canon*.[3] Any attempt to understand Buddhism apart from its social dimension is fundamentally a mistake. Until Western Buddhists understand this, their embrace of Buddhism will not help very much in the efforts to bring about meaningful and positive social change, or even in their struggle to transform their ego. I agree with Trevor Ling when he says that Buddhism can be regarded as a prescription for both restructuring human consciousness and restructuring society.[4]

In South and Southeast Asia, Buddhists have long been concerned with both the attainment of personal liberation and the maintenance of proper social order. Religion and politics are perceived as two interrelated wheels. The wheel of righteousness (*dhammacakka*) must influence the wheel of power (*anacakka*). For Buddhism to survive, according to the scriptures, it must be supported by a just ruler (*dhammaraja*), a king who turns the wheel of state in the name of justice. The king rules in subordination to one power only, the Dharma. Kings in Theravadin Buddhist countries since Emperor Asoka have strived for this ideal. It is the ruler's duty to restrain the violent elements in society, discourage crime through the alleviation of poverty, and provide the material necessities to enable the state's citizens to pursue the religious life unhindered.[5] If this ideal is not carried out, the tension between the two wheels causes the wheel of power to collapse, and a new ruler will take over. The wheel of righteousness is represented by the sangha. While the sangha is not directly involved with the wheel of power, it can affirm or deny the government's legitimacy. Indeed, support of the state from the sangha is a necessity for the political, social, and economic well-being of the community. To suggest that Buddhism has been unconcerned with the organization of society is to ignore history. Traditionally, Buddhism has seen personal salvation and social justice as interlocking components.

The Sarvodaya Movement in Sri Lanka is an effort to reconstruct society in a Buddhist manner.[6] In Vietnam, the Venerable Thich Nhat Hanh founded Van Hanh University and the School of Youth for Social Service. During the war in his country, members of both institutions showed great courage and compassion. Despite this, or because of it, the founder is still not allowed to return home. Many years ago, he proposed that modern Buddhists need retreat monasteries and spiritual centers that would be places of serenity and retreat. For those of us who work constantly in the city, daily mindfulness practice alone may not build enough strength, so Thich Nhat Hanh proposed that clergy and laypeople who care for the social welfare of others retreat regularly to such centers. Without renewing their inner strength, social workers will find it difficult to endure the tumultuous world outside. Nhat Hanh proposed the establishment of an Institute for Buddhist Studies, not as a place for degrees and diplomas in order to get jobs, or for Buddhism to be studied in the abstract, but as a place for a living community of those who truly seek to understand a spiritual way of thought and explore the social and artistic life of the Buddhist tradition.

Buddhism as practiced in most Asian countries today serves mainly to legitimize dictatorial regimes and multinational corporations. If we Buddhists want to redirect our energies towards enlightenment and universal love, we should begin by spelling Buddhism with a small *b*. Buddhism with a small *b* means concentrating on the message of the Buddha and paying less attention to myth, culture, and ceremony. We must refrain from focusing on the limiting, egocentric elements of our tradition. Instead, we should follow the original teachings of the Buddha in ways that promote tolerance and real wisdom. It is not a Buddhist approach to say that if everyone practiced Buddhism, the world would be a better place. Wars and oppression begin from this kind of thinking.

Buddhism enters the life of society through the presence of men and women who practice and demonstrate the Way (*magga*) toward the ultimate goal of nirvana through their thought, speech, and actions. The presence of Buddhist adepts means the presence of wisdom, love, and peace. The leaders of most societies are themselves confused and engrossed in greed, hatred, and delusion. They are like the blind leading the blind. If they do not have peace of mind, how can they lead others? In Buddhism, we say that the presence of one mindful person can have great influence on society and is thus very important. We use the term "emptiness of action" or "nonaction" to mean to act in a way that influences all situations nonviolently. The most valued contribution of masters of the Way is their presence, not their actions. When they act, however, their actions are filled with love, wisdom, and peace. Their actions are their very presence, their mindfulness, their own personalities. This nonaction, this awakened presence, is a most fundamental contribution.

The presence of virtuous people is the foundation for world peace. This belief is found not only in the Buddhist tradition, but in almost all of Asian civilization. A Chinese sage said, "Whenever an enlightened person appears, the water in the rivers turns clearer and the plants grow greener." Cultivators of Zen would say that we need "a person of no rank."

The presence of individuals who have attained awakening is not passive or lacking in zeal. Those who have attained the Way are living individuals who speak a living language. Their thoughts, speech, and actions express their views toward contemporary life and its problems. If spiritual leaders speak only in clichés and words that have no meaning for the modern world, their religions will die. There may be many churches, temples, pagodas, and ritual, but these are only outward forms of religious practice without spiritual depth or content. For masters who live their religion, awareness is born from their own experience, not just from books or tradition.

True masters may be theologians, philosophers, scientists, artists, or writers. Their awareness is not of the intellect, nor is it based on the views of partisan groups or ideologies. They live according to their own true self and not according to public opinion or the pronouncements of authorities. Their thoughts, science, and art are permeated with the characteristics of love, wisdom, and humanism, and they reject the path of war and ideological conflict. They envision and work for a society that unites humanity. The influence of compassion and serenity can be seen in the cultural and artistic works of India, Sri Lanka, Southeast Asia, China, Korea, Japan, and Tibet, through poetry, architecture, painting, and other arts. Through thought and art, the source of Buddhist wisdom has reached teachers, scientists, and politicians.

Buddhism is simply a way of mindfulness and peace. The presence of Buddhism does not mean having a lot of schools, hospitals, cultural institutions, and political parties run by Buddhists. Rather, the presence of Buddhism means that all these things are permeated and administered with humanism, love, tolerance, and enlightenment. These are characteristics that Buddhism attributes to opening up and developing the best aspects of human nature. This is the true spirit of Buddhism. All our efforts to preserve Buddhism or Buddhist society may fail, or they may succeed. The outcome is irrelevant. Our goal is to develop human beings with enough inner strength and moral courage to begin restructuring the collective consciousness of society.

Since the time of the Buddha, there have been many Buddhists who were very involved with society. But there have also been meditation masters who, although they seem not to be involved with society, have also made great contributions to the community of men and women. Their very lives are proof that saints are still possible in this world. Without persons like these, our world would be poorer, more shallow. These meditation masters—monks and nuns who spend their lives in the forests— are important for all of us. We who live in society can benefit greatly from them. From time to time we can study and meditate with masters like these, so they can guide us to look within. In the crises of the present day, those of us who work in society, who confront power and injustice on a regular basis, get beaten down and exhausted. At least once a year, we need to visit a retreat center to regain our spiritual strength so that we can continue to confront society. Spiritual masters are like springs of fresh water. We who work in society need to carry that pure water to flood the banks and fertilize the land and the trees, in order to be of use to the plants and animals, so that they can taste something fresh and be revitalized. If we do not go back to the spring, our minds will get polluted, just as water becomes polluted, and we will not be of much use to the plants, the trees, or the earth. At home, we must practice our meditation or prayer at least every morning or evening.

We who work in society must be careful. We become polluted so easily, particularly when we are confronted by so many problems. Sometimes we feel hatred or greed; sometimes we wish for more power or wealth. We must be clear with ourselves that we do not need much wealth or power. It is easy, particularly as we get older, to want softer lives and more recognition, and to be on equal terms with those in power. But this is dangerous. Religion means a deep commitment to personal transformation. To be of help we must become more and more selfless. To do this, we have to take moral responsibility for our own being and our own society. This has been the essence of religion from ancient times right to the present.

The Buddhist tradition focuses on looking within as the means to achieve this. Meditation is the most important and distinctive element of Buddhism. Through deepening awareness comes acceptance, and through acceptance comes a seemingly miraculous generosity of spirit and empowerment for the work that compassion requires of us. With this self-awareness, we can genuinely join those of other faiths to work for our mutual betterment.

The world today has become a very small place. In order to build mutual understanding and respect among people of diverse religions and beliefs, we need an alternative to living by ideology. We must see things as they are and then act from that awareness. Ken Jones, of the Network of Engaged Buddhists in the United Kingdom, put it succinctly: "The greatest religious problem today is . . . how to combine the search for an expansion of inner awareness with effective social action, and how to find one's true identity in both."[7] For me, this means practicing buddhism with a small *b*.

NOTES

1. Max Weber, *The Religion of India* (New York: The Free Press, 1958), 213.
2. T.R.V. Murti, *The Central Philosophy of Buddhism: A Study of the Madhyamika System* (London: G. Allen and Unwin, 1955), 263.
3. See, e.g., Thich Nhat Hanh, *Old Path White Clouds: Walking in the Footsteps of the Buddha* (Berkeley: Parallax Press, 1991).
4. Trevor O. Ling, *The Buddha: Buddhist Civilization in India and Ceylon* (New York: Scribner, 1973), 183.
5. See the following for a full treatment of this subject: Bardwell Smith et al. (eds.), *The Two Wheels of Dhamma: Essays on Theravada Tradition in India and Ceylon* (Chambersburg, Pa.: American Academy of Religion, *Studies in Religion* No. 3, 1972); R. S. Sharma, *Aspects of Political Ideas and Institutions in Ancient India*, 2nd edition (Delhi: Motilal Banarsidass, 1968), 64–77; and B. G. Gokhale, "Early Buddhist Kingship," in *Journal of Asian Studies*, vol. 26, no. 1 (Nov. 1966): 33–36, and his "The Early Buddhist View of the State," in *Journal of the American Oriental Society*, vol. 89, no. 4 (Oct.–Dec. 1969): 731–738.
6. See D. L. Wickremsingha, "Religion and the Ideology of Development," in N. Jayaveera, ed., *Religion and Development in Asian Societies* (Colombo, 1973); and Joanna Macy, *Dharma and Development* (West Hartford, Conn.: Kumarian Press, 1983).
7. Ken Jones, *The Social Face of Buddhism* (Boston: Wisdom Publications, 1988).

Blue Mountains Constantly Walking

GARY SNYDER

FUDO AND KANNON

The mountains and rivers of this moment are the actualization of the way of the ancient Buddhas. Each, abiding in its own phenomenal expression, realizes completeness. Because mountains and waters have been active since before the eon of emptiness, they are alive at this moment. Because they have been the self since before form arose, they are liberated and realized.

This is the opening paragraph of Dogen Kigen's astonishing essay *Sansuikyo*, "Mountains and Waters Sutra," written in the autumn of 1240, thirteen years after he returned from his visit to Song-dynasty China. At the age of twelve he had left home in Kyoto to climb the well-worn trails through the dark hinoki and sugi (cedar-and-sequoia-like) forests of Mt. Hiei. This three-thousand-foot range at the northeast corner of the Kamo River basin, the broad valley now occupied by the huge city of Kyoto, was the Japanese headquarters mountain of the Tendai sect of Buddhism. He became a novice monk in one of the red-painted shadowy wooden temples along the ridges.

"The blue mountains are constantly walking."

In those days travelers walked. The head monk at the Daitoku-ji Zen monks' hall in Kyoto once showed me the monastery's handwritten "Yearly Tasks" book from the nineteenth century. (It had been replaced by another handwritten volume with a few minor updates for the twentieth century.) These are the records that the leaders refer to through the year in keeping track of ceremonies, meditation sessions, and recipes. It listed the temples that were affiliated with this training school in order of the traveling time it took to get to them: from one day to four weeks' walk. Student monks from even those distant temples usually made a round trip home at least once a year.

Virtually all of Japan is steep hills and mountains dissected by fast shallow streams that open into shoestring valleys and a few wider river plains toward the sea. The hills are generally covered with small conifers and shrubs. Once they were densely forested with a cover of large hardwoods as well as the irregular pines and the tall straight hinoki and sugi. Traces of a vast network of well-marked trails are still found throughout the land. They were tramped down by musicians, monks, merchants, porters, pilgrims, and periodic armies.

We learn a place and how to visualize spatial relationships, as children, on foot and with imagination. Place and the scale of space must be measured against our bodies and their capabilities. A "mile" was originally a Roman measure of one thousand paces. Automobile and airplane travel teaches us little that we can easily translate into a perception of space. To know that it takes six months to walk across Turtle Island/ North America walking steadily but comfortably all day every day is to get some grasp of the distance. The Chinese spoke of the "four dignities"—Standing, Lying, Sitting, and Walking. They are "dignities" in that they are ways of being fully ourselves, at home in our bodies, in their fundamental modes. I think many of us would consider it quite marvelous if we could set out on foot again, with a little inn or a clean camp available every ten or so miles and no threat from traffic, to travel across a large landscape—all of China, all of Europe. That's the way to see the world: in our own bodies.

Sacred mountains and pilgrimage to them is a deeply established feature of the popular religions of Asia. When Dogen speaks of mountains he is well aware of these prior traditions. There are hundreds of famous Daoist and Buddhist peaks in China and similar Buddhist and Shinto-associated mountains in Japan. There are several sorts of sacred mountains in Asia: a "sacred site" that is the residence of a spirit or deity is the simplest and possibly oldest. Then there are "sacred areas"— perhaps many dozens of square miles—that are special to the mythology and practice of a sect with its own set of Daoist or Buddhist deities—miles of paths—and dozens or hundreds of little temples and shrines. Pilgrims might climb thousands of feet, sleep in the plain board guesthouses, eat rice gruel and a few pickles, and circumambulate set routes burning incense and bowing at site after site.

Finally, there are a few highly formalized sacred areas that have been deliberately modeled on a symbolic diagram (mandala) or a holy text. They too can be quite large. It is thought that to walk within the designated landscape is to enact specific moves on the spiritual plane.[1] Some friends and I once walked the ancient pilgrimage route of the Omine Yamabushi (mountain ascetics) in Nara prefecture from Yoshino to Kumano. In doing so we crossed the traditional center of the "Diamond-Realm Mandala" at the summit of Mt. Omine (close to six thousand feet) and four hiking days later descended to the center of the "Womb-Realm Mandala" at the Kumano ("Bear Field") Shrine, deep in a valley. It was the late-June rainy season, flowery and misty. There were little stone shrines the whole distance—miles of ridges—to which we sincerely bowed each time we came on them. This projection of complex teaching diagrams onto the landscape comes from the Japanese variety of Vajrayana Buddhism, the Shingon sect, in its interaction with the shamanistic tradition of the mountain brotherhood.

The regular pilgrimage up Mt. Omine from the Yoshino side is flourishing—hundreds of colorful Yamabushi in medieval mountain-gear scale cliffs, climb the peak, and blow conches while others chant sutras in the smoky dirt-floored temple on the summit. The long-distance practice has been abandoned in recent years, so the trail was so overgrown it was almost impossible to find. This four-thousand-foot-high direct ridge route makes excellent sense, and I suspect it was the regular way of traveling from the coast to the interior in paleolithic and neolithic times. It was the only place I ever came on wild deer and monkeys in Japan.

In East Asia "mountains" are often synonymous with wilderness. The agrarian states have long since drained, irrigated, and terraced the lowlands. Forest and wild habitat start at the very place the farming stops. The lowlands, with their villages, markets, cities, palaces, and wineshops, are thought of as the place of greed, lust, competition, commerce, and intoxication—the "dusty world." Those who would flee such a world and seek purity find caves or build hermitages in the hills—and take up the practices which will bring realization or at least a long healthy life. These

hermitages in time became the centers of temple complexes and ultimately religious sects. Dogen says:

> Many rulers have visited mountains to pay homage to wise people
> or ask for instructions from great sages. . . . At such time these
> rulers treat the sages as teachers, disregarding the protocol of the
> usual world. The imperial power has no authority over the wise
> people in the mountains.

So "mountains" are not only spiritually deepening but also (it is hoped)
independent of the control of the central government. Joining the hermits
and priests in the hills are people fleeing jail, taxes, or conscription.
(Deeper into the ranges of southwestern China are the surviving hill
tribes who worship dogs and tigers and have much equality between the
sexes, but that belongs to another story.) Mountains (or wilderness) have
served as a haven of spiritual and political freedom all over.

Mountains also have mythic associations of verticality, spirit, height,
transcendence, hardness, resistance, and masculinity. For the Chinese
they are exemplars of the "yang": dry, hard, male, and bright. Waters
are feminine: wet, soft, dark "yin" with associations of fluid-but-strong,
seeking (and carving) the lowest, soulful, life-giving, shape-shifting. Folk
(and Vajrayana) Buddhist iconography personifies "mountains and waters" in the *rupas*—"images of Fudo Myo-o (Immovable Wisdom King)
and Kannon Bosatsu (The Bodhisattva Who Watches the Waves). Fudo
is almost comically ferocious-looking with a blind eye and a fang, seated
or standing on a slab of rock and enveloped in flames. He is known as an
ally of mountain ascetics. Kannon (Kuan-yin, Avalokitesvara) gracefully
leans forward with her lotus and vase of water, a figure of compassion.
The two are seen as buddha-work partners: ascetic discipline and relent-
less spirituality balanced by compassionate tolerance and detached for-
giveness. Mountains and Waters are a dyad that together make wholeness
possible: wisdom and compassion are the two components of realization.
Dogen says:

> Wenzi said, "The path of water is such that when it rises to the
> sky, it becomes raindrops; when it falls to the ground, it becomes

rivers." . . . The path of water is not noticed by water, but is realized by water.

There is the obvious fact of the water cycle and the fact that mountains and rivers indeed form each other: waters are precipitated by heights, carve or deposit landforms in their flowing descent, and weight the offshore continental shelves with sediment to ultimately tilt more uplifts. In common usage the compound "mountains and waters"—*shan-shui* in Chinese—is the straightforward term for landscape. Landscape is "mountains and waters pictures." (A mountain range is sometimes also termed *mai*, a "pulse" or "vein"—as a network of veins on the back of a hand.) One does not need to be a specialist to observe that landforms are a play of stream-cutting and ridge-resistance and that waters and hills interpenetrate in endlessly branching rhythms. The Chinese feel for land has always incorporated this sense of a dialectic of rock and water, of downward flow and rocky uplift, and of the dynamism and "slow flowing" of earth-forms. There are several surviving large Chinese horizontal handscrolls from premodern eras titled something like "Mountains and Rivers Without End." Some of them move through the four seasons and seem to picture the whole world.

"Mountains and waters" is a way to refer to the totality of the process of nature. As such it goes well beyond dichotomies of purity and pollution, natural, and artificial. The whole, with its rivers and valleys, obviously includes farms, fields, villages, cities, and the (once comparatively small) dusty world of human affairs.

THIS

"The blue mountains are constantly walking."

Dogen is quoting the Chan master Furong. Dogen was probably envisioning those mountains of Asia whose trails he had walked over the years—peaks in the three- to nine-thousand-foot range, hazy blue or blue-green, mostly tree-covered, maybe the steep jumbled mountains of coastal South China where he had lived and practiced thirteen years earlier. (Timberline at these latitudes is close to nine thousand feet—none of these are alpine mountains.) He had walked thousands of miles. ("The Mind studies the way running barefoot.")

> If you doubt mountains walking you do not know your own walking.

Dogen is not concerned with "sacred mountains"—or pilgrimages, or spirit allies, or wilderness as some special quality. His mountains and streams are the processes of this earth, all of existence, process, essence, action, absence; they roll being and nonbeing together. They are what we are, we are what they are. For those who would see directly into essential nature, the idea of the sacred is a delusion and an obstruction: it diverts us from seeing what is before our eyes: plain thusness. Roots, stems, and branches are all equally scratchy. No hierarchy, no equality. No occult and exoteric, no gifted kids and slow achievers. No wild and tame, no bound or free, no natural and artificial. Each totally its own frail self. Even though connected all which ways; even *because* connected all which ways.

This, *thusness*, is the nature of the nature of nature. The wild in wild.

So the blue mountains walk to the kitchen and back to the shop, to the desk, to the stove. We sit on the park bench and let the wind and rain drench us. The blue mountains walk out to put another coin in the parking meter, and go on down to the 7-Eleven. The blue mountains march out of the sea, shoulder the sky for a while, and slip back into the waters.

HOMELESS

The Buddhists say "homeless" to mean a monk or priest (in Japanese, *shukke*—literally "out of the house"). It refers to a person who has supposedly left the householder's life and the temptations and obligations of the secular world behind. Another phrase, "leaving the world," means getting away from the imperfections of human behavior—particularly as reinforced by urban life. It does not mean distancing yourself from the natural world. For some it has meant living as mountain hermits or members of religious communities. The "house" has been set against "mountains" or "purity." Enlarging the scale of the homeless world, the fifth-century poet Zhiang-yan said the proper hermit should "take the purple heavens to be his hut, the encircling sea to be his pond, roaring with laughter in his nakedness, walking along singing with his hair hanging down."[2] The early Tang poet Han-shan is taken as the veritable model of a recluse—his spacious home reaches to the end of the universe:

> I settled at Cold Mountain long ago,
> Already it seems like years and years.
> Freely drifting, I prowl the woods and streams
> And linger watching things themselves.
> Men don't get this far into the mountains,
> White clouds gather and billow.
> Thin grass does for a mattress,
> The blue sky makes a good quilt.
> Happy with a stone underhead
> Let heaven and earth go about their changes.

"Homeless" is here coming to mean "being at home in the whole universe." In a similar way, self-determining people who have not lost the wholeness of their place can see their households and their regional mountains or woods as within the same sphere.

I attended the ceremonies at the shrine for the volcanic mountain of Suwa-no-se Island, in the East China Sea, one year. The path through the jungle needed brushing, so rarely did people go there. Two of us from the Banyan Ashram went as helpers to three elders. We spent the morning cutting overgrowth back, sweeping the ground, opening and wiping the unpainted wood altar-structure (about the size of a pigeon coop), and then placing some offerings of sweet potatoes, fruit, and *shochu* on the shelf before the blank space that in fact framed the mountain itself. One elder then faced the peak (which had been belching out ash clouds lately) and made a direct, perfunctory personal speech or prayer in dialect. We sat on the ground sweating and cut open watermelon with a sickle and drank some of the strong *shochu* then, while the old guys told stories of other days in the islands. Tall, thick, glossy green trees arched over us, roaring with cicada. It was not trivial. The domestic parallel is accomplished in each household with its photos of ancestors, offerings of rice and alcohol, and a vase with a few twigs of wild evergreen leaves. The house itself, with its funky tiny kitchen, bath, well, and entranceway altars, becomes a little shrine.

And then the literal "house," when seen as just another piece of the world, is itself impermanent and composite, a poor "homeless" thing in its own right. Houses are made up, heaped together, of pine boards, clay tiles, cedar battens, river boulder piers, windows scrounged from wrecking yards, knobs from K-Mart, mats from Cost Plus, kitchen floor of sandstone from some mountain ridge, doormat from Longs—made up of the same world as you and me and mice.

> Blue mountains are neither sentient nor insentient. You are neither sentient nor insentient. At this moment, you cannot doubt the blue mountains walking.

Not only plum blossoms and clouds, or Lecturers and Roshis, but chisels, bent nails, wheelbarrows, and squeaky doors are all teaching the truth of the way things are. The condition of true "homelessness" is the maturity of relying on nothing and responding to whatever turns up on the doorstep. Dogen encourages us with "A mountain always practices in every place."

LARGER THAN A WOLF, SMALLER THAN AN ELK

All my life I have been in and around wild nature, working, exploring, studying, even while living in cities. Yet I realized a few years ago that I had never made myself into as good a botanist or zoologist or ornithologist as so many of the outdoor people I admire have done. Recalling where I had put my intellectual energies over the years, it came to me that I had made my fellow human beings my study—that I had been a naturalist of my own species. I had been my own object-of-study, too. I enjoy learning how different societies work out the details of subsistence and celebration in their different landscapes. Science, technology, and the economic uses of nature need not be antithetical to celebration. The line between use and misuse, between objectification and celebration, is fine indeed.

The line is in the details. I once attended the dedication of a Japanese temple building that had been broken down and transported across the Pacific to be resurrected on the West Coast. The dedication ceremony was in the Shinto style and included offerings of flowers and plants. The difficulty was that they were the plants that would have been used in a traditional Japanese dedication and had been sent from Japan—they were not plants of the new place. The ritualists had the forms right but clearly didn't grasp the substance. After everyone had gone home I tried to make brief introductions myself: "Japanese building of hinoki wood, meet manzanita and Ponderosa Pine . . . please take care of yourself in this dry climate. Manzanita, this building is used to damp air and lots of people. Please accept it in place of your dusty slopes." Humans provide their own sort of access to understanding nature and the wild.

The human diverseness of style and costume, and the constant transformations of popular culture, is a kind of symbolic speciation—as though humans chose to mimic the colors and patterns of birds. People from the high civilizations in particular have elaborate notions of separateness and difference and dozens of ways to declare themselves "out of nature." As a kind of game this might be harmless. (One could imagine the phylum Chordata declaring, "We are a qualitative leap in evolution representing something entirely transcendent entering what has hitherto been merely biology.") But at the very minimum this call to a special destiny on the part of human beings can be seen as a case of needlessly multiplying theories (Occam's razor). And the results—in the human treatment of the rest of nature—have been pernicious.

There is a large landscape handscroll called "Interminable Mountains and Streams" (attributed to Lu Yuan of the Ching dynasty; now in the Freer). We see, within this larger scope of rocks, trees, ridges, mountains, and watercourses, people and their works. There are peasants and thatched huts, priests and complexes of temples, scholars at their little windows, fishermen in their boats, traveling merchants with their loads, matrons, children. While the Buddhist tradition of North India and Tibet made the mandala—painted or drawn charts of the positions of consciousness and cause-and-effect chains—their visual teaching aids, the Chan tradition of China (especially the Southern Song) did something similar (I will venture to suggest) with landscape painting. If a scroll is taken as a kind of Chinese mandala, then all the characters in it are our various little selves, and the cliffs, trees, waterfalls, and clouds are our own changes and stations. (Swampy reedy thicket along a stream—what does *that* say?) Each type of ecological system is a different mandala, a different imagination. Again the Ainu term *iworu*, field-of-beings, comes to mind.

> All beings do not see mountains and waters in the same way. . . . Some see water as wondrous blossoms, hungry ghosts see water as raging fire or pus and blood. Dragons see water as a palace or a pavilion. . . . Some beings see water as a forest or a wall. Human beings see water as water. . . . Water's freedom depends only on water.

One July walking down from the headwaters of the Koyukuk River in the Brooks Range of Alaska I found myself able to look into the realm of Dall (mountain) sheep. The green cloudy tundra summer alps—in which I was a frail visitor—were the most hospitable they would ever be to a hairless primate. The long dark winters do not daunt the Dall sheep, though—they do not even migrate down. The winds blow the scant loose snow, and the dried forbs and grasses of arctic summer are nibbled through the year. The dozens of summer sheep stood out white against green: playing, napping, eating, butting, circling, sitting, dozing in their high smoothed-out beds on ledges at the "cliff-edge of life and death." Dall sheep (in Athapaskan called *dibee*) see mountains—Dogen might say—"as a palace or pavilion." But that provisional phrase "palace or pavilion" is too high-class, urban, and human to really show how totally and uniquely *at home* each life-form must be in its own unique "buddha-field."

> Green mountain walls in blowing cloud
> white dots on far slopes, constellations,
> slowly changing, not stars, not rocks

"by the midnight breezes strewn"
cloud tatters, lavender arctic light
on sedate wild sheep grazing
tundra greens, held in the web of clan
and kin by bleats and smells to the slow
rotation of their Order living
half in the sky—damp wind up from the
whole North Slope and a taste of the icepack,
the primus roaring now,
here, have some tea.

And down in the little arctic river below the slopes the Grayling with their iridescent bodies are in their own (to us) icy paradise. Dogen again:

Now when dragons and fish see water as a palace, it is just like human beings seeing a palace. They do not think it flows. If an outsider tells them, "What you see as a palace is running water," the dragons and fish will be astonished, just as we are when we hear the words, "Mountains flow."

We can begin to imagine, to visualize, the nested hierarchies and webs of the actual nondualistic world. Systems theory provides equations but few metaphors. In the "Mountains and Waters Sutra" we find:

It is not only that there is water in the world, but there is a world in water. It is not just in water. There is a world of sentient beings in clouds. There is a world of sentient beings in the air. There is a world of sentient beings in fire. . . . There is a world of sentient beings in a blade of grass.

It would appear that the common conception of evolution is that of competing species running a sort of race through time on planet earth, all on the same running field, some dropping out, some flagging, some victoriously in front. If the background and foreground are reversed, and we look at it from the side of the "conditions" and their creative possibilities, we can see these multitudes of interactions through hundreds of other eyes. We could say a food brings a form into existence. Huckleberries and salmon call for bears, the clouds of plankton of the North Pacific call for salmon, and salmon call for seals and thus orcas. The Sperm Whale is sucked into existence by the pulsing, fluctuating pastures of squid, and the open niches of the Galápagos Islands sucked a diversity of bird forms and functions out of one line of finch.

Conservation biologists speak of "indicator species"—animals or birds that are so typical of a natural area and its system that their condition is an indicator of the condition of the whole. The old conifer forests can be measured by "Spotted Owl," and the Great Plains once said (and would say it again) "bison." So the question I have been asking myself is: what says "humans"? What sucks *our* lineage into form? It is surely the "mountains and rivers without end"—the whole of this earth on which we find ourselves more or less competently at home. Berries, acorns, grass-seeds, apples, and yams call for dextrous creatures something like us to come forward. Larger than a wolf, smaller than an elk, human beings are not such huge figures in the landscape. From the air, the works of humanity are scratches and grids and ponds, and in fact most of the earth seems, from afar, to be open land. (We know now that our impact is far greater than it appears.)

As for towns and cities—they are (to those who can see) old tree trunks, riverbed gravels, oil seeps, landslide scrapes, blowdowns and burns, the leavings after floods, coral colonies, paper-wasp nests, beehives, rotting logs, watercourses, rock-cleavage lines, ledge strata layers, guano heaps, feeding frenzies, courting and strutting bowers, lookout rocks, and ground-squirrel apartments. And for a few people they are also palaces.

DECOMPOSED

"Hungry ghosts see water as raging fire or pus and blood . . ."

Life in the wild is not just eating berries in the sunlight. I like to imagine a "depth ecology" that would go to the dark side of nature—the ball of crunched bones in a scat, the feathers in the snow, the tales of insatiable appetite. Wild systems are in one elevated sense above criticism, but they can also be seen as irrational, moldy, cruel, parasitic. Jim Dodge told me how he had watched—with fascinated horror—Orcas methodically batter a Gray Whale to death in the Chukchi Sea. Life is not just a diurnal property of large interesting vertebrates; it is also nocturnal, anaerobic, cannibalistic, microscopic, digestive, fermentative: cooking away in the warm dark. Life is well maintained at a four-mile ocean depth, is waiting and sustained on a frozen rock wall, is clinging and nourished in hundred-degree desert temperatures. And there is a world of nature on the decay side, a world of beings who do rot and decay in the shade. Human beings have made much of purity and are repelled by blood, pollution, putrefaction. The other side of the "sacred" is the sight of your beloved in the underworld, dripping with maggots. Coyote, Orpheus, and Izanagi cannot help but look, and they lose her. Shame, grief, embarrassment, and fear are the anaerobic fuels of the dark imagination. The less familiar energies of the wild world, and their analogs in the imagination, have given us ecologies of the mind.

Here we encounter the peculiar habitat needs of the gods. They settle on the summits of mountains (as on Mt. Olympus), have chambers deep below the earth, or are invisibly all around us. (One major deity is rumored to be domiciled entirely off this earth.) The Yana said that Mt. Lassen of northern California—"Waganupa" in Ishi's tongue, a ten-thousand-foot volcano—is home to countless *kukini* who keep a fire going inside. (The smoke passes out through the smoke-hole.) They will enjoy their magical stick-game gambling until the time that human beings reform themselves and become "real people" that spirits might want to associate with once again.

The spirit world goes across and between species. It does not need to concern itself with reproduction, it is not afraid of death, it is not practical. But the spirits do seem to have an ambivalent, selective interest in cross-world communication. Young women in scarlet and white robes dance to call down the gods, to be possessed by them, to speak in their voices. The priests who employ them can only wait for the message. (I think it was D. H. Lawrence who said, "Drink and carouse with Bacchus, or eat dry bread with Jesus, but don't sit down without one of the gods.")

(The *personal* quality of mountain dreaming: I was half asleep on the rocky ground at Tower Lake in the Sierra. There are four horizontal bands of cream-colored rock wavering through the cliff face, and the dream said "those rock bands are your daughters.")

Where Dogen and the Zen tradition would walk, chant a sutra, or do sitting meditation, the elder vernacular artisans of soul and spirit would play a flute, drum, dance, dream, listen for a song, go without food, and be available to communication with birds, animals, or rocks. There is a story of Coyote watching the yellow autumn cottonwood leaves float and eddy lightly down to the ground. It was so lovely to watch, he asked the cottonwood leaves if he might do it too. They warned him: "Coyote, you are too heavy and you have a body of bones and guts and muscle. We are light, we drift with the wind, but you would fall and be hurt." Coyote would hear none of it and insisted on climbing a cottonwood, edging far out onto a branch, and launching himself off. He fell and was killed. There's a caution here: do not be too hasty in setting out to "become one with." But, as we have heard, Coyote will roll over, reassemble his ribs, locate his paws, find a pebble with a dot of pitch on it to do for an eye, and trot off again.

Narratives are one sort of trace that we leave in the world. All our literatures are leavings—of the same order as the myths of wilderness peoples, who leave behind only stories and a few stone tools. Other orders of beings have their own literatures. Narrative in the deer world is a track of scents that is passed on from deer to deer with an art of interpretation which is instinctive. A literature of bloodstains, a bit of piss, a whiff of estrus, a hit of rut, a scrape on a sapling, and long gone. And there might be a "narrative theory" among these other beings—they might ruminate on "intersexuality" or "decomposition criticism."

I suspect that primary peoples all know that their myths are some-how "made up." They do not take them literally and at the same time they hold the stories very dear. Only upon being invaded by history and whipsawed by alien values do a people begin to declare that their myths are "literally true." This literalness in turn provokes skeptical questioning and the whole critical exercise. What a final refinement of confusion about the role of myths it is to declare that although they are not to be believed, they are nonetheless aesthetic and psychological constructs which bring order to an otherwise chaotic world and to which we should willfully commit ourselves! Dogen's "You should know that even though all things are liberated and not tied to anything, they abide in their own phenomenal expression" is medicine for that. The "Mountains and Waters Sutra" is called a sutra not to assert that the "mountains and rivers of this moment" are a text, a system of symbols, a referential world of mirrors, but that this world in its actual existence is a complete presentation, an enactment—and that it stands for nothing.

WALKING ON WATER

There's all sorts of walking—from heading out across the desert in a straight line to a sinuous weaving through undergrowth. Descending rocky ridges and talus slopes is a specialty in itself. It is an irregular dancing—always shifting—step of walk on slabs and scree. The breath and eye are always following this uneven rhythm. It is never paced or clocklike, but flexing—little jumps—sidesteps—going for the well-seen place to put a foot on a rock, hit flat, move on—zigzagging along and all deliberate. The alert eye looking ahead, picking the footholds to come, while never missing the step of the moment. The body-mind is so at one with this rough world that it makes these moves effortlessly once it has had a bit of practice. The mountain keeps up with the mountain.

In the year 1225 Dogen was in his second year in South China. That year he walked out of the mountains and passed through the capital of the Southern Song dynasty, Hang-zhou, on his way north to the Wan-shou monastery at Mt. Jing. The only account of China left by Dogen is notes on talks by the master Ru-jing.[3] I wonder what Dogen would have said of city walking. Hang-zhou had level broad straight streets paralleling canals. He must have seen the many-storied houses, clean cobbled streets, theaters, markets, and innumerable restaurants. It had three thousand public baths. Marco Polo (who called it Quinsai) visited it twenty-five years later and estimated that it was probably the largest (at least a million people) and most affluent city in the world at that time.[4] Even today the people of Hang-zhou remember the lofty eleventh-century poet Su Shi, who built the causeway across West Lake when he was governor. At the time of Dogen's walk, North China was under the control of the Mongols, and Hang-zhou would fall to the Mongols in fifty-five more years.

The South China of that era sent landscape painting, calligraphy, both the Soto and Rinzai schools of Zen, and the vision of that great southern capital to Japan. The memory of Hang-zhou shaped both Osaka and Tokyo in their Tokugawa-era evolution. These two positions—one the austere Zen practice with its space, clean halls, the other the possibility of a convivial urban life rich in festivals and theaters and restaurants—are two potent legacies of East Asia to the world. If Zen stands for the Far Eastern love of nature, Hang-zhou stands for the ideal of the city. Both are brimming with energy and life. Because most of the cities of the world are now mired in poverty, overpopulation, and pollution we have all the more reason to recover the dream. To neglect the city (in our hearts and minds for starters) is deadly, as James Hillman says.[5]

The "Mountains and Waters Sutra" goes on to say:

> All waters appear at the foot of the eastern mountains. Above all waters are all mountains. Walking beyond and walking within are both done on water. All mountains walk with their toes on all waters and splash there.

Dogen finishes his meditation on mountains and waters with this: "When you investigate mountains thoroughly, this is the work of the mountains. Such mountains and waters of themselves become wise persons and sages"—become sidewalk vendors and noodle-cooks, become marmots, ravens, graylings, carp, rattlesnakes, mosquitoes. *All* beings are "said" by the mountains and waters—even the clanking tread of a Caterpillar tractor, the gleam of the keys of a clarinet.

NOTES

1. Allan Grapard, "Flying Mountains and Walkers of Emptiness: Toward a Definition of Sacred Space in Japanese Religions." *History of Religions*, February 1982.
2. Burton Watson, *Chinese Lyricism: Shih Poetry from the Second to the Twelfth Century* (New York: Columbia University Press, 1971).
3. Takashi James Kodera, *Dogen's Formative Years in China* (Boulder: Prajna Press, 1980).

4. Jacques Gernet, *Daily Life in China: On the Eve of the Mongol Invasion* (Stanford, Calif.: Stanford University Press, 1962).
5. James Hillman, *Blue Fire* (New York: Harper & Row, 1989).

River Seeing the River

John Daido Loori

Prologue

Morning dew on the tips of ten thousand grasses reveals the truth of all of the myriad forms of this great earth. Have you seen it? The sounds of the river valley sing the eighty-four thousand hymns of Suchness. Have you heard them? Pervading throughout these forms and sounds is a trail far from words and ideas. Have you found it? If you wish to enter, look, listen, then enter, right there.

Main Case

The river is neither strong nor weak, neither wet nor dry, neither moving nor still, neither cold nor hot, neither being nor nonbeing, neither delusion nor enlightenment. Solidified, it is harder than diamond: who could break it? Melted, it is softer than milk: who could break it? This being the case, we cannot doubt the many virtues realized by the river. We should then study that occasion, when the rivers of the ten directions are seen in the ten directions. This is not a study only of the time when humans or gods see the river: there is a study of the river seeing the river. The river practices and verifies the river; hence, there is a study of the river speaking river. We must bring to realization the path on which the self encounters the self. We must move back and forth along, and spring off from, the vital path on which the other studies and fully comprehends the other.

CAPPING VERSE

The mind empty of all activity,
Embraces all that appears,
Like gazing into the jeweled mirror,
Form and reflection see each other.
No coming or going; no arising or vanishing; no abiding.
The ten thousand hands and eyes manifest of themselves,
Each in accord with circumstances—
Yet never forget the way.

This case is taken from the "Mountains and Rivers Sutra," one of the fascicles of Master Dogen's *Shobogenzo* or *Treasury of the True Dharma Eye*. The "Mountains and Rivers Sutra" is the seed of Zen practice here, on Mount Tremper. Somehow our monastery ended up on a mountain with two rivers crossing in front: the Esopus and the Beaverkill. The Chinese art of geomancy claims that this configuration of landscape is one of the most powerful places to locate a spiritual center. Partly because of this location, we called our order the Mountains and Rivers Order. This order is essentially a way of studying the Buddhadharma. Our way of study comes directly out of the "Mountains and Rivers Sutra." Also these teachings of mountains and rivers have a direct bearing on ecological concerns which have been very important to us through the years.

This section of the "Mountains and Rivers Sutra" has to do with the third of the Five Ranks of Master Tozan—a subtle and profound teaching which provides a matrix for and way of appreciating the relative and absolute aspects of reality. This third rank comments on the development of maturity in practice—the functioning of emptiness in everyday life, the emergence of compassion and its activity in the world.

Dogen was a great lover of nature, an incredible poet and mystic. He located his monastery deep in the mountains on the Nine-headed Dragon River. He did much of his work in a hermitage on the cliffs of the mountain. He was intimate with the mountains. But the mountains and rivers Dogen speaks of here are not the mountains and rivers of the poet, the naturalist, the hunter, the woodsman. They are the mountains and rivers of the Dharmadhatu, the Dharma realm.

Mountains and rivers are generally used in Buddhism to denote samsara—the world of delusion, the pain and suffering of the world, the ups and downs of phenomenal existence. What we have here is not a sutra about mountains and rivers in that sense, but the revelation of the mountains and rivers themselves as a sutra, as a teaching. The river Dogen speaks of is the river of the Dharmadhatu, the phenomenal realm, the realm of the ten thousand things. We've created a mandala of mountains and rivers here on this peak—and at its center, as well as at its edges—pervading everywhere are the mountains and rivers. Rivers, like mountains, have always had a special spiritual significance. A lot of spiritual history has happened along the banks of the Ganges in India, and on the Yangtse River of China. Much of the Dharma and the teachings of Christianity and Judaism have emerged on the banks of rivers throughout the world.

Thoreau said of the Merrimack: "There is an inward voice that in the stream sends forth its spirit to the listening ear, and in calm content it flows on, like wisdom, welcome with its own respect, clear in its breast like all these beautiful thoughts. It receives the green and graceful trees. They smile in its peaceful arms."

The first part of this case reads:

The river is neither strong nor weak, neither wet nor dry, neither moving nor still, neither cold nor hot, neither being nor nonbeing, neither delusion nor enlightenment. Solidified, it is harder than diamond. Who could break it? Melted, it is softer than milk. Who could break it? This being the case, we cannot doubt the many virtues realized by the river. We should then study that occasion when the rivers of the ten directions are seen in the ten directions.

Many of you may remember Herman Hesse's book *Siddhartha*. For me, that book was a very powerful teaching. When I returned to this book many years after originally studying it in school, I remember how troubled that time of my life was. Somehow, this book had not sunk in when I was younger. But at this later time, the reading of *Siddhartha* brought me to the Delaware River. Going to the river became a pilgrimage for me, a place to go to receive the river's spirit, to be nourished. I didn't know what was going on, but I was moved by what Hesse had to say about Siddhartha and the river. Each time I went to the Delaware, it was like a clear, cool, refreshing drink of water, soothing a fire inside me. I didn't understand, but I kept going back. I photographed the multiplicity of the river's faces and forms revealed at different times. I found myself traveling the river, immersing myself in it. This went on for years, and for years the river taught me. Then, finally, I heard it. I heard it speak. I heard what it was saying to Siddhartha, to Thoreau.

If you remember Hesse's story, Siddhartha was in great pain and misery. He was wandering in the forest, and he finally came to a river—the river that earlier in the book a ferryman had taken him across. Of course in Buddhist imagery that river and that crossing over is the *prajna paramita*, "Go, go, hurry, cross over to the other side." We can understand that crossing over in many ways. We can understand the other shore as being none other than this shore. We can also understand that the other shore crosses over to us, as well as that we cross over to the other shore.

At this point in the novel, Hesse writes of Siddhartha:

> With a distorted countenance he stared into the water. He saw his face reflected and spat on it. He took his arm away from the tree trunk and turned a little, so that he could fall headlong and finally go under, bent, with closed eyes towards death. Then, from a remote part of the soul, from the past of his tired life he heard the sound. It was one word, one syllable, which without thinking he spoke instinctively. The ancient beginning and ending of all Brahmin prayers, the holy "OM," which had the meaning of the Perfect One, or perfection. At that moment, when the sound of OM reached Siddhartha's ears, his thundering soul suddenly awakened, and he recognized the folly of his action.

The book goes on for several pages describing the further teachings of the river, and then says:

> I will remain by this river, thought Siddhartha. It is the same river which I crossed on my way to town. A friendly ferryman took me across. I will go to him. My path once led from his hut to a new

life which is now old and dead. He looked lovingly into the flowing water, into the transparent green, into the crystal lines of its wonderful design. He saw bright pearls rise from the depths, bubbles swimming on mirror, sky blue reflected in them. The river looked at him with a thousand eyes, green, white, crystal, sky blue. How he loved this river! How it enchanted him! How grateful he was to it! In his heart, he heard the newly awoken voice speak. And it said to him, "Love this river, stay by it, learn from it." Yes, he wanted to learn from it. He wanted to listen to it. It seemed to him that whoever understood this river and its secrets would understand much more, many secrets, old secrets.

Dogen Zenji addresses the secrets of the river and of all water. "The river is neither strong nor weak, neither wet nor dry, neither moving nor still, neither cold nor hot, neither being nor nonbeing, neither delusion nor enlightenment." It is none of the dualities. Water is H_2O, composed of two parts hydrogen and one part oxygen. Two odorless and tasteless gases. You bring them together and you get water. But water is not oxygen, and it is not hydrogen. It is not a gas. It is what D.H. Lawrence calls in one of his poems "the third thing." It is the same way with absolute and relative, with all the dualities. It is not either one or the other; it is always the third thing. The third thing is not strong or weak, not wet or dry, not moving or still, not cold or hot, not being or not-being, not delusion or enlightenment. What is the third thing that Dogen speaks of, that the sutra speaks of, that the river speaks of?

Master Tozan is one of the founders of the Soto school of Zen that is part of our tradition. Tozan is also one of the foremost teachers of the Five Ranks. The Five Ranks have to do with the relationship between dualities. Once when Tozan was crossing the river with Ungo Dojo, who was his successor in the lineage, he asked Ungo, "How deep is the river?" Dojo responded, "Not wet." Tozan said, "You clod." "How would you say it, Master?" asked Ungo. Tozan said, "Not dry." Does that reveal the third thing? Is that neither wet nor dry?

"Harder than diamond, softer than milk." "Harder than diamond" expresses the unchanging Suchness of all things, the Thusness of all things. On the wall of the dokusan room is a calligraphy for *nyorai*, which means Thus, Such. The way the strokes of the calligraphy are formed looks like Thusness, too. Just this moment! "Softer than milk" refers to the conditioned Suchness of things. Dogen talks in another part of the "Mountains and Rivers Sutra" about the stone woman giving birth to a child in the night. The stone woman is a barren woman and, of course, it is impossible for such a woman to give birth to a child. Dogen goes on to say that this event is "incomprehensible." This refers to the incomprehensibility of something that is without any fixed characteristics whatsoever, without any existence, being able to give rise to conditioned existence, to the multiplicity of things. That this is nevertheless true is the basis of the codependence of the whole universe, what we call the Diamond Net of Indra—totally interpenetrated mutual causality and co-origination. There is no way that you can affect one aspect of this net, without affecting the totality of it. With these two phrases, "harder than diamond, softer than milk," Dogen presents the conditioned and the absolute aspects of reality.

Then Dogen says:

> We should then study the occasion when the rivers of the ten directions are seen in the ten directions. This is not only a study of the time when humans or gods see the river. There is a study of the river seeing the river. The river practices and verifies the river. Hence, there is a study of the river speaking river. We must bring to realization the path on which the self encounters the self. We must move back and forth along, and spring off from, the vital path on which the other studies and fully comprehends the other.

What is the path on which the self meets the self, and the other meets the other? It is the practice of the river seeing the river, seeing itself. Dogen expresses it slightly differently in another one of his fascicles, "Genjokoan." He says, "To study the Buddha Way is to study the self. To study the self is to forget the self. And to forget the self is to be enlightened by the ten thousand things." When you study the self, you begin to realize that it is the self-created idea. We create it moment to moment. We create it like we create all the ten thousand things, by our codependency and our co-origination. What happens when the self is forgotten? What remains? The whole phenomenal universe remains. The whole Dharmadhatu remains. That's what it means, "To forget the self is to be enlightened by the ten thousand things." That is, we see the ten thousand things as our own body and mind. In one of his poems Master Tozan talks about the old grandmother looking in the mirror seeing her reflection. "Everywhere I look, I meet myself. It is at once me, and yet I am not it." You and I are the same thing, but I am not you and you are not me. Both of those facts exist simultaneously, but somehow that doesn't compute. Our brains can't deal with it. The two things *seem* mutually exclusive. That's why practice is so vital. You need to see it for yourself, and see that words don't reach it. There is no way this reality can be conveyed by words, any more than the taste of the crystal-clear water of the spring can be conveyed in any other way than by tasting it.

The Prologue says: "The morning dew on the tips of the ten thousand grasses reveals the truth of all the myriad forms of this great earth." Each thing, each tip of grass, each dewdrop, each and every thing throughout the whole phenomenal universe contains the totality of the universe. That's the truth of the myriad forms of this great earth.

"The sounds of the river valley sing the eighty-four thousand hymns of Suchness. Have you heard them?" The songs don't just say OM. They sing the eighty-four thousand hymns, the eighty-four thousand gathas, the teachings, the sermon of rock and water. "Pervading throughout these sounds and forms is a trail far from words and ideas. Have you found it? If you wish to enter it, simply look and listen." But look with the whole body and mind. See with the whole body and mind. Listen and hear with the whole body and mind, and then you'll understand them intimately. That's the entry. If you go chasing it, you won't find it. "To carry the self forward and realize the ten thousand things is delusion," as Master Dogen said. "That the ten thousand things advance and realize the self is enlightenment." You see? The other shore arrives.

What does it mean that "the river practices and verifies the river"? it means that you practice and verify yourself, and in so doing, it is the practice and verification of all Buddhas, past, present and future. Supposedly Buddha predicted that there will be a time when Buddhism will disappear from the face of the earth. He defined that time as a time in which there would be no masters alive, no sutras, nobody sitting zazen, no realized beings. He characterized it as a time of great darkness, supposedly sometime in the future. Let's say that that time of great darkness has appeared. Let's say it goes on for five hundred years. In such a case one would have to wonder about the mind-to-mind transmission. Even now there are historical gaps in the mind-to-mind transmission. From the point of view of the lineage, we chant the lineage list as though it were a continuum. In Chinese culture there was a great need for ancestral continuity. If there was no legitimate ancestor, they would take a likely name and splice it in, and everybody was happy. Nowadays historians sometimes find out that these names are not the proper successors. And the scholars say, "Aha! Mind-to-mind transmission doesn't exist. This teacher died and a hundred years later this other teacher, who supposedly got mind-to-mind transmission from him, was just born. There was no-mind-to-mind transmission." That's why they're scholars! From the point of view of the Dharma, if mind-to-mind transmission disappeared from the face of the earth for a million years, one person doing zazen, realizing the true self, would have the same realization of the Buddhas of the past, and the gap of a million years would be filled in an instant, mind-to-mind.

It is as if electricity disappeared from the face of the earth and someone, a billion years from now, created a generator, started turning it, and coiled a wire and attached it to the generator; the more they turned, the hotter the wire got until finally it glowed and light appeared. It would be the same light that is produced by lightbulbs, the same electricity. All that needed to be done was to produce the electricity. In the case of the Buddhadharma, all that needs to be done is to realize it. What do you realize? What you realize is that Buddha mind has always been there. You do not attain it, you were born with it. Zen did not come to America from Japan, it was always here, always will be here. But like the lightbulb, electricity itself is not enough. You need to plug in the bulb to see the light. In the Dharma you plug in people; the Buddhadharma shines through humans, through Buddhas. Only Buddhas can realize Buddha. Dogen says that when we realize Buddha, "We must bring to realization the path on which the self encounters the self. We must then move back and forth along, and spring off from, this living path on which one studies and fully comprehends other."

One of the characteristics of the Third Rank of Tozan is maturity of practice, emptiness functioning as the basis of daily activity. This functioning is none other than the ten thousand hands and eyes of great compassion—Kannon Bodhisattva. She always manifests according to circumstances. In her manifesting there is no sense of separateness. That realization of seeing our own face everywhere we look becomes action. Not just seeing or knowing our own faces, our true selves, but acting on the basis of this knowledge. This is called the action of nonaction. Compassion is not the same as doing good, or being nice. Compassion functions freely, with no hesitation, no limitation. It happens with no effort, the way you grow hair, the way your heart beats, the way you breathe, the way your blood circulates, or the way you do all the ten thousand other things you do moment to moment. It does not take any conscious effort. Someone falls, you pick them up. There is no sense of doer, or what is being done. There is no separation.

The capping verse says:

The mind, empty of all activity,
Embraces all that appears.
Like gazing into a jeweled mirror,
Form and reflection see each other.
No coming or going, no arising or vanishing, no abiding.
The ten thousand hands and eyes manifest of themselves,
Each in accord with circumstances—
Yet never forget the way.

The first lines of this verse refer to a line from Tozan's "Jeweled Mirror of Samadhi." The meaning of these lines is the same as the meaning of "the ass seeing the well and the well seeing the ass" which Dogen refers to elsewhere—an image which indicates the interdependence of phenomena.

"No coming or going, no arising or vanishing, no abiding." There is no sticking, no holding on to one place. "The ten thousand hands and eyes manifest of themselves / Each in accord with circumstances— / Yet never forget the way." Without coming and going, arising or vanishing, abiding, these ten thousand hands and eyes of compassion manifest of themselves. Kannon Bodhisattva always manifests in a form that's in accord with circumstances. That's the meaning of the lines, "Each in accord with circumstances— / Yet never forget the way." The great blue heron comes and goes every day, like clockwork. I know where to be with my camera, or my eyes, to experience it. And yet, it knows how to go its own way, it knows how to step outside of that pattern. It never forgets its own way.

If you want your practice to manifest in the world, if you want to help heal this great earth of ours which is groaning in sickness, you need to realize what we've been talking about. All you need to do to realize it is listen, and through the hum of the distant highway, you can hear the thing itself, the voice of the river. Can you hear it? That's it. . . . Is that the third thing?

The Third Turning of the Wheel
A Conversation with Joanna Macy

WES NISKER WITH BARBARA GATES
FOR *Inquiring Mind*

INQUIRING MIND: How has your meditation practice and your study of Buddhism been a basis for your action in the world?

JOANNA MACY: The real philosophical grounding of my work comes from the Buddha's central teaching of *paticca samuppada* or dependent co-arising, the understanding that everything is intrinsically interrelated. The Buddha said, "He who sees the Dharma sees dependent co-arising, and he who sees dependent co-arising sees the Dharma." When I first encountered Buddhism, the teaching of causality was the farthest thing from my interest or inclination; but after I explored it a little, I began to see what the Buddha meant by dependent co-arising, and how radical and profound that insight really was. With it—with his "turning of the wheel of the Dharma"—he turned the thinking of his time on its head. And that teaching is central now to our enterprise of living and to our liberation.

Let me go back and start with the Buddha's idea of change, *anicca*. That also turned the thought of his age inside out. The philosophical thinking of the Indian subcontinent at the Buddha's time was similar to what was happening in Greece—I think it might be related to the patriarchal cast of mind. That mindset equated reality with the changeless: what is *really real* does not change. Now you can't prove that one way or the other, but once you make that axiomatic move it affects everything else. What it leads you to is a rejection of empirical experience: since everything I experience by my senses is changing—my face in the mirror gets another wrinkle every day and the weather changes and my hopes change—then this world of my experience is less real. If you've made the supposition that what is real is unchanging, as Plato also did, then this world, this changing dimension, becomes illusory in some way. Then the spiritual journey—the project of liberation—is to try to get to the ultimate, unchanging, disembodied reality. We move away from the phenomenal world, seeing it as less real and less valuable. A split is created.

Gautama followed that path for a while; he tried, and excelled in, all the Hindu ascetic practices of denying and mortifying the flesh. The idea was to transcend this changing world of matter and phenomenality, which is less real than something else that doesn't change, which must be something abstract, purely mental.

IM: That was the prevailing Hindu idea at the time, that there was a *moksha* or *nirvana*, a place which was unchanging and different than *maya*, or *samsara*, this conditioned reality.

JM: That's right. That thinking reached its peak of expression in the *Upanishads*. This idea has been very present in Western thought as well; when you equate the real and the valuable with what is changeless, you get the same mind-matter split. You also get the disastrous split between humans and the rest of nature. Now what the Buddha did was to slip right out of that dichotomy. He said, what is real is change itself: "*Sabbe anicca.*" Everything is without a permanent, changeless self—including you. You are not separable from your experience. This insight arises in vipassana practice—and it just blows your mind! You're watching and watching these dharmas—or psycho-physical events—come up, and it begins to dawn on you that among the things that are coming up on the screen you never see a little sandwich board saying, "I." It dawns on you that there's no experience of self separate from the experience of everything else.

So, the Buddha said that change is what is real. Heraclitus did that too, right? But the Buddha also said that there's order in that change. Now this is an amazing move, because the previous mindset—you can see it both in Vedic India and in the Greeks—is to assume that order requires stability, that order requires permanence or freezing something in place. But the Buddha turned that inside out, too! He said that the order is *in* the change. And that is the meaning of dependent co-arising. "This being so, that is." "When this arises, that arises." "If this does not arise, that does not arise." So the change is not chaotic. He made the radical assertion that the change is orderly, that order is intrinsic to change. What that also says is that there's not some mind up there, some "Big Daddy Mind" that is making this happen and making that happen, imposing order on otherwise random events. Orderliness is simply "how things work." That is the very meaning of the word *dharma*. It means, "That's how things are ordered."

For generations, most Western scholars of Buddhism didn't really grasp the teaching of dependent co-arising, because they came to it with unconscious assumptions about linear causality. Now, thanks to modern physics and systems theory and systems cybernetics, we are beginning to move beyond linear causality.

IM: So it's like the current scientific understanding that each subatomic event is conditioned by every other subatomic event, even if separated by great distances. It's as if everything is embedded in this interlocking web of occurrences. There may be no obvious or apparent connection, but everything is affecting everything else.

JM: Right. Take the Karl Pribram's holographic image of the universe. It is close to the Buddha's understanding that all is intrinsically interrelated, everything occurs in relationship. The psychic corollary is that instead of being condemned to the isolation cell of your individual ego, you can enter into this web of co-arising and know that all of life is flowing through you all the time, that you are inseparable from it. Through our action in the world there is a release into our true nature, because our true nature is interactive. We enter into our co-arising as into a dance.

IM: In some sense the dependent co-arising, the idea of everything affecting everything else, can also say to me that my freedom is limited.

JM: This was a burning question for many people who came to the Buddha. Some seekers, as the suttas show, came from schools that were very deterministic—like the Jains, who believed that your karma was cast in concrete, set by previous actions and previous incarnations, and that all you could do was to wear it away, usually by severe ascetic practices. But the Buddha said repeatedly that he taught the Dharma—or *paticca-samuppada*—for the sake of freedom. So that you will "have reason for doing this rather than doing that." In other words, the interdependence, the reciprocal action between the factors that condition us, is such that you can alter it in one place and the house of cards tumbles, pull out one factor here or another there and the structure collapses. Each recognition of an attachment or an aversion frees you from the vicious circle of ignorance and gives you choice.

This recognition can either come in action or in meditation. Shantideva, the great eighth-century saint-scholar, tells us that to act for others can be as good a way to discover "no self" as sitting in meditative practice.

IM: This whole interpretation of the Buddha's teachings seems to undercut the idea of nirvana, the unconditioned state, and along with it the Theravada emphasis on getting off the wheel, reaching a place where there is no longer change.

JM: Theravadin teachings tend to be imbued with the Theravadin Abhidharma, and especially the commentaries on this Abhidharma, which evolved several centuries after the Buddha. The Theravadin Abhidharma commentator, like Buddhaghosa, altered the earlier presentation of *paticca-samuppada* in significant ways. First, they affirmed that there are unconditioned dharmas, namely in nirvana. Prior to that, in the Vinaya and the *Sutta Nikayas*, there is nothing that is seen as unconditioned or arising independently.

IM: What you seem to be saying is that those earliest teachings are closer to Mahayana Buddhism than to the Theravada understanding.

JM: The seeds of the Mahayana, particularly the Madhyamika, are right there in the Pali texts, and that's why when the Mahayana actually does break on the scene around the first century, it is called "the second turning of the wheel." The turning of the wheel is the perception of dependent co-arising, *paticca-samuppada*. That is the Dharma. And the Mahayanist wisdom texts return to that perception and make a very clear statement that there is no nirvana without samsara, and that form and emptiness are one.

What had happened that necessitated that "second turning of the wheel" were assertions by influential Theravadin Abhidharma commentaries, which said that there were unconditioned dharmas and an unconditioned state. It was a reification of some place outside of the Dharma, outside of experience, outside of the laws of change.

IM: What would be the alternative understanding of nirvana? If it's not the unconditioned state, what is it?

JM: It is the capacity, moment by moment, to be free. And it's there right now. You can have it right now by breaking free from the attachments and aversions that bind you to small self. Nirvana is not a place; it's an event. It's the experience, as the Buddha said, of "the calming down" of self-strivings and strategies. The experience of it ignites in successive moments, as Shariputra describes when he says, "Just as a fire is blazing, one flame arises and another flame fades out, so does one perception arise and another fade out. This is nibbana." So in the very heart of change, in the very midst of the phenomenal world of samsara, comes the recognition: "I don't have to be trapped."

When the Buddha described what happened for him under the bodhi tree, his enlightenment is portrayed in terms of what he saw—and it did not remove him from the world of flux. He beheld *paticca-samuppada*, "And then, brethren, then light arose, vision arose, joy arose, knowledge arose, and I sat there watching the arising and the ceasing." He was just there with reality without trying to manipulate it and without trying to judge it and without trying to stop it. But when you make nirvana a place to go, a place to be removed from change, then, of course, it shapes everything else. Then you start to think of this world as a trap and you are always looking for the exit sign. The whole enterprise shifts from transformation of life to escape from life. And if the world is a trap, it's easy to feel resentful of it and not care what happens to it.

In order to understand this better, we should look at the cultural context in which the Buddha was teaching. All teaching took place "in the forest" and there were a number of forest teachers, each with his own disciples—bands of dropouts who were seeking cultural and spiritual alternatives to the established order. And the norm for these seekers was ascetic. If we were there, we would be going around in robes and shaven heads. This would be the way to unhinge ourselves from the dominant culture and its ways of thinking. In that context the Buddha was accused of being soft and indulgent, because he was less ascetic than the other forest teachers. He refused to hate the body or fear it as a source of attachment, delusion, and suffering. In fact, he said that it is better to identify with the body than with the mind, because the mind changes even faster than the body. He taught that of the four kinds of grasping, only one is after objects of sense desire; all the others are mental.

In order to get perspective on the world-rejecting flavor of the Pali texts, it is also well to remember that they were transmitted through the Theravadins, the most monastic of all the eighteen early schools of Buddhism. Theravadins assigned great value to maintaining the purity of the monks' practice; hence the ascetic and reclusive flavor of their texts—and also, I would add, their misogyny.

In the later Abhidharma texts of the Theravada, three fundamental shifts occurred that many people erroneously assign to the Buddha himself. One, as I said, was to classify nirvana as an unconditioned dharma. Another was to interpret the wheel of causation as a chronological sequence of *three* lives, thereby weakening the perception of reciprocity between all the factors. A third was the idea of momentariness or *khanika*, where the dharmas (units of experience) are taken as occurring so rapidly that they don't last long enough to affect each other. As with Hume, the British philosopher, what you get then is sequence, not causation. This view can undermine the idea that one might be an effective presence in the world.

You see, in focusing on proving that there is no self, and that you can take the self apart like a chariot until you just have its component parts, the Abhidharmists analyzed and dissected experience into its psychophysical elements or dharmas. They systematically categorized and classified these dharmas, almost as if they were real, discrete entities. The second turning of the wheel at the outset of the Mahayana blew all this apart with the affirmation that not just the self, but the dharmas too, and our concepts as well, are all empty of own-being. It returns to the original import of *paticca-samuppada*.

When I was with the Sarvodaya movement in Sri Lanka, I noticed that in the training of monks to work in village development, they had dropped the Abhidharma. That is pretty amazing, since these are Theravadin monks. I asked the Reverend Nyanaseeha, director of the training school, about this and he said, "The suttas (the earlier texts) are more appropriate." His own teaching focused less on the annihilation of the self than on the experience of extension into and through other beings, into wider and wider circles.

IM: So you move beyond the self by submerging it, dissolving it in all of life.

JM: In "the second turning of the wheel," that idea comes to the fore in the literature called the *Perfection of Wisdom*. That's when the bodhisattva idea is born, vowing to save all beings, knowing that there are no separate beings. Now let me just say that what we're having now in our time, I'm convinced, is a third turning of the wheel. The metaphor of the three turnings of the Wheel of Dharma has been taken in a variety of ways. For example, Mahayanist historians use it to refer to the Abhidharma, Madhyamika, and Yogachara schools of thought, while in Tibetan Buddhism it often refers to the Hinayana, Mahayana, and Vajrayana traditions. In a similar way, I see these turnings as a spiral, circling back to the original teaching of *paticca-samuppada* and embracing it in a wider, contemporary context. Note the emphasis now, in our time, on moving beyond separateness into interconnectedness and interbeing. That is the central thrust of Thich Nhat Hanh's teaching.

IM: It is also the approach of the "deep ecology" movement, and seems to fit in with the whole concept of Gaia, the one living organism. These new progressive philosophical movements seem to have that same understanding of conditioned co-arising. It's the Buddha's wisdom come around in different form.

JM: Right. So in the third turning of the wheel we've got the earliest teachings of the Buddha, picked up again as the wheel just—whooosh!—spins again. And the ecologists are on it and the feminists are on it.

It is the old teaching and also new again, at the same time. We can imagine ourselves released from the squirrel cage of ego, released from the terrible trips we play on and lay on ourselves, released from our own addictions, and from the behavior that devastates the world. For centuries we have focused on the fetters and suffering that we seek release *from*. Now, with this third turning of the wheel, our eyes are turning to what we're released *into!* We're released into interbeing, into the dance of the holographic universe, where the part contains the whole. We suddenly find that we live and act on behalf of all beings and by virtue of all beings.

And it's not a moral trip. It's not some kind of righteous burden that says, "On top of everything else I've got to do, I've got to go stand at the polls." Rather it springs naturally from the ground of being. It is not something *more* we ask of our self, but rather the release from that self—release *through* action, and *into* action.

IM: What role does meditation practice have to play in this third turning of the wheel?

JM: I believe that in this third turning there will be no split between meditation and action in the world. These two dimensions of experience seem to have become polarized. For example, when I was in graduate school in the early 1970s, I wanted to do a tutorial on meditation and revolution, and my department advisor said, "Well, that's a contradiction in terms; those are polar opposites." Now that view is beginning to change. You don't want to lose the distinctions between the two, but instead to see how they are mutually reinforcing—like our friends who are doing meditation out on the railroad tracks at the Concord Naval Weapons Station.

IM: There are some who would say that going and sitting in a cave and meditating is also social action. Purification of your own "self" also helps purify the web. You might say, "They also serve, who only sit."

JM: I agree and would add that the reach of their practice extends farther than one would think, because the part contains the whole. We're so interconnected that someone who, let's say, is on retreat or working alone to restore a tract of wilderness, is actually affecting us all, not just because it's arithmetically true that one billionth of the world is getting cleaner, but because there's a co-arising dynamic there. The whole is intrinsically altered, and each of us with it.

IM: That's the one hundredth monkey business.

JM: *(Laughs)* Yes. That's it. With the third turning of the wheel we see that everything we do impinges on all beings. The way you are with your kid is a political act, and the products you buy and your efforts to recycle are part of it, too. So is meditation. Just trying to stay awake and aware is a tremendous task and of ultimate importance. We're trying to be present—to ourselves and to each other—in a way that can save our planet.

IM: Saving the planet implies taking responsibility for the future as well.

JM: Well, lately I have been practicing co-dependent arising with beings who aren't born yet. I evoke them, I see them—they become very real to me. You see, I have been working on the issue of radioactive waste. The reality of it is so overwhelming that it's easy to give in and think there's nothing we can do. That is when I feel the presence of the beings who are not born yet. It's like they say to me, "This is a real important time, and we're with you. We know you're working for our sake." I feel a great love for them, these beings of the future time. Sometimes with workshop groups I've tried letting them be present, too—in councils in New Mexico and Massachusetts, where we let the future beings speak through us as to what they want us to do with this radioactive waste. At one point, we talked as if we were the future beings; at another we made a tape recording for them. In doing this I felt heartened by the teaching of *paticca samuppada*. In the Dharma we are here for each other, and to sustain each other, over great distances of space and time.

IM: Do you think it is possible to have that vital insight of dependent co-arising without meditating? Can that understanding be taught or realized in other ways?

JM: I really don't know. I don't see how, personally, you can sustain that insight without meditating, but that doesn't mean that in order for our world to heal we've got to get 5.2 billion people sitting on *zafus*.

IM: Whew!

JM: I think it will be like what Robinson Jeffers called "falling in love outwards." That's our mission, to fall in love with our world. We are made for that, you see, because we are dependently co-arising. It is in the dance with each other that we discover ourselves and lose ourselves over and over.

IM: So in this third turning of the wheel, there is also the building of sangha, the creation of community. Maybe not all 5 billion of us need to get on *zafus*, but perhaps in the building of community we can see the dependent co-arising and lose our sense of separate self. You saw how that worked in Sri Lanka, and yet it may be more difficult here in this culture where we are so isolated, not only as separate selves but as separate cells in our nuclear family houses. We have very little sense of community.

JM: And that is one of the great sufferings of our time. So, yes, the building of community is a great part of the third turning, because community is where the interdependence is visible, manifest, an agent for healing. There's a wonderful book called *No Contest*, by Alfie Kohn. It challenges the great American myth that competition is innate, healthy, and productive. In reality, competition distorts and isolates and makes us sick. We've been in an insane asylum where we've been told that what we are is limited to what's in this bag of skin. This is a terrible thing we've been doing to ourselves.

IM: And that we're in competition with all the other bags of skin.

JM: Right. And so we need therapy, we need communal forms of therapy. We have to learn a new concept of self—self as all beings, self as planet.

We have to be faithful with each other. We have to build ourselves into one another's lives in new ways, and let structures arise by which we live together, and work and play and pray together. . . .

This third turning of the wheel is central, I think, to what Buddhism has to offer to our world in this time, and it is also what we see happening within the Buddhist movement. It is of great depth and great promise, and involves much that we are only now beginning to conceptualize. In this turning of the wheel, as we noted, the spiritual goal is not escape from the world, but transformation of the world. The practice is not for perfection, but for wholeness. As Carl Jung foresaw coming for us at the end of the Piscean age—we let go of the intrinsic dualism of striving to be perfect, and seek instead to restore connection, coming round to a place of vast inclusion.

IM: In this third turning of the wheel, we go from personal salvation to planetary salvation, back to the community of all.

JM: Yes! And it all comes back to co-arising again, to reciprocal action. The motto of the Sarvodaya movement was, "We build the road and the road builds us." Through that which we seek to heal will we be healed.

PART THREE

BUDDHISM
in the
WORLD

I believe that we must consciously develop a greater sense of universal responsibility. We must learn to work not just for our own individual self, family, or nation, but for the benefit of all mankind. Universal responsibility is the best foundation for our personal happiness, and for world peace, the equitable use of our natural resources, and, through a concern for future generations, the proper care for the environment.

—*The Dalai Lama*

INTRODUCTION

✳

WHEN ONE SURVEYS THE STATE OF THE ENVIRONMENT in predominantly or formerly Buddhist countries, the report is grim. Vietnam and Cambodia still suffer the devastating environmental consequences of war—bomb craters breeding malarial mosquitoes, farm fields riddled with explosive mines. Thailand and Japan have been swept up in surges of rapid economic development and unrestrained consumerism. Tibet's remote mountains and plains are under assault from Chinese logging and uranium-waste dumping. Ladakh's ancient culture is being shoved aside for cash crops and tourist trade. Throughout Asia, pollution threatens rural waterways, forests are stripped for export products, and high-rise offices loom over Buddhist temples.

How are Buddhist activists and religious leaders responding to this frightening state of affairs? The Dalai Lama advocates demilitarization of the entire planet, beginning with the difficult task of inner disarmament through love and compassion. Thai monk Prayudh Payutto assesses the devastating role of greed, hate, and delusion, which seem to be out of control on many levels. International organizer Sulak Sivaraksa shows what happens when Western-style consumerism becomes the dominant ethic in Southeast Asia. As an alternative, he offers examples of Buddhist development projects oriented toward community-building rather than economic profit.

Certainly a Buddhist heritage is no guarantee of ecological awareness; contradictions between theory and practice abound. Thus Buddhist activists are often compelled to draw attention to environmentally destructive projects close to home. Monks perform ceremonial tree ordinations to stop wanton logging. Villagers walk from town to town to expose the serious pollution of Thailand's biggest lake. Citizens of many nationalities work together to resist the Chinese occupation and environmental degradation of Tibet and the construction of the Yadana pipeline in Burma.

Now that it is possible to speak of a global Buddhism, those who benefit from the teachings feel compelled to address the plight of the tradition's source lands. Western Buddhists are in fact as much a part of the equation as Asian Buddhists. Products sold to consumers in the West leave large ecological footprints in the East: teak benches for American gardens are made from slashed forests in Thailand; cheap oil for Western industry means destruction of native lands in Burma. A Buddhist approach to these complex international dilemmas requires full acknowledgment of the suffering involved for *all* members of the interdependent web—native peoples, consumers, governments, forests, lakes. To what degree can the resolute force of spiritual development counter the driving force of economic development? There are no easy answers, but skillful means may emerge in the difficult work ahead.

GLOBALIZATION, POPULATION, AND DEVELOPMENT

❋

The True Source of Political Success
THE DALAI LAMA

TODAY'S WORLD REQUIRES US to accept the oneness of humanity. In the past, isolated communities could afford to think of one another as fundamentally separate. Some could even exist in total isolation. But nowadays, whatever happens in one region eventually affects many other areas. Within the context of our new interdependence, self-interest clearly lies in considering the interest of others.

Many of the world's problems and conflicts arise because we have lost sight of the basic humanity that binds us all together as a human family. We tend to forget that despite the diversity of race, religion, ideology, and so forth, people are equal in their basic wish for peace and happiness.

Nearly all of us receive our first lessons in peaceful living from our mothers, because the need for love lies at the very foundation of human existence. From the earliest stages of our growth, we are completely dependent upon our mother's care and it is very important for us that she express her love. If children do not receive proper affection, in later life they will often find it hard to love others. Peaceful living is about trusting those on whom we depend and caring for those who depend on us. Most of us receive our first experience of both these qualities as children.

I believe that the very purpose of life is to be happy. From the very core of our being, we desire contentment. In my own limited experience I have found that the more we care for the happiness of others, the greater is our own sense of well-being. Cultivating a close, warm-hearted feeling for others automatically puts the mind at ease. It helps remove whatever fears or insecurities we may have and gives us the strength to cope with any obstacles we encounter. It is the principal source of success in life. Since we are not solely material creatures, it is a mistake to place all our hopes for happiness on external development alone. The key is to develop inner peace.

Actions and events depend heavily on motivation. From my Buddhist viewpoint all things originate in the mind. If we develop a good heart, then whether the field of our occupation is science, agriculture, or politics, since the motivation is so very important, the result will be more beneficial. With proper motivation, these activities can help humanity; without it, they go the other way. This is why the compassionate thought is so very important for humankind. Although it is difficult to bring about the inner change that gives rise to it, it is absolutely worthwhile to try.

When you recognize that all beings are equal and like yourself in both their desire for happiness and their right to obtain it, you automatically feel empathy and closeness for them. You develop a feeling of responsibility for others—the wish to help them actively overcome their problems. True compassion is not just an emotional response but a firm commitment founded on reason. Therefore, a truly compassionate attitude towards others does not change even if they behave negatively.

I believe that we must consciously develop a greater sense of universal responsibility. We must learn to work not just for our own individual self, family, or nation, but for the benefit of all mankind. Universal responsibility is the best foundation for our personal happiness, and for world peace, the equitable use of our natural resources, and, through a concern for future generations, the proper care for the environment. My own ideas about this are still evolving, but I would like to share some of them with you.

I believe it is important to reassess the rights and responsibilities of individuals, peoples, and nations in relation to each other and the planet as a whole. This has a direct bearing on human rights. Because it is very often the most gifted, dedicated, and creative members of our society who become victims of human rights abuses, the political, social, cultural, and economic developments of a society are obstructed by the violations of human rights.

Therefore, the acceptance of universally binding standards of human rights is essential in today's shrinking world. Respect for fundamental human rights should not remain an ideal to be achieved, but a requisite foundation for every human society. But when we demand the rights and freedoms we so cherish, we should also be aware of our responsibilities. If we accept that others have an equal right to peace and happiness as ourselves, do we not have a responsibility to help those in need?

A precondition of any discussion of human rights is an atmosphere of peace in society at large. We have recently seen how newfound freedoms, widely celebrated though they are, have given rise to fresh economic difficulties and unleashed long-buried ethnic and religious tensions that contain the seeds for a new cycle of conflicts. In the context of our newly emerging global community, all forms of violence, especially war, have become totally unacceptable as means of settling disputes. Therefore, it is appropriate to think and to discuss ways of averting further havoc and maintaining the momentum of peaceful and positive change. . . .

Faced with the challenge of establishing genuine world peace and preserving the bountiful earth, what can we do? Beautiful words are not enough. Our ultimate goal should be the demilitarization of the entire planet. If it were properly planned and people were educated to understand its advantages, I believe it would be quite possible.

But if we are to have the confidence to eliminate physical weapons, to begin with some kind of inner disarmament is necessary. We need to embark on the difficult task of developing love and compassion within ourselves. Compassion is, by nature, peaceful and gentle, but it is also very powerful. Some may dismiss it as impractical and unrealistic, but I believe its practice is the true source of success. It is a sign of true inner strength. To achieve it we do not need to become religious, nor do we need any ideology. All that is necessary is for us to develop our basic human qualities.

Ultimately, humanity is one and this small planet is our only home. If we are truly to help one another and protect this home of ours, each of us needs to experience a vivid sense of compassion and responsibility.

Only these feelings can remove the self-centered motives that cause people to deceive and misuse one another.

No system of government is perfect, but democracy is closest to our essential human nature; it is also the only stable foundation upon which a just and free global political structure can be built. So it is in all our interests that those of us who already enjoy democracy should actively support everybody's right to do so. We all want to live a good life, but that does not mean just having good food, clothes, and shelter. These are not sufficient. We need a good motivation: compassion, without dogmatism, without complicated philosophy, just understanding that others are our human brothers and sisters and respecting their rights and human dignity. That we can help each other is one of our unique human capacities.

We accept the need for pluralism in politics and democracy, yet we often seem more hesitant about the plurality of faiths and religions. It is important to remember that wherever they came from, all the world's major religious traditions are similar in having the potential to help human beings live at peace with themselves, with each other, and with the environment. For centuries, millions of individual followers have derived personal peace of mind and solace in times of suffering from their own particular religious tradition. It is evident too that society in general has derived much benefit from religious traditions in terms of inspiration to ensure social justice and provide help to the needy.

Human beings naturally possess diverse mental dispositions and interests. Therefore, it is inevitable that different religious traditions emphasize different philosophies and modes of practice. Since the essence of our diverse religious traditions is to achieve our individual and collective benefit, it is crucial that we are active in maintaining harmony and mutual respect between them. Concerted efforts to this end will benefit not only the followers of our own faith, but will create an atmosphere of peace in society as a whole.

In the world at present, if we are serious in our commitment to the fundamental principles of equality which I believe lie at the heart of the concepts of human rights and democracy, today's economic disparity between the north and south can no longer be ignored. It is not enough merely to state that all human beings must enjoy equal dignity. This must be translated into action. We have a responsibility to find ways to reduce this gap. Unless we are able to address this problem adequately, not only will it not go away, but it will fester and grow to give us further trouble in the future. . . .

A new way of thinking has become the necessary condition for responsible living and acting. If we maintain obsolete values and beliefs, a fragmented consciousness and a self-centered spirit, we will continue to hold to outdated goals and behaviors. Such an attitude among a large number of people would block the entire transition to an interdependent yet peaceful and cooperative global society.

If we look back at the development in the twentieth century, the most devastating cause of human suffering, of deprivation of human dignity, freedom, and peace, has been the culture of violence in resolving differences and conflicts. In some ways the twentieth century can be called the century of war and bloodshed. The challenge before us, therefore, is to make the next century a century of dialogue and of peaceful coexistence.

In human societies there will always be differences of views and interests. But the reality today is that we are all interdependent and have to coexist on this small planet. Therefore, the only sensible and intelligent way of resolving differences and clashes of interests, whether between individuals or nations, is through dialogue. The promotion of a culture of dialogue and nonviolence for the future of mankind is thus an important task of the international community. It is not enough for governments to endorse the principle of nonviolence or hold it high without any appropriate action to promote it.

It is natural that we should face obstacles in pursuit of our goals. But if we remain passive, making no effort to solve the problems we meet, conflicts will arise and hindrances will grow. Transforming these obstacles into opportunities for positive growth is a challenge to our human ingenuity. To achieve this requires patience, compassion, and the use of our intelligence.

Buddhist Solutions for the Twenty-first Century

PRAYUDH PAYUTTO

WITH THE END OF THE COLD WAR, the tension and fear resulting from the threat of confrontation between the two superpowers and a world divided into ideological camps seemed to dissolve. This was around the end of the twentieth century. Many people felt that in the approaching twenty-first century, the human race would be blessed with a much more peaceful existence, that the world would live in peace.

But it soon became apparent that this was not to be. The threat of the Cold War was a very definite, tangible one, a threat that could be focused on quite easily. The wars that have since sprung up all over the globe are much more difficult to control.

Although the ideological wars seem to have passed on, we now have more wars arising from racial and religious confrontation, which are much more passionate and brutal.

Hatred, discrimination, and mutual distrust are intensified by the struggle for natural resources. The avaricious competition to amass natural resources not only leads to strife within human society. These resources must be found within the natural environment, which gives the problem a double edge. On one hand, there are problems with the environment, in the form of depletion of natural resources. On the other hand, there is an intensification of mutual human destruction.

The environmental crisis and the shortage of natural resources began to become really clear only toward the end of the twentieth century. Twenty-first-century man will inherit the fruits of twentieth-century man's destruction of the environment. The enormous amount of natural resources on this planet, amassed over a period of hundreds of millions of years, have mostly been consumed by humanity in a period of only one or two hundred years.

All of these problems stem from the problem of hatred or violence perpetuated under the power of what we call in Buddhism *dosa*, or aversion, and *lobha*, desire or greed. These two forces, greed and hatred, are very important forces in the mind. With the development of technology, and in particular, so-called high technology, which deals with information and communications, greed and hatred have acquired much more effective tools.

Technology has become a tool of greed and hatred, and technological progress, in the form of industrial development, has been used almost exclusively to their ends. Science, technology, and the development of information and communications technology have been used to lull humanity into heedless consumption, dullness, and intoxication in various forms, rather than for the development of the human being or quality of life. They have been used as tools for seeking objects with which to nourish greed, and in so doing, have fired hatred through the contention and dispute over material wealth.

Greed and hatred, which are natural conditions within the human mind, would be much easier to control, and would be much shorter lived, if it were not for the influence of a third condition, which in Buddhism we call *ditthi*, views and beliefs. Ideologies, religious beliefs, and social values are all aspects of *ditthi*. Whenever greed, anger, and hatred are reinforced with beliefs and social values, they acquire a clearer direction, an impetus which channels them into much more destructive activities.

Briefly speaking, the beliefs that have held control over modern human civilization can be grouped into three main perceptions:

1. The perception that mankind is separate from nature, that mankind must control, conquer, or manipulate nature according to his desires.

2. The perception that fellow human beings are not fellow human beings. Rather than perceiving the common situations or experiences shared among all people, human beings have tended to focus on the differences between themselves.

3. The perception that happiness is dependent on an abundance of material possessions.

The first perception is an attitude toward nature; the second perception is an attitude toward fellow human beings; the third perception is an understanding of the objective of life.

These three beliefs or perceptions have determined the direction of human development and undertaking. The development of human society is guided by the *kamma*, or actions, of human beings blinded by these three views or perceptions.

Even the different sciences and branches of learning which have been responsible for the material progress of humanity in recent times, and on which modern civilization is founded, have unknowingly developed under the influence of these three perceptions or attitudes.

Broadly speaking, without going into detailed analysis, we might say that the natural sciences have developed under the influence of people who had a tendency to aspire to conquering nature, who perceived human beings as separate from nature. The social sciences have developed under the influence of those who perceived not the similarities in human beings, but the differences, seeing human beings as divided into different groups, tending to look at society in terms of the struggle for power. Thirdly, the humanities have developed under the influence of those who see freedom, the goal of life, as an external condition, as the power to control other things, such as nature or fellow human beings. This kind of freedom seeks to have power over external conditions, and as such influences the development of the natural and social sciences. When freedom is seen in this way, happiness is likewise perceived as being intimately related to the power to control external circumstances, which in turn can be used to satisfy personal desires.

In coming years the population of the world will continue to increase, the resources of the world will continue to dwindle, and the environment will continue to deteriorate. These three attitudes or beliefs will escalate these problems to more critical dimensions. While the population of the world is increasing, and the natural resources of the world dwindling, human beings still perceive their happiness as dependent on sensual pleasures and material possessions. They still perceive freedom as the power to control external conditions, and fellow human beings as rivals and hostile groups.

In the past, the largest proportion of religions has helped only select groups of people, fostering harmony and friendship within the group, but greeting others with hostility. This is why religion has been such a divisive force in human history, a catalyst for war and destruction.

Many teachings which were suitable for small groups of people are no longer effective in today's global village. They are not up to the current situation. In the present time, material development has led us to a world that is linked over the whole planet, but religious teachings are still addressing the human situation in terms of small groups. As a result, human beings are not yet ready to live together on a global level.

So it seems that personal human development is not commensurate with the physical world situation. Religions are not yet attuned to addressing the needs of people on a global level. Instead of being a factor for mutual peace and harmony in the world, we find that religions are a cause of more and more contention and strife, wars, and bloodshed.

The concept of human rights arose from a historical background of division, segregation, and competition. Human rights are a necessary protection from aggression from other parties, an answer to a negative situation. The concept of human rights is useful in an age of fighting and contention, or when human thinking is divisive and separatist, but is not enough to lead humanity to true peace and harmony.

While we must acknowledge the needs of human rights activists, in order to understand the situation more clearly, we must analyze the quality of mind within the activists themselves. When we look into the mental motivations behind many, or even most, of the demands for human rights, we will find that they are often based on or influenced by aversion or resentment. As long as this aversion is within the mind, it will be very difficult to obtain truly efficacious results from human rights activities, because the basic feeling behind them is not truly harmonious. Aversion is the inspiration which decides the direction of this activity, making the resulting behavior too aggressive to obtain the required result, instead escalating the problem.

In order to really address this problem it is necessary to address the basic state of mind within each individual, which is a concern of human development.

From what I have said so far, it seems that it is necessary for us to proceed to a way of thinking, or a perception of human relations, which is more positive. We must develop thinking which sees human beings as both equal and united. There has been much talk of equality in recent times, but it tends to be a divisive or contentious kind of equality. It is an equality that is based on competition, suspicion, and fear. In order to prevent the drive for equality from being divisive, there must be unity. Unity is the desire and inclination to live together. It is an attitude that leads to cohesion and alliance.

We must delve into the third basic attitude that has colored human perception. If we cannot solve this third view, we will not be able to deal successfully with the first two. This third attitude is a perception of life on the personal level, the understanding of the basic meaning or objective of life.

Human beings aspire to freedom, but freedom has many different meanings. As I have already mentioned, the perception of freedom prevalent in modern civilization is of freedom from external limitations and restrictions, including the ability to control other people and the natural world. Seeing freedom in this way conditions the way we see other qualities in life, such as happiness. If we see freedom as the ability to control or manipulate other things, such as by amassing a wealth of material possessions or controlling nature, then we will feel that the more material possessions we have, the more happiness we will have.

This kind of perception has bogged down in the present time with the deterioration of the environment, and we find that the natural resources are no longer able to support the increasing population. It has led to a situation where we are forced to compromise. In much the same way as we are forced to compromise with each other, we are forced to compromise with nature. If humanity were to consume or seek happiness to the fullest extent, we would manipulate nature without restraint. But if we did so, the situation would be dangerous to us. As world resources are depleted and the environment is damaged, we ourselves are threatened, and so we must compromise.

Simply speaking, for human beings to live happily there must be freedom on three levels.

The first freedom is the freedom to live with nature and the environment. We could call this physical freedom. This is freedom from want and deprivation, an adequate supply of the four basic necessities of life—food, clothing, shelter, and medicine.

Secondly, in our relationships with fellow humans, we must have social freedom—that is, to be able to live safely together without being exploited by others.

However, these first two kinds of freedom will not be truly effective if they are not connected to the third kind of freedom, which is inner freedom, freedom on the personal level. Human development on the personal level is the most important kind of development, that which leads to inner freedom. What is inner freedom? Having physical and social freedom, people must learn to live independently, to be happy and contented within themselves.

This is a happiness that is more independent of externals, no longer dependent on having to exploit nature or our fellow beings. We become more and more capable of finding contentment within our own minds and through our own wisdom. With a more independent kind of happiness, social and physical freedom will be preserved and strengthened. Human beings will then have the best possible relationship with both the natural environment and human society.

Internal freedom is the foundation or the guarantee on which social and physical freedom can be grounded. Conversely, without inner freedom, human happiness must be dependent on manipulation of the external environment and social exploitation. Physical and social freedom will not be feasible realities as long as there is such exploitation. At best, there must be compromise, a situation where people are forced to do something in order to preserve the state of the environment. If, however, there is inner freedom, it is very possible that a harmonious attitude to the external environment will be developed, and humanity will attain to true happiness that is possessed of both harmony and balance.

Human beings possess the potential for a very high level of freedom, but because of the wrong view that happiness lies in material possessions and consumption of sense experiences, human happiness is very much tied to material objects. People these days find it impossible to experience contentment within themselves, forcing them to exploit both nature and their fellow man in order to find the happiness they hope for from outside. The more they do this, the more problems arise. Not only do we not have any true freedom and happiness within our own lives, we lose our freedom on the physical and social levels. And so it turns out that the more material progress there is, the more do human beings lose their ability to experience happiness within themselves.

Ultimately, human development leads to freedom from the internal enemies, to minds that are completely freed of the oppressive influence of greed, hatred, and delusion. When our minds are completely freed of mental defilements, we will also be freed of mental suffering, which is the main cause of human problems with the physical and social environment. When there is internal freedom, it is no longer necessary for us to exploit the external environment; we can instead live in a way that is truly beneficial to both the physical and social environments.

Our relationship with the natural environment should be a balanced one, one that avoids extremes. One extreme is to concentrate wholly on manipulating the external environment. The other extreme is to completely disregard the external environment.

It is worth noting that those who aspire to conquer nature and manipulate it to their needs tend to see nature as an entirely external object. When confronted with problems pertaining to internal human nature, such as when asked why they do not do something about selfishness and hatred, they tend to counter that these things are natural conditions for human beings. They feel that the internal nature should be left to operate unrestrained. Their perception of nature is incomplete and inconsistent. Aspiring to conquer only external nature, they do not consider that internal nature is also a condition which can be conquered.

For a correct relationship with nature, we must see our situation in a more profound way, seeing ourselves as part of the whole interrelated natural world, not as separate entities or owners or controllers of nature.

In the field of politics, democracy now rides triumphant. In reality, however, its merit is not yet beyond question, and its saving power is still doubtful. We can say in passing that so long as democracy is dominated by the three wrong views, it will not lead mankind to real peace and security. Its ideological foundation must be rectified before democracy can realize its ideal.

Today there seems to be an attempt to pair or even identify democracy with capitalism, as in "democracy and free market economy" and "free market democracy." It is doubtful whether democracy can ultimately be paired or identified with capitalism, or whether democracy paired or identified with capitalism is really good democracy. Capitalism and socialism, ostensibly two different and opposing systems, are both, in reality, united under materialism and are both founded on the three types of aggressive and divisive thinking. The collapse of communist socialism does not spell the soundness of capitalism. On the contrary, it implies that, of the two predominant forms of materialism, as the failure of one has been witnessed, that of the other can be expected. Economics needs not only reformation or transformation, but a conversion in its theoretical foundation.

The situation now is that in order to provide happiness for a small group of people, the larger group of people and the natural environment at large must suffer. Even if the whole of nature were destroyed in the process of seeking happiness, human beings would not find happiness. The Buddha once said that even a whole mountain of gold would not be enough to render a single human being truly satisfied. Even if people were to fight each other until the whole of society disintegrates, they would find no happiness. Everybody would be searching and struggling for happiness, but no one would find it.

If we turn to skillful harmonious views and encourage the development of happiness within, this inner happiness will help to successfully bring about our three objectives: living together in peace, the relief of human suffering, and the preservation of the planet. These are all directly related to personal human development and the achievement of true inner freedom.

The human social world is getting smaller and smaller, now becoming a global community. The time has come to learn to live together, and this will only be possible when human beings are able to develop the freedom that is not dependent on the external environment, and instead learn to help support the external environment. In this way human beings will be able to experience the taste of true freedom and true happiness.

The Religion of Consumerism

SULAK SIVARAKSA

WESTERN CONSUMERISM is the dominant ethic in the world today. You cannot walk down the streets of Bangkok, for example, without being bombarded by billboards touting the benefits of various soft drinks. Streets here are jammed with expensive, foreign cars that provide the owners with prestige and the city with pollution. Young people define their identities through perfumes, jeans, and jewelry. The primary measure of someone's life is the amount of money in his or her checkbook. These are all liturgies in the religion of consumerism.

Although Siam was never colonized by a Western power, in many ways we have been more devastated by this insidious force than those who were. In 1855, with the arrival of Sir John Bowring, the British began to pressure us to open our ports to foreign trade, under their so-called open door policy. King Mongkut, known worldwide from the play *The King and I*, had been a Buddhist monk for twenty-six years. He realized that if we did not agree to open the country to the British, we would be colonized by them. So he invited in the British, and simultaneously the Swedes, the French, and the Germans. The ploy succeeded, and we preserved our political independence. But then our elites in Bangkok began to ape Western ways of life and thought, and our intellectual colonization began.

Mongkut's son, King Chulalongkorn, reigned from 1868 to 1910. He sent his sons to be educated abroad, and when they came back, they had retained their Buddhist heritage and Thai culture, but they were overly enamored of the Western way of life. Gradually, they introduced Western education, medicine, technology, and administration into Siam. In the past, education and culture had been the domain of the Buddhist sangha, the community of monks, but with the introduction of so many Western notions, the traditional Buddhist methods of education lost government support. Buddhism became formalized as a state religion, like the Church of England, and lost much of its vitality.

Today, spiritual advisors to the nation's leadership are no longer members of the *sangha*. Buddhist monks still perform state ceremonies, but they have to be careful to confine their sermons to those subjects that provide spiritual solace to political leaders and have little or no relevance to society. The new "spiritual" advisors are from Harvard Business School, Fletcher School of Law and Diplomacy, and London School of Economics. Although many of them are well-meaning natives of Buddhist lands, most no longer understand the message of Buddha. One Burmese expert even claimed that his country's economic stagnation was caused by Buddhism, and one Thai psychiatrist said that mental illness in Bangkok was due to the Buddhist practice of mindfulness. Had these so-called experts not been educated abroad, no one would have taken them seriously.

Today Bangkok is a third-rate Western city. The department stores have become our shrines, and they are constantly filled with people. For the young people, these stores have replaced the Buddhist temples as centers of social life. And the shadow of Bangkok is spreading over the countryside. In former times, we never had absentee landlords, but today city people are "investing" in rural land, while developers are acquiring and destroying more and more forests. "Development" has become a euphemism for greed.

When they were colonial powers, the British and French maintained some semblance of environmental balance in South and Southeast Asia, replanting trees, for example, so that future timber supplies would be assured. But following World War II, the Americans began to exploit the natural wealth of our country as quickly and efficiently as possible. Bangkok began to develop at a hyperactive pace, consumer culture flourished, and the decadent aspects of Western development—sexual exploitation, violence, and drug abuse—became the norm.

Our educational system teaches the young to admire urban life, the civil service, and the business world, and, as a result, we are "brain-draining" our rural areas. If you go to the villages today, you will find only old people. The young people with ambition and intelligence are in Bangkok, and those who cannot compete there go overseas to serve as cheap labor in the Middle East or as prostitutes in Japan, Germany, or Hong Kong. This new religion of consumerism exploits the minds and bodies of the young and is entirely dysfunctional. Modern Siam is an eroding society.

❋

Traditional Asian cultural values stress the spiritual side of a person as well as the group to which he or she belongs. Personal growth is always related to social well-being. A person is taught to respect other living beings, including animals and plants. Personal achievement at the expense of others is frowned upon. Exploitation, confrontation, and competition are to be avoided, while unity, community, and harmony are encouraged. Those who have become rich or powerful are still expected to treat others kindly and with respect. Conspicuous consumption is scorned. In traditional societies, the rich exhibit their wealth only on certain festival days. In everyday life, they eat and dress the same as everyone else.

A central principle of Buddhist philosophy is that it is more noble to give than to take. In traditional life, we practiced generosity, offering to each other whatever we could. Harmony was always the highest priority. When conflicts arose between individuals and the family, or between families and the village, the former always gave in to preserve the harmony of the larger unit. Confucianism takes this even further. Since the state is larger and more important than towns, villages, or families, the wishes of the Confucian rulers and lawmakers were always respected. The Indian concept of the *Dhammaraja,* "righteous ruler," also carries this notion of obedience from the citizens.* In both Chinese and Indian social hierarchies, the status of merchants was third, far below the king (whose primary duty was to administer the kingdom justly, not to accumulate wealth or power) and the scholars or brahmans (who also served a higher social purpose). As recently as the last century, a Siamese king died with only 1,000 taels of silver in his palace, having spent most of the royal treasury on maintaining Buddhist monasteries. Religion, whether Bud-

---

*The negative side of this obedience in most Asian political systems is that there is not enough public participation. At the local village levels, people may participate in a more democratic way, but at the higher levels of government, the Asian model is too hierarchical. Kings were often regarded as divine, and they began to look down upon the people from whom they came. The concept of divine and sacred rulers promoted superstition and ignorance. The historical residue of this can be seen today in Asian countries' tolerance of authoritarian leaders.

dhism, Hinduism, Islam, or Taoism, has played a strong role in shaping the ideals of the state in most Asian societies.

Even before the advent of the great traditions of Asia, animism contributed toward the cultural concepts of peace and social justice, encouraging respect for natural phenomena. We were taught to revere the spirits that look after the forests and oceans. At each meal, we expressed gratitude to the Rice Goddess to remind us not to eat wastefully and to be aware of all the human labor and natural resources that went into each plate of food. Traditional rites of the field also contributed to an awareness of and gratitude toward nature. Local festivals promoted communal spirit, reminding us that rice is for collective consumption rather than individual wealth. If a family had a surplus of rice, clothing, utensils, or medicine, it was offered to the temple for the monks and the needy.

In the traditional Thai worldview, work and play were both a part of life. The Thai word *sanuk* means "to enjoy life in a relaxed way." Cooperation, rather than competition, was admired. Monks were respected for living a virtuous and ethical way of life. Temples were not only the center of social and spiritual life, they were also ecological centers. All life was spared there. Fishing in the canals and rivers of temple grounds was not allowed, and animals could take refuge in the temple grounds.

I do not want to over-glorify traditional, rural society and its values. People's lives were difficult. But people did respect one another and the wisdom of their elders. In every Thai village, the temple was the center of spiritual, educational, and social life. This model sustained itself for over 700 years in my country, and much longer in other parts of the world.

Within my lifetime, there has been a complete reversal of almost all of these values. All over the world, self-supporting, self-sustaining societies have not been able to resist the pressures of consumerism. Why is consumerism so powerful that it erodes these worthwhile values?

According to Buddhism, there are three poisons: greed, hatred, and delusion. All three are manifestations of unhappiness, and the presence of any one poison breeds more of the same. Capitalism and consumerism are driven by these three poisons. Our greed is cultivated from a young age. We are told that our desires will be satisfied by buying things, but, of course, consuming one thing just arouses us to want more. We all have these seeds of greed within ourselves, and consumerism encourages them to sprout and grow.

Consumerism also supports those who have economic and political power by rewarding their hatred, aggression, and anger. And consumerism works hand in hand with the modern educational system to encourage cleverness without wisdom. We create delusion in ourselves and call it knowledge. Until the schools reinvest their energy into teaching wholesome, spiritual values instead of reinforcing the delusion that satisfaction and meaning in life can be found by finding a higher-paying job, the schools are just cheerleaders for the advertising agencies, and we believe that consuming more, going faster, and living in greater convenience will bring us happiness. We don't look at the tremendous cost to ourselves, to our environment, and to our souls. Until more people are willing to look at the negative aspects of consumerism, we will not be able to change the situation for the better. Until we understand the roots of greed, hatred, and delusion within ourselves, we will not be free from the temptations of the religion of consumerism, and we will remain stuck in this illusory search for happiness.

I am not suggesting that we replace Western ways wholesale with cultural patterns that were suitable for a simple agrarian society. But I am suggesting that we look deeply into our own traditions to find solutions to the problems of a modern, industrialized world. Instead of just absorbing Western values, derived from the Greco-Roman and Judeo-Christian traditions at the expense of our own indigenous models, we must find a "middle path," applying the best of both in an intelligent way. To date, "Westernization" has been largely uncontrolled in Asia (and throughout much of the so-called Third World). Western material values have not merged with Asian culture; they have overwhelmed and diluted it.

We cannot turn back the clock to the "good old days," but, with awareness of the models that our ancestors left us, we can evaluate and apply all development models and begin to build a society worth living in.

Development As If People Mattered

Sulak Sivaraksa

From the Buddhist point of view, the generally recognized goals of development are completely backward. Economists measure development in terms of increasing currency and material items, fostering greed. Politicians see development in terms of increased power, fostering hatred. Both measure the results strictly in terms of quantity, fostering delusion. From the Buddhist point of view, development must aim at the reduction of these three poisons, not their increase. We must develop our spirit. Cooperation is always better than competition.

In Buddhism, development can be attained in stages as negative desires are overcome. The goals of development are perceived differently. From the usual standpoint, when desires are increased and satisfied, development can proceed. From the Buddhist standpoint, when there are fewer desires there can be greater development. It is the reduction of desires that constitutes development. This is the opposite of the materialist notion that dominates our conventional thinking.

The influence of Christianity, or at least real Christian spiritual values, has eroded to the extent that Western civilization has become merely capitalistic or socialistic, in both cases aiming to increase material goods in order to satisfy craving.

In the 1920s, Max Scheler said:

We have never before seriously faced the question whether the entire development of Western civilization, that one-sided and over-active process of expansion outward, might not ultimately be an attempt using unsuitable means—if we lose sight of the complementary art of inner self-control over our entire underdeveloped and otherwise involuntary psychological life, an art of meditation, search of soul, and forbearance. We must learn anew to envisage the great, invisible solidarity of all living beings in universal life, of all minds in the eternal spirit—and at the same time the mutual solidarity of the world process and the destiny of its supreme principle, and we must not just accept this world unity as a mere doctrine, but practice and promote it in our inner and outer lives.*

This reflects the spirit of Buddhist development, where the inner strength must be cultivated, along with compassion and loving kindness.

Perhaps a truly developed city would not be distinguished by a multitude of skyscrapers, but by the values attendant in its growth: simplicity, comfort, and respect for the community of life around it. People would enjoy a simpler, healthier, and less costly diet, lower on the food chain and without toxic additives or wasteful packaging. Animals would no longer be annihilated at the rate of 500,000 per hour merely to be an option on every menu. A new work ethic could be to enjoy our work and to work in harmony with others, as opposed to getting ahead of others and having a miserable time doing it.

In *Small Is Beautiful*, E. F. Schumacher reminds us that Western economics encourages the maximization of material gain without regard for people. He presents Buddhist economics as a study of economics as if people mattered, saying that Buddhist concepts of development avoid gigantism, especially of machines, which tend to control rather than to serve human beings. If we can avoid the extremes of bigness and greed, we may be on a middle path of Buddhist development, creating a world in which industry and agriculture are meaningful and satisfying for all beings.

I agree with Schumacher that small is beautiful in the Buddhist concept of development, but I feel it is important to emphasize that cultivation must come also from within. What is most basic is to work on ourselves. In Sri Lanka, the Sarvodaya Shramadana movement always applies Buddhism first to the individual, and then to the village. At the foundation of the Sarvodaya movement are the Four Abodes: loving kindness, compassion, sympathetic joy, and equanimity. Loving kindness is cultivated toward oneself and others. Through observing precepts and practicing meditation, we can create a state of happiness in our minds that is then spread to others as we render assistance. Compassion is culti-

*Max Scheler, *Selected Philosophical Essays* (Evanston: Northwestern University Press, 1973).

vated by recognizing the suffering of others and wanting to bring it to an end. Sympathetic joy is cultivated by rejoicing when others are happy or successful. Joy without envy is the only true and sustainable happiness. Equanimity is cultivated when the mind is evenly balanced. Whether faced with success or failure, we can remain calm. Trying to do our best to alleviate suffering, we accept our limits and are not disturbed about things we cannot control.

The Four Abodes can be developed step by step, and they build on each other. Even though we are not perfect, we can continue to set our minds on this goal. When we are oriented toward happiness and tranquility rather than material accumulation, we have already begun to develop our community.

Even with all the violence and instability Sri Lanka and Burma have experienced in recent years, they still have a greater chance of true awakening than Siam, which has lost confidence in its Buddhist heritage. The Western model of development has come too far during the last two decades. It would take a major transformation for Siam to choose a middle path of development. Yet, we must live in hope and practice as well as we can.

The goals of Buddhist development are equality, love, freedom, and liberation. The means for achieving these lie within the grasp of any community—from a village to a nation—once its members begin the process of reducing selfishness. To do so, two realizations are necessary: an inner realization concerning greed, hatred, and delusion, and an outer realization concerning the impact these tendencies have on society and the planet.

The Buddha taught that the first awareness is that suffering indeed exists throughout the world. It is our task as intelligent practitioners to be aware of suffering and to apply the insights of the Buddha to our own social setting. We have to translate his essential teaching to address the problems of today. Until we see that the way to be free from suffering is through mindfulness and nonviolence, there is little possibility of overcoming suffering, either personally or societally.

I would like to offer two examples of monks who are applying the insights of the Buddha in contemporary Siam. In Surin province in the impoverished northeast, an abbot recalled that when he was young, the people seemed happier. The people got along with each other and there was that *sanuk* feeling among them. The villages were surrounded by jungles, and elephants roamed freely. The people were poor, but they managed to produce enough food for their families, as well as for the monks. They had the four essentials of food, clothing, shelter, and medicine. Over the last thirty years, the abbot witnessed constant development and construction. Today, the jungle and the elephants have disappeared, and the people are suffering.

The abbot knew that something was wrong. Local products were going to Bangkok to the multinational corporations, and then to the superpowers. He told the people, "Meditation must not be only for personal salvation but for the collective welfare as well. There needs to be collective mindfulness. We need to look to the old traditions that sustained us for so many centuries." When he started to speak this way, people didn't believe him, but they listened out of respect. He said, "Let us try alternative ways." He used controversial words, like "communal farming." In Siam, anticommunism is very strong, and if you use words like "communalism," you can be accused of being a communist. But when a monk who is pure in conduct spoke this way, he aroused the interest of the people.

He encouraged people to farm together and to share their labor with each other. He explained that ambition and competitiveness had only brought them more suffering. The abbot suggested starting rice banks to overcome the shortage of rice, and the village temples cooperated. Whatever was cultivated that was left over was offered to the temple, where the grain was kept for anyone in need to receive free of charge. In this way, the traditional concept of giving alms to the temple was translated to address the social reality of today.

The next project he started was a buffalo bank. Being Buddhists, we don't like to kill buffalos. So the temple kept the buffalos and offered the offspring to those who could not afford to buy one. The only conditions were that the buffalo had to be treated kindly and that 50 percent of all future offspring would be returned to the buffalo bank. This abbot's approach to development based entirely on traditional values and practices is innovative and exemplary.

Another monk who practices the true spirit of Buddhism is Phrakru

Sakorn. A Thai monk in his fifties who only completed elementary education, he is the abbot of Wat Yokrabat in Samut Sakorn province, one province away from Bangkok. Most people who live there are impoverished, illiterate farmers. The province is usually flooded with sea water, which perennially destroys the paddies, leaving the people with little or no other means of subsistence.

Many of the people had been driven to gambling, drinking, or playing the lottery. Aware of the situation, Phrakru Sakorn decided to help the people before making any improvements in his own temple or spending a lot of time preaching Buddhist morals. Phrakru organized the people to work together to build dikes, canals, and some roads. He realized that poverty could not be eradicated unless new crops were introduced, since salt water was ruining the ricefields. He suggested planting coconut trees, based on the example of a nearby province.

Once the people of Samut Sakorn started growing coconuts, Phrakru advised them not to sell the harvest, because middlemen kept the price of coconuts very low. He encouraged them to make coconut sugar using traditional techniques. With assistance from three nearby universities that were interested in the development and promotion of community projects, the people of Samut Sakorn began selling their coconut sugar all over the country. Phrakru has since encouraged the growing of palm trees for building material and the planting of herbs to be used for traditional medicine.

These two monks are exemplars of socially engaged Buddhism. In Buddhism we speak of *kalyana mitta*, good friends. We must understand and help each other. If we want social justice, one village has to be linked with other villages. One country has to be linked with other countries. The Third World has to be linked with the First World. Poor fishermen must help working women, and working women must help industrial workers. We must all start relating to each other. We have to cultivate that understanding.

In this regard, some positive messages have been coming from the so-called First World. There are people in the West beginning to realize the harm caused by their way of life. Their recognition of the limits of Western Cartesian thought, beliefs, and values is the first step toward humility and the willingness to learn from other societies. It is a profound change. This kind of awareness and understanding will help Siam and other developing countries tremendously.

An illustration of this comes from Ladakh, in northern India. Ladakh is in a corner of the Tibetan plateau. The ecology is extremely delicate, with only a few inches of rainfall a year. Up until the 1970s, the people of Ladakh were proud. They were isolated from "civilization" as we know it. By Western standards, they were poor, but they were self-sufficient and were a fairly happy community. Then the Indian government built roads up there, tourists began to arrive, and the Ladakhis began to imitate the tourists, desiring Coca Cola and other Western goods.

Helena Norberg-Hodge, an English woman who has lived in Ladakh for nearly twenty years, has written a play. In it some Ladakhis go to New York and return home. People ask what it was like, and they reply that in New York, the poor people want to dress fashionably. They eat white bread like the bread the Indians sell the Ladakhis. But the richer people eat natural food like that of our forefathers. They wear cotton clothes, buying a lot of it from this part of the world.

This demonstrates that development is a two-way street. The educated, more enlightened people in the West are beginning to realize that development is not purely material; they reject many of the things promoted by the consumer culture. They feel respect for nature. We have these things in our traditions, but we have been brainwashed by advertising. The most important task for those of us in the Third World is to help our people get back in touch with our roots.

Southeast Asia is now a major destination for American and European tourists, as well as Japanese tourists who behave exactly like their Western brethren. They trot all over the globe spending money, flying on Japanese airlines, eating Japanese food, using Japanese guides, speaking only their own language, and returning home no wiser. Siam has a special attraction to foreign visitors. Japanese, European, and Middle Eastern men come to Siam as "sex tourists" to enjoy the prostitutes. In Bangkok they can have girls, boys, anything they want for very little money. It is really dreadful, and in this age of AIDS, also deadly. It would be better for tourists like this to stay home and watch films on television about the world, and pay detailed attention to the explanations therein.

But we cannot stop people from spending their money. We can only educate them to spend it wisely.

Some of us are trying to build up an alternative tourism. If tourists are serious, they can see the reality of Bangkok and the surrounding cities. Most tourists do not realize that when they buy local goods cheaply, they are buying the products of child laborers and others who are denied even a subsistence wage. Westerners who understand the situation often ask, "Is it better to buy or not to buy? Should one support the individual laborer despite the corrupt system in which he lives?" This is a complicated question, and there are no easy answers. If you do not buy, you are not helping the individual; if you do buy, it does not really help either. A Buddhist answer is to make an effort to understand as deeply as possible, to try to see the whole picture. By raising people's consciousness to the negative as well as the positive aspects of a country, we hope to cultivate real communication with those from wealthier countries.

The first step in becoming a "conscious tourist" is to go with goodwill. The second step is to be willing to change your consciousness, and the third is to get more facts and then to try to alert the people at home about the situation. If enough Westerners protested the existence of sex tourism to the Thai government or stopped patronizing the sections of Bangkok where it is rampant, the structures would begin to disappear and alternative models might develop. It is essential for us to meet people from other countries so that we may learn from each other. With enough understanding and goodwill, the people of the Third World and those of the developed countries will work together to build a more just world.

Is advanced technology contrary to Buddhist values? In one way I think it is. People speak about technology as if it were value-free, when in fact it is not. The metaphysical assumption of technology is that man is a supreme being. Man can destroy anything in the name of progress. Most importantly, advanced technology belongs to a development path that pays no attention to the needs of people. Robots may produce faster, but they create human unemployment. This is contrary to human and Buddhist values.

The restoration of balance and flexibility in our economics, technologies, and social institutions will be possible only with a profound change of values. Contrary to conventional belief, value systems and ethics are not peripheral to science and technology. In fact, they constitute the basic assumptions and the driving force of science. A shift of values from self-assertion and competition to cooperation and social justice, from expansion to conservation, from material acquisition to inner growth would be of prime importance in creating a new science and a new technology. Those who have already begun to make this shift have found it liberating and enriching.

Many young people who are concerned with spiritual growth rather than material well-being devote themselves to social justice and have great respect for indigenous peoples who are fighting to preserve their ways of life. Some even risk their own lives to enact social change. This is a return from the profane to the sacred, from an artificial, unsustainable lifestyle to a human scale, and it bodes well for our future together. To return to a more human scale will not mean a return to the past. It will require the development of new forms of technology and social organization. Much of our conventional, resource-intensive, and highly centralized technology has become obsolete, and it needs to be replaced by new forms of technology that incorporate ecological principles and some traditional values.

Many alternative technologies are already being developed. They are often called "soft technologies," because their impact on the environment is greatly reduced by the use of renewable resources and recycling of materials. These technologies tend to be small-scale and decentralized, responsive to local conditions and designed to increase self-sufficiency and flexibility. As our physical resources become scarcer, we need to invest more in people, a resource we have in abundance. Ecological balance requires full employment, and the new technologies facilitate this. Being small-scale and decentralized, they tend to be labor-intensive.

"Deep ecology" recognizes the urgent need for profound changes in our perception of the role of human beings in the ecosystem. Asia's new vision of reality must be spiritual and ecological. If we can develop in this way, the future may be bright.

BUDDHIST COUNTRIES IN ENVIRONMENTAL TROUBLE

✺

Thailand's Ecology Monks

PIPOB UDOMITTIPONG

A SHORT TIME AFTER the First National Economic Development Plan was drafted some thirty years ago, the government prohibited Buddhist monks in Thailand from preaching *santutthi*, the teaching of austerity or contentment with what one has. This action was sanctioned by the Sangha Authority, the official governing body of the monks. The reasoning behind this decree was that the government believed that the teaching of *santutthi* was opposed to the ideals of economic growth, and hence opposed to development.

This is merely one example of the many ways in which the government has attempted to confine the role of religion to the performing of rituals. Social activism of the Thai Sangha has been significantly eroded during this century.

The late Buddhadasa Bhikkhu, a revered Thai monk, argued against the government ruling which prohibits the teaching of *santutthi*. He pointed out that this teaching contributes to real human progress, which must focus upon the development of wisdom rather than material assets.

Due to the rapid surge of Western influences into our society, even with the immense potential of our Buddhist teachings, monks no longer play major roles in their communities. Their traditional roles have been taken over by modern institutions such as schools and hospitals. In addition, the state has attempted to centralize power over every aspect of life, and monks have been largely brought under its control through the two Sangha Acts.

The first act was passed during the period of administrative reform around a hundred years ago in response to pressure from foreign powers demanding an opening of the country. Religious affairs were brought under control of the government. The second act was passed under a dictatorial regime in 1951. This legislation was aimed at using the monks to promote the material development of the nation as envisaged by the state. It resulted in the creation of a governing body with absolute authority over the monks.

Monks have been disadvantaged in the area of education. There are few higher learning institutions for monks and they are allocated much smaller per capita budgets than secular universities. Monks, for the most part, are not allowed to enroll in secular universities.

All of these factors largely impact the ability of Thai monks to become involved in social development along Buddhist lines. However, there are a few monks who are able to continue their spiritual duties while adapting their practices to be more beneficial to their communities and to the larger society.

In the following section, I would like to present two cases of Buddhist monks who have successfully applied their Buddhist principles and wisdom, in conjunction with indigenous beliefs, to address environmental problems within a social context.

TREE ORDINATION

Siam has been known for her abundance of natural resources. Lush forest-covered mountains once filled the northern part of the country. The name Siam comes from a Pali word meaning green.

It is ironic that, as the Forestry Department celebrates 100 years of controlling forests across the land, forest cover has declined to approximately 20 percent. This is an official figure and is thought to be overestimated. Forest coverage in one province in the northeast has declined to just 1 percent. If it is true, as demonstrated through laboratory experiments, that 40 percent forest cover is needed to balance the atmosphere, the depletion of the forests in Thailand is catastrophic. The impact of the loss of the moderating effects of forests has already become clear in some areas. Flooding, drought, and climatic changes have been recorded more often in recent years.

As Thailand marches toward modern industrialization, prospects for her forests look dim. Some Buddhist monks, however, stand out as a source of hope and inspiration as they draw upon traditional cultural and spiritual values to address the environmental crisis.

The ordination ceremony is usually performed for men as a ritual signifying their entrance into the monkhood. This ceremony has recently been adapted to sanctify trees. In a tree ordination, saffron robes are wrapped around the trunk of a tree to signify its sacredness. Traditionally, bodhi trees on the temple grounds are blessed in this way.

Phrakhru Manas Natheepitak, the abbot of Wat Bodharma in northern Thailand, is generally credited with being the first to adapt the ordination ritual to sanctify trees. After realizing that people did not link the rise in the incidence of drought with past deforestation, he developed the ritual as a tool to educate people about the environmental importance of the forest and the dangers of logging. In 1992, he said:

> If a tree is wrapped in saffron robes, no one would dare cut it down. So I thought that perhaps this idea could be used to discourage logging, and I began performing ceremonies on trees in the forest near the temple. I called the ritual an "ordination" to give it more weight. The term "tree ordination" sounds weird to Thai people since an ordination is a ritual applied only to men. This weirdness has helped spread the news by word of mouth.

In 1987, a local logging company began felling trees on the last plot of forest left in the abbot's area. Deforestation in the north has been taking place since the British forced the Thais to open their country to British trade over 100 years ago. Phrakhru Manas, who is greatly respected by the local people, began pleading with the logging company to halt their activities in 1988, but to no avail. He organized local resistance to the logging efforts, but realized that this resulted only in delaying these efforts. He then came up with the idea of tree ordinations and contacted various nongovernmental organizations (NGOs) and media people. This time he was successful in putting a halt to the logging.

Upon receiving complaints from the logging company, the Sangha authorities severely reprimanded Phrakhru Manas, but he stood his ground. He felt that local people must have a say in managing local resources, and argued for the protection of nature by drawing upon Buddhist teachings.

Since that time, he has continued his work. He also organizes forest treks and exposure trips to other watershed areas for local people, and incorporates environmental education in his preaching. The villagers now better understand that droughts and flooding can result from the removal of the stabilizing influence of forest cover.

EVOLUTION OF THE TREE ORDINATION

The work of Phrakhru Manas Natheepitak has helped raise environmental awareness nationwide. The government imposed a logging ban the following year due to the monk's effort and the disaster which was caused by floods and storms in southern Thailand, and other monks began adopting the tree ordination as a means of preserving the forests.

Phra Prajak Kuttajitto, a well-known conservationist monk in Dong-yai Forest in northeastern Thailand, began ordaining trees in 1989. He has been threatened with jail for his environmental activities, and was recently forced to disrobe.

In recent years, local authorities in Chiang Mai, Thailand's second largest city, have adopted the ritual to protect large teak trees lining the road to Lamphun. Government agencies and NGOs have now become interested in the Buddhist principles of natural conservation.

Phrakhru Pitak Nanthakun has been most successful in applying the ordination ritual to his environmental preservation work. He is from Nan, a mountainous province in the northern region which was once known for its lush forests. After thirty years of national development, however, forest cover in Nan is down to 30 percent.

Historically, logging was initiated by Western corporations, particularly British companies, who took the largest trees. Local logging companies then began consuming the medium-sized trees to be used to dry tobacco and sold for domestic use. In the 1960s, cash cropping, particularly the growing of corn, increased rapidly and resulted in the clearing of large tracts of forest to make way for "slash and burn" agriculture. In addition to this, roads were constructed as part of the government's counter-insurgency campaign in the north, which facilitated all of the extractive activities mentioned above.

Phrakhru Pitak began campaigning for forest preservation in Nan in 1975 as a seventeen-year-old novice monk. He tried to educate the people in Kew Muang, his home village, about the importance of the forest, and to encourage reforestation. Since he was the most educated person in the village, the local people listened to him, and his efforts were largely successful. Teak and other trees were planted in degraded areas and watersheds were preserved. Each year his activities expanded. He also facilitated other activities such as the construction of roads and reservoirs, the initiation of local cooperative shops, and the introduction of alternatives to cash cropping and logging. When he left for three years to continue his studies and gain practical training in community development, his environmental activities were continued by the villagers.

Upon returning, he led a protest against the provincial plan to create eucalyptus plantations to stimulate economic growth in Nan. The type of eucalyptus tree chosen would severely deplete the soil. Forests were to be cleared to create these plantations. He wrote a letter protesting the plan which eventually wound up in a national paper. The provincial governor complained bitterly to the Sangha Authorities, and Phrakhru Pitak was brought before them. Fortunately, he was successful in convincing them of the dangers of eucalyptus cultivation, and so was able to save hundreds of acres of forest in his home area.

By then, however, forestry officials had already begun clearing small portions of land for the eucalyptus plantations. Phrakhru Pitak's response was to bring together NGOs and local people to protest. This brought the project to a halt.

In 1987, the area experienced a severe drought. The root cause of the problem was the continuing deforestation, especially in the watershed areas. After the drought, the villagers became more committed to preserving the forests. Phrakhru Pitak's activities were expanded to encompass the Pong Mountains which surround the Pong watershed. Protecting only one part of the watershed was insufficient. In 1988, he initiated the Kew Muang Conservation Club, and expanded his conservation activities into six villages. Local committees were set up to manage local forests. This time, however, the government threatened to designate the community forests as sanctuaries, which would be off-limits to local people.

Phrakhru Pitak encouraged the local people to intensify their planting activities in the forest to show the government that local people were highly skilled at managing their own resources. He was worried that the government would use any excuse to expropriate the forests and then turn around and lease them to logging companies.

Throughout 1989, he sought to raise environmental awareness by organizing trainings and forest treks for novice monks and local children. Over 200 novices enrolled in his program that year. He provided education, not only about the forest, but about environmentally friendly agricultural methods as well. Phrakhru Pitak feels that once children are educated, they are able to raise awareness among their parents as well.

ADAPTING BUDDHIST RITUALS TO ENHANCE PRESERVATION

Phrakhru Pitak, having heard of the successful application of the tree ordination ceremony by Phrakhru Manas Natheepitak, started his own campaign.

He combined the tree ordination with a *phaa paa*, a traditional Buddhist ceremony in which lay people offer money and goods to the monks. This ceremony has been successfully adapted to secure tree seedlings rather than funds or goods. In 1991, he performed his first tree ordination and tree seedling *phaa paa* in Kew Muang. Local villagers, government officials, and NGO workers participated in the ceremonies and helped plant trees. A Buddha image and spirit house were placed beside the largest tree of the forest. The forest was sanctified.

The following year, he performed another tree ordination in the Pong watershed area. This time, he invited media people to the event, which further strengthened the growing environmental awareness in the area. Phrakhru Pitak feels that the success of the programs would not be possible without the cooperation of a number of NGOs and government agencies. His role is to act as a link between the people and the government.

In 1991, he set up the Hag Muang Nan Group (Love Nan Group), which brought together local village groups, government agencies, and NGOs. The Hag Muang Nan Group (HMN) is itself an NGO, and acts as an umbrella organization, coordinating the activities of its various members. The group has also provided training and materials aimed at enhancing environmental awareness to various groups in Nan.

Under the HMN, Phrakhru Pitak has initiated the "Love for the Nan River" project. The Nan River, a major water artery in Thailand, was surveyed to determine its condition, and a campaign to educate people about the river was introduced. In 1993, a ritual to prolong the life of the river was held. This ritual is usually applied to humans or livestock. Monks chanted and the river was blessed and sanctified. Hundreds of people participated in the ceremony. A certain portion of the river was declared a sanctuary to allow fish populations to regenerate, similar to the sanctuaries traditionally created on temple grounds. Birds and wildlife are allowed to live free from harm on temple lands.

These activities have inspired other monks along the Nan River to adopt the ritual and create fish sanctuaries. To date, nine sanctuaries have been established. It seems that, though Phrakhru Pitak Nanthakun initially began his work in the mountains, his activities have widened to touch the lowlands and the streams.

Tree Ordination in Thailand

SUSAN M. DARLINGTON

TREE ORDINATION CEREMONIES (*buat ton mai*) are performed by many participants in the Buddhist ecology movement in order to raise the awareness of the rate of environmental destruction in Thailand and to build a spiritual commitment among local people to conserving the forests and watersheds. Some large-scale ordinations have been carried out for publicity and public sympathy to make the government see the environmental impact of some of its economic development plans. This was the case in the southern province of Surat Thani in March 1991, when over fifty monks and laypeople entered a national park to wrap monks' robes around all the large trees in a rainforest threatened by the construction of a dam (Pongpet 1991). Most tree ordinations are aimed at local areas, and villagers, through their participation in these ceremonies, signify their acceptance of this adaptation of a Buddhist ritual to sanctify the forest and thereby protect it. The regulations the monks establish limit the villagers' use of the forest, forbidding the cutting of any trees or killing of any wildlife within it.

In July 1991, I attended a tree ordination ceremony in Nan Province in northern Thailand sponsored by Phrakhru Pitak Nanthakhun. Although the tree ordination was the culmination of months of preparation and was one aspect of a larger conservation program, the actual ceremony involved only a day and a half of activities. Phrakhru Pitak invited over twenty monks from Nan and other northern provinces to assist in performing the ceremony. Recognizing the importance of gaining the support of the Sangha hierarchy and the local government for the project's success, Phrakhru Pitak consulted with and involved members of the province's Sangha organization, especially the seniormost monk in the three subdistricts of the ten participating villages, the District Officer, and other local bureaucrats.[1] Many local government officials and mid-level members of the Sangha hierarchy participated in the ceremony. Given the independent nature and potentially controversial aspects of the activities of most socially engaged monks, Phrakhru Pitak's attention to convincing the Sangha hierarchy and the government of the project's importance was significant for assuring its success. The night before the ceremony, representatives of Wildlife Fund Thailand (an affiliate of World Wildlife Fund) showed slides to the villagers. WFT's cosponsorship of the project placed Phrakhru Pitak's work on a national stage and gave it further legitimacy. Not only is WFT one of the largest environmental NGOs in Thailand, but it also has royal patronage. The involvement of NGOs in the work of ecology monks is essential to much of their success, although at the same time it raises potential political issues, as many NGOs are openly critical of government policy.

The ordination ceremony began in the morning with a modification of a traditional ritual, *thaut phaa paa* (the giving of the forest robes). Traditionally, this ritual is performed by Thai laypeople to donate robes, money, and other necessities to monks for religious merit. The funds support the monks and the upkeep of the temple. Since the 1980s this ritual has been increasingly used across the nation to raise funds for local development projects; those contributing offerings to the monks gain merit, and the monks allow the money donated to be used for projects ranging from building or repairing a school to establishing a local credit union or village cooperative store. People's commitment to such projects is often stronger because of the religious connotations behind the source of the funds—they not only gain merit from the original donations at the *phaa paa* ceremony but from supporting the development project sanctioned by the monks as well.

Phrakhru Pitak added a new twist to this ceremony. Several nurseries around the provincial capital and some wealthy patrons offered 12,000 seedlings to the monks. Along with the donation of seedlings, there were several other innovations. The villagers paraded their offerings in three groups, representing the three subdistricts in which the ten participating villages belonged. While they carried model trees with simple offerings of money and necessities, they did not dance, drink, or play the traditional music that usually accompanies a *phaa paa* parade (Darlington 1990:132–37). Rather, each of the three groups performed skits they had prepared, which presented their ideas of conserving the forest. Two were straightforward; for example, one group pantomimed planting seedlings. The most dramatic of the three included political commentary. The villagers acted out an incident of the forest being cut down, passing the blame from the minority hill people to the northern Thai villagers, until it finally settled on the government for not protecting the forest. The political debate concerning forest conservation and the economic interests involved in its destruction underlies all conservation activities.[2] It is unusual, however, for these issues to be brought so openly to the surface, especially during a Buddhist ritual. All three skits emphasized the urgent need for the villagers to conserve the forest.

Once the forest robes were ritually accepted by Phrakhru Pitak, he and the highest-ranking monk present accepted the seedlings, thus sanctifying them and conferring merit on the donors and the participants. A few of the seedlings were planted around the temple grounds and at the site of the tree ordination as part of the ceremony. Most were given to the villagers to reforest areas that had been denuded, following the pattern established by *phaa paa* ceremonies conducted to raise development project funds. These new trees were chosen carefully; they were species, such as fruit trees, that were profitable without having to be cut down. Having been sanctified and given by the monks further protected them, as the villagers would see cutting them as a form of religious demerit (*baap*).

After planting the trees at the temple, the participants climbed into trucks, vans, and buses to make the five-kilometer trip into the mountains to the tree chosen to be ordained. Over 200 people accompanied the more than twenty monks to the site, which had earlier been prepared by volunteer development workers and villagers. A four-foot-tall Buddha image had been placed on a concrete stand at the base of the giant tree. The thick vegetation around the site had been trimmed, and a tent for the monks put up. Phrakhru Pitak commented that over twenty years ago, when he walked the eight kilometers from his village through the deep forest to school along this route, this tree was not unusual for its height or size. Now it clearly stood out as the tallest remaining tree. One could now see for miles across a landscape dotted with nearly vertical maize fields, visible because of the deforested hillsides.

It is important to note that in this ceremony, as in all tree ordinations, the monks did not claim to be fully ordaining the tree, as that status is reserved for humans only. The ceremony was used symbolically to remind people that nature should be treated as equal with humans, deserving of respect and vital for human as well as all life. The opportunity of the ordination was used to build spiritual commitment to preserving the forest and to teach in an active and creative way the value of conservation. The main emphasis of Phrakhru Pitak's sermon during the ritual was on the relationship between the Buddha and nature, and the interdependence between the conditions of the forest and the villagers' lives.

During the ritual, at the same point in which a new monk would be presented with his robes, two monks wrapped orange robes around the tree's trunk, marking its sanctification. A crowd of photographers from local and Bangkok newspapers and participating NGOs, one anthropologist, and two video camera crews documented the quick act. The robes stood as a reminder that to harm or cut the tree—or any of the forest— was an act of demerit. While it was not unusual to find bodhi trees (the tree under which the Buddha achieved enlightenment) wrapped with sacred cloth, in those cases the tree was already seen as holy; the cloth served more to honor the tree than to sanctify it. The innovation here was that the tree ordained was not already treated as sacred but was made so through the ritual. The orange robes symbolized its new status.

As in most ordinations, the ritual included the sanctification of water in a monk's alms bowl. A small Buddha image was placed in the bowl and candle wax dripped into the water while the monks chanted. Traditionally, this holy water (*nam mon*) is sprinkled on the participants, conferring a blessing on them. This water is seen as ritually very powerful, and people always make sure to receive some of the drops from the monk (Olson 1991). On this occasion, Phrakhru Pitak used the blessed water in an original manner. Each of the headmen from the ten villages drank some of the water in front of the large Buddha image to seal their pledge to protect the forest. This use of a sacred symbol to strengthen such an oath was another innovation which reinforced the notion of environmentalism as a moral action. It made the protection or destruction of the forest karmic action: protecting it would confer good merit (*bun*), destroying it would bring demerit, the balance ultimately affecting one's rebirth or even quality of living in this life. Beyond that, it drew on the belief of the villagers in the magical powers of the holy water; while specific sanctions were not mentioned for failing to uphold the headmen's pledge, the implications were that breaking it would involve going against the power secured by the use of the water.

Perhaps the most telling aspect of the ceremony (the one which in itself raises the most questions or is open to the greatest variety of alternative interpretations) is the plaque that was nailed to the tree prior to the ordination. No formal mention of the sign was made during the ritual, nor was much discussion or fanfare made concerning its content or placement. Yet it always draws the most attention and discussion from Thai who are introduced to it. The sign reads, *"Tham laay paa khee tham laay chaat,"* which can be translated, "To destroy the forest is to destroy life." The word *chaat* (life) is problematic and can carry several meanings, all of which relate to the issue of conservation on various levels.[3] *Chaat* can mean life, birth (as in rebirth), or nation. The sentence could thus be read, "To destroy the forest is to destroy life, one's rebirth, or the nation."

The first meaning is the most straightforward from the point of view of environmentalists whose concerns do not necessarily involve either religious or nationalist connotations. Yet it also implies the Buddhist idea that one should respect and care for all life because any being could have been one's mother in a previous life. The second meaning, to destroy one's rebirth, invokes the concept of *kamma*. It raises the idea that destroying the forest is an act of demerit and consequently has a negative influence on how one is reborn in one's next life. The third possibility, that of destroying the nation (meaning both territory and people; Reynolds 1977:274, 1994:442), is the most complex. It evokes nationalist feelings, linking the condition of the forest with that of the state. It draws upon the moral connection between nation (*chaat*), religion (*satsana*), and monarchy (*mahakeset*), the trinity of concepts which supposedly makes up Thailand's identity (Reynolds 1977, 1994). Even this meaning is double-edged. While it invokes the villagers' loyalty to the nation and the king in protecting the forest, it also calls upon the nation itself to uphold its moral responsibility to preserve the forest. Given the political undertones of the conservation issue, it is unlikely that this implicit meaning is present by mere coincidence.

The use of the word *chaat* on the sign demonstrates the complexity and significance of the tree ordination. Concepts of religion are being reinterpreted to promote environmentalism at the same time the latter is linked through moral ties with local and national political and economic issues. Throughout the ordination, and the larger project of which it was a part, Phrakhru Pitak extended his traditional role as spiritual and moral leader of lay villagers to embrace an activism which necessitates political involvement. The same kind of role enlargement is recreated in every project run by ecology monks, from tree ordinations and the establishment of sacred community forests to tree-planting ceremonies and exorcisms or long-life ceremonies at sites threatened by ecological destruction.

Monks are not supposed to be concerned with worldly issues such as politics. At the same time, however, the ecology monks see environmental destruction as a crucial factor in their main concern—human suffering. They cannot avoid a certain degree of involvement in the former if they are to deal with the latter. They feel a responsibility as monks to teach people environmental awareness and show them the path to relieving their suffering. The root causes of suffering are, in Buddhist philosophy, greed, ignorance, and hatred. As the destruction of the forest is caused by these evils, the monks see it as their duty to adapt traditional religious concepts and rituals to gain the villagers' acceptance and commitment to their ecological aims.

NOTES

1. In later projects, Phrakhru Pitak involved provincial government officials and Sangha, including the governor and military leaders.
2. Economic enterprises that destroy natural forests include the creation of eucalyptus plantations and logging hardwood trees such as teak. The former is occurring primarily in the northeast legally, and at a rapid rate (see Lohmann 1991; Sanitsuda 1992a, 1992b), while the latter continues throughout the country despite a national ban passed in 1989. The widespread belief is that both frequently occur with the backing of factions within local, regional, and national governments and the military (Pinkaew and Rajesh 1991).
3. I thank Dr. Thongchai Winichakul and Dr. Robert Bickner for pointing out to me the several meanings of *chaat* as used in the sentence on the plaque.

BIBLIOGRAPHY

Chatsumarn, K. 1987. How Buddhism Can Help Protect Nature. In *Tree of Life: Buddhism and Protection of Nature*, ed. S. Davies, pp. 7–16. Geneva.

———— 1990. Buddhist Monks and Forest Conservation. *Radical Conservatism: Buddhism in the Contemporary World*, ed. Thai Inter-Religious Commission for Development and the International Network of Engaged Buddhists, pp. 301–309, Bangkok.

Darlington, S. M. 1990. "Buddhism, Morality and Change: The Local Response to Development in Thailand." Ph.D. Dissertation, University of Michigan, Ann Arbor.

———— n.d. Practical Spirituality and Community Forests: Monks, Ritual and Radical Conservatism in Thailand. *Environmental Discourses and Human Welfare in South and Southeast Asia*, eds. A. L. Tsing and P. Greenough.

Harris, I. 1991. How Environmentalist is Buddhism? *Religion* 21:101–14.

Hirsch, P. 1993. *Political Economy of Environment in Thailand*. Manila.

———— 1996. Environment and Environmentalism in Thailand: Material and Ideological Bases. *Seeing Forests for Trees: Environment and Environmentalism in Thailand*, ed. P. Hirsch, pp. 15–36. Chiang Mai.

Kingshill, K. 1965 (1960). *Ku Daeng—the Red Tomb*. Bangkok.

Local Development Institute. 1992. Community Forestry; Declaration of the Customary Rights of Local Communities. Thai Democracy at the Grassroots. Bangkok.

Lohmann, L. 1991. Peasants, Plantations and Pulp: The Politics of Eucalyptus in Thailand. *Bulletin of Concerned Asian Scholars* 23(4):3–17.

Olson, G. 1991. Cries over Spilt Holy Water. *Journal of Southeast Asian Studies* 22:75–85.

Pei S. 1985. Some Effects of the Dai People's Cultural Beliefs and Practices on the Plant Environment of Xishuangbanna, Yunnan Province, Southwest China. *Cultural Values and Human Ecology in Southeast Asia*, eds. K. L. Hutterer, A. T. Rambo, and G. Lovelace, pp. 321–39. Ann Arbor.

Pinkaew L., and N. Rajesh (eds.). 1991. *The Future of People and Forests in Thailand after the Logging Ban*. Bangkok.

Pongpet M. 1991. Stopping the Chainsaws with Sacred Robes. *Bangkok Post*, March 29, pp. 27–28.

Queen, C. S., and S. B. King (eds.). 1996. *Engaged Buddhism: Buddhist Liberation Movements in Asia*. Albany.

Renard, R. D. n.d. Using a Northern Thai Forest: Approaches by a Conservationist Monk, Thai Lowlanders, Hmong Highlanders, and International Development. *Ecology, Ethnicity and Religion in Thailand*, eds. L. E. Sponsel and P. Natadecha-Sponsel.

Reynolds, F. E. 1977. Civic Religion and National Community in Thailand. *Journal of Asian Studies* 36(2):267–82.

———— 1994. Dhamma in Dispute: The Interactions of Religion and Law in Thailand. *Law and Society Review* 28(3):433–51.

Rigg, J. 1995. Counting the Costs: Economic Growth and Environmental Change in Thailand. *Counting the Costs: Economic Growth and Environmental Change in Thailand*, ed. J. Rigg. pp. 3–24. Singapore.

Saneh C., and Yos S. (eds.) 1993. *Paa Chumchon nai Prathetthai: Naewthaang kaan Phadthanaa (Community Forests in Thailand: The Direction for Development)*. Bangkok.

Sanitsuda E. 1992a. Torn from the Land: How Tree-Planting Uproots Whole Villages. *Bangkok Post*, 23 January, pp. 23, 42.

———— 1992b. Man and Forest. *Bangkok Post*, 24 January, pp. 27, 48.

Somboon S. 1987. *Kaanphadthanaa Taam Naew Phuthasaasanaa: Karanii Phra Nak Pha-dthanaa (A Buddhist Approach to Development: The Case of "Development Monks").* Bangkok.

—— 1988. A Buddhist Approach to Development: The Case of "Development Monks" in Thailand. *Reflections on Development in Southeast Asia,* ed. L. T. Ghee, pp. 26–48. Singapore.

Sponsel, L. E., and P. Natadecha. 1988. Buddhism, Ecology, and Forests in Thailand: Past, Present, and Future. *Changing Tropical Forests,* eds. J. Dargavel, K. Dixon, and N. Semple, pp. 305–25, Canberra.

Sponsel, L. E., and P. Natadecha-Sponsel. 1995. The Role of Buddhism in Creating a More Sustainable Society in Thailand. *Counting the Costs: Economic Growth and Environmental Change in Thailand,* ed. J. Rigg, pp. 27–46. Singapore.

Stott, P. 1991. *Mu'ang* and *Pa*: Elite Views of Nature in a Changing Thailand. *Thai Constructions of Knowledge,* eds. M. Chitakasem and A. Turton, pp. 142–54. London.

Suchira P. 1992. Changing Provinces of Concern: A Case-Study of the Social Impact of the Buddhadasa Movement. *Sojourn* 7(1):39–68.

Tambiah, S. J. 1970. *Buddhism and the Spirit Cults in North-east Thailand.* Cambridge.

—— 1976. *World Conqueror and World Renouncer: A Study of Buddhism and Polity in Thailand against a Historical Background.* Cambridge.

—— 1984. *The Buddhist Saints of the Forest and the Cult of Amulets.* Cambridge.

Taylor, J. 1993a. *Forest Monks and the Nation-State: An Anthropological and Historical Study of Northeastern Thailand.* Singapore.

—— 1993b. Social Activism and Resistance on the Thai Frontier: The Case of Phra Prapak Khuttajitto. *Bulletin of Concerned Asian Scholars* 25(2):3–16.

—— 1996. *"Thamma-chaat":* Activist Monks and Competing Discourses of Nature and Nation at Northeastern Thailand. *Seeing Forests for Trees: Environment and Environmentalism in Thailand,* ed. P. Hirsch, pp. 37–52. Chiang Mai.

Thai Inter-Religious Commission for Development. (1992. *Kaanoprom Phrasong kap Kaanunak Thammachaat Khrang thii 3 (Training Monks and Nature Conservation).* Meeting Number 3 Sekhiyatham 2(11):26–31.

Thai Inter-Religious Commission for Development and the International Network of Engaged Buddhism. 1990. *Radical Conservatism: Buddhism in the Contemporary World.* Bangkok.

Thurman, R. A. F. 1984. Buddhist Views of Nature: Variations on the Theme of Mother-Father Harmony. *On Nature,* ed. L. S. Rouner, pp. 96–112. Notre Dame.

Trébuil, G. 1995. Pioneer Agriculture, Green Revolution and Environmental Degradation in Thailand. *Counting the Costs: Economic Growth and Environmental Change in Thailand,* ed. J. Rigg, pp. 67–89. Singapore.

Dhamma Walk around Songkhla Lake

SANTIKARO BHIKKHU

"SI NUAN, SI NUAN." These were the most commonly heard words in our circumambulation of Siam's largest lake.* *Si Nuan* literally means soft tan color, and is the name of the dog that adopted us from day one. She originally came along with the temple boys from Wat Talae Noi whom we pressed into carrying our lead banner. Her name was introduced to thousands of villagers around the lake and fans who followed the progress of the walk through call-in radio programs. So it was that people who had never seen her before called out her name as she wandered among our straggling crew of monks, lay folks, students, and foreigners.

The Songkhla Lake Dhamma Walk (*Dhammayatra*) was conceived and planned by national and local members of Phra Sekhiyadhamma with help from southern NGOs (nongovernmental organizations), village leaders, and some government officials. Phra Sekhiyadhamma is a small but growing network of grassroots monks struggling to integrate the study and practice of Buddha-Dhamma with responsibility for the communities, culture, and society crumbling around us. Modernity brings many wonders, but we ponder why so much must be destroyed in exchange. Further, we ask why the poor, ordinary majority of people seem to pay the most and benefit the least from the wonders of *lokanuivat*, "spinning according to the world"—the most common Thai translation for "globalization," with little or no say in decisions that affect them.

The members of Phra Sekhiyadhamma believe that Buddha-Dhamma is relevant to all forms of suffering, including these. We believe that Sangha is more than yellow-robed shavelings chanting for meals and ought to be a "Sangha of the People," fully engaged in solving communal, ecological, and economic problems. We dedicate ourselves to *sekhiya-*

---

*On the use of "Siam" rather than "Thailand," see page 438, note 20.—ED.

dhamma, literally "the Dhamma for training ourselves," which enables us to serve the Triple Gem and all beings within the present realities of suffering.

Our network organized the Dhammayatra walk to test the value and effectiveness of peace walks as a form of moral persuasion with Thai Buddhist and Muslim cultures. Our first goal was to help bring attention to the dilemma of Songkhla Lake, Siam's largest lake, a uniquely complex and prolific ecosystem. We wanted to establish a middle way between protest marches and apathetic silence. Some of us see ever more violent clashes over natural resources in Siam's future and hope that Buddhist leaders can help mediate just and peaceful resolutions. A second goal was to help build up the people's network around the lake in order to provide a greater local voice in working out policies and projects. We see a natural role for monks as network facilitators and wanted to encourage local monks to participate in the walk. A few were already involved in their own areas but were not yet cooperating with other monks, village leaders, and NGO workers concerned with the lake. Our third goal was to identify local monks who would be willing to join us in our engaged Buddhist work, both around the lake and on national issues.

We were moderately successful in these goals. We stirred up publicity for the lake and for the people living close to it. We were accepted and praised by some senior monks, with no serious criticism. We were blessed with the presence and advice of Samdech Maha Ghosananda from Cambodia, an internationally recognized leader of engaged Buddhism. A precedent has been set. We proved that such walks are possible here and that they have potential for popularity. And the strands of a Songkhla Lake network are now being woven together.

THE ISSUES

We presented ourselves to the people living around the lake as concerned outsiders who wanted to learn more about what the residents themselves thought, rather than offer our own analysis and solutions. We wanted to strengthen the voice of the lake's people, especially the poor and marginalized. Though we did hold a certain bias for the poor community members, we tried to avoid being against the developers, land speculators, factory owners, middle-class suburbanites, and others who are slowly buying off, tempting away, and pushing out the locals. The more privileged group already has a well-established voice, plenty of influence, and significant political-economic power. We felt it was crucial to create a space in which the ignored members of society—the intimidated and downtrodden silent majority—were encouraged to speak.

Five main issues concerning the lake were identified by various representatives of the people.

1. *No fish to eat.* The amount and diversity of fish and shrimp have deteriorated grievously, especially within the last five years. Many species have disappeared, including delicious ones. We heard stories of how fish used to jump into peoples' boats, there were so many! People blamed the problem on overfishing by themselves and others; use of intensive fishing technology such as drag nets, electric shocks, and poisons; fishing during spawning seasons; and the deterioration of the water. Manmade disruptions in the normal circulation of sea, rain, and brackish water through connecting channels have interfered with migrations of fish fry that once swam in the interchanging currents. Destruction of mangroves and other spawning grounds due to development and prawn farms has undercut marine life reproduction.

2. *Bad water and reduced water levels.* Either the water is much more shallow than before, the bottom is silting up, or the whole system is drier. The remaining water is dirty and unable to cleanse itself naturally. Erosion due to mountain deforestation to the north and east, conversion of wetlands to rice fields, and road building has led to dramatic levels of siltation. Further, the roads that now encircle the lake block the natural drainages into it. Pollution from towns, factories, agricultural chemicals, and prawn farms is poisoning the water. In some places along the walk, bathers ended up with skin rashes.

3. *Theft of water.* Increasingly, water is taken up for urban and industrial uses, resulting in less drainage into the lake. The town of Had Yai is the primary reason for a proposed dam that most of the lake

people do not want. This is on top of the use of lake water for irrigation and prawn farms.

4. *Loss of land.* With the spread of Had Yai and other large southern towns, an increasing amount of land is covered with concrete sub-divisions for the professional and business class. Wetlands are turned into "Songkhla Laguna" housing developments, while the former residents are denied entry or even passage through these new villages.

5. *Breakdown of community.* With the loss of traditional livelihoods, the siphoning off of the young into towns, the relocation of homes, the domination of formal village leaders by the government, and the deterioration of the temples, the lake communities have little left to hold them together. Too often, the only unifying factor is the lack of opportunity elsewhere. This is a tragic di-lemma for a society to impose on its people—to deprive them of old joys, bonds, and strengths while denying them new ones. Seeing this convinced many of us that ecological problems are inevitably cultural and moral problems.

I was shocked to find that the northwest shore of the Upper Lake area we passed through at the beginning of the walk, which had been converted from rich and diverse flood forests into rice fields, was as poor as areas in Siam's Isaan. Isaan, the Northeast, with poor soils, a harsh climate, and more patient, docile inhabitants, is the poorest part of the country; the South is much richer in resources and income. Why was there such poverty here? The common denominator was rice. Farmers have been taught to deplete their soils and invest in chemicals. If they only kept books, they would realize that there is no way they can make a profit on rice. Thus, poverty by policy.

There is not yet a strong enough coalition of grassroots leaders to arrive at the consensus needed to save the lake and its human and natural resources. We often heard villagers in one area blaming their difficulties on peers in another part of the lake. We suspect this tension is encouraged by government agents. We tried to be a channel through which villagers could begin to hear one another and visit their counterparts around the lake. By identifying the main issues, we are hoping to work toward such a consensus so the people themselves will have a determining role in the efforts to preserve the lake's ecological and cultural systems. We believe that a comprehensive approach would include:

1. dialogue among village and religious leaders from all around the lake;
2. collective analysis of the problems and their causes;
3. freedom from domination by the government, politicians, and business interests (although these sectors must be brought into the process eventually);
4. a solidarity plan of action determined by the people themselves, supported by NGOs and the government, with the moral guidance of engaged religious leaders.

Such an approach will not happen easily. The people have been effectively brainwashed against such action.

WALKING LESSONS LEARNED

In addition to what we learned about the lake, we were forced to rethink the walk itself. There were surprises and disappointments. There is always the danger that such walks will be seen merely as a form of protest. A walk led by monks could come under much criticism for overt protesting, especially when many of us were from outside the area. Fortunately we were able to establish a middle way of walking. Our role was to listen to the people rather than tell them what was going on or what to do. We avoided taking sides, although individual walkers often had their own points of view.

With monks in the lead, a number of Buddhist customs and traditions came into play. At times, we didn't know what to do with the flood of donated food. People kept giving us water bottled in throw-away plastic. We had not taken precautions to avoid this and similar ecologically destructive habits. The expectation of a sermon delayed our setting out until the sun was high up in the sky, blazing hot in the middle of the dry season. On the other hand, lots of people came out to see us, and this raised our spirits.

We were warned to avoid the word *environment* by Ven. Payutto, Siam's leading scholar-monk and advisor to Phra Sekhiyadhamma. He feels that the word betrays its Western origins, separating human beings from the rest of nature. In Buddhism, we ought to speak of nature or ecology as inclusive of everything, especially ourselves.

Those who came out to the temples and joined us on the roads were primarily the old. This partly reflects the reality of village Buddhism, trapped in a time no longer relevant to the young. It also reflects the economic reality that young people are collected each day in pickup trucks to work in fish- and prawn-packing factories. Many of the old people were delighted to see us walking. In their youth, everyone walked daily. A ten-kilometer trip to the market was not unusual. Now the young need motor scooters to get anywhere. It was much harder to get the young to join us for a stroll to the next village.

As a minority of the community around the lake are Muslim, we hoped to involve them in the walk, too. With some exceptions, we were not very successful in this. The exceptions give us hope that we can do better in the future. Perhaps a few Muslim leaders will join us later in reflections about the walk.

Monks and NGOs have had little experience working together beyond the personal level. This was the first time we know of that a group of monks worked with NGOs to plan a large-scale activity. A lot of learning and unlearning was required. Different working cultures, turf battles, prejudices, and communication styles got in the way. But in the end, we found that we could work together in the spirit of Dhamma. Sometimes the monks were able to help the NGO workers let go of an attachment; sometimes it was the other way around.

The presence of foreigners—American, Bangladeshi, Chakma, Australian, Haitian, and Canadian—clearly helped to spark interest among local residents and to spread the word to other countries. "If foreigners have come from far away to walk around our lake, maybe something important is going on here." Walking together offered many opportunities for making friends, sharing hardships and joys, learning and growing in Dhamma. These opportunities can be nurtured with good group process, which must be adequately prepared for in advance. When we were able to include time for interpersonal work, the results were satisfying and conflicts dissolved. The many friendships forged and strengthened are an important sign of the walk's value. Initiated by Cambodia by our Khmer friends, the Dhammayatra is now set to be accepted as a legitimate form of social statement in Siam. With popularity, however, will come the danger that the Dhamma is watered down or filtered out by special interest groups. For this reason Phra Sekhiyadhamma and its friends must remain mindfully vigilant.

Si Nuan, our faithful companion, was adopted by Phramahá Jaroen Dejadhammo, the leading "development monk" at the south end of the lake. She was a bit ragged at the end of the first walk, but her tail kept wagging through all the meetings.

SECOND AND THIRD WALKS

Throughout the first Dhammayatra, villagers asked if we would be back the following year. Our reply was always, "It depends on whether local groups care enough to do the organizing." At the closing sessions, the walkers themselves overwhelmingly wished for another walk. Some even wanted two: a second around the lake and another elsewhere in Siam (tragically, there is plenty of ecological and cultural destruction going on in this "Tiger Cub" for a plentitude of walks). Some southern NGOs and local monks agreed to help organize it, so a second Dhammayatra took place mid-April through mid-May 1997.

This walk circumambulated the lake clockwise and passed through the major towns around it: Songkhla, Had Yai, and Phattalung. It was longer in both time (one month) and distance (450 kilometers). We chose to walk through the cities in an attempt to reach city folk, and had to face new challenges, such as more apathy than in the villages and not antagonizing city dwellers by obstructing traffic. The greater distance, as well as some logistical miscalculations, meant that on some days the walking was far more rigorous than before. Nonetheless, the character of the walk stayed much the same as the first year and further developed the Dhammayatra practice. We saw the same problems but tried to focus more attention on the solutions proffered by local people. The most significant developments were a more diverse group of organizers and more attention to group process.

A third walk took place in May 1998, lasted two weeks, and followed the Utapao River for about 140 kilometers. Rather than walk around the lake as in the past, we walked from the hills near the Malay border down to the southern end of the lake, following the major tributary of the lower lake. By doing so, we hoped to draw attention to the linkages between the no-longer-forested hills, the rubber plantations, the urban centers, and the lake. The shorter walk allowed more intensive preparation, which led to more activities with local communities, such as planting trees, debates with government officials, cleaning up temples, and rituals to symbolically extend the life of the river and lake. Another important change was to walk less each day and to provide more time for meditation, chanting, and group process. For example, skits were used throughout the walk to share observations and feelings, and base groups met daily to share responsibilities, fun, and needs. Further, there was greater local involvement in organization and decision making. These improvements helped to rejuvenate some local conservation groups that had been rather dormant.

The second Dhammayatra occurred just before the *baht* nose-dived in June 1997. Thus, the third Dhammayatra took place in the wake of Asia's so-called economic crisis. This encouraged us to keep expenses low and to deemphasize fund raising. Nonetheless, we again had a small budget surplus. We also found ourselves explaining the International Monetary Fund to each other and many of the communities we visited, then critiquing the impact of this powerful, faraway bureaucracy on our lives.

The Songkhla Lake Dhammayatra has even attracted its own chronicler. Ted Mayer, a Ph.D. candidate from Wisconsin, has been following us in more ways than one and helping to document the evolution of our thinking and responses. Mayer observes:

> I believe the lake walks have created a unique kind of public space in which a very broad range of issues can be explored by participants and observers. These issues include not only the current state of human relationships with nature at the local and global level, but also the meaning and significance of Buddhist practice, the possi-

bilities and problems of cultivating relations of trust between people of very diverse backgrounds, and the challenges of designing effective strategies for social change. The breadth and openness of this space makes it possible, I believe, for a unique kind of spiritual and social creativity to take place. That same breadth and openness, however, also increases the range of difficulties that may be encountered.*

Due to the slowly building successes of the walks held so far, and their imitation elsewhere in Siam, the informal group that has been organizing them has decided to develop a less ad hoc organizational form. At this writing, we are still working out the details; however, a few major tendencies can be shared here.

We intend to maintain the *ngan boon* (meritorious activity or volunteerism) that has characterized all of the walks. Previously, we had no paid or full-time staff, and no one organization in control. While we will have two full-time coordinators for the next year, they will not receive salaries. Rather, they will receive a living allowance that liberates them from remunerated jobs so that they, unlike the rest of us, can focus their time and energy on walk-related duties that require timely and consistent responses. Nonetheless, and this is crucial, the two coordinators will work as colleagues of the rest of us and have no more authority than anyone else in decision making. Anybody can have a say who adheres to the agreed-upon principles of the Dhammayatra and contributes goodwill, time, and energy.

Thus, we are exploring a new model of organization that consciously avoids the funding-driven structure of most NGOs. That it is religiously based and involves monks, while pursuing social aims, makes the new project unique in Siam.

Finally, the Dhammayatra will continue to be the main activity of the project. It will also try to follow up contacts built with local communities and generally support a greater role for religious principles, perspectives, and methods in solving the social problems of southern Thailand.

---

*From an unpublished version of an article that appeared in *Seeds of Peace*, vol. 14, no. 3 (Sept.–Dec. 1998). Some of Mayer's reports were used in preparing this essay.

BUDDHIST REVIVAL

At heart, Phra Sekhiyadhamma is working for a revival of Thai Buddhism. We fear that the current hierarchy, used by politicians and bedazzled by the wealthy, is leading Thai Buddhism astray. Along the walk, we saw pathetic signs of decay: *wat*s (temples) cluttered with garbage left over from festivals—the festivals put on by businessmen (not community members) who make big profits off the gambling and drinking (and give the *wat* a percentage); monks hanging out all day with cigarettes drooping from bored lips, eyes gazing blankly; the *wat*s' crockery tossed into back rooms with no respect for the donors; many *wat*s with just one octogenarian monk unable to look after the place or to communicate with people less than half his age.

Yet all was not hopeless. There were also many well-kept *wat*s and alert monks along the route. The people came out en masse at *wat* after *wat* to greet and feed us. Seeds of faith remain, but must be watered with Dhamma teachings and cultivated with community empowerment. Thus, we see grassroots engaged Buddhism as one way to salvage what is alive in the tradition and adjust to the future. It is a crucial element in any reversal of the cultural decay that is taking the Thainess out of Thailand. The basic responsibilities of study, meditation, and service must be rejuvenated and encouraged in all monks, especially the young, often aimless ones. Then they will be able to find their way in partnership with the people. Although we have not found many nuns, they too must be supported to grow into a meaningful role within the temples and communities.

Si Nuan died last year. She was older than we thought. After almost dying on the second walk, which was much tougher than the first, she didn't make it to the third. May she join future walks in spirit.

Resisting the Yadana Gas Pipeline

PARVEL GMUZDEK

EARLY IN THE MORNING ON JUNE 3, 1997, a group of about forty activists and media observers gathered in front of the National Museum in Bangkok and boarded a brightly colored '70s model Mercedes bus. The group was bound for the Thong Pha Phum region in the Kanchanaburi province, the site of a section of the Burmese-Thai Yadana pipeline now under construction. In broad terms, the purpose of the trip was to voice opposition to the project. The actual goals and hopes for specific outcomes of the protest varied, however, from person to person, according to the various affiliations of the participants. Some were concerned about the environmental impacts of the project and wanted to have a first-hand look at the construction site. Others had been involved in activities in support of human rights and democracy in Burma (officially called the Union of Myanmar). Their main interest was to postpone the construction until the political climate in that country changed. Others went along to document the event and in that way widen the forum for public discussion.

This protest was a brainchild of the Kalayanamitra Council, a group of Thai as well as North American and European activists, formed in 1996 under the guidance of Sulak Sivaraksa. Although the Council intends to be involved broadly in the area of human rights and environmental protection in Thai-Burmese development projects, its formation was prompted in particular by the controversy around the Yadana pipeline. Joining the Kalayanamitra Council were numerous other organizations, notably the Thai Action Committee for Democracy in Burma (TACDB), and the Kanchanaburi-based Thai branch of Earth-Rights International, and the All Burma Students' Democratic Front (ABSDF). Among the participants were a number of Thai Buddhist monks, a group of young people from Moo Ban Dek Children's Village School in Kanchanaburi, and a few Western observers.

While I was frantically jotting down these names and abbreviations on the way to the site, the bus suddenly came to the end of the paved surface and began to bump along a narrow dirt road. In a short while we stopped in front of a small forest monastery. After transferring our modest luggage onto four-wheel-drive trucks, we gathered inside the main building. From here on we were to continue on foot. One of the monks briefly spoke about contemplative walking in nature, emphasizing awareness of our immediate surroundings. Up to this point I had not been deeply involved in the pipeline issue. So I came wanting to bear witness before making any judgments. Being wholly present and aware of where I was and how I was feeling was exactly what I needed to do.

Although I had experienced the Thai rainforest before, I soon began to realize how much I had forgotten. Tall trees and oppressive humidity, refreshingly cool rivers, respectably large red ants, steep cliffs with black dots marking the bat caves, spiders the size of a child's fist, and, of course, the bloodthirsty mosquitoes—in this region a particularly risky factor due to the heavy presence of malaria. The jungle is not the most comfortable place for the average urban dweller—nor should it be or need be. The longer we walked and the deeper I immersed myself in the forest, the more I saw how remarkable the place was. The plants and the animals have adjusted to the difficult conditions and managed to strike an admirable degree of balance in the environment—so admirable, and yet so sensitive to disturbances of the kind humans are capable of!

Just as I was playing with this idea, we stopped at a small clearing which turned out to be a favorite spot of wild elephants. We learned that a herd of as many as twenty elephants likes to come here from Burma to take advantage of the hot springs and the adjacent wetland. In other words, this was an elephant bath. Apparently, city humans are not the only ones in the market for hot water! Hot springs, incidentally, signal an area of seismic activity. Indeed, almost the entire length of the Thai section of the pipeline runs parallel to the Three Pagodas Fault, where six earthquakes of magnitudes between 4.1 and 4.5 on the Richter scale were recorded between 1983 and 1988.

There is also the problematic issue of animal migration. The corridor proposed for the service road and the pipeline itself will effectively slice the forest in half, thereby cutting off the elephants' migration route. So the outlook for the elephants' moonlight bathing parties is bleak. I scooped up a handful of warm water and smelled it. Sulfur. Maybe it helps them control parasites? Maybe they've been coming here for centuries.

We reached the campsite just before dusk. Most of us elected to jump immediately into the nearby river to cool off and soak away our travelers' pains. I walked upstream a bit and found a small pool just big enough for me to lie down in it. I watched a spider make an intricate web stretching from one bank to the other, and I listened to the unfamiliar voices of the forest. The feeling was that of peace. Then I made my way back to the camp, carefully avoiding the newly built spider webs. I was just in time for a delicious vegetarian meal, followed by evening prayer and meditation. The monks told us that because we were of several differ-ent faiths, we should pray to nature as that is what connects all of us regardless of our beliefs. There could hardly be a more appropriate place to say this. The speaker of the evening, Phra Kosin, went on to talk about death and fear. We all are afraid to die, and this includes the animals and the trees. Many trees will die here so that people can have natural gas. Had we thought about this? he asked.

The next morning we joined the monks in meditation at 4 A.M. At the crack of dawn we packed up and began to walk to the actual site of the pipeline. It was a long hike up the hill, and the path was narrow and winding. I tried to imagine bulldozers and other heavy machinery coming through here on their way to the construction site, and it all seemed ridiculous. I thought of a Karen farmer who lived in this area all his life growing rice and corn, on his way to visit relatives in the neighboring village, suddenly coming to a huge hole in the ground with a pipe in it and shaking his head. From what I read and was told, the public discus-sion among the local people concerning the pipeline is minimal. Many in this remote area cannot read and are not thoroughly informed about the implications of a project such as this. Although there are a number of local organizations engaged in the public discussion, even they admit it is not enough. They say if nothing else comes out of this protest besides greater awareness of the need for public discussion of big projects, they will have accomplished something.

Finally, we reached our destination on the top of a hill. The con-struction had not started here yet, so this was an opportunity to see the site in its original state. Nothing suggested that this was the place, except for stakes in the ground and bright red markings on the trees that were to come down for the pipeline. One of the Burmese friends looked over toward the next ridge and pointed out that we were looking at Burma. In Burma the construction of the pipeline has other implications, as important as the ecological ones but certainly more pressing. The Tennasserim region (on the Burmese side) is a home for ethnic minorities, notably the Mon and Karen. In order to build the pipeline, the ruling Burmese government, known as SLORC (State Law and Order Restoration Council), has stationed more troops in the region to provide security and to control the local movements opposed to the project and to SLORC itself. Associated with these actions are numerous human rights abuses such as relocation of villages, forced labor, rape, and even killings of those suspected of being associated with the opposition Karen National Union or the Mon National Liberation Army. All of these facts have been systematically documented in a book called *Total Denial*, published in 1996.

What causes so much suffering? The people in Burma suffer, nature suffers, and what for? To answer this question we have to come back to ourselves. I recalled how on the way to the site the bus stopped briefly to refuel at a PTT gas station. PTT stands for the Petroleum Authority of Thailand, one of the four main shareholders in the Yadana project. How interesting, I thought. We so strongly oppose some of the activities of this company, yet we are dependent on that very company for many of our privileges. Something here does not make sense. We take for granted the services that we receive as a result of using fossil fuels. We are happy to use fossil fuels, but not nearly as willing to take responsibility for the consequences. If we truly want to preserve the forest in Kanchanaburi and protect Burma's minorities, what choices are we going to have to make in our personal lives? This is a question worth considering while sitting in the shade of a two-hundred-year-old tree soon to be dead in the name of supplying power for our computers and stereos. I find the Buddhist philosophy of attaining awakening through awareness pointing those who are interested in the same direction. What are the implications of our daily actions? Of course, the other part of the equation is the possibility of generating electricity from renewable resources, such as solar (a plentiful resource base in Thailand). Undoubtedly there are ways to have a good degree of comfort without destroying the Thong Pha Phum forest and other people's livelihoods.

On the way back down to the valley, some of the monks and the local guides kept finding different edible plants in the forest—nuts in the ground, roots, fruits on the trees. I realized that they could survive here quite easily, that this was indeed their home. A friend of mine in the United States recently suggested that if a company wants to build a large retail shopping mall or a factory in a previously undeveloped area, the corporate executives should first go and live on that land for several weeks. This would accomplish many things, but mainly it would enable them to gain some understanding of not only the economic implications of their decisions (i.e., the profit that can be made) but also the implications for the environment and people immediately affected by those decisions. The advantage of the locals is that they already understand this. They live here, know what they need to survive and how to obtain it. For that reason, it is essential that they be deeply involved in a discussion of any major project in their area.

Later in the afternoon we left the Thing Pha Phum forest and moved further south to a different part of the pipeline route. In this section the construction is already well under way. Here the number of people tripled as the participants in this year's International Network of Engaged Buddhists conference joined the protest. With them were a number of media reporters, including several from such unlikely countries as the Netherlands and the Czech Republic. The Venerable Maha Ghosananda, a charismatic Buddhist spiritual leader from Cambodia, described the Buddhist teaching that happiness comes from charity rather than greed. In this context he addressed the Right Livelihood aspect of the Eightfold Path to the Cessation of Craving. Following his speech, we stood for five minutes in silence in front of the half-finished pipeline. It was very quiet during that time. The presence of the monks suggested a peaceful, loving atmosphere, even in the face of the violence and destruction inherent in the scene. The monks then led both groups on a contemplative walk along the construction area. At one point a few of us stopped to talk with two workers subcontracted by Mannesmann from the United States to lay the pipeline (Mannesmann is a German company in charge of completing the Thai side of the project). They said they had not heard about any controversy surrounding the project but were quite willing to listen and share their professional opinions about the construction. They pointed out that the pipe used is a much heavier gauge than needed for a purpose such as this. It is relatively very flexible, so in case of an earthquake the chances are that the pipe will withstand it without problems. With a bit of optimism one could call this a bright spot of the day.

It was getting late, and many of us were beginning to feel in our joints the kilometers walked, but there was one final event to go. This was in the Kanchanaburi township, where the local leaders and activists had organized a march and a public demonstration in support of the cause. Many local people stopped and listened to the speeches of human rights activists and environmentalists. This is encouraging, because whether people support the issue or not, they should have access to all the available information, as well as the opportunity to engage in the discussion. It is my sincere belief that the Yadana pipeline protest will be remembered as an important call not only to prevent this project from being completed in the form presently planned, but also as a wider challenge to the governments and public officials of all countries. This is the challenge to employ ethical and ecological investment strategies, and to invite broad and thorough public discussion of those strategies. It is a challenge for all of us to critically examine our consumer habits and how they impact the natural world.

The Agony of Tibet

GALEN ROWELL

IN 1981, I SET OFF to lead the first two American expeditions allowed into the back country of Tibet since the Chinese invasion three decades earlier. For a photographer, it was the chance of a lifetime. I thought little of politics or human rights. I simply wanted to climb mountains and take photographs of the mysterious land I had read so much about.

I never dreamed that I would make five visits to Tibet over the next eight years, become the subject of diplomatic complaints, be held by soldiers overnight against my will, and see many of my articles go unpublished in the United States out of fear of Chinese retribution. If I had it to do all over again, there is only one thing I would have done differently. I would not have compromised the story of Tibet's environmental destruction as much as I did. Then, I was worried about going back. Now I simply want to tell the story.

Before 1981, the remote parts of Tibet were shrouded in mystery. All the modern naturalists knew about the region came from reports at least three decades old. "I have never seen so many varieties of birds in one place," wrote British explorer Kingdon Ward in 1920. "One great zoological garden," Joseph Rock wrote in a 1930 *National Geographic*. "Wherever I looked I saw wild animals grazing contentedly." In the thirties, a German traveler named Dalgleish reported sighting a herd of 10,000 *chiru*, a Tibetan antelope now rarely seen. In the forties, Leonard Clark reported, "Every few minutes, we would spot a bear or a hunting wolf, herds of musk deer, *kyang*s, gazelles, bighorn sheep, or foxes. This must be one of the last unspoiled big-game paradises."

This glory was what I had come to see. For an exorbitant fee— $50,000 to guide several naturalists for three weeks in the Anye Machin mountains of northeast Tibet—our Chinese hosts promised "a wealth of rare birds and animals . . . thick virgin forests where deer, leopards, and bear thrive, while the grasslands and gravel slopes near the snow line are alive with hordes of gazelles, wild asses, and rare musk deer."

For three weeks, we walked—over a hundred miles in all. We saw virtually nothing. The wildlife had disappeared.

My other trek that year was to the Tibetan side of Mount Everest. I drove through over 1,000 miles of back roads without seeing a single wild large mammal. My negative results confirmed those of Pema Gyalpo, who had led a delegation the previous year that traveled 8,000 miles overland. She made the trip for the Tibetan government-in-exile in Dharamsala, India, whose head of state is her brother, the Dalai Lama. "On long journeys," she wrote, "you used to see more gazelles, deer, and antelope than people. Now, in three months of extensive traveling in Tibet, I did not see any of these creatures."

In 1950, Mao's People's Liberation Army invaded Tibet. Nine years later, the Tibetan people rebelled after China's promises of religious and personal freedom proved false. The revolt was brutally crushed, and the Dalai Lama fled into exile in India. More than 80,000 Tibetans were killed in the immediate aftermath, and observers estimate 1.2 million Tibetans have died at the hands of Chinese soldiers or as a result of imprisonment or starvation in the last thirty years. This carnage is just a fraction of the roughly 35,000,000 victims of China's four decades of Maoist rule, but it represents a fifth of the Tibetan population. During the subsequent decade, more than 6,000 monasteries, temples, and historic structures were razed. Alexander Solzhenitsyn calls China's administration of Tibet "more brutal and inhumane than any other communist regime in the world."

Before the arrival of the Chinese, Tibet had its own separate language, religion, currency, government, and postal system. It also had the most successful system of environmental protection of any inhabited region in the modern world. There were no parks or wildlife preserves in the Western sense. Formal protection of wildlife and wildlands was unnecessary in a land where devout Buddhist compassion for all living beings reigned supreme.

Tibetan Buddhism essentially prohibits the killing of animals. Children are taught from birth that all life is sacred. In his classic work, *Seven Years in Tibet*, Heinrich Harrer wrote of the frustration of working with Tibetans on the dike that to this day protects the capital city of Lhasa from flooding. "There were many interruptions and pauses. There was an outcry if anyone discovered a worm on a spade. The earth was thrown aside and the creature put in a safe place."

The Buddhist ethic pervades all aspects of Tibetan culture. "I have never seen less evidence of hatred, envy, malice and uncharitableness," wrote British India's trade consul in Tibet, Hugh Richardson, after living in Lhasa in the 1940s. "The Tibetan system produced a people who in the upper levels were self-controlled, intelligent, often deeply learned, capable, unpretentious, dignified, humane and friendly. The majority of people made efforts to live as much as possible with nature, not against it."

The 1950 invasion of Tibet, justified on the false grounds that Mao's China was simply restoring historical borders, was in many ways the consummation of China's long-standing desire to gain control of Tibet's natural resources. The Chinese know Tibet as Xizang, which translates as "western treasure house," a name that was born in the ancient myth that Tibet contained gold and other riches. Chinese infiltration into the country had already begun at the turn of the century, when settlers began to deforest the border regions. By 1910, the Chinese had established schools along the border that outlawed the Tibetan language and customs. In 1911, Tibet expelled all Chinese from its borders and was free of foreign control for nearly four decades.

After the invasion, China set out to "liberate" Tibet by systematically destroying its culture. Farmers were forced into collectives and required to grow winter wheat instead of the traditional barley. The policy produced bumper crops for a few years before depleting the soil and ruining the harvest. To make matters worse, China brought much of the wheat home to feed a population cut off from other sources of grains as a result of the 1959 break with the Soviet Union. Tibet was plunged into a famine, the first in recorded history, which lasted through 1963. Another period of famine followed from 1968 to 1973.

The invaders made a sport of shooting indiscriminately at wildlife. In 1973, Dhondub Choedon, a Tibetan now in exile in India, reported that "Chinese soldiers go on organized hunts using machine guns. They carry away the meat in lorries and export the musk and furs to China." Important habitat for vast herds of animals was soon overgrazed as the Chinese forced nomadic families into communes to raise livestock for export instead of their own subsistence. Tibetans, including the children, were forced to kill "unnecessary animals" such as moles and marmots that vied with humans for grain and dug up valuable grazing land. Children were given a quota for small animals to kill that, if not met, resulted in beatings and other forms of punishment.

My first attempts to quantify environmental conditions in Tibet failed. Chinese officials either refused to give me statistics, or interpreters sensed what I was up to and stopped translating. I soon discovered, however, that if I feigned interest in increased productivity under the communist regime, I could glean some alarming statistics. The general secretary of a poor county in the mountains of Amdo province dug out papers and proudly rattled off figures that confirmed my worst suspicions about habitat destruction.

"Before we had communes we had just 7,000 animals. Now the same 700 square kilometers has 70,000 yaks and sheep. Since 1979, many people own their own animals as well. Our comrades are doing very well now. Each makes thirty to forty yuan ($18–$24 at the time) a month, but through personal sales many make 100 yuan a month."

The general secretary admitted that much of the extra income came from the slaughter of wild musk deer. When queried about this apparent violation of Chinese law, he said that special dispensations were granted by the commune leader.

"What happens if a musk deer is killed illegally?" I asked. Such crimes meant a big fine, he responded, although he admitted he could not remember the last time a person had been fined. As it turned out, not one person in recent years had been fined for the poaching, but several bounties of fifteen yuan had been paid for the pelts of snow leopards, which are officially protected as an endangered species in China by international agreement. Many ten-yuan bounties had been paid on wolves as well.

At the end of the first two trips in 1981, I joined several of the scientists who had traveled with me at a press conference in Beijing. We laid out the facts for the reporters. "The wildlife of this region has been decimated," said Rodney Jackson, whose snow leopard studies formed the basis of a *National Geographic* cover story in June 1986. "We come to Tibet because of inaccurate information given us by the Chinese about the presence of wildlife in an area they charged us dearly to visit. This, plus attitudes that endorse irresponsible wildlife depletion, can adversely affect China's friendship with other nations if they are allowed to continue."

The Associated Press (AP) bureau chief demanded exclusivity and promised to send me copies of the story. It was never published. An AP correspondent in the United States later told me that they couldn't afford to run "unnecessarily negative China material" that might put their Beijing bureau in jeopardy. When Jackson took his story to several U.S. wildlife organizations that fund research in China, he was again rebuffed. Criticism of China was not allowed in this close-knit scientific community, Jackson discovered. If he continued to threaten the relationship these organizations had cultivated with Beijing, he could not expect to get money for his research.

After I returned home that year, my proposals for articles about the difficulties facing researchers and the environmental holocaust in Tibet were turned down. I was well connected with many national magazines, and I asked the editors why. "Our readers want upbeat stories," came the chorus. "And besides, China is our friend." The strongest motive, future press access, went unspoken. I began to see how the Chinese could censor the American press almost as successfully as their own.

My first major article appeared in the February 1982 *National Geographic*. I wanted to focus on the false promise of Tibet's "wildlife," but I didn't have the photographs to support such a story. I had no direct documentation of the killing, except for a picture of Rodney Jackson examining a fresh snow leopard pelt hanging on a commune wall. The editors and I agreed that shots of empty plains are not only inconclusive, but rather boring. The focus of the article was thus tightened into "Nomads of China's Wild West," a cultural profile of an armed and surprisingly independent Tibetan tribe called the Goloks. But I held out, bravely I thought, for at least one photo caption that mentioned the environment.

Beneath my photo of an overgrazed landscape ran a quote from me about the promise of "blue sheep, gazelles, bears, wolves, and deer—a richness of animal life touted to me by the Chinese authorities in Beijing. The Chinese also spoke of dense virgin forests. In fact, we saw almost no wildlife and . . . no forests at all."

Upon publication, the Chinese embassy lodged a formal complaint: I was guilty of an intentional political act that jeopardized Sino-American friendship. As I was planning to return to Tibet the following year as climbing leader of the first American expedition permitted to attempt Mount Everest's West Ridge, I heeded the Chinese authorities' demand that I write a letter of self-criticism. Beneath a haze of murky Latin-based words, I confessed how unwise I had been to say what I did if I ever planned to return to Tibet again.

For the next six years, I wrote with a split personality. For my own book, *Mountains of the Middle Kingdom,* published by the Sierra Club in 1983, I wrote a tell-all account, but for periodicals that might reach Beijing, I omitted all strong personal observations and opinions.

Despite this self-censorship, I again incurred the wrath of the Chinese authorities. My *National Geographic* assignment in 1988 was to document the Tibetan side of a proposed joint Chinese-Nepalese national park surrounding Mount Everest. My wife, Barbara, and I traveled with representatives of the Woodlands Mountain Institute of West Virginia, which had been working with both governments to create the park. As we left the United States in May 1988, we were told that China would announce the establishment of the park within days.

We were accompanied during our three weeks in the field by Yin Binggao, director of forests for Tibet, along with several of his employees. Despite Tibet's high altitude, large forests are nurtured by monsoon rains in parts of southeastern Tibet and also along the Nepalese border, where river valleys cut through the rain shadow of the Himalayas.

One of these valleys is on the east side of Mount Everest. While the rest of my group stayed in a 14,000-foot camp, I crossed a high pass and hiked into the fabled Valley of Flowers, discovered by the first British Everest expedition in 1921. Here, amid twenty colors of native rhododendron blossoms, I was shocked to see trees being felled by the thousands. I photographed a convoy of Tibetan women carrying fresh hundred-pound beams over the pass directly through our camp. The operation appeared to be centrally organized. Lumber was cut on the spot and piled into four-cornered stacks that formed orderly rows across the valley.

Yin Binggao said he knew nothing about the timber operation. He suggested it must be Tibetans cutting wood on their own. A day later, we saw Chinese trucks in the village of Kharta loaded with the same wood bound for towns on the treeless plains to the North. There, virtually all new construction is undertaken by Chinese residents or officials. Embarrassed now, Yin Binggao promised to report the situation immediately to the closest forest official. I later found out the nearest office was in Shigatse, hundreds of miles from any forest.

The entire forestry department of Tibet employs just thirteen people. According to official documents, $54 billion of timber has been cut within the borders of old Tibet since 1959. As Tibetans do not use much wood for fuel or to frame ordinary houses, the majority of this timber is destined for China. The deforestation is aided by the forced labor of thousands of Tibetan prisoners in the southeastern part of the country. In Amdo, nearly 50 million trees have been felled since 1955, and millions of acres at least 70 percent cleared, according to the Dalai Lama's exiled government in India. Roughly 70,000 Chinese workers have been brought to the region or have traveled there voluntarily, in large part to cut down the rich stands of trees.

My colleague assigned to cover the Nepalese side of Everest and I reached the same conclusion: the environment on both sides of the mountain was being destroyed. Neither government indicated it was planning to declare a joint park, although the Nepalese had long maintained the rather ineffectual Sagarmatha National Park at the core of the proposed area.

National Geographic had hoped for an upbeat story, but instead of killing it entirely, they ran it as "Heavy Hands on the Land," a litany of wildlife and land-use problems surrounding a seemingly immutable mountain. Soon after publication, the Woodlands Institute informed me that, according to the Chinese government, my article was in error. I had stated that the park would not be created in the near future, but a document contradicting my claim had been forwarded to *National Geographic* by the institute.

In typically vague phrases, a Chinese official stated it was indeed the government's intention to proceed toward the goal of creating a natural preserve near Mount Everest, someday. I was surprised, since I had been present at meetings with the top two officials in the Tibetan government, both of whom refused to sign any letter of intent. Scanning the letter, I noticed that their names were indeed absent. It was signed by Yin Bing-gao. As of this writing, the intent to create the park remains on paper only.

But that was not the end. Upon my return to the United States, I was notified that I had been tried and convicted in absentia for "sedition." During my trip I had given a picture of the Dalai Lama to the patriarch of a nomad family that gave us splendid hospitality for three days and opened up his family's lives for us to photograph. This was, using phrases that commonly issue from Beijing, "wanton intrusion in China's internal affairs and overt support for the separatist Dalai-clique."

As I had become accustomed to doing, I sat down and wrote the obligatory letter to the Chinese Embassy, explaining that I had no political motivation in giving the photo and apologizing for any trouble I might have caused. It was simply a gift, I explained, to a man who invited me into his home and allowed me to photograph his family. But as I did this, I felt humiliated and compromised in a way I never had before. Something inside of me finally snapped. Whatever the consequences, I vowed then that I would no longer just stand by and watch the power of my work be diluted.

Since my last journey to Tibet in 1988, much has happened. There are fewer wild animals and trees, more prisoners and paper promises, but still no parks or real progress toward environmental protection. Peaceful demonstrations for Tibetan independence in Lhasa in 1987 became riots after Chinese soldiers fired into unarmed crowds, killing Buddhist monks and nuns. Observers estimate that at least 600 Tibetans have been killed and thousands of Tibetans imprisoned and tortured in the subsequent crackdown. The Chinese government instituted a year of martial law in Tibet in March 1989. Three months later, the government in Beijing unleased its tanks on the students occupying Tiananmen Square. And in December 1989, the Dalai Lama was awarded the Nobel Peace Prize.

The most bizarre manifestations of China's ideological rule, such as the killing of all "unnecessary" animals, have disappeared. What remains is a steady consolidation of China's domination of the country, aided by naked political oppression. As Tibet's animal and plant resources are destroyed, Beijing is now gearing up to extract gold and minerals, including uranium. China's armed forces have established nuclear missile bases on

Tibet's high plateau and are now rumored to be preparing a high-level nuclear-waste dump that would accept nuclear reactor fuel from China as well as Western Europe.

Despite the attention focused on the plight of Tibet in the last year, no country has gone on record as supporting Tibet's right to independence, for fear of angering Beijing. In the wake of the Nobel committee's decision to award its peace prize to the Dalai Lama, China has made it as difficult as possible for any nation extending support to the exiled leader. The government in Beijing even threatened to cut all economic ties to Norway if its king attended the prize ceremony. Although the United States Congress passed a resolution condemning China's treatment of Tibet, President Bush refused to meet with the Dalai Lama, preferring instead to send emissaries on a secret mission to China. To this date, no U.S. president has ever shaken hands with the exiled head of state.

In May 1989, I traveled to Dharamsala with my wife to meet the Dalai Lama and discuss a book we were preparing together called *My Tibet*, published by the University of California Press. After several hours of interviews about the past, present, and future of Tibet's environment, we found him to be deeply concerned, well versed in the natural history of his country, and surprisingly hopeful and compassionate in his outlook. The Dalai Lama believes that behind every apparently bad event lurks some hidden goodness. With the right attitude, he avows, our worst enemies aid us in becoming clear and strong. Despite the desperate situation in his country, the Dalai Lama consistently argues against taking up arms against the Chinese. He remains confident that Tibet will emerge from Chinese oppression with greater compassion and unity than ever before.

It came as no surprise to us that a few months later, the Nobel committee made special mention of the Dalai Lama's commitment to the environment, the first time a Nobel citation has made specific reference to the ecological crisis. As he looked at some of my pictures of Tibet's last remaining wildlife that I planned to include in the book, he commented on the way his people used to coexist with humans and animals before the invasion. "Some of that harmony remains in Tibet today," he told me, "and because it happened in the past, we have some genuine hope for the future."

Make Tibet a Zone of Peace

THE DALAI LAMA

A S YOU KNOW, TIBET HAS, for forty years, been under foreign occupation. Today, more than a quarter of a million Chinese troops are stationed in Tibet. Some sources estimate the occupation army to be twice this strength. During this time, Tibetans have been deprived of their most basic human rights, including the right to life, movement, speech, worship, only to mention a few. More than one sixth of Tibet's population of 6 million died as a direct result of the Chinese invasion and occupation. Even before the Cultural Revolution started, many of Tibet's monasteries, temples, and historical buildings were destroyed. Almost everything that remained was destroyed during the Cultural Revolution. I do not wish to dwell on this point, which is well documented. What is important to realize, however, is that despite the limited freedom granted after 1979 to rebuild parts of some monasteries, and other such tokens of liberalization, the fundamental human rights of the Tibetan people are still today being systematically violated. In recent months this bad situation has become even worse.

If it were not for our community in exile, so generously sheltered and supported by the government and people of India and helped by organizations and individuals from many parts of the world, our nation would today be little more than a shattered remnant of a people. Our culture, religion, and national identity would have been effectively eliminated. As it is, we have built schools and monasteries in exile and have created democratic institutions to serve our people and preserve the seeds of our civilization. With this experience, we intend to implement full democracy in a future free Tibet. Thus, as we develop our community in exile on modern lines, we also cherish and preserve our own identity and culture and bring hope to millions of our countrymen and women in Tibet.

The issue of most urgent concern at this time is the massive influx of Chinese settlers into Tibet. Although in the first decades of occupation a considerable number of Chinese were transferred into the eastern parts of Tibet—in the Tibetan provinces of Amdo (Chinghai) and Kham (most of which has been annexed by the neighboring Chinese province)—since 1983, an unprecedented number of Chinese have been encouraged by their government to migrate to all parts of Tibet, including central and western Tibet (which the PRC refers to as the so-called Tibet Autonomous Region). Tibetans are rapidly being reduced to an insignificant minority in their own country. This development, which threatens the very survival of the Tibetan nation, its culture and spiritual heritage, can still be stopped and reversed. But this must be done now, before it is too late.

The new cycle of protest and violent repression, which started in Tibet in September of 1987 and culminated in the imposition of martial law in the capital, Lhasa, in March of this year [1989], was in large part a reaction to this tremendous Chinese influx. Information reaching us in exile indicates that the protest marches and other peaceful forms of protest are continuing in Lhasa and a number of other places in Tibet despite the severe punishment and inhumane treatment given to Tibetans detained for expressing their grievances. The number of Tibetans killed by security forces during the protest in March and of those who died in detention afterwards is not known but is believed to be more than 200. Thousands have been detained or arrested and imprisoned, and torture is commonplace.

It was against the background of this worsening situation and in order to prevent further bloodshed that I proposed what is generally referred to as the Five Point Peace Plan for the restoration of peace and human rights in Tibet. I elaborated on the plan in a speech in Strasbourg last year. I believe the plan provides a reasonable and realistic framework for negotiations with the People's Republic of China. So far, however, China's leaders have been unwilling to respond constructively. The brutal suppression of the Chinese democracy movement in June of this year, however, reinforced my view that any settlement of the Tibetan question will only be meaningful if it is supported by adequate international guarantees.

The Five Point Peace Plan addresses the following principal and interrelated issues. It calls for (1) transformation of the whole of Tibet, including the eastern provinces of Kham and Amdo, into a Zone of *Ahimsa* (nonviolence); (2) abandonment of China's population-transfer policy; (3) respect for the Tibetan people's fundamental human rights and democratic freedoms; (4) restoration and protection of Tibet's natural environment; and (5) commencement of earnest negotiations on the future status of Tibet and of relations between the Tibetan and Chinese peoples. In the Strasbourg address, I proposed that Tibet become a fully self-governing democratic political entity.

I would like to take this opportunity to explain the Zone of Ahimsa or peace sanctuary concept, which is the central element of the Five Point Peace Plan. I am convinced that it is of great importance not only for Tibet, but for peace and stability in Asia.

It is my dream that the entire Tibetan plateau should become a free refuge where humanity and nature can live in peace and in harmonious balance. It would be a place where people from all over the world could come to seek the true meaning of peace within themselves, away from the tensions and pressures of much of the rest of the world. Tibet could indeed become a creative center for the promotion and development of peace.

The following are key elements of the proposed Zone of Ahimsa:

- The entire Tibetan plateau would be demilitarized.
- The manufacture, testing, and stockpiling of nuclear weapons and other armaments on the Tibetan plateau would be prohibited.
- The Tibetan plateau would be transformed into the world's largest natural park or biosphere. Strict laws would be enforced to protect wildlife and plant life; the exploitation of natural resources would be carefully regulated so as not to damage relevant ecosystems; and a policy of sustainable development would be adopted in populated areas.
- The manufacture and use of nuclear power and other technologies which produce hazardous waste would be prohibited.
- National resources and policy would be directed toward the active promotion of peace and environmental protection. Organizations dedicated to the furtherance of peace and to the protection of all forms of life would find a hospitable home in Tibet.

- The establishment of international and regional organizations for the promotion and protection of human rights would be encouraged in Tibet.

Tibet's height and size (the size of the European Community), as well as its unique history and profound spiritual heritage, make it ideally suited to fulfill the role of a sanctuary of peace in the strategic heart of Asia. It would also be in keeping with Tibet's historical role as a peaceful Buddhist nation and buffer region separating the Asian continent's great and often rival powers.

In order to reduce existing tensions in Asia, the president of the Soviet Union, Mr. Gorbachev, proposed the demilitarization of Soviet-Chinese borders and their transformation into a "frontier of peace and good-neighborliness." The Nepal government had earlier proposed that the Himalayan country of Nepal, bordering on Tibet, should become a zone of peace, although that proposal did not include demilitarization of the country.

For the stability and peace of Asia, it is essential to create peace zones to separate the continent's biggest powers and potential adversaries. President Gorbachev's proposal, which also included a complete Soviet troop withdrawal from Mongolia, would help to reduce tension and the potential for confrontation between the Soviet Union and China. A true peace zone must, clearly, also be created to separate the world's two most populous states, China and India.

The establishment of the Zone of Ahimsa would require the withdrawal of troops and military installations from Tibet, which would enable India and Nepal also to withdraw troops and military installations from the Himalayan regions bordering Tibet. This would have to be achieved by international agreements. It would be the best interest of all states in Asia, particularly China and India, as it would enhance their security, while reducing the economic burden of maintaining high troop concentrations in remote areas.

Tibet would not be the first strategic area to be demilitarized. Parts of the Sinai peninsula, the Egyptian territory separating Israel and Egypt, have been demilitarized for some time. Of course, Costa Rica is the best example of an entirely demilitarized country.

Tibet would also not be the first area to be turned into a natural preserve or biosphere. Many parks have been created throughout the world. Some very strategic areas have been turned into natural "peace parks." Two examples are the La Amistad park, on the Costa Rica–Panama border, and the Si A Paz project on the Costa Rica–Nicaragua border.

When I visited Costa Rica earlier this year, I saw how a country can develop successfully without an army to become a stable democracy committed to peace and the protection of the natural environment. This confirmed my belief that my vision of Tibet in the future is a realistic plan, not merely a dream.

Let me end with a personal note of thanks to all of you and our friends who are not here today. The concern and support which you have expressed for the plight of the Tibetans has touched us all greatly and continues to give us courage to struggle for freedom and justice; not through the use of arms, but with the powerful weapons of truth and determination. I know that I speak on behalf of all the people of Tibet when I thank you and ask you not to forget Tibet at this critical time in our country's history. We too hope to contribute to the development of a more peaceful, more humane, and more beautiful world. A future free Tibet will seek to help those in need throughout the world, to protect nature, and to promote peace. I believe that our Tibetan ability to combine spiritual qualities with a realistic and practical attitude enables us to make a special contribution in however modest a way. This is my hope and prayer.

In conclusion, let me share with you a short prayer which gives me great inspiration and determination:

> For as long as space endures,
> And for as long as living beings remain,
> Until then may I, too, abide
> To dispel the misery of the world.

Thank you.

PART FOUR

*

ENVIRONMENTAL ACTIVISM

as

BUDDHIST PRACTICE

If the world is to be healed through human efforts, I am convinced it will be by ordinary people, people whose love for this life is even greater than their fear, people who can open to the web of life that called us into being, and who can rest in the vitality of that larger body.

—*Joanna Macy*

INTRODUCTION

❁

Tree-sitters, vegetarians, environmental lawyers, and re-cyclers are spurred to engage in environmental activism for many different reasons. They may have been inspired by Thoreau's philosophy of simplicity, by John Muir's celebration of the divine universe, or by Rachel Carson's scientific rigor in exposing pollution. Activists who base their environmental work in *Buddhist* thought and practice have appeared more recently, but their numbers are growing. Some persevere on their own. Some find colleagues and support among Buddhists engaged in other arenas—hospice care, prison projects, refugee relief. And some work collaboratively with environmentalists motivated by Christianity, Hinduism, or other religions/spiritual traditions. As new links are forged between traditional contemplative disciplines and modern forms of en-gagement, the practice of Buddhist environmental activism takes shape.

How is Buddhist practice relevant to the task of caring for the earth? The Buddhist vision of dependent origination, in which everything de-pends on everything else, can function both as an insight into the nature of reality and as a basis for analysis of environmental problems. Under-standing the self from an interdependent ecological perspective radically recasts the task of protecting the planet. What does it mean to feel the pain of a blue whale or rainforest as one's own? John Seed declares, "I visualize myself as being one leaf on the tree of life . . . and I realize that the sap of that tree runs through every leaf, including me."

In the first set of readings, Buddhist teachers elucidate some of the principles that sustain Buddhist environmental practice. Zen teacher Philip Kapleau shows how social action, undertaken in the proper spirit, can be a form of meditation; at the same time, he encourages Buddhists to critique the social conditions that increase suffering. Zen priest Norman Fischer reiterates the value of wholehearted engagement in the work that needs to be done. Drawing on Tibetan practices, Chögyam Trungpa and Jeremy Hayward recommend the cultivation of fearlessness. In this tradition, a person who has grasped the *vajra* sword of insight is able to cut through delusion and release the brilliant energy of the universe.

But everyday ecological-Buddhist practice is demanding. Christopher Titmuss asks, "When governments and business are actively destroying the earth, how can one give loving-kindness to that?" He and Joanna Macy emphasize the importance of intention in counteracting the anger and despair that can overwhelm activists. They believe that trying to be heroic does not help, because self-aggrandizement strengthens the isolated ego. Casting blame on a supposed enemy likewise misfires, for it reinforces dualistic thinking. The great challenge is to negotiate the dynamic interplay of action and nonaction, engaging completely while avoiding attachment to visible results.

In the second set of readings, Buddhist activists on the front lines share the fruits of their experience defending sentient beings and reducing suffering. Vanya Palmers takes on the cruel factory farming of pigs; Erin Volheim protests the logging of old-growth redwoods. Following a strong call from the rainforest, John Seed leads ritual gatherings that help people overcome their separation from the earth. For the sake of future beings, Joanna Macy proposes a Nuclear Guardianship Project to contain the poison fire of nuclear waste.

Awakening to the pain of the world can become a powerful crucible for motivated action. The discipline of mindfulness can help to illumine difficult questions about what to eat and how to live. These writers model the way of environmental activism as practice path—one life, serving all beings.

FOUNDATIONS OF
ACTIVISM

❉

Responsibility and Social Action
PHILIP KAPLEAU

I N ZEN BUDDHISM, RESPONSIBILITY MEANS responsiveness. Responsiveness is responsibility. To respond fully to every situation that comes your way, from a call for help of one kind or another to just talking with someone, and to give all of yourself to it—this is responsibility.

A developed, compassionate, loving person influences people unself-consciously, motivates them, and inspires them to act in similar ways. The whole community benefits. Even just doing zazen in the zendo has a powerful, invisible effect. People find it hard to believe that there can be social usefulness in just sitting and meditating. And yet the truth is that if you purify your mind, even to a small degree, and transcend ego-attachment, you are at the same time purifying other minds. The effect on other people—on your family, on your circle of acquaintances—grows and grows.

Everything depends on your mind-state, and on what your conscience dictates. In Buddhism, compassion and wisdom are the qualities that develop out of your practice. Gradually you can act without being attached to the result and simply do what you feel needs to be done. Some people feel called upon to deal with social injustice and other inequities of life in an active way. The important thing is how you do that. If you're striving for particular results, then you're attached. If you're striving to be unattached, then you're committing another kind of subtle fault.

When we get deeper in our practice, we give our all and at the same time simply spontaneously respond to the needs of the situation. Then we do what our karma, which means our whole pattern of life, dictates. And that's always changing. We must remember that karma is not a fixed thing. The relation between cause and effect is dynamic, and it is constantly changing. The more we practice, the more we become aware of these things. The more we become aware of these things, the more our past karma changes. Gradually our future karma will be created from a different base—a base of awareness.

There's really no distinction between "being" and "doing." Being is an aspect of doing; doing is an aspect of being. Without an awareness of being, there can be no truly meaningful doing. Any doing that lacks awareness of the being aspect becomes a frenzied thing, a do-gooding, that will often do more harm than good. Eric Fromm, in his book *The Art of Loving*, says, as I remember it, that in our Western culture, a person, to be active, must always be doing something. It is the active person who is always right. And to be active means to be working, to be studying or doing sports, and so on. He goes on to say that what's not taken into account is the motivation behind the acting. For example, somebody could be doing something out of tremendous ambition to make money, or for fame or position, or one could be driven for certain psychological reasons. There could be a compulsive driving of yourself, in which case the activity becomes a passivity, because one is not the actor but, rather, one is being acted upon, one is being driven. And so he says that actually the highest activity is zazen. (He used the word *meditation*.) Because, when it is done under the proper circumstances, the proper mind-state, it is a free act and therefore the highest kind of activity. And this is certainly true enough.

Sitting in this way, one develops a sensitivity after a while, and one feels the pain of the world very strongly. One feels part of everything else. You find in Zen two feelings about this, side by side. There have been Zen masters who have encouraged social action, and in Buddhism as a whole there has been at certain times great social concern. We find it with the Buddha himself. But probably the greater weight of the evidence leans toward developing one's own self first, that is, before trying to do good works on a grand scale.

Until one develops compassion and sympathy, one is not rightly attuned. Of course, this doesn't come entirely through enlightenment. But certainly with enlightenment and the dropping away of habitual self-concern, feelings are liberated that allow us to become more deeply sensitive to every kind of situation. Some people, however, try to help others on a large scale before they're ready. Remember Milarepa, the great Tibetan Buddhist teacher, who says, "There will never be any end of people to help. Till the end of the world there will always be people to help." But to help people without hurting them at the same time, or hurting yourself, means that we must first work on ourselves. Certainly this does not exclude helping in emergencies or times of crisis or simply whenever you're asked. Nor does it exclude doing whatever might be useful or beneficial in general. If you can see it, then you can do it. This is a natural part or practice, but we must not become attached to it. In *The Three Pillars of Zen*, Yasutani Roshi talks about the difference between a bodhisattva and a buddha: a bodhisattva, he says, is still attached to the idea of saving or helping people, whereas a buddha spontaneously does these things wherever he or she can. A buddha is one who is constantly helping but has no self-conscious thought, no special intention, about it.

A Middle Way alternates between the life of inward meditation and the life of action-in-the-world, the twin poles of nirvana and samsara that are ultimately one. What we take in through meditation we must give out in love and action on behalf of our fellows on this earth—humans and nonhumans.

Social action is itself a kind of meditation and can be a great ripener of compassion and equanimity. It is also an act of giving what we can. This corresponds to the eighth precept: not to withhold material or spiritual aid.

The Buddha said, "Whoever nurses the sick serves me."

The object of gaining an insight into the inner truth of things is really to qualify oneself for greater compassionate action in the world.

A Zen master said, "Zen [training] is a preparation for life in the world, not the goal of life in the world." Buddhists do not take a fatalistic view of karma. Rather, Buddhist teaching has always urged practitioners to make every effort to remove disease and war.

In short, the relation to cause and effect is not fixed but constantly changing. Men and women make their own history, but they make it under specific karmic conditions inherited from previous generations, collectively as well as individually.

More than any previous society in human history, capitalist industrial society has created conditions of extreme impermanence, terrifying insubstantiality, and a struggling dissatisfaction and frustration. It would be difficult to imagine any social order for which Buddhism was more relevant and needed. Surely Buddhists should be sharp and active critics of all social conditions and values that move deluded and struggling humanity to increase pain and suffering, greed and violence. At the same time, they must remain compassionately responsive toward the individual men and women who drive others and are themselves driven by their own undisciplined impulses. Is not a Buddhism that lectures individuals on their delusions, but has nothing to say about the deluding political and economic conditions that reinforce these, merely hypocrisy? Here again our way is the Middle Way, concerned with individual change and also with the context of social change, yet ultimately with something greater than either or both.

The Buddhist Way, with its compassion, equanimity, tolerance, concern for self-reliance and responsibility—above all, its cosmic view—can be a model for society.

What are needed are political and economic relations and a technology that will: (a) help people to overcome ego-centeredness through cooperation with others instead of subordination, exploitation, and competition; (b) offer to each a freedom that is conditional only upon the freedom of others, so that individuals may develop a self-reliant social responsibility rather than being the conditioned pawns of institutions and ideologies; (c) encourage people to concern themselves primarily with the material and social conditions of personal growth, and only secondarily with material production.

"He alone can do good who knows what things are like and what their situation is," quotes E. F. Schumacher in his classic, *Small Is Beautiful*. To a world knotted in hatreds and aggression, Buddhism offers a unique combination of an unshakable equanimity and a deeply compassionate practical concern.

He who clings to the Void
And neglects compassion
Does not reach the highest stage.
But he who practices only compassion
Does not gain release from the toils of existence.
He, however, who is strong in the practice of both
Remains neither in samsara nor in nirvana.

A major task for Buddhism in the West, it seems to me, is to ally itself with religious and other concerned organizations to forestall the potential catastrophes facing the human race: nuclear holocaust, irreversible pollution of the world's environment, and the continuing large-scale destruction of nonrenewable resources. We also need to lend our physical and moral support to those who are fighting hunger, poverty, and oppression everywhere in the world.

To remain silent or indifferent in the face of the challenges in today's imperiled world is, in the end, to give aid and comfort to forces of reaction and bigotry, and to weaken the effectiveness of those seeking to combat such negative forces. Let your practice go with you out of the zendo and see what happens. Let the world's pain come into your zazen and see the great exertion that will emerge.

Zen Work

NORMAN FISCHER

PAI CHANG WAS THE ZEN MASTER famous for establishing the Zen monastic rule. He was always very insistent on working every day. When he was old he persisted in this, and the monks felt sorry for him so they hid his tools. He said, "I have no virtue. Why should others work for me?" And he refused to eat. He said, "A day of no work is a day of no eating." This saying became very famous in Zen circles, and to this day the Zen schools are noted for their practice of work.

Once Yun Yen asked Pai Chang, "Every day there's hard work to do. Whom do you do it for?" Pai Chang said, "There is someone who requires it." Yun Yen said, "Why not have him do it himself?" Pai Chang said, "He has no tools."

If you really think about what work is, you see that everything is work—being alive and in a body is already work. Every day there is eating and shitting and cleaning up. There is brushing and bathing and flossing. Every day there is thinking and caring and creating. So there's no escape from work—it's everywhere. For Zen students there's no work time and leisure time; there's just lifetime, daytime and nighttime. Work is something deep and dignified—it's what we are born to do and what we feel most fulfilled in doing.

Even within conventional notions of work there are a lot of kinds of work. There's administrative work, clerical work, creative work, and emotional work. Clearly all these forms of work are important and useful, but in religious practice, especially in Zen, there is a special place given to physical work and the dignity of physical work.

I am a little embarrassed to be speaking about physical work because I don't do that much of it these days and haven't done that much of it throughout my life. When I was young I used to have very little use for it. But probably the most important thing I have learned in my years of Zen practice is to appreciate physical work and to honor it as a special practice. So even though I do not have great skills as a worker, I hope I have a good spirit for work. Most of the physical work I do nowadays is housework—dishes and bed-making and taking out the garbage and compost and recycling. And I always enjoy our temple communal work times, hoeing together in the early mornings, or digging, or planting potatoes, or the long temple-cleaning periods every month.

I think we are lucky at Green Gulch to have as much work as we do. Work brings us together and makes us into a real community. There are many places to do sesshins and retreats, but it's not the same when the members of a community don't have real work they need to accomplish together. When there's real physical work, we struggle together and create a place together, and that place then inspires our practice on a daily basis because we know we have worked to make it.

At Green Gulch we have good basic work—taking care of land, growing flowers and food that will actually be used by people, making good soil and a sustainable agriculture and horticulture. We also have the practice of cooking food and of cleaning up after cooking. And we have the practice of taking care of guests—making beds and cleaning the guest house, making spaces feel beautiful and warm. And we have the very fundamental work of stewardship of the physical plant—making sure the invisible things like sewage and water, as well as the visible things like buildings and walkways and cars and trucks—will be in working order when we need them. All these forms of work are really wonderful. We couldn't ask for more straightforward and meaningful work.

I recently gave a weekend poetry workshop at Green Gulch. One man, an older retired man who had lived a full life, was very moved by the weekend, but his being moved had nothing to do with the poetry. What moved him was the feeling he had about our community. He said he was so touched by the way the guest house was taken care of, the way the dining room was taken care of, the quality of the food, the way people treated him and seemed to treat each other. He had gone into the kitchen at midnight and found fresh bread there with butter, freely offered—this really impressed him! He said that after a whole lifetime of working within organizations he had become pretty cynical, that he'd seen many organizations begin with lots of idealism but very soon devolve into battles for turf and the usual pettiness and meanness, and he had the strong view that all organizations must be this way. So he was very surprised by his feeling that our organization was somehow different. I didn't bother to mention to him that we too have our turf battles and our pettiness, because our life here at Green Gulch is not so different from anywhere else. And yet I think there is something else that happens at Green Gulch that comes from our commitment to the bodhisattva path, a commitment that isn't just theoretical or emotional, but is grounded in the daily activity of our shared work.

✻

I would like to distinguish between two modes of work practice. One is work as meditation, and the other is work as giving, or work as love, or maybe simply work as offering.

Work as meditation happens when the work you are doing is very simple and repetitive, and it can involve an actual meditation practice that you do as you are working—like being aware of your hands and feet, or of your tool as it moves, or of the rhythm of your movements in the work. Most physical work involves some sense of rhythm or timing. When you can enter into this timing and flow with it, you can work very efficiently and at the same time be very relaxed. You enter into something bigger than the thoughts inside your head or your distractions and complaints. Work as meditation can also involve periodic pauses during the work to recollect yourself—to go to your breath, or stop for a moment to come back to the present if your mind is wandering. In some of our work places we have the custom of striking a bell every now and then to bring us back. Just as in zazen, you can be aware of your mind as you work and keep trying to bring it back to the task at hand all the time, even when there is no bell or no special pause.

In this kind of work there isn't too much thinking or planning or conceptualizing. There's no worry about how much you are getting done, though you do try to do what you are doing efficiently and beautifully, without hurrying. This is the kind of work we do during work periods in sesshin or during temple-cleaning periods: not rushing to get the dishes washed or the compost buckets emptied so we can get onto the more important job, which is the way I used to view physical work before I began my Zen study, but just appreciating work for what it is—a thoroughgoing engagement with our life. We have a custom during our monastic training periods at Tassajara of assigning the cleaning of the toilets to the head monk. The head monk is a highly honored person in the practice period, and assigning him or her this job is a way of saying that even this work, which may seem lowly, is special work when it is practiced in the spirit of meditation.

There are a few important ways to practice with this kind of work. One important way is silent work. When we work silently we put ourselves more fully into our actual working, with more clarity and with more gusto. Silent work isn't strictly silent. It's OK to talk about the task—where we put something or where to get something or how to do something, but we don't have conversations or make social talk. There's a time for that too, but if we always chat when we work we won't appreciate the depth of the work, and we also won't appreciate how wonderful it is to chat together.

Second, there is bowing in and bowing out. Beginning work together with incense and a bow really helps to remind us that we're working together, even if we go off to different locations, and it helps to remind us that our work is an offering.

Next is cleaning up and caring for our tools. If we do a flurry of work and don't leave time to care for our tools or clean up, we'll come back to work the next time and we won't be able to begin well. We'll end up having to look for something we've misplaced, or we'll have a sour feeling seeing such a mess. It's good to start every work session with our workspace and tools in order. This can be hard to do—in fact it's one of my biggest problems in my personal work. I get confused and sidetracked, and I don't leave things in a good state when I stop work, and this snowballs. But I am very clear about the consequences of this—it leaves me in an even bigger state of confusion. So I am working hard on this myself, and it is definitely improving. It's important to have a sense that we have finished something before we go on to the next thing. Even if we can't finish a task, we can try to bring it to a place that has a feeling of finishing, to a particular stage, and we can take a moment at least to consider where we have gotten before we go on to something else, rather than just dropping one task and flying off into something else. And this includes cleaning and maintaining our tools.

The second kind of work practice, work as giving or as offering, is not as simple as this kind of work, and sometimes it's not so relaxing.

The essential characteristic of work as offering is not the how of the work—because there may be a variety of ways to accomplish the work depending on the situation. Here the crucial factor is the underlying attitude and purpose of the work. Our work is an offering: we are accomplishing it for the benefit of Buddha, Dharma, and Sangha—in other words, for the benefit of others. So work as offering is a kind of burning up of the self in the activity of work, just doing it completely without holding anything back. There's no sense of an observer or of any practice at all. There's just doing what you do completely with a good spirit.

This reminds me of the story about Pai Chang. We work hard because there is someone who requires it. Who is that someone? We can say all beings, we can say reality itself, we can say Buddha, but none of these is quite accurate. Someone requires it and maybe it is best to say we don't know who that someone is. Why doesn't this person do it herself? Because we are her tools. Our body, our mind, and our whole life are her tools. So we throw ourselves into our work with a lot of verve and joy.

In this kind of work there may be lots of planning and organizing and concern about how much money we make or how much work we get done. But the reason we are concerned about all this is not because we want to get rich or become famous or get a promotion—the reason is that we love the one who requires us to work, and we want to do as good a job for that one as possible. So this kind of work is a little difficult, and we have to take care of ourselves in the midst of it, but it is also very fascinating, because every task requires a different kind of effort, and we need to discover the kind of effort that is appropriate. And we need always to reflect on our attitude and to see how we are doing. Complaining a lot or feeling like we're working too hard or joylessly are signs that we're forgetting to *offer* our work—we're sliding into a conventional view of work for pay or profit or promotion, a view that serves no one. It takes the joy out of work. It makes us feel pressured; it grinds us down. No amount of money and prestige justifies wasting our precious time, our precious life, doing something that isn't important to us. We need to feel that we are choosing to work because a human being works for the one who requires it. This is what a human being does. Fish swim and birds fly; humans work. This is our life and our joy.

As some of you may know, I have been exploring the possibility of setting up a restaurant in the new shopping development in Marin City near Green Gulch. I believe this Zen approach to work is important for everyone, not just Zen students, and especially for people for whom the most creative jobs in our society are not an option. Social welfare people say it's not enough to get someone off dope or out of jail—they have to have hope, and this means a job. And the dream for this restaurant is that it would provide jobs for people in Marin City and eventually be owned and operated by people in Marin City.

But the truth is, just having a job isn't enough to give you true hope. A lot of ex-cons do get jobs, but they end up going back to jail because, although they have a job, they don't have a vision for how to do that job in a way that makes it fulfilling. If you don't see how you can become fulfilled through your job, then it is natural that you will feel taken advantage of, and the job will become not a source of hope but another way for you to feel denigrated and exploited. I imagine a restaurant in which every worker can practice making an offering. When we make wholehearted offerings, we always receive more than we have given. We receive our freedom and our dignity.

The other day, I drove by a garden under construction in Mill Valley. All of the men working in the garden were Hispanic. And it reminded me that in most of the Western world white people do the management, and people of color do the physical work. I saw it in Israel when I visited there some years ago, and it is the case in many European countries as well.

Everyone loses in a situation like this. The managers begin to develop the idea that physical work is beneath them, and the physical workers begin to overlay their work with a sense of its inferiority. So the managers lose their bodies and their connection to the actual tasks that support their lives. They become abstract and ideological; they become ungrounded. And the physical workers lose their sense of dignity and ownership of the work they do. Such a social situation can't be healthy. How can there be justice if management people can't understand or appreciate working people? And how can working people grow and develop if they don't have a sense of the dignity of their work?

The training that we do together through physical work in places like Green Gulch is important not only for us but in a wider context as well. As we learn distinct skills—like cooking, cleaning, bread-making, carpentry, plumbing, farming, gardening—we also learn to appreciate the beauty of physical work, and we develop an attitude and an understanding of work that we will carry throughout our lives.

Encouraging Words for Activists

JOANNA MACY

H OW CAN WE ENGAGE IN ACTION on behalf of earth and not get consumed, not go crazy? We who have aligned ourselves with this effort to transform a civilization so that complex forms of life can continue are faced with something very different from the kinds of challenges that our foremothers and forefathers faced.

I'd like to begin by reflecting on some peculiarities of our situation in the twilight of the twentieth century here on planet earth. Six occur to me. First of all, there is the staggering range of the crisis, from the soil to the forest to the air to the seas to the rivers to the spasms of extinction. It's overwhelming for any single pair of eyes.

Second and concurrent to that, there is an overwhelming amount of data. You never know enough. Every time you hear mention of a new development, you think, "I'd better bone up on that, too." When can you draw a free breath?

Third, it appears that our chances of pulling through are slim. We recognize this, but we don't say it much. For example, the chlorofluorocarbons we've already put into the biosphere will still be eating the biosphere for the next fifteen years. How do you find the energy and motivation to act when it may be too late?

The fourth and related peculiarity is the taboo against acknowledging the situation—aside from the occasional letter from Nobel laureates on the thirty-fourth page of the newspaper—against speaking out and naming what we're doing to ourselves. It still feels inappropriate to acknowledge this in polite society. On one level we really intuit the severity of the crisis we're in, and on the other we're just going along with business as usual. The press helps us by treating everything as if it were separate—wars and hunger, radiation and AIDS, the floods in Bangladesh and the floods in the Midwest.

The fifth feature is that it's increasingly dangerous to act on behalf of earth because of repressive actions of the FBI (as in infiltrating Earth First!) and attacks on environmentalists by corporate-sponsored movements like Wise Use. I know for myself when I do speak out, I sometimes hear ancestral voices whispering, "Shut up or you will be burned." We carry this fear.

Lastly, we feel so pressed—the letters to answer, the lobbying, the meetings, the fundraising, the calls to make. We get sick and tired, and we get tired and sick. Some of the people I most admire work around issues of contamination and are themselves ill. It's not an easy time to charge out, although it is the most natural choice in the world to move out and act when our larger body is threatened. It's good to be able to name why it's hard for us to do that.

I'd also like to reflect on some things that have helped me act for earth. What do we have going for us? I've come to realize that we have a lot going for us. First, it helps to remember your true nature. Action is not something you do, it's something you *are*. In other words, you are not a noun, you're a verb. That is our true nature. In our old paradigm, the substantialist view of the world, rocks, atoms, molecules, trees, people, nation-states were seen as separate entities, and what happened between them—in terms of interchanges, communications, messages, relationships—was considered less real because you can't see it or weigh it or touch it. And that was true for Aristotle, Newton, Galileo. Now in the view that has emerged in our time, natural scientists see reality as flows, interconnecting currents of matter, energy, and information. They see that what appeared to be separate entities are patterns made by flows and sustained by flows. This reversal of perspective is happening now, and we can live it in our lives. Systems thinker Norbert Weiner said, "We are not stuff that abides, we are patterns . . . in a river of ever-flowing water." Or, to use another image, we are flames that keep our shape by burning, by the act of combustion—matter in and matter out.

So action isn't a burden to be hoisted up and lugged around on our

shoulders. It is something we are. The work we have to do can be seen as
a kind of coming alive. More than some moral imperative, it's an awakening to our true nature, a releasing of our gifts. This flow-through of energy and ideas is at every moment directed by our choice. That's our role
in it. We're like a lens that can focus, or a gate that can direct this flow-
through by schooling our intention. In each moment we can give it
direction.

❊

This true nature of ours tells us what our power is. Understanding power
is absolutely critical because you can have all the smarts and devotion and
information to carry forth a campaign of action, but if you are still falling
for the old notion of power you are crippling yourself. The old notion
tells us that power is what one substance does to another piece of substance. And what can it do? It can push it around. It can exert its will.
Hence we have identified power with domination—power over. And
we've imagined that power means having strong defenses, really being
invulnerable so others don't push *us* around. In contrast, an image frequently used by systems thinkers is the nerve cell. In a neural net, nerve
cells are constantly interacting and interdependent, allowing flows of
matter and energy and information among them and transforming those
flows. What is the power of one nerve cell in relation to another? It's not
power over or the power of being invulnerable. If a nerve cell were to
build strong defenses to protect itself from painful information, it would
die. An effective nerve cell lets the charge through. It communicates and
develops collaborative assemblies or networks. We can call that power
with, or as systems theorists say, synergy. So when we remember our true
nature as change, as action, we remember also the true collaborative nature of our power.

A second thing that helps is *mudra*. We go from philosophy to gesture. There are two symbolic gestures, or mudras, in Buddhism that help
me a lot. The *abhaya* mudra, palm outward, means "Fear not." Don't be
afraid. It arose with the teachings about impermanence and interbeing.
When I wonder where is my refuge, my safe haven, it reminds me that
my real refuge is in my action, in the flow going out of the heart, in the
connection. The other mudra is the gesture of touching the ground.

When the Buddha was sitting under the bodhi tree, Mara said, "By what authority are you doing this?" Gautama didn't recite his pedigree or what he had accomplished in his life; he reached down and touched the earth. *This* is my right to be here; this is my right to seek freedom from endless suffering and inflicting of suffering. The scriptures say that when he did that, the earth roared.

Knowing this, we know we don't need to fear pain. We can see our pain for the world as flow-through of information in the great net. Grief can ambush us at any time, and our power doesn't have anything to do with being immune to that. It derives rather from our capacity to suffer with—the literal meaning of compassion. To be able to suffer with is good news because it means you can share power with, share joy with, exchange love with. Let your pain tell you that you are not alone. What we thought might have been sealing us off can become connective tissue.

Third, it has been helpful to me, too, to reflect on the meaning of apocalypse. A theologian brother who knew his Greek told me that the real meaning of the word is to uncover, to disclose. What can be disclosed in us? If we really face the magnitude of the dangers—the possibility that this may be the end of the road for our species—what can be revealed in us? People think that if we allow ourselves to experience this fear, it will paralyze us. And they think that if we don't look at it, we won't be paralyzed. But what if we were to live each moment as if it were our last? That's a central spiritual teaching—the death meditation in Buddhism or medieval Christianity's mystery play *Everyman*. Look into apocalypse and let that free you from triviality, evasion. If you're in a game and the chances of winning are minimal, and it is only minutes to the end, what does the coach say to you? He doesn't say, "It'll turn out okay, just relax," but rather, "The odds are overwhelmingly against us: go out and give it all you've got." Use that sense of being on the brink to come alive, to discover who you really are, to let all the falseness that we imprison ourselves in be stripped away. Before Lakota warriors went into battle, they said: Today is a good day to die.

❋

It also helps a lot to remember that each one of us has been called into being at this time. I am convinced of that. We are not here by accident.

Is it my imagination to think that we have chosen this? Is it not a privilege to be incarnating at a time when the stakes are really high, at a time when everything we've ever learned about interconnectedness, about trust, about courage, can be put to the test? Each one of us, I believe, is a gift the earth is giving to itself now, a unique gift. Every anguish, betrayal, disappointment can even help prepare us for the work of healing. You don't need to be extraordinary. If the world is to be healed through human efforts, I am convinced it will be by ordinary people, people whose love for this life is even greater than their fear, people who can open to the web of life that called us into being, and who can rest in the vitality of that larger body.

Last, we need to be ready for surprises. The first property of systems is that the whole is more than the sum of the parts. Each time new systemic patterns form, through interaction, something emerges that wasn't there before—that is a systemic property of life. You cannot predict what is going to emerge. That is why it's okay not to have a blueprint. Unburden yourself of the notion that you have to carry around a master plan to know what is the best thing to do. Lewis Mumford saw this years ago when he said that the era of the individual savior, a Buddha, a messiah, or a Christ, was over, and that the wisdom was going to erupt through each and all of us. Transformation now is a collective event.

Practicing with Passion

CHRISTOPHER TITMUSS

WHAT DOES "SPIRITUAL" ACTUALLY MEAN FOR US? The original meaning of this word is from the Latin word *spirare*, "to breathe." So to be spiritual is to breathe, and what does it mean to breathe? What does it mean for life to breathe? We sometimes get trapped in the rhetoric of spirituality, the language of spirituality, and we become servants of the ideology. And I say, let's not be concerned with "spirituality." Let's not be concerned with being "Green," being "environmentalist." Let's really look at life, and if at times those words are useful and applicable, fine. But let's not make too much fuss about them. Because it's an invitation to conflict and division.

From a spiritual standpoint, intention is extraordinarily significant. The Buddha gives a remarkable analogy. He said it's as though people sometimes find themselves stuck at the bottom of an extremely dark well. Somebody passes by, and they have a rope with them, and they throw the rope down to the bottom of the well. And then the Buddha asks, What are the conditions for this person at the bottom of the well to come out of the situation? Two things have to take place. The person at the top of the well has to take the strain of the rope. And equally important, the person at the bottom has to be willing to take hold of it. In other words, the intention must be there. The intention for change, for liberation, for awakening, must be there.

In the movement for social change and justice, one of the biggest factors contributing to stress and burnout is that there is a dependency on result. Last January, I was in Bodghaya teaching, and information came on the shortwave that the Persian Gulf war had started. On this retreat we had an Iraqi from Baghdad, and seven Israelis who were deeply concerned about the Scuds; there was a lot of fear and concern. We organized a peace pilgrimage to the Bodhi tree. It began with Westerners and a handful of Thais and Tibetans. We walked with a single candle each, and soon there were hundreds of people. It was a small but beautiful expression of our concern. We didn't think we were going to stop the war.

Focusing too much on results brings nightmares—literally and metaphorically. There is a perversion of perception, and this is something that each one of us must watch with the same kind of vigilance as if we had a cobra in a small room with us. The ego comes up in the form of "I" or "we" and says, "We are so small. I am so small. We can't ever confront the huge circumstances and crises of life." This has a paralyzing effect on emotional life. It deadens the spirit. And this wretched system we live under, day in and day out, is putting out that message. The media conspire with this. We get blinded by the media—appalling magazines like *Time* and *Newsweek*—which are the servants of government.

One of the ways media conspire is in the language of "militant" and "moderate." When people in a factory, working in the most foul working conditions—health, safety, financial, etc.—begin to voice their concern, they are called "militant." When the women set up a peace camp at Greenham Common during the 1980s, they were all described as "militant." Militant is anything that upsets the status quo. It's part of a conspiracy to marginalize the work for peace and social justice. So we really have to look into the way we speak. Even the word "activist"—say you're an activist, and the reaction is, "Oh, God, not one of them . . ." That's media influence. So let's not use language that works against us.

Another important message of the Dharma for a spiritual life—a life which can breathe—is to avoid an obsession with the future. And I think the Green movement has made some errors here, by putting out information that says, "In the future, this is going to happen unless we do thus and so." Especially in the United States, where there's an extraordinary belief in progress, this creates the attitude that things will get better once we "get it right."

When we talk about the future, it touches a place of fear. We feel anxious about the Earth and our future, and this constant anxiety leaves us feeling horror or guilt or despair, essentially insecure. And what happens when people feel insecure? They go to the sacred shrine in their home, called the refrigerator, and open up the inner tabernacle and stuff themselves. We contribute to consumerism by plaguing people with fears of the future. Unless we look at the emotional content of fear and aggression and liberate ourselves, awaken our hearts, we are as much part of the problem as anyone.

The Buddhist world in Asia is in a severe state of historical crisis. That shows itself in the tyranny of government, in Burma, Tibet, Thailand, Kampuchea, and Sri Lanka, where leaders claim to be upholding Buddhist tradition while they incarcerate, torture, and murder thousands of citizens, while they actually destroy the Buddhist tradition, Buddhist values, a Buddhist way of life. It's important that we who have a love and concern find ways to express our concern. Because, like it or not, there are millions of people in other parts of the world who look to the West, and who think of the West as where it's all going—to this nightmare. I think we have a very valuable function to play in showing what postconsumerism is: something other than this selfish, individualistic form of living. We need new ambassadors to show there are people in this society who are saying, This is rotten, and I don't want to live like this. And that's where the Dharma teachings clearly have a potency, because they're so flexible. We don't have to use the word "Buddha," or "Dharma," "Sangha," or any of that.

One concern I have is that we liberate ourselves from anger. I can't support what I sometimes feel is a rationalization of "righteous anger," which is to me a contradiction in terms. Anger by its character, by its definition, is harmful. Usually we do one of two things: we either fight the person who is angry, or we defend our position. And the force of anger goes against what we want. When we're angry with people, they tighten up. They become more ideological about their belief, and we have given support to it through the nature of dependent arising. But on the other hand, Buddhists—who are painfully nice people, and that disturbs me as much as those who are angry—will sometimes say, Let's direct some loving-kindness toward the people we're angry at. I take a different view. When governments and business are actively destroying Earth, how can one give loving-kindness to that? We need to hear the voices of the people and animals who have no voice, and our kindness needs to go to those who are disadvantaged by the system. If one is trying to be too kind, the passion is watered down. One is afraid to be passionate for justice, because one confuses passion with anger. And it's up to us to acknowledge the difference between anger and loving life passionately and tenaciously.

The Buddha's teaching states this very succinctly. He says the most noble forms of human consciousness are embodied in four areas: *metta*—which isn't wishy-washy-let's-be-nice-to-each-other, but is an active force of friendship, a very deep friendship for life which is unshakable in the force of circumstances. The other is *karuna*, compassion, which we think is a feeling of pity for someone, but it's the action which relieves suffering. It's not just sitting and having some nice concerned thoughts about the injustice and suffering in the world. The third noble state is *mudita*, which means spiritual joy—a joy with no limit. It's not just being engaged in meditation and feeling happiness. It's gladness at the good fortune of others. The fourth, *upekkha*, is translated as equanimity. But that has kind of a passive note to it. I think true equanimity is the capacity to stand steady in the face of painful circumstances. The Buddha made it quite clear: to stand steady when one is besieged with the forces of pleasure and pain. So equanimity is active, it's not afraid, it's direct, and it's willing to challenge the forces that are unsatisfactory, whether they are embodied in the Henry Kissingers of the world or elsewhere.

At particular times, there is an active interest in a particular area of concern. Sometimes it's crime, sometimes it's AIDS, South Africa, sometimes overpopulation, women's rights. But an obsession with the fashion of the moment is a situational response. People are talking about it; there is a huge outpouring of publicity, demonstrations, public meetings, leafletting. Then that wave passes. It's the responsibility of people who've gone deeper than the situational response—toward transcendence—to ground things in the here and now. Then we're not so dependent on situational response, because we've touched something deeper, which has a liberating fortitude to it. The teachings give mettle to awareness, to wisdom; they give a sustainability to it. We go steady, steady, steady, because the work of liberation and awakening the heart can't be a situational response. The Dharma teachings are about transcendence, and therefore it's a lifelong commitment. There is no retirement.

Renunciation and Daring

CHÖGYAM TRUNGPA

I

Imagine that you are sitting naked on the ground, with your bare bottom touching the earth. Since you are not wearing a scarf or hat, you are also exposed to heaven above. You are sandwiched between heaven and earth: a naked man or woman, sitting between heaven and earth.

Earth is always earth. The earth will let anyone sit on it, and earth never gives way. It never lets you go—you don't drop off this earth and go flying through outer space. Likewise, sky is always sky; heaven is always heaven above you. Whether it is snowing or raining or the sun is shining, whether it is daytime or nighttime, the sky is always there. In that sense, we know that heaven and earth are trustworthy.

The logic of basic goodness is very similar. When we speak of basic goodness, we are not talking about having allegiance to good and rejecting bad. Basic goodness is good because it is unconditional, or fundamental. It is there already, in the same way that heaven and earth are there already. We don't reject our atmosphere. We don't reject the sun and the moon, the clouds and the sky. We accept them. We accept that the sky is blue; we accept the landscape and the sea. We accept highways and buildings and cities. Basic goodness is that basic, that unconditional. It is not a "for" or "against" view, in the same way that sunlight is not "for" or "against."

The natural law and order of this world is not "for" or "against." Fundamentally, there is nothing that either threatens us or promotes our point of view. The four seasons occur free from anyone's demand or vote. Hope and fear cannot alter the seasons. There is day; there is night. There is darkness at night and light during the day, and no one has to turn a switch on and off. There is a natural law and order that allows us to survive and that is basically good, good in that it is there and it works and it is efficient.

We often take for granted this basic law and order in the universe, but we should think twice. We should appreciate what we have. Without it, we would be in a total predicament. If we didn't have sunlight, we wouldn't have any vegetation, we wouldn't have any crops, and we couldn't cook a meal. So basic goodness is good *because* it is so basic, so fundamental. It is natural and it works, and therefore it is good, rather than being good as opposed to bad.

The same principle applies to our makeup as human beings. We have passion, aggression, and ignorance. That is, we cultivate our friends, we ward off our enemies, and we are occasionally indifferent. Those tendencies are not regarded as shortcomings. They are part of the natural elegance and equipment of human beings. We are equipped with nails and teeth to defend ourselves against attack, we are equipped with a mouth and genitals to relate with others, and we are lucky enough to have complete digestive and respiratory systems so that we can process what we take in and flush it out. Human existence is a natural situation, and like the law and order of the world, it is workable and efficient. In fact, it is wonderful, it is ideal.

Some people might say this world is the work of a divine principle, but the Shambhala teachings are not concerned with divine origins. The point of warriorship is to work personally with our situation now, as it is. From the Shambhala point of view, when we say that human beings are basically good, we mean that they have every faculty they need, so that they don't have to fight with their world. Our being is good because it is not a fundamental source of aggression or complaint. We cannot complain that we have eyes, ears, a nose, and a mouth. We cannot redesign our physiological system, and for that matter, we cannot redesign our state of mind. Basic goodness is what we have, what we are provided with. It is the natural situation that we have inherited from birth onwards.

We should feel that it is wonderful to be in this world. How wonderful it is to see red and yellow, blue and green, purple and black! All of these colors are provided for us. We feel hot and cold; we taste sweet and sour. We have these sensations, and we deserve them. They are good.

So the first step in realizing basic goodness is to appreciate what we have. But then we should look further and more precisely at what we are, where we are, who we are, when we are, and how we are as human beings, so that we can take possession of our basic goodness. It is not really a possession, but nonetheless, we deserve it.

Basic goodness is very closely connected to the idea of *bodhicitta* in the Buddhist tradition. *Bodhi* means "awake" or "wakeful" and *citta* means "heart," so *bodhicitta* is "awakened heart." Such awakened heart comes from being willing to face your state of mind. That may seem like a great demand, but it is necessary. You should examine yourself and ask how many times you have tried to connect with your heart, fully and truly. How often have you turned away, because you feared you might discover something terrible about yourself? How often have you been willing to look at your face in the mirror, without being embarrassed? How many times have you tried to shield yourself by reading the newspaper, watching television, or just spacing out? That is the sixty-four-thousand-dollar question: how much have you connected with yourself at all in your whole life?

The sitting practice of meditation is the means to rediscover basic goodness, and beyond that, it is the means to awaken this genuine heart within yourself. When you sit in the posture of meditation, you are exactly the naked man or woman that we described earlier, sitting between heaven and earth. When you slouch, you are trying to hide your heart, trying to protect it by slumping over. But when you sit upright but relaxed in the posture of meditation, your heart is naked. Your entire being is exposed—to yourself, first of all, but to others as well. So through the practice of sitting still and following your breath as it goes out and dissolves, you are connecting with your heart. By simply letting yourself be, as you are, you develop genuine sympathy toward yourself.

When you awaken your heart in this way, you find, to your surprise, that your heart is empty. You find that you are looking into outer space. What are you, who are you, where is your heart? If you really look, you won't find anything tangible and solid. Of course, you might find something *very* solid if you have a grudge against someone or you have fallen possessively in love. But that is not awakened heart. If you search for awakened heart, if you put your hand through your rib cage and feel for it, there is nothing there except for tenderness. You feel sore and soft, and if you open your eyes to the rest of the world, you feel tremendous sadness. This kind of sadness doesn't come from being mistreated. You don't feel sad because someone has insulted you or because you feel impoverished. Rather, this experience of sadness is unconditioned. It occurs because your heart is completely exposed. There is no skin or tissue covering it; it is pure raw meat. Even if a tiny mosquito lands on it, you feel so touched. Your experience is raw and tender and so personal.

The genuine heart of sadness comes from feeling that your nonexistent heart is full. You would like to spill your heart's blood, give your heart to others. For the warrior, this experience of sad and tender heart is what gives birth to fearlessness. Conventionally, being fearless means that you are not afraid, or that, if someone hits you, you will hit him back. However, we are not talking about that street-fighter level of fearlessness. Real fearlessness is the product of tenderness. It comes from letting the world tickle your heart, your raw and beautiful heart. You are willing to open up, without resistance or shyness, and face the world. You are willing to share your heart with others.

2

The situations of fear that exist in our lives provide us with stepping stones to step over our fear. On the other side of cowardice is bravery. If we step over properly, we can cross the boundary from being cowardly to being brave. We may not discover bravery right away. Instead, we may find a shaky tenderness beyond our fear. We are still quivering and shaking, but there is tenderness, rather than bewilderment.

Tenderness contains an element of sadness, as we have discussed. It is not the sadness of feeling sorry for yourself or feeling deprived, but it is a natural situation of fullness. You feel so full and rich, as if you were about to shed tears. Your eyes are full of tears, and the moment you blink, the tears will spill out of your eyes and roll down your cheeks. In order to be a good warrior, one has to feel this sad and tender heart. If a person does not feel alone and sad, he cannot be a warrior at all. The warrior is sensitive to every aspect of phenomena—sight, smell, sound, feelings. He appreciates everything that goes on in his world as an artist does. His experience is full and extremely vivid. The rustling of leaves and the sounds of raindrops on his coat are very loud. Occasional butterflies fluttering around him may be almost unbearable because he is so sensitive.

Because of his sensitivity, the warrior can then go further in developing his discipline. He begins to learn the meaning of renunciation.

In the ordinary sense, renunciation is often connected with asceticism. You give up the sense pleasures of the world and embrace an austere spiritual life in order to understand the higher meaning of existence. In the Shambhala context, renunciation is quite different. What the warrior renounces is anything in his experience that is a barrier between himself and others. In other words, renunciation is making yourself more available, more gentle and open to others. Any hesitation about opening yourself to others is removed. For the sake of others, you renounce your privacy.

The need for renunciation arises when you begin to feel that basic goodness belongs to you. Of course, you cannot make a personal possession out of basic goodness. It is the law and order of the world, which is impossible to possess personally. It is a greater vision, much greater than your personal territory or schemes. Nonetheless, sometimes you try to localize basic goodness in yourself. You think that you can take a little pinch of basic goodness and keep it in your pocket. So the idea of privacy begins to creep in. That is the point at which you need renunciation— renunciation of the temptation to possess basic goodness. It is necessary to give up a localized approach, a provincial approach, and to accept a greater world.

Renunciation also is necessary if you are frightened by the vision of the Great Eastern Sun. When you realize how vast and good the Great Eastern Sun is, sometimes you feel overwhelmed. You feel that you need a little shelter from it, a roof over your head and three square meals a day. You try to build a little nest, a little home, to contain or limit what you have seen. It seems too vast, so you would like to take photographs of the Great Eastern Sun and keep them as a memory, rather than staring directly into the light. The principle of renunciation is to reject any small-mindedness of that kind.

The sitting practice of meditation provides an ideal environment to develop renunciation. In meditation, as you work with your breath, you regard any thoughts that arise as just your thinking process. You don't hold on to any thought and you don't have to punish your thoughts or praise them. The thoughts that occur during sitting practice are regarded as natural events, but at the same time, they don't carry any credentials. The basic definition of meditation is "having a steady mind." In meditation, when your thoughts go up, you don't go up, and you don't go down when your thoughts go down; you just watch as thoughts go up and thoughts go down. Whether your thoughts are good or bad, exciting or boring, blissful or miserable, you let them be. You don't accept some and reject others. You have a sense of greater space that encompasses any thought that may arise.

In other words, in meditation you can experience a sense of existence, or being, that includes your thoughts but is not conditioned by your thoughts or limited to your thinking process. You experience your thoughts, you label them "thinking," and you come back to your breath, going out, expanding, and dissolving into space. It is very simple, but it is quite profound. You experience your world directly and you do not have to limit that experience. You can be completely open, with nothing to defend and nothing to fear. In that way, you are developing renunciation of personal territory and small-mindedness.

At the same time, renunciation does involve discrimination. Within the basic context of openness there is a discipline of what to ward off, or reject, and what to cultivate, or accept. The positive aspect of renunciation, what is cultivated, is caring for others. But in order to care for others, it is necessary to reject caring only for yourself, or the attitude of selfishness. A selfish person is like a turtle carrying its home on its back wherever it goes. At some point you have to leave home and embrace a larger world. That is the absolute prerequisite for being able to care for others.

In order to overcome selfishness, it is necessary to be daring. It is as though you were dressed in your swimsuit, standing on the diving board with a pool in front of you, and you ask yourself: "Now what?" The obvious answer is: "Jump." That is daring. You might wonder if you will sink or hurt yourself if you jump. You might. There is no insurance, but it is worthwhile jumping to find out what will happen. The student warrior has to jump. We are so accustomed to accepting what is bad for us and rejecting what is good for us. We are attracted to our cocoons, our selfishness, and we are afraid of selflessness, stepping beyond ourselves. So in order to overcome our hesitation about giving up our privacy, and in order to commit ourselves to others' welfare, some kind of leap is necessary.

In the practice of meditation, the way to be daring, the way to leap, is to disown your thoughts, to step beyond your hope and fear, the ups and downs of your thinking process. You can just be, just let yourself be, without holding on to the constant reference points that mind manufactures. You do not have to get rid of your thoughts. They are a natural process; they are fine; let them be as well. But let yourself go out with the breath, let it dissolve. See what happens. When you let yourself go in that way, you develop trust in the strength of your being and trust in your ability to open and extend yourself to others. You realize that you are rich and resourceful enough to give selflessly to others, and as well, you find that you have tremendous willingness to do so.

But then, once you have made a leap of daring, you might become arrogant. You might say to yourself: "Look, I have jumped! I am so great, so fantastic!" But arrogant warriorship does not work. It does nothing to benefit others. So the discipline of renunciation also involves cultivating further gentleness, so that you remain very soft and open and allow tenderness to come into your heart. The warrior who has accomplished true renunciation is completely naked and raw, without even skin or tissue. He has renounced putting on a new suit of armor or growing a thick skin, so his bone and marrow are exposed to the world. He has no room and no desire to manipulate situations. He is able to be, quite fearlessly, what he is.

At this point, having completely renounced his own comfort and privacy, paradoxically, the warrior finds himself more alone. He is like an island sitting alone in the middle of a lake. Occasional ferry boats and commuters go back and forth between the shore and the island, but all that activity only expresses the further loneliness, or the aloneness, of the island. Although the warrior's life is dedicated to helping others, he realizes that he will never be able to completely share his experience with others. The fullness of his experience is his own, and he must live with his own truth. Yet he is more and more in love with the world. That combination of love affair and loneliness is what enables the warrior to constantly reach out to help others. By renouncing his private world, the warrior discovers a greater universe and a fuller and fuller broken heart.

This is not something to feel bad about: it is a cause for rejoicing. It is entering the warrior's world.

3

We are going to discuss the obstacles to invoking drala,* which must be overcome before we can master the disciplines of invoking external, internal, and secret drala. One of the important points in invoking drala is to prepare a ground of gentleness and genuineness. The basic obstacle to gentleness is arrogance. Arrogance comes from hanging on to the reference point of *me* and other. You may have studied the principles of warriorship and Great Eastern Sun vision, and you may have received numerous teachings on how to rest in nowness and raise your windhorse, but if you regard those as your personal accomplishment, then you are missing the point. Instead of becoming gentle and tamed, you could become extremely arrogant. "I, Joe Schmidt, am able to raise windhorse, and *I* feel good about that. I am beginning to accomplish something, so I am a big deal."

Being gentle and without arrogance is the Shambhala definition of a gentleman. According to the *Oxford English Dictionary*, one of the definitions of a gentleman is someone who is not rude, someone whose behavior is gentle and thoroughly trained. However, for the warrior, gentleness is not just politeness. Gentleness is consideration: showing concern for others all the time. A Shambhala gentlewoman or gentleman is a decent person, a genuine person. He or she is very gentle to himself and to others. The purpose of any protocol, or manners, or discipline that we are taught is to have concern for others. We may think that if we have good manners, we are such good girls or good boys; we know how to eat properly and how to drink properly; we know how to behave properly; and aren't we smart? That is not the point. The point is that, if we have bad table manners, they upset our neighbors, and in turn our neighbors develop bad table manners, and they in turn upset others. If we misuse

---

*The Tibetan word *drala* refers to the living patterns of energy accessible to human perception—ED.

our napkins and our silverware because we are untrained, that creates problems for others.

Good behavior is not meant to build us up so that we can think of ourselves as little princes or princesses. The point of good behavior is to communicate our respect for others. So we should be concerned with how we behave. When someone enters a room, we should say hello, or stand up and greet them with a handshake. Those rituals are connected with how to have more consideration for others. The principles of warriorship are based on training ourselves and developing self-control so that we can extend ourselves to others. Those disciplines are important in order to cultivate the absence of arrogance.

We tend to think that the threats to our society or to ourselves are outside of us. We fear that some enemy will destroy us. But a society is destroyed from the inside, not from an attack by outsiders. We may imagine the enemy coming with spears and machine guns to kill us, massacre us. In reality, the only thing that can destroy us is within ourselves. If we have too much arrogance, we will destroy our gentleness. And if we destroy gentleness, then we destroy the possibility of being awake, and then we cannot use our intuitive openness to extend ourselves in situations properly. Instead, we generate tremendous aggression.

Aggression desecrates the ground altogether: the ground that you are sitting on, the walls around you, the ceiling and windows and doorways. In turn, you have no place to invite the dralas to come in. The space becomes like an opium den, thick and heavy, and the dralas say, "Yuck, who wants to go in there? Who's inviting us? Who's invoking us with their deception?" They won't come along at all. When the room is filled with *you* and your trip, no sensible person is attracted to that space. Even *you* aren't.

When the environment is stuffy and full of arrogant, self-styled men and women, the dralas are repelled. But then, what happens if a warrior, someone who embodies nonaggression, freedom from arrogance, and humbleness, walks into that room? When such a person enters an intense situation full of arrogance and pollution, quite possibly the occupants of the room begin to feel funny. They feel that they can't have any fun and games anymore, because someone who won't collaborate in their deception has walked in. They can't continue to crack setting-sun jokes or indulge and sprawl on the floor, so usually they will leave. The warrior is left alone, sitting in that room.

But then, after a while, a different group of people may walk in, looking for a fresh room, a clean atmosphere. They begin to assemble— gentle people who smile without arrogance or aggression. The atmosphere is quite different from the previous setting-sun gathering. It may be slightly more rowdy than in the opium den, but the air is cheerful and fresh. Then there is the possibility that the dralas will begin to peek through the doors and the windows. They become interested, and soon they want to come in, and one by one they enter. They accept food and drink, and they relax in that atmosphere, because it is pure and clean. Because that atmosphere is without arrogance, the dralas begin to join in and share their greater sanity.

When the warrior-students experience an environment where the dralas are present, where reality is present, where the possibility of sanity is always there, they can appreciate the mountains, clouds, sky, sunshine, trees, flowers, brooks, the occasional cries and laughter of children. That is the main point of invoking drala: to appreciate reality fully and properly. Arrogant people can't see intensely bright red and blue, brilliant white and orange. Arrogant people are so involved with themselves and they are competing so much with others that they won't even look.

When you are fully gentle, without arrogance and without aggression, you see the brilliance of the universe. You develop a true perception of the universe. You can appreciate green, nicely shaped blades of grass, and you can appreciate a striped grasshopper with a tinge of copper color and black antennae. It is so beautiful sitting on a plant. As you walk toward it, it jumps off the plant. Little things like that are not boring sights; they are new discoveries. Every day you see different things. When I was in Texas a few years ago I saw thousands of grasshoppers. Each one of them had its own approach, and they were striped with all sorts of colors. I didn't see any purple ones, but I saw copper, green, beige, and black ones, with occasional red spots on them. The world is very interesting wherever you go, wherever you look.

Whatever exists in our world is worth experiencing. Today, perhaps, there is a snowfall. There is snow sitting on the pine trees, and we can watch as the mountains catch the last rays of sun above their deep iron-blue foreground. When we begin to see details of that nature, we feel that the drala principle is there already. We can't ignore the fantastic situations in the phenomenal world. We should actually take the opportunity, seize it on the spot. Invocation of the drala principle comes from that fascination that we have, and that we *should* have—without arrogance. We can appreciate our world, which is so vivid and so beautiful.

Meeting the Dralas

JEREMY HAYWARD

W E EXIST IN A SPACE OF INSEPARABLE AWARENESS and energy. Even the words *space, energy,* and *awareness* are only concepts that point to an essentially unconditioned and unbounded presence.

This space of energy-awareness is both outside and inside of us, because the distinction of "outside" and "inside" does not apply to it. It cannot be conceived, but it can be experienced now, directly and personally.

Most spiritual traditions recognize this simple presence. And it is compatible with scientific fact, though perhaps not with what most scientists want to believe. This common realm also manifests as physical energy that enlivens and nourishes our body/mind. It is important to understand this if we are to overcome the split between "spirituality" and the "ordinary world" we experience with our senses.

Chinese *chi gong* and Tai Ch'i masters demonstrate the physical effects of this basic energy-awareness, which they call *qi* or *ch'i*. The shared space of energy-awareness shows in subtle perceptions and communication that many people experience and are sometimes called "extrasensory," but are actually quite ordinary.

The sixteenth-century Chinese sage Wang Shihuai explains:

The name "mind" is imposed on the essence of phenomena. The name "phenomena" is imposed on the functioning of mind. In reality there is just one single thing, without any distinctions of inside and outside and this and that. What fills the universe is both all mind and all phenomena.

Students wrongly accept as mind the petty, compartmentalized mind that is vaguely located within them and wrongly accept as phenomena the multiplicity of things and events mixing together outside of their bodies. Therefore they pursue the outer or they concentrate on the inner and do not integrate the two. This will never be sufficient for entering the Path.

Fundamental energy-awareness is the ground of all that is, and within it new patterns and meanings arise constantly in a self-created cosmic display.

The world that we perceive and think we know, with all its boundaries and distinctions, is just the surface of reality. It is an elaborate play, like a holographic sound and light show, but including smell and the other senses. And our bodies and minds, feelings and perceptions, and the "things" that make up our world, are all part of that show. Nothing has a fundamentally separate existence.

This grand dance is happening everywhere and throughout time, at every level from the infinitesimally small to the infinitely large. You can see the dance in a swarm of gnats flitting back and forth in the last rays of the evening sun, in the force of a hurricane as it sweeps the coast, or in the majestic but momentary burst of a comet in the night sky.

You can see the cosmic dance in the smallest thought flitting repetitively through your mind, in the movement of a herd of animals, or in the compassionate action of a great leader. There are also energy patterns that are not so obvious, but that you can feel when you are willing to open to the unexpected in your world.

*

When we open our heart/mind/body to our real, direct connection with the sacred world, we tune in to energy patterns that are like the veins and arteries of the world, carrying the world's life-energy.

The energy of the world courses through these channels, and since we are part of that world, the energy of the world runs through our veins and arteries and nerves as well. When we can feel those energy patterns, we can draw upon the nourishment and power of the unseen fullness supporting the world of superficial appearances.

We can feel these energy patterns in the quality of things. When we see only the surface appearance of separate things, we deaden them, and the world becomes flat and meaningless. But if we are open to the connections among things and to the quality of things—the blueness of sky, solidness of rock, swirlingness of wind, hauntingness of a loon's cry—then we feel their energy. We feel it running through us so that we can respond to it, and it can respond to us.

I am not talking about anything dramatic here—no sudden flashes of cosmic light or visitors from outer space. I am talking about responsiveness to subtle energies through which we can communicate with the sacred world.

This principle of communication is found in almost every human group as far back as we know. The principle is found in the ancestors, helpers, and spirits of the Native American tradition; in the pagan gods of the Greek, Roman, Germanic, and Nordic peoples; among African tribes and Australian aboriginals; in the Japanese *kami*, which are the basis of the naturalistic, shamanistic Shinto tradition. In every culture we find human collaboration with these cosmic energies.

Like electricity, the energy patterns themselves are fundamentally neutral. Whether the outcome of collaboration is beneficial or harmful depends on the training and intention of the people involved. In the Shambhala teachings, living patterns of energy that we can feel and with which we can communicate are called *drala*s.

Drala is a Tibetan word that means "transcending enemies." The "enemy" in this sense is the aggression that creates boundaries and territoriality, that severs the world so that one part is separate and hostile to another.

The drala energy of the world is not fundamentally separate from your own energy and wisdom. You can feel it when you go beyond the self-imposed limitations in your own perception. You may feel the world as strange beyond the cozy boundaries of the familiar, yet at the same time it is brilliant, energetic and sacred. Everything is included here. There is no separation between "sacred" and "profane."

There are energies connected with space and the elements, and energies attracted to particular places. Some places seem to have more power than others. When you are open you can discover these places and take care of them. There are magnetic spots, or power spots, on the earth where the energy can be felt almost as if it were tangible.

Some people can actually hear the hum of the earth at such spots. There are such power spots wherever you look. If you open your heart and mind and then look at a hillside on the opposite side of the valley, your eye will naturally gravitate to particular spots where the energy of the hill is concentrated. It is as if the landscape has nerves running through it and these spots are the nerve centers.

Animals naturally find the power spots of a place—cows in a field tend to congregate around them, deer sleep on them, birds land on certain trees. A majestic outcropping of rock; the small group of ancient trees standing on a patch of high ground; a quiet pool in the middle of a forest, fed by a series of waterfalls—all can be places for the drala energies to arrive.

Often, these places have very healthy vegetation, sometimes lots of wildflowers. Ancient monasteries and churches were often built on these places. Such spots can be places of healing and power, exuding tremendous energy. They are places where we can invoke the patterns of energy—good places to build a house, or to sit and be healed through our connection with the earth.

When we restore our connection with the energies of the sacred world, we restore our harmony with what dwells on, in, and above the earth. And in turn we are nourished and strengthened through that connection.

Kenchen Thrangu Rinpoche spoke of the dralas in a talk at Gampo Abbey, the Buddhist monastery founded by Trungpa Rinpoche, who presented extensive teachings on connecting with the dralas. Thrangu Rinpoche told the students:

> Trungpa Rinpoche said to me that although there was great development of wealth in the Western world, through a lot of manufacturing, mining of the earth and so forth, much of the vitality of the land had been harmed, and because of that the dralas had departed.

As a method for restoring the vitality and healing a wounded situation he had given the practice of dralas, so that people could bring brilliance and dignity to their physical world and body, potency to their speech, and courage and strength of heart to their minds. He gave these extremely important instructions so that from the point of view of both spiritual activity and worldly activity, people could experience brilliance and dignity.

How, then, can you begin to connect in practice with the drala energies of your own life and environment? Appreciating sacredness begins by taking an interest in all the details of life. Even seemingly mundane aspects of your life—where you live, what you wear, what bowls or plates you eat from—can contribute to this overall sense of sacredness and the feeling of the presence of the dralas. When we appreciate the world, we experience it as sacred and want to take care of it.

The drala energies can enter into empty places, gaps in space or in time or in thought. A small opening in a rock can have an intense living quality; a moment of silence is often called "pregnant," for good reason. Whatever creates a gap in our thoughts—a sacred space, a powerful object, a moment of sudden recognition of connection, an auspicious coincidence, repeating patterns of a ritual—if we are present to these places and moments, we may encounter the living energies of the dralas.

Mythologist Joseph Campbell was in Japan for a conference on religion when he overheard another American delegate, a social philosopher from New York, say to a Shinto priest, "We've been to a good many ceremonies and seen quite a few *kami* shrines, but I don't get your ideology, I don't get your theology."

The Japanese paused as though in deep thought and then slowly shook his head, saying, "I think we don't have ideology, we don't have theology . . . we dance."

To invoke the dralas you have to pay attention, especially to the patterns in your life. When something sudden happens in your life it cuts through your habitual daydreams, and if you pay attention, it could wake you up.

It might be just a flash of color abruptly calling your attention; it might be the sudden sound of a siren a block away; it might be a brief moment of silence in a roomful of chattering people. Or it could be a forceful turn of events in your life, like losing a job, hearing of the death of a friend, someone insulting you out of the blue, a check arriving in the mail . . . anything. If we pay attention to these things we can hear the dralas.

We can open to the drala energies if we are willing to listen to our intuition and willing to give in to it. Perhaps we have a strange feeling that a friend is in trouble and needs a call from us, or we feel uncomfortable as we are driving that all is not well at home. We may feel a sudden urge to begin a new form of artistic work, or an intuition that we should form a business partnership, or seek a friendship with a relative stranger. We should pay attention to these intuitive feelings.

Simple experiences like this may not seem to have much to do with patterns of energy. But it is precisely that intuitive insight, that sense of knowing without knowing how we know, that is the inner ear with which we can hear the dralas.

These energies do not abide permanently in a place, but they arrive and then depart in their own time. So waiting and repetition, perhaps in ritual and ceremony, are important aspects of invoking the energy of the dralas.

Ritual can be simply sitting paying attention to your breath repetitively, over and over, perhaps for days and weeks, going through boredom and fear. It can involve fasting and sleeplessness, and endless repetition of spoken phrases, drumming, chanting, dancing, and so on. Or ritual can be practicing a skill—working with brush strokes, wood chisel cuts, or musical scales. Perseverance and repetition, with joy and humor and playfulness, not solemn religiosity, is key to invoking dralas.

If we refine and cultivate our environment, we invite energy into it. We can invite energy into specially reserved, protected spots. In Japan, for example, the countryside is filled with small shrines to the *kami*, placed at such power spots.

Every garden and home has at least one shrine marking the power spot of the garden. The shrine is not elaborate; it could be nothing but a rope or a group of rocks marking off an area. Or it could be a small wooden dwelling with an opening in which to place flowers.

These energies are attracted to an environment that is uplifted and elegant, spotless and loved. You don't have to have an expensive home, but wherever you live, you can take care of it. You can keep it clean, uncluttered, maybe adorn it with fresh flowers, as if to welcome an honored guest.

You could create a special space in your home—a special room or simply a small corner of your apartment. You could place a flower arrangement there, and a calligraphy or picture. This can be your sacred place to practice in. If you take care of that place, simply going there can create a gap in thought and bring freshness and energy into your daily life.

If we take an attitude of loving care toward objects and spaces in our life, their sacredness shines out and attracts further drala energy. When you care about something you take care of it; when you care about someone you take care of him or her. Your continued care for the objects and people in your life maintains the drala energy and keeps it contained. Otherwise it seeps out and the connection is lost. If you treat your world kindly and gently, with affection and appreciation, that makes a lot of room for energy to enter and remain.

Likewise, treating our own body with care and affection attracts dralas. How we dress, clean, and nourish our bodies affects our state of mind, heart, and energy. We don't have to wear expensive clothes or eat extravagantly, but we can dress and eat with an attitude of respect and appreciation for our bodies.

This includes a certain quality of formality. We lose our connection with the energy patterns when we become completely casual. Special scarves, lapel pins, or hats attract energy—anything we wear around our head and shoulders that uplifts us.

We need to be inquisitive and look into things more; to listen to people, to frogs, to the sounds of rain; to see deeply rather than glancing at things casually. We need to let our hearts be touched; to stop thinking about things as problems to be solved and start appreciating the magic and mystery of our life. If we live our life with these attitudes and intentions, then we attract the dralas so that they can help us wake up to the harmony, beauty, and power of the sacred world.

DEFENDING
SENTIENT BEINGS

❊

What Can I Do?

VANYA PALMERS

WE HUMANS ARE OPTICAL ANIMALS; we relate to the world
predominantly through our eyes. So it's not surprising that it was
a picture that first triggered my interest in animal rights. It showed a
monkey in a "restraining chair," immobilized in the technical surroundings of screws, wires, and plexiglass. My one-year-old daughter probably
had something to do with the fact that this picture grabbed me. In the
frightened, confused face of the monkey I saw—not just with my eyes but
with my heart and body—the face of my daughter. It haunted me for days
and nights.

Up until this point, I had not been particularly interested in animal
rights. Of course I didn't think we should mistreat animals, but I left it to
elderly ladies who doted on their pets to worry about animal rights. As
for me, my primary concern was *bodhicitta*, the mind of enlightenment,
and my social conscience was appeased by writing letters for Amnesty
International. But looking at the monkey's face, I felt that something was
very wrong, and I wanted to know more about it. At that time, I was
living at Tassajara Zen Mountain Center, and our contact with the outside world was limited to the mail and the monthly town trip.

It was Peter Singer's book *Animal Liberation* that gave me the information and the language to talk about what was burning inside of me. In
1982, educated and motivated by this excellent book, some friends and I
at Zen Center started an organization called Buddhists Concerned for

Animals, and over the next few years we published several newsletters. We used donations to send Peter Singer's book and other material to all the North American Buddhist centers we knew of.

When it was time for us to leave the monastery and return to the marketplace, our opportunities increased. We gave talks, showed slides and videos, organized rallies, conducted anticruelty investigations, filed lawsuits, and networked with other concerned people.

In terms of outreach, the Buddhist part of our name eventually outlived its usefulness. We also felt the need to concentrate our energies in order to be more effective, and so we chose to focus on the relatively unknown subject of factory farming.

Brad Miller, a fellow practitioner at San Francisco Zen Center, founded the Humane Farming Association in 1985, and it turned out to be a tremendous success story. (I can say this without self-praise, because by that time I had returned to Europe.) With 70,000 members and a dedicated core group, the Humane Farming Association now has the muscle and political weight to effect real change. The Boycott Veal campaign, for example, has been putting a lot of pressure on farmers to stop the extremely cruel treatment of calves who spend all of their short lives locked in dark boxes too small for them to turn around in, and the campaign has reduced veal production by 60 percent nationwide.

After getting settled again in Switzerland with my wife and daughter and helping to establish a Zen center here, I was ready to turn my attention back to animal rights. This time it was pigs.

I wanted to learn how pigs would live without human interference. The pig is the smartest of domestic animals, somewhere between a dog and a monkey in terms of intelligence. We are told that the pig has been domesticated for so long that it has lost most of its original instincts. But students of ethology (animal behavior) in Europe started a project in which pigs from a commercial pig farm were released into a large, nearly wild territory. Within hours, they started to behave just like their wild sisters and brothers. They formed packs of several adults and their offspring, and built themselves nests.

Pigs have highly differentiated sound communications and tight family bonds. When the mother pig is ready to give birth, she withdraws from the group and finds herself a protected place where she builds a special soft nest, about six feet in diameter and several feet deep, out of ferns, moss, grass, and twigs. If she is on a factory farm, she looks frantically for a place to build a nest, postponing giving birth for several hours. In nature, she and her litter remain apart from the group for about ten days. She suckles her piglets for about sixteen weeks, and they stay with her until they are grown. If a nursing mother dies, the piglets are suckled by another sow in the family. The males leave the family group at about a year, while the females remain. If the group becomes too large, it divides in two.

On a factory farm, baby pigs are separated from their mothers at three or four weeks of age. At this point their tails are cut off, their canine teeth extracted, and the males are castrated—all without anesthetic. They are put into dark, crowded cages with slatted floors, where they will spend the rest of their lives living just above their own excrement. Pigs are famous for their sensitive noses. They can smell roots and insects two feet under the ground, which is why they make such good truffle hunters. Factory pigs live with no sun, no jumping, no grasses, no wind, no mother, and no escape, until the final nightmare of transportation to the *parinirvana* of the slaughterhouse.

We spent three years studying the technical details of factory farming and the law, lobbying, holding endless meetings, breaking into locked buildings, filing charges over a hundred times against agricultural schools, farms, and administrative departments; organizing rallies, writing articles, informing the public with slide shows and videos, and staging dramatic direct actions. For me, one of the most satisfying actions was showering the Swiss capital of Bern with down feathers (from old pillows) to protest the import of "battery eggs," which are eggs from chickens who live their whole lives in wire cages with an eight-inch square per chicken. Battery eggs were outlawed in Switzerland by public vote twelve years ago.

Another one of our actions is to take live piglets, eight to twelve weeks old, to schools and public places. Most people have never met a pig except on their plate, and children especially love to feed and scratch them and play with them. We make an event out of it, with T-shirts, balloons, and things to paint, cut out, and glue together. For this we have a little bus and a wagon for the pigs.

We have also created a forty-five-second spot film which is shown in movie theaters as our finances allow. The first shots are of free-range pigs building a nest, and of piglets jumping and playing in the woods; then come pictures of screaming pigs locked in separate cages; and the last shots are of a group of animal rights activists ranging in age from twelve (my daughter) to eighty. A narrator's voice asks people to eat less meat and to support our work for animal rights.

We've done other things, too. A friend came back from Russia with a film about fur-farming, which he was able to show on Swiss TV during prime time. A few days later we organized a simultaneous demonstration in every city in Switzerland, in which people poured red paint on the sidewalks in front of fur shops. This action received good press coverage and good response from the public.

A few weeks ago I was on a retreat with Sister Phuong, the Vietnamese nun who works with Thich Nhat Hanh, and I asked her about this kind of aggressive action. She said that the spirit in which we act and speak is of crucial importance. I'm happy to report that throughout the action at the fur shops we were joyful and peaceful.

We've also had a good time recently with His Most Serene Highness, Prince Hans Adam II of Liechtenstein. His land holdings in Austria contain that country's largest pig factory. He may not even have known this before, but he certainly knows it now. After unsuccessful attempts to have a dialogue with him, we filed suit, charging him with cruelty to animals and with false advertising. (His labels claim his pig factory is "animal-friendly," "ecological," etc.) We distributed photographs of the princely pig cages to every household in Liechtenstein. The largest daily newspaper in Switzerland picked up the story and gave it big headlines.

But in spite of three years of activism, the conditions for pigs on factory farms in Austria and Switzerland haven't changed much, and it doesn't look as if they will in the near future. So our new focus is to urge people to eat less meat and dairy products, and we do this by educating them as to the destructive effects of eating meat on their health and the health of the whole planet.

A few months ago, a friend of mine who is a Catholic priest in Vienna brought a Zen master from Morocco to visit me, accompanied by six practitioners. They were friendly, and experienced in the practice. But I couldn't help feeling distressed when, at dinner, all of them ordered heavy meat dishes. It's hard for me to understand how such awake people can have what seem to me to be such blind spots, but I know that cultural conditioning and lack of information have a lot do with it. I didn't say anything at dinner, but later I had a lively correspondence with the Moroccan Zen master, an open-minded man in his seventies. I argued that it wasn't just a question of the precept of not killing (although Shakyamuni considered it important enough to put it at the top of the list). Eating meat causes problems that didn't exist 2,500 years ago, or even a few decades ago, just as the nuclear threat, global warming, and the ozone hole didn't exist. I sent him pictures, and once again, these were the persuasive argument.

The suffering inflicted in the course of today's meat production is enormous, and I can't imagine that anyone who learns about it would want to support it, least of all a Buddhist.

May all beings be happy!

Universal Chainsaw, Universal Forest

ERIN VOLHEIM

HEADWATERS FOREST IN NORTHERN CALIFORNIA contains six virgin groves of old-growth redwoods, and is home to many endangered species. This 60,000-acre ecosystem was logged by Pacific Lumber in a relatively sustainable manner until 1985, when it was taken over in a hostile buy-out by the Texas-based Maxxam Corporation, whose CEO is Charles Hurwitz. At that point Maxxam began logging at an alarming rate in order to pay off Hurwitz's debts resulting from a savings-and-loan failure.

For over ten years, concerned citizens have ben protesting the destruction of this precious forest. While Hurwitz is awaiting trial for the S&L failure, the government has arranged to buy 7,500 acres of Headwaters for $380 million, an acreage that falls far short of the 50,000 acres that would constitute a biologically viable forest. The terms of this deal allow Maxxam to cut the remaining 52,500 acres with no restrictions or consideration of endangered species habitat. Activists are asking for a debt-for-nature swap, whereby Hurwitz would pay his debt by giving all 60,000 acres to the government for conservation. Activists are also pressing for an effective Habitat Conservation Plan.

In the middle of a September night, our caravan of cars transporting twenty Zen students is stopped by a thin man with scraggly long hair wearing a rain poncho, jeans, and cowboy boots. We are at the end of the off ramp to Stafford in Humboldt County, a small town five hours north of San Francisco. Motioning with a cup of coffee toward a grassy lot, he tells us where to park. Instead of waiting for a ride to the Headwaters rally base camp a half mile away, we decide to walk into a night of light rain.

For some, Zen training and activism don't mix, but for the members of Ecosattva, they are inseparable. Ecosattva is an affinity group formed at Green Gulch Farm, the Zen center in Marin County where most of us live. "Eco" means home and "sattva" means being, and so we are "homebeings." A week before the rally, to prepare us for the possibility of civil disobedience, trainers from the Bay Area Coalition for Headwaters came to Green Gulch and gave us a nonviolence training, and during that half day we realized how well we worked together as a group. A strong vow to examine our relationship to world suffering shone through.

Walking quietly down the street of this rural area, we see signs on fences that say "Trespassers Shot" and "This Family Supported by the Timber Industry." Most of these residences are owned by employees and retirees of Pacific Lumber (PL), the largest employer in the area. Some of these workers wake up earlier than Zen students to drive trucks laden with ancient redwood trees to lumber mills, like the one in Carlotta thirty minutes away. They have a steady outdoor job with good pay, yet overnight, thousands of strangers are streaming into their neighborhood to protest the cutting at their job site, also known as Headwaters Forest, Strangers like us are asking them to reconsider their livelihood and the scruples of the company they work for.

At the same time we walk this street, a red tree vole nibbles on redwood needles in her treetop home an hour south of Stafford, in the

60,000 acres of the Headwaters Forest complex. Several trees over, a pair of endangered marbled murrelets, seabirds that nest only in inland old-growth trees, are sleeping. Government biologists have designated the next day as the end of murrelet nesting season, and this means Pacific Lumber will now have the legal right to cut in the oldest groves, whether the birds fly to the ocean on schedule or not. That's why the Headwaters rally has been planned for this weekend.

The endangered spotted owl calls to its mate while hunting the northern flying squirrel, and in the Elk River's rain-teased pools, threatened Coho salmon drift. After several more years of clearcutting there will be no more Headwaters Forest, no shelter for all this life. Originally there were 2 million acres of old growth redwood forest here; now only 5 percent remains.

Our questioning mind leads us along the back country road to the Stafford base camp. We sign in at the entrance table and admire the organizers' thoroughness. Scouting out a place for a group camp, we pass by hundreds of cars, trailers, and campers. On the far end of the acreage we find a large clearing, and we set up our circle of tents. It is after midnight. We are tired but excited. We don't know what will happen in the morning. We learn that there may not be massive civil disobedience this year. In 1996, 1,033 citizens were arrested for crossing onto Pacific Lumber's sawmill property in Carlotta, but this year the local sheriff's department has announced that only protesters who cross a police barricade will be arrested. Since this entails touching a police officer, it can be considered assault, resulting in a felony charge. The news is disheartening. Our sense of our role in the rally is muddied by the possibility of a long jail term and potential violence. But we can still act as witnesses and support the collective effort. Around 2 AM a heavy rain drives us to bed.

The morning sun touches our soggy tents with its bright heat, waking the light sleepers. In five hours the noon rally will begin. Some of us get breakfast at the free vegan kitchen.

While chatting in the kitchen tent over stale bagels, we find out that the rally will be held right here at the Stafford base camp and that civil disobedience for today is discouraged. We also hear that the National Guard is on call in the town of Carlotta, the site of past rallies. So, to avoid a violent confrontation there, we will stay where we are and rally on the thirteen-acre base camp site donated by a Stafford resident. This resident's support for the protest was amplified by the loss of his house in January 1997. A mudslide caused by a Pacific Lumber clearcut destroyed his home. Six other families lost their homes due to PL's negligence, and the stripped hills may slide again this winter. To prevent further tragedy, demonstrators are filling sandbags down by the Eel River adjacent to the base cam property. Later that afternoon a chain of people will pass along these sandbags one by one until they make a protective wall around a Stafford resident's house.

Unknowingly, we have arrived at our final destination. We go to the sound stage to announce that the Buddhist Peace Fellowship is inviting everyone to an 11 AM meditation. With the BPF banner strung on a fence above our sitting spot, we form a circle in the grass around a makeshift altar. We begin with twenty people, and soon the circle grows. As we sit still in the midst of hundreds who are talking, singing, playing drums, and blaring announcements from the sound stage, we experience pure silence. By the end of the period there are at least fifty people chanting the *Metta Sutta*.

Soon after the sitting, the rally begins. Singing, dancing, and inspirational speeches fill the Eel River valley. Grandmothers, neo-hippies, Christians, homeless people, loggers, lawyers, and Zen priests move their bodies to the music of Bonnie Raitt and others. This looks a lot like any summer festival in California.

In the afternoon we gather under BPF banner and start to walk back to Highway 101. Giant puppet representations of Bill Clinton and Charles Hurwitz bob on sticks behind us while drums urge us onward. People dressed like trees are surrounded by a dancing spotted owl and murrelet and salmon puppets, with a lumberjack and his ax not far behind. Up ahead are the police officers in riot gear blocking the freeway ramps. They stand in defensive formation with clubs in hand and hefty cans of pepper spray on their belts. In this peaceful march, people sing and call out their pleas for these old redwoods and all they represent. "No compromise—60,000 acres!" echoes as we walk through the underpass. Soon we reach the demolished houses and mud-filled yards lined with silent police and flashing police cars on either side. The sandbagging of a resident's house is in process. In the end, a check from Headwaters activists for $10,000 is given to Stafford residents to help with rebuilding.

There is a saying at Green Gulch Farm: "Working hard, accomplishing nothing." The Headwaters Forest has not been saved. We had many expectations for this journey, and every event broke free from our grasp. There was no climax, no dramatic accomplishments. But the intimacy of our group experience engendered powerful feelings, and the future will tell us about the connections made at the rally. We will learn whether our dedication sparked the interest of others. The impact on police, residents, PL employees, and one another is a slow-burning ember.

We came together at Headwaters to honor our bodhisattva vow to benefit all beings. We sat together to affirm our commitment. We marched together to give legs to our despair.

The Rainforest as Teacher
A Conversation with John Seed
WES NISKER FOR *Inquiring Mind*

THERE ARE MANY GATES TO THE GATELESS, and many ways to learn about the Way. John Seed gave up his practice of insight meditation after the rainforest suddenly took over as his teacher of truth. In the last decade, since hearing the call of the wild, Seed has become a leading environmental activist as well as a theoretician and teacher of deep ecology. He travels around the world organizing and leading groups called the Council of All Beings, a workshop he developed with Joanna Macy based on her despair-and-empowerment work. The Council of All Beings uses ritual, visualization, movement, and breath work to help people overcome their narrow anthropocentric views, and to experience interconnectedness with the earth and other life forms. According to Seed, this radical change in human consciousness is required if nature is to survive.

INQUIRING MIND: Begin by telling us about your background in Buddhist meditation.

JOHN SEED: I did several meditation retreats in Bodhgaya, India, in 1972, two with S.N. Goenka and one with Tibetan Lama Yeshe. Then I went back to Australia and continued to practice, and meanwhile began looking for people to join me in forming a meditation community. We built a meditation center near Lismore and New South Wales, and I began organizing retreats. Just after a retreat led by Christopher Titmuss in 1975, we organized Bodhi Farm, which was a meditation community. From 1972 until 1979, I did several ten-day meditation retreats every year, and kept up a regular daily practice, and that was the foundation of my life.

Then in 1979, although I had no conscious interest in the issue, I got involved in a demonstration to save a rainforest located about five miles down the road from where I lived. Somehow I found myself involved in what turned out to be the first direct action in Australia—or in the world for that matter—in defense of the rainforests. All of a sudden, the forest was inside me and was calling to me, and it was the most powerful thing I have ever felt. Very soon after that I stopped meditating. My practice just dropped away. I wasn't looking inside anymore. And I didn't have any particular explanation for this. I must say, at first it caused me quite a lot of anguish, and for a while the only reason I was sitting was some kind of vague dread or guilt that if I stopped something terrible would happen. But all the other motivation to meditate had gone, and pretty soon the guilt was gone too, and then I was just out there in the world of direct action. I was getting a very strong message from the rainforest and I followed it.

IM: So now the rainforest is your practice?

JS: Definitely. I receive great spiritual nourishment from the forest itself. Furthermore, I have the scientific understanding that we humans spent 125 million of the last 130 million years evolving within this rainforest, and that our cells and our very psyche are infused with the intelligence of the forest. The fact that the forest communicates so strongly to me is not surprising.

What also turned me toward the forest were the statistics I began reading from the United Nations Environment Program and from various ecologists, which indicate that we are the last generations of human beings that are going to be in a position to turn this thing around—to prevent the destruction of complex life on earth. That kind of information burnt away all the distractions in my life, the kinds of things that at one time had been obstacles to my meditation practice. But again, it was not so much the intellectual knowing as it was just being in the forest. That experience was what made it possible for me to apply myself to the environmental work with a kind of urgency and commitment that I was never able to apply to my sitting practice.

IM: Do you feel your meditation practice had anything to do with your subsequent involvement in environmental work?

JS: I have no doubt that it was the same warm current that led me from LSD to meditation, which then picked me up again and took me into the forest. My sense is that I'm not getting lost from the path. This is what I'm meant to be doing. Perhaps one day that current will pick me up and I'll start meditating again. I haven't lost confidence in the practice. It's just that I was led somewhere else.

IM: Do you find any correspondence between meditation and the environmental work you are doing now?

JS: I think I developed some qualities in meditation that are very useful in environmental work, such as being able to focus on the process rather than the goal. That is very useful, since the fruits of environmental action can be pretty bitter at the moment. For every forest we save, we can't help but notice that a thousand forests disappear. So the sitting practice taught me how to work joyously without seeing any sweet fruits of my action.

There is also a definite correspondence for me in the realization of no-self. I find myself surrendering completely to the rainforest. The closest thing to meditation practice for me now is to lie down in the forest when it's dry, cover myself in leaves, and imagine an umbilical cord reaching down into the earth. Then I visualize myself as being one leaf on the tree of life, both as myself personally and as a human being, and I realize that the sap of that tree runs through every leaf, including me, whether I'm aware of it or not.

I don't believe this to be a mystical notion. It's very matter of fact. In reality, every breath of air we take connects us to the entire life of the planet—the atmosphere. I feel it very physically. I'm part of the water cycle. The sun lifts the water up into the atmosphere and then it comes down, lubricating and giving life to everything. Eighty to 90 percent of what I am is just this water.

I help organize and lead gatherings called the Council of All Beings, and the exercises we do at these gatherings give us a sense that we are not so much a personality as an intersection of these great cycles. We begin to break the illusion of being separate from the rest of creation. I can lie on the ground and feel the vibration of this earth which gave rise to me and which has sustained my ancestors and everything else for four thousand million years in incredible intelligent harmony.

It's only recently that I as a human being have lost the ability to dance to that tune which promises hundreds and thousands and millions of years of continued evolution. I started creating my own tune, the human tune, which has become so loud in my ears that I can't hear the sound of the earth's cycles or the music of the spheres. We need to check into those other tunes through ritual and ceremony, or else we sign our own death warrant and the death warrant of everything around us. We can't replace the life support systems. We can't destroy the atmosphere or the water or the soil with impunity.

IM: It sounds as though these exercises and rituals you've created for the Council of All Beings are designed to give people a visceral feeling or actual experience of being a part of the earth and the various cycles of nature.

JS: That's right. And when I first started doing this, I felt so separate from nature that I thought it was going to be a huge undertaking, that it would be a vast voyage before I could reconnect. But to my amazement, I found the illusion of separation to be very flimsy, and that there are just a few conceptual filters that prevent us from reuniting with the earth. Just hold your breath for two minutes and you will understand the illusion of separation. There's no separation possible. We're constantly cycling the water and air and earth through us. Furthermore, we don't walk on the earth. The air is part of the earth. We walk *in* the earth. It really helps if we realize these things.

Recognizing our connection with nature is very simple and accessible regardless of where we are living. We may think we're surrounded by concrete and plastic, but then we think a little further and realize that the concrete is sand and the bodies of shellfish. The plastic is a product of the rainforest laid down during the carboniferous era 130 million years ago and turned into oil. Look just under the surface, and the unnaturalness of things starts to disappear.

That's what we work on in the Council of All Beings. We present a series of rituals and ceremonies intended to dispel the illusion of separation and alienation. All indigenous cultures have, at the very center of their spiritual life, similar kinds of ritual and ceremony that acknowledge and nurture human interconnectedness in the larger family of life. What has happened to modern humans is that we have become arrogant. It stems perhaps from the Judeo-Christian idea that we are the center of it all, the crown of creation, and the rest of the world is just resources. We look at the nature rituals and ceremonies of indigenous people as nothing but primitive superstition and pagan mumbo jumbo. We think we're enlightened, and that means we are above nature, and out of that arrogance we are threatening to destroy ourselves.

Everything about our society is based on this idea of ourselves as specially created apart from the rest of nature. We don't have to believe this intellectually to be completely enthralled by it. As long as we think of "the environment" we are objectifying it and turning it into something over there and separate from ourselves. Even if we don't believe in any particular theory of economics, our whole life is conditioned by an economic system based upon the principle that the earth has no value until human labor is added to it. The earth is just a bunch of dirt, and we are so clever we can mold that dirt and turn it into spaceships and into great long electric wires to carry our messages. We think we are the miracle, and we've refused to recognize the miracle of the dirt which composes us. Any miracle that we have is only miraculous because we are made of this incredible dirt—miracle dirt which will agree to do everything we ask of it. We refuse to recognize any of that. All that we know is, "Aren't I fantastic?" That's our downfall.

IM: It also sounds like the Council of All Beings is a kind of therapy group for existential despair.

JS: It's interesting that you mention therapy, because I've recently met a couple of therapists who share similar attitudes, and we're going to write a few articles for the community of therapeutic professionals. We will start with the assertion that most therapies don't work, and the reason for that is because the self they are trying to heal is a fiction. It's a social fiction. There's no such thing as this "self." It's an illusion, and you can't heal illusions. The actual self that requires healing includes water, air, and soil. And if we think we can conceptually deny that reality and remove a piece of it and heal it, then we are bound to fail. We are ignoring the act that we are polluting and destroying the cycles which, in a very fundamental way, compose and underpin the very personality we are try-ing to heal. My experience is that when people have a profound awaken-ing of their interconnectedness with nature, the healing of the personality just follows. You don't have to concentrate on that anymore because you are engaged in the larger concern of evolution. A lot of the things that troubled me so much about myself while I was meditating don't disturb me any longer. I don't know whether I've solved anything. I've even for-gotten what was troubling me. I can't remember what it felt like to have any kind of interest in personal enlightenment. But now I feel very happy and alive. I feel like I don't care what happens to me.

IM: Perhaps nature is teaching you the same thing that meditation pro-poses to teach.

JS: And maybe the sitting made it possible. I feel very supported by the fact that people like Gary Snyder and Joanna Macy, who have a much more solid Buddhist practice than me, also share my feelings and concern for nature.

IM: Have you considered the extinction of the human species, or even the earth itself, as a natural phenomenon, a part of evolution?

JS: Of course, everything dies, and we're going to have to let go of this planet sooner or later. The sun is going to go into nova in four thousand million years, and then the earth is going to fry up in a crisp. So what am I going to do about it? Tear my hair?

Once I was swimming at sunrise on the coast of New South Wales when I was attracted to a rock that was covered with incredible life: sea weed, crabs, shellfish. And as I began to embrace this life, all of a sudden I was embracing the living rock underneath, and I could feel the molecular continuity between the rock and the life it was supporting and my own physical being. I experienced that all of the molecules and atoms were the same, and that somehow the rock had the potential and, I would have to say, the desire or the propensity to transform itself into all kinds of soft stuff, like seaweed and human flesh. I realized that the sharp distinction between cellular life and what preceded it was actually just in my mind. The universe was miraculous and seamless. The miracle didn't start when humans came along or for that matter when life began. When a bolt of lightening fertilized the bowl of molecular soup, it was ready and waiting. I have a visceral understanding of this process, and a deep feeling of connection. Therefore I don't have a great deal of anxiety about the result.

I was afraid to accept that realization at first. I struggled against it. I was afraid that I might lose my motivation by letting in the good news that everything was all right whatever happens. The atoms which had done this before, for whatever imponderable reasons, were obviously capable of doing it again. And nothing I did could touch those bigger processes.

But my motivation to save complex life was undiminished by this realization. Somehow I have surrendered the interests of my personality. I say regularly to my DNA, "Just tell me what to do. I'm working for you now." I'm not working for "the man" anymore.

The music that evolved me for four thousand million years—I can hear that again. It says to me, "Save the planet. Save complex life. Protect biological diversity. Try and keep gene pools intact wherever possible. That's what I want you to do."

Then I think, well, maybe the earth is dead already, and we're the decomposing bacteria or the maggots, and it's our job to eat the corpse, to multiply until the corpse is totally consumed. What if that is the case? Then here I am, this reluctant maggot, not doing my job of consuming the resources of the earth as fast as possible. It's actually the James Watts and the Ronald Reagans who are doing their job properly. And I'm just some kind of a demented maggot that refuses to fulfill its role because of some weird ideas that have come into my head. So, maybe it will take five minutes longer to consume the corpse because I am dragging my heels. But maybe the final decision hasn't been reached yet. Maybe it's in our hands.

Meanwhile, what I notice is that when I live committed like this, my life is full of joy. I was sitting on a train in Tokyo on my way to do a Council of All Beings and I looked around at the people on the train, the wealthiest people in the world, and saw that they were so unhappy. I don't want that life. My life feels very joyful and exciting to me right now. In this day and age, if you end up with a joyful and exciting life, feeling at one with all things, you really can't complain, regardless of the outcome.

Guarding the Earth
A Conversation with Joanna Macy
WES NISKER AND BARBARA GATES FOR
Inquiring Mind

INQUIRING MIND: In the Nuclear Guardianship Project, you call for citizen involvement in the responsible care of radioactive waste. How are the teachings of mindfulness incorporated into guardianship training to help us and future generations participate in the guardianship of the waste?

JOANNA MACY: Mindfulness teaches us that we don't have to like something to look at it. We can actually free ourselves from constantly saying, "This is terrible, isn't this disgusting?" or "I can't stand this." Mindfulness helps us disidentify. We don't have to approve or disapprove of what we're being mindful about. Whatever we're looking at is just there. And this stance helps us a lot in being present to it.

Neither government nor industry has an impressive record in preparing people for working with the "poison fire" (what we call radioactive waste). The training is notoriously sloppy. Along with training in technical procedures, *mindfulness* is the training that is required. You and others who do sitting practice have been engaged in guardianship training already, and you didn't even know it!

IM: After having looked deeply into ourselves, we then have more capacity to face anything.

JM: Exactly. To look at the external poison fire will be a piece of cake after having confronted some of what comes up within us. It builds courage. The Tibetan community that I've been involved with invited me back to India this past summer to instruct me in a practice that they consider important for dealing with the poison fire. It has to do with building fearlessness.

You see, if you're going to watch the poison fire, then you have to find out if there's anything else you'd rather not see. In other words, you can't watch the poison fire if you're keeping inner toxic wastes buried out of sight and out of mind.

IM: Could you give a more specific example?

JM: I remember thinking as I prepared to go to India: Okay, kiddo, you want to be able to look at the poison fire, then you've got to be able to face the horrors in your own life, too. And—pow! Once that willingness was there, a buried memory surfaced that was extremely painful. I had virtually erased that experience for almost fifty years. When it came up, flooding me with grief and rage, it felt like it would undo my life—challenging all my beliefs in sanity and decency. I thought, Oh, Joanna, all these years that you've gone into religion—into biblical history, then world religions, then the Dharma and meditation—was it just to prettify reality? Was it because all the while you sensed the horror at the heart of it all?

When I went to India, I told the Rinpoche, "I've lost my sense of what end's up, and my faith that there are objective structures to reality." He just beamed and said, "Very good. This is going to save us a lot of time." He knew, of course, that if you're attached to an ideology or a faith system, it'll get in the way of that guardian eye, of that capacity to be totally, radically present.

JM: How did the Guardianship Project come into being?

IM: I've been in a kind of dance with radioactive waste for the last fourteen years. Back in Washington, D.C., in 1978 I engaged in a citizens' lawsuit to stop faulty storage of high-level waste at a nearby nuclear reactor. While our citizens' group lost its case against the Virginia Electric Power Company, working on the suit taught me a lot. Night after night, to substantiate our legal claims, I had sat up studying the statistics, trying to understand the phenomenon called ionizing radiation. Not only does radioactivity cause cancers, immune diseases, stillbirths, sterility, and genetic mutation, but the wastes that release this radioactivity are frighteningly mismanaged.

This introduction to the enormity of the problem also led me to develop the Despair and Empowerment work that I have conducted around the world during the intervening years. I tried to confront our capacity for denial. I could see how we as a society were ready to turn our faces away from the radioactive waste, as well as other horrors we didn't want to see. For me this became the big koan, the big mystery—have we finally created something that we cannot face?

In 1988, I began to study the issue of radioactive waste in a more systematic way. I called ten friends together: a nuclear engineer, a poet, an environmental lawyer, a cosmologist, a psychotherapist, some ordinary folks like me, and said, "Will you work with me for six months? We'll meet once a month to study and teach one another about radioactive waste, and, because it's so hard to look at, we'll blend together the three S's: study, strategy, and spiritual practice." In the process of studying the poison fire, our "guardian group" learned how voluminous and pervasive the problem truly is.

IM: Can you give us a hint to the dimensions of the problem?

JM: It's difficult to find a way of describing it that we can digest or relate to. . . . As Ralph Nader's organization stated in a recent overview: the radioactivity generated by nuclear waste every year in the United States alone—and we only have a quarter of the world's reactors—is equal to

240 times the radioactivity released by the Chernobyl disaster. And don't forget that this radiation has a hazardous life of up to 250,000 years. Some of it, like the nickel in reactor containments, lasts for *millions* of years.

Now statistics about the waste are misleading because of what they *don't* include: Everything connected with the fuel cycle and nuclear-weapons production becomes radioactive. Nuclear waste is not just some by-product; every building, every truck, every pipe, every piece of equipment every step of the way becomes not only contaminated but contaminat*ing*. In that sense, the poison fire is almost mythic in nature. Like King Midas in his greed, it transforms what it touches.

And nobody wants to look at it, even many environmental activists. On Earth Day 1990, radioactive waste was barely mentioned. We allow ourselves to believe that there's nothing that we can do—except, as the government proposes, bury it deep under the ground.

IM: What are the potential problems in burying the waste?

JM: In burying it, we are pretending to ourselves that we have a final solution to the problem. We are saying to ourselves, all right, now we've buried it, and it's gone. We don't need to think about it anymore. But there is no final solution here. No containers last as long as the radioactivity they contain, and when sealed off underground, they will be inaccessible for repair and replacement. After you bury them, the casks corrode, the earth shifts, and the radioactivity seeps into the ground water. For instance, in the case of Carlsbad, the radioactivity will seep into the Pecos River, into the Rio Grande, and on out into the Gulf of Mexico.

When I was at Los Alamos last month, I learned that a group of scientists who had worked on Star Wars are now busy exploring ways that nuclear waste might be transmuted. They've actually found a way on paper to do it. They figured out how that by using a half-mile-long accelerator, you can add neutrons to the nucleus of radioactive waste elements. At the present time, the process would be prohibitively expensive, but it may someday be feasible. Perhaps we may even get smart enough to do something beneficial with the waste. These scientists now recognize that the waste must be kept accessible, and that if we hide it, we can't get it back to transmute it.

Some antinuclear activists want to wish the waste away; they say,

"Not in my backyard!" This in known as the NIMBY syndrome. Others call for a new Manhattan Project, a mammoth government research campaign to develop practical technology for the transmutation of the waste. I say, that's great, go ahead. But meanwhile don't lose sight of the fact that we already have the technology to contain the waste. It's a technology of the heart. It's a technology of mindfulness. All we need to do is to pay attention to it. Thanks to present machineries of monitoring and repair, this attention will be sufficient to keep the radioactivity out of the biosphere and out of the bodies of living beings. But *no* technology for long-term care exists if it subtracts the essential factor of human intention and involvement.

IM: What is a potential scenario for guarding it and containing it?

JM: We decide that for the sake of the future beings and for the sake of this generation, too, we're going to take care of the poison fire. That means wherever it's generated, we keep it on-site. We don't transport it because the transportation is very risky. We've already had hundreds of accidents on the highways with this stuff. So local communities take political responsibility for citizen-controlled guardianship, both in the decisions about how to handle it and in actually overseeing the monitoring.

IM: Describe what would happen at a Guardian Site.

JM: At these Guardian Sites, the waste containers would be religiously monitored and repaired. This means continually watching, testing the soil, testing the water and air. It means to repair as embrittlement, leaks, and seepage occur. The people who would be doing the technical work would be the nuclear engineers we've been training over the last fifty years. In addition to the technicians, countless others—people like you and me—would go to the Guardian Sites as well to support the technicians and ensure public safety. We would also be guardians.

As a species, we humans have always honored the extraordinary gift of attention. Because attention to the poison fire would ensure the health of all beings and our genetic continuity, it would be a sacred act. And it would be viewed as such.

The Guardian Sites—Rancho Seco, Three Mile Island, Hanford, etc.—would become places of attention and remembering, of remembering the story that produced the poison fire. You might go on a pilgrimage to, say, Seabrook or Rocky Flats to pay homage to the guardians or for the spiritual renewal involved in this act of homage. You might go for the great Remembering, because it is there that the stories are told about how we almost destroyed our planet with nuclear weapons and nuclear power.

When I think about how beings of the future will relate to our radio-active legacy, an unexpected danger occurs to me: the danger that they may not take seriously the toxicity of these wastes. The beings of the future need to believe the danger, that is, believe that their ancestors knowingly produced plutonium that cripples and kills for one quarter of a million years. They will have to come to terms with that.

IM: And the future generations need to remember this again and again because they could easily convince themselves that no one could ever have unleashed something so awful.

JM: Yes. We cannot uninvent the nuclear technology, so we must remember what happened at Alamagordo, at Hiroshima, at Nagasaki, at the testing site in the Nevada desert, what happened to the people around Hanford. This must be enshrined in our collective memory so that we can learn from it and be vigilant.

The challenge for the beings of the future will be in accepting what their ancestors have done, and for that acceptance to occur, a measure of forgiveness will also be necessary.

So these sites will be places of remembering, of acceptance and for-giveness. They will also be places of moral vigilance. We might go to them for merit. We might go to offer gifts. And, just as we now go to Barre or to Spirit Rock for meditation retreats, we might go to a Guard-ian Site for meditation practice, or to teach meditation—because we need, at these places, to harness the technology, so to speak, of cultivating vigi-lant awareness. I don't see the practice of vipassana as being undercut or invalidated by doing it at a Guardian Site. Quite the contrary. There would be times of intensive practice, watching what comes up in the body and mind. Then there would be shifts for watching the monitors. It's like when you're in a monastery, you sit and walk and sit again, and then you go out and sweep the temple compound. You sweep up every piece of trash and you do that very, very attentively.

So this poison fire would be watched, and that very act of attention and commitment to life would not be that different from the spiritual practices that people have seen as valuable over the millennia.

In the coming times, I imagine, people will look back at our religious traditions and notice how much they feature fire. In the Old Testament, there's Moses and the burning bush; you can't get too close to the fire. In the *Bhagavad Gita*, there are the great flames of Vishnu when Krishna turned into fire on the battlefield. If I were looking back from a future perspective, when our spiritual calling was to guard the poison fire, then how would I read these scriptures? I would say, "Oh, these were given to us to help us have the courage and understanding to guard the poison fire."

The guardianship of this poison fire can continue through generations that will wonder if perhaps this was a sacred gift given to us to help us wake up.

IM: So perhaps the shape of the nuclear cooling tower will become the shape of the new temple . . .

JM: After the guardianship idea took hold in my mind, I went on a pilgrimage to Three Mile Island. It was in 1984, five years after the accident there. As I was coming down from our summer cabin in Central New York into the Susquehanna Valley, I imagined bands of future pilgrims coming down to the great monastery at Three Mile Island. I came over the hill and looked down to the river. My God! I saw the island in the Susquehanna and these enormous cooling towers. They take your breath away. I experienced a rush of awe, the way you feel looking at a pyramid or Chartres cathedral. I could see how people in the future (if we make it so that there *are* any people in the future) might look at these towers. They dwarf everything else, and rise in a sweeping curve like giant vases set down by the gods.

I called up the utility company and said, "I'd like to come visit the plant because I'm writing a story about it." They said, "You need to write a letter requesting a visit and then we'll let you know." And I said, "I'm only here for one more day." And they said, "What kind of story?" And I said, "It's a story about the future monastery at Three Mile Island." And they said, "Oh, it's fiction!" "It's not fiction," I said. "It just hasn't happened yet!" And they said, "If it's fiction, we don't see why you need to come, because you can make it all up." And so I said, "Well, the citizen groups I've talked to have been very helpful, and *they* were happy to talk with me." Then the authorities said, "Okay, okay, okay." They sent a car for me, and I went and spent the day.

It was an amazing day. They began showing me more and more. They had taken the lid off the reactor where the accident had occurred and lowered a video camera in. They had just screened the video for the first time. So they said, "Come on, you've got to watch this!" On the screen I could see a landscape of cliffs and rubble. My guide pointed: "Now, those are the remaining fuel rods, and this shows it really was a meltdown. . . ." I said, "This experience that you are accumulating is so important for all of us, because you are among the first to deal with the problems of cleanup, and this is going to be the big preoccupation of generations to come. I hope that you realize how valuable your work is and let us all know about it."

I recognized then that the people working to clean up the utility were guardians, but they weren't treated as such. And right near here, in Sacramento, there is a Guardian Site at the Rancho Seco nuclear plant even though its employees don't know it. They're sitting there guarding the highly radioactive fuel rods because the reactor has been closed down by popular vote.

IM: But these nuclear technicians haven't been through your guardian-ship training. In addition to mindfulness practice, what other training is important for guardianship?

JM: At our guardian group meetings, we use imagination to help us get our minds around the nature of this waste. For example, at our last meeting, one of the members had made a huge map of the United States. It filled our living room. We moved back the furniture, spread it out, took off our shoes, and walked around on it. On the map you could see all the nuclear reactors, the uranium mines, the radioactive dumps, and the transportation routes to bring the waste to Yucca Mountain and Carlsbad, etc. We did a drama right on the map where we identified with the poison fire in a particular site. This was such an amazing learning tool. In the process, we were building our moral imagination. That has to be trained as well. We have to build the moral imagination to imagine what is already at hand. We must imagine the real because the world we've created is so outrageous that we have to use our imagination to even believe what is so.

We must also use our imaginations to encompass the time span of the poison fire and its effects. In our guardian group, we've become interested in the question of time itself and in those philosophers and mystics who were looking beyond chronological time to other dimensions where things are simultaneous. We've discussed the way chronological time is a function of our kind of consciousness. When we develop packets for organizing guardian groups around the country and around the world, we plan to include ways of exploring this. I've already been doing workshops on time, or, as we call it, "deep time." We're going from deep ecology to deep time. Deep ecology occurs in deep time; it means that we not only dependently co-arise with other beings now, but with beings of the past and future as well.

IM: With radioactive waste and the war in the Persian Gulf and the effects of these on beings of the future . . . the whole space-time continuum is like a Guardian Site.

JM: Yes. I have come to see that the guardian stance, the intention to sustain the gaze, is necessary to the guardianship of our earth, at every stage.

One of the things that has scared me the most about the war in the Persian Gulf is how ready we humans are to lie to each other. As they say, "The first casualty of war is truth." We see this in the administration's speeches and press conferences, and we see it in ourselves; it's easier to accept a lie than to look at our own doubts, our own pangs, our own sense of dread about what this war might be. So we ride along with the Pentagon's reports and the current spasms of patriotism, but inside us is a yearning for fresh air.

Truth is as precious as air when someone has got a pillow over your face or is holding your head under water. And if we do nothing else but just protect our capacity to see truth, we're doing crucial work. We're never going to be able to self-correct from our disastrous course if we don't keep the feedback loop open. We need to maintain true contact with the world out there, so we don't get mesmerized in our own dream.

IM: What an incredible task. If we're going to really look at nuclear waste or at the war, then the enormity of our greed, hatred, and delusion is exposed. This could be extremely painful.

JM: Yes, but we can reframe our pain as compassion. As we open to our anguish, we can see it as our ability to share in the suffering of our world. And that is the literal meaning of compassion: to suffer with. This transmutes the pain into the power to act.

At a conference in New Mexico, a psychiatrist who had been at a presentation of the Nuclear Guardianship Project made this comment: "Just to hear about the possibility of relating to nuclear waste in this way is healing, regardless of what the practical steps may be. Until now, we have felt such a deep, unconscious shame about what we have created, material that will poison the world and the DNA of future beings for the next three million years. It has cut us off from our future—from a spiritual relationship with future generations. So when we hear about the Guardianship Project, an intention springs up—the intention to be responsible—and we think, 'Yes, I can watch the radioactive waste.' At that moment within us our relationship with future generations is healed." That moved me a lot, because it put into words what I've felt—and what has been motivating me all along.

*

HOME
PRACTICE,
WILD PRACTICE

The snow across the river glows, and the rocks and peaks, the serpentine black stream, the snows, sky, stars, the firmament—all ring like the bell of the universal Buddha. *Now!* Here is the secret! *Now!*

—*Peter Matthiessen*

INTRODUCTION

✻

CENTURY AFTER CENTURY, SEEKERS OF TRUTH have been drawn to the unadorned teachings of the natural world. Chinese hermits in high mountain huts, Thai monks in rain-drenched forests, and now American students of Dharma backpacking in open country—all follow a time-honored path. To integrate spiritual awakening and ecological awakening is to become part of an ancient lineage of nature practice.

Home practice, wild practice can mean many things. Thunderstorms, icy winds, a line of geese across the sky, the heart's pulse in a warm body—what is *not* practice with nature? Paying attention to everything that comprises a place, or a self, or a breath is an inexhaustible lifetime practice. To practice with nature is also to learn the myriad faces of suffering and impermanence, to penetrate the secrets of abundance and no self. In garden or forest, city park or meadow, deep insight can arise spontaneously, vividly. All my relations! No separation!

At the turn of the twenty-first century, wild nature is disappearing at an alarming rate. Entire species and ecosystems are severely threatened. Global needs for food and water are putting pressure on every remaining acre of arable land. Citizens, corporations, and whole societies show widespread disregard for the most minimal standards of sustainability and right livelihood. In the space of a generation, the world has already lost a catastrophic proportion of its biological riches.

What is effective practice under these unprecedented circumstances? Aspiring green Buddhists attempt to answer this question at home, in communities, and in the wild, inventing and adapting practice forms to include environmental concerns. Patrick McMahon takes walking meditation into the Sierra Mountains; Elias Amidon brings mindfulness to a shopping mall. Gardener Wendy Johnson struggles with the dilemmas of pests and compost; Peter Matthiessen seeks answers tracking the elusive snow leopard. When spiritual discipline and ecological sensitivity inter-sect, perception of place and other beings is significantly enhanced. As these authors explore and reflect, they open up new paths for Buddhist environmental practice.

Religious traditions in many ages have promoted specific food prac-tices as links to spiritual well-being. The concluding essays of this section examine ways to practice in relation to food, food production, industrial agriculture, eating meat or no meat. It can now be demonstrated that most acts of producing food cause some ecological harm. In the complex global marketplace, how can one minimize suffering? Helen Tworkov, Philip Glass, and Bodhin Kjolhede discuss ways to become more con-scious of the food choices one makes. Taking these concerns into the world of economics and public policy requires an even greater commit-ment. Gary Snyder writes:

> To nourish living beings, we must not be content simply to have a virtuous diet. To save all beings, we must work tirelessly to main-tain the integrity of these mandala-like places of habitat, and the people, creatures, and Buddhas who dwell in their palace-like spaces.

Ecological practice requires dedication and creativity. Spiritual awakening is both a goal and a path. Wild mind, earth mind, bodhisattva mind—how can these ripen together?

＊

The Attentive Heart

STEPHANIE KAZA

BREATHING IN, BREATHING OUT. Slow deep inhale, slow deep exhale. Quieting the body, quieting the mind. I woke up this morning under the graceful, arching branches of bay laurels and Douglas firs. All night the trees have been conversing under the full moon, weaving me into their stories, capturing my dreams with their leaning limbs and generous trunks. Breathing together as I slept, as they rested, we danced quietly in the summer night. Their great confidence framed a circle for my waking; their sturdy presence offered an invitation to be still.

I arrived last night to join others on retreat in a small community in Anderson Valley near Mendocino. On this flat, gentle river bottomland the trees have grown up in easy conviviality, nurtured by floodplain water and the protection of the valley. Below the knoll the creek winds its way through a lazy channel, limpid with the slow movement of late summer. The central grassy area is open and spacious, framed by the comfort and stability of trees. Tall, straight redwoods and firs emerge above the rounded coast live oaks, bays, and madrones, filling the sky with quiet companions.

Inside this large ring of trees lies an island of stillness, a protected area in a war zone. These several hundred acres have been designated for slowing down, for listening to the calls of the heart. Their purchase was an act of intention on behalf of trees and people, that they might find a more peaceful way together. Up and down the valley, stands of redwoods are being turned into lumber and cash at an alarming rate. The tension over trees in this county is palpable. The high price for rare clear-grained heartwood is a driving force behind more and more logging. The economic machine justifies and perpetuates the killing in this war. For some the price is too high, since logging also causes fragmentation of wildlife habitat, severe soil erosion, and widespread loss of salmon runs. The battle involves private property rights and the defense of ecological integrity. Tree lovers prefer the trees alive; the timber companies want them dead. The two desires are completely incompatible.

The meditation retreat, however, is not about trees; it is about the attentive heart, the heart that feels the presence of others and the call to respond, the heart that lives in relationship with other beings. The attentive heart is not a purchasable item; its value cannot be measured in economic terms. The capacity for compassion and response grows slowly from cultivation and practice. In this retreat we are practicing the traditional Buddhist methods of mindfulness and intention. Breathing in, breathing out, with awareness, over and over again, we are trying to pay attention to what we are actually doing moment to moment. The instructions are simple, but the practice is very difficult. The mind is so naturally slippery, so deftly agile, so quick and ready to dart off in any new direction. To notice even ten breaths in a row seems an impossible task. Like practicing scales on an instrument, watching the breath can be tedious, even boring; and in this lies the great challenge to keep coming back, to keep trying to settle the scattered mind.

Though there is no escaping the local tree war, I find it stabilizing to focus on one activity, one motion at the center. Breathing slowly, the monkey mind finds a place to rest, to empty out, to pry loose from the paralyzing traps of self-absorption. After an hour of sitting silently, we step outside for a period of walking meditation. Each time the mindfulness bell rings, we pause and breathe deeply three times, noticing the detail of where we are. We walk so slowly, it actually makes me laugh. The retreatants look odd drifting across the lawn like misplaced jellyfish or banana slugs. One step, breathing in, one step, breathing out. Paying attention to the feet, paying attention to the breath, noticing the body moving through the landscape.

I walk with bare feet, soaking up the sunlight in the grass, crinkling the green leaves with my toes. In the center of the soft lawn I bump into the roots of an old Douglas fir stump. A tiny oak seedling has taken shelter in a crack of the stump, drawing on the tree's remaining nourishment. The tree roots protrude a few inches above the ground, marking the space of its former water territory. Worn and smooth, they are like firm hands touching my feet. My feet, the tree's feet—we meet each other in the deep breathing that connects body to ground. I touch the tree's presence by walking the length of its roots. Next to the ephemeral exuberance of the grass, the roots provide depth and grounding, a testimony to the history of the tree.

In the slow time of meditation I practice observing each sound with attention. A bumblebee on the lawn works the tiny plantain blossoms, methodically gathering the morning pollen with self-absorbed buzzing. A large blue dragonfly whirs through the open air. Up in the trees scrub jays squabble with squirrels over territorial rights. Acorn woodpeckers call back and forth, scolding intruders. Each sound is surrounded by a generous spaciousness. Each sound is connected to a specific individual and event. In the silence of walking I hear each relation.

Cultivating this practice of mindfulness is painstaking and demanding. In each moment of observing a leaf, a squawk, a firm touch, there is the temptation to make it something more than it is—an object of fascination, a delirium of nature bonding, a symphony of deliberate orchestration. There is also the danger of thinking it something less than it is, missing the context and history of the tiny event striking the senses. Either way one falls off the impossibly thin razor's edge of bare attention. Fall and return, err and correct. Like riding a bicycle, the mind aims for balance, seeking to stabilize the wobble between the pulls toward falling.

Each step, listen, breathe. Each step, note what is actually happening. It is difficult to hold the tension of these instructions in my body. I want to run away from them, hurl myself horizontally through space rather than drop vertically through time. Slow people moving like molasses on the lawn—we are all so serious about this! Couldn't I go up and tickle someone? Wouldn't it be fun to break their attention with peals of laughter? I feel impatient and mischievous with the slowness of this practice. Breathe, relax, observe the mind of resistance. Slowing down again, I walk with grass, roots, sky, clouds, watching the emotional waves rise and fall, surge and pass away. Emptying out of self-referential ideas, emptying out of the tendency for distraction, I am trying to maximize the possibility of being completely here. But every second there is a tug in the web that pulls on my attention.

Loud, heavy, gear-grinding, gas-guzzling noises invade the island of stillness. My body tenses. I recognize the sound of a logging truck on the local transport route between forests and cities. I know more than I want to about the sound of this logging truck. The roaring engine sets off an internal alarm tied to fear, protectiveness, uncertainty, helplessness. *The forests! the forests!* the voice of concern calls out. Breathe, walk, listen, observe. The tension sinks into my stomach and tightening hands. I try to stay present to the whole causal net, to the desire to escape it, to the tension of the conflict, to the sense of threat to my survival. I know the trucks are carrying trees stripped naked into logs, their arms hacked off and left to rot or burn. I know that a logging operation can quickly turn a living forest community into an unofficial burial ground. I imagine the trucks as hearses in a long and very drawn-out funeral procession. A wave of great grieving washes over me. I struggle with this slow walking, torn between acting and not acting. It seems like an indulgence to take the time to cultivate mindfulness when so much is being lost.

But this is the tension—to find a considered way of acting not based on reaction. Building a different kind of sanity requires a stable base for careful action. It means being willing to know all the dimensions of the reality of destruction, being willing to breathe with the tension of emotional response, being willing to cultivate tolerance for unresolved conflict. This nonverbal form of ethical deliberation depends on the careful work of paying attention to the whole thing. Meditating, walking slowly, calming the mind by centering on the breath—these painstaking, deliberate practices increase the odds for acting intelligently in the midst of crisis.

The bell sounds to close the period of walking meditation and to begin the break. I am longing to shake off the tension of the logging dilemma. Between the orchard and the kitchen, a small path drops over the hill and winds through a sloping oak woodland. I follow it intuitively toward the low places, hoping to find water and the company of alders. To my delight my first encounter on the floodplain is an exquisite and abundant community garden, source of our soups and salads. Six-foot tomato plants droop with the weight of juicy red fruit, a fencerow of peas hang ripe for the picking. The quiet eye leaps for joy at the brilliant orange and yellow chrysanthemums, coreopsis, and poppies. After a morning of silence and restraint, my senses feast on the stimulating sight.

Past the lettuce, past the eggplant, past the zucchini, I aim for the faint sound of water over rocks. My feet want to stand in cool water, my hands yearn to splash wetness on my face. Stepping over the cowpies and fallen oak twigs, I leave the path and wander down to a shallow stream. Warm and almost stagnant, the water is barely moving. Near an over-hanging alder the creek is a foot deep; I slip out of my meditation clothes and into my fish body. Wriggling, squirming, splashing, cleansing—for a few moments the existence of suffering is a distant thought. The tension of human confusion slides away; I bask in the apparent simplicity of animal life.

Stretching out in the midday sun, I let go of the strain of knowing so much and paying attention with such discipline. I doze on the warm rocks, resting like a lizard. Wavering on the edge of consciousness, my mind drifts with the sounds of the stream and the warmth of the sun. Thoughts skim across the surface, finding no anchoring place in the pond of my imagination. The tension of acting/not acting is swallowed up in a yawn as I turn on my back to face the full sun.

By late afternoon we have been sitting and walking silently for several hours. I fight it less, willing now to just do the practice, just put in the time. The logging trucks still roll by with disturbing regularity, but the day has ripened, slowing my reactivity and emotional responses. The accumulation of warmth and sunshine has softened the field of green bordering the trees. My companions walking slowly across the lawn seem more like trees than people; they are less awkward, more comfortable, less ruffled around the edges. We are absorbed in the practice of remembering where we are, remembering our relations, noting the suffering of ethical tension. It takes time to see the deeply encoded patterns of destruction and transgression against trees and other nonhuman beings. It takes time to cultivate a relational sensitivity that is compassionate and not pathological. It takes time to embrace wholeheartedly the complexity of living with trees.

I find some comfort in our communal clumsiness. We each stumble along the uncharted path. Practicing with others is a useful antidote to the isolation of insight. We walk together sharing the silence, giving each other support as we investigate our lives. We forget and remember, moment after moment, each of us making an effort to deepen our capacities for observation of self and other. By learning in community, we practice breathing in a circle of friends and companions. Against the backdrop of ecological uncertainty, this retreat seems like a very small contribution of attention. Though I cannot know how it will affect the large-scale patterns of social relationships with trees, I make an effort anyway. The choice to practice awareness, over and over in each moment, is the cultivation of intention, a quiet, fierce kind of passion that supports the capacity to act with restraint.

Old tree stump, young oak sprouting, jay, and woodpecker—with your company I am just breathing, just walking, trying not to stumble on the irregular terrain. In this steady silence I ask for help to walk more gracefully, for patience to cultivate an attentive heart.

Meditating with Mountains and Rivers

PATRICK MCMAHON

I SOMETIMES FORGET THE MILES Shakyamuni Buddha walked before sitting down under the Bo Tree, the seat of his enlightenment. Recently returning from a week of walking practice in the Clan Alpine Range of central Nevada, I'm vividly reminded of his long path.

In the middle of the night, it seems, I'm startled out of sleep by a long wail. There it is again . . . and again. I lie in my sleeping bag and wonder: railroad whistle, animal, bird, or the trumpet of the Last Judgment? Then it comes back to me. This is the Mountains and Rivers backpack sesshin, and that's the wakeup call. I stick my head out the tent. Starlight illumines stones and sagebrush and the surrounding hills. My companions are already up and meandering their ways toward the meditation circle. No time to lose. I dress, splash water on my face, and stumble after them. Putting down my cushion in the circle, I scrooch knees into gravel, straighten the back and pull my woolly hat over my ears. The bell sounds us into silence.

For a decade now, once or twice a year, for a week at a time, I've been walking the trails of California, Nevada, Utah, and Wyoming with my Zen sangha. We call these excursions Mountains and Rivers sesshins, after the *Mountains and Rivers Sutra* of thirteenth-century Japanese Zen master Dogen. Pioneered in North American by poet Gary Snyder, these "gatherings of the mind" bring the practices of Zen—sitting, walking, chanting, Dharma discussions and interviews, cooking, and cleaning—out of the meditation hall and into the open.

Each spring and summer we get out our topographical maps, assemble provisions, pack gear, and head for the back country. On foot once again, we rediscover the Way as a literal trail, of gravel and sand, dust and mud, pine needles and pumice. We remember that realization is not fixed, but moves with every step.

Likewise we experience once more the particular nature of this Mountains and Rivers practice, not set down in a fixed and unvarying form, as temple practice sometimes seems to be, but evolving. Going over the ancient ground, we freely find new ways, trying what works, abandoning what doesn't. Too much walking, too little sitting? We revise. Too much talking, not enough silence? We shut up. Too much silence, not enough communication? We speak up.

I'm warm enough as long as I'm sitting, but when we stand for walking meditation the morning chill slips through my layers of clothes to tender skin. I brace myself against the desert just outside this small circle of humans. Inevitably, though, in the rhythm of the morning meditation— sitting, walking, sitting, walking, sitting, walking, sitting—the imagined chasm between me and the cosmos closes, and I become almost comfortable.

It's with reluctance, then, that midway through the meditation block I abandon the comfort of the meditation circle for an interview out there in the darkness with my Zen teacher. Ours is a koan practice, of trying to make sense of the seemingly nonsensical words of our Ch'an and Zen ancestors. This morning I'm particularly tangled in those words, and even though disinclined to face the cold and dark, I need help. As I sit in the waiting line, my confusion, the darkness, and the cold fuse into one hard ball. Before long, though, I find myself settling into this shelterless place too: after all, in the desert at this hour, where is there to go? By the time I hear the teacher's summoning bell I'm warmed and ready. Candle lanterns light the way along a dry creekbed to an opening between a stunted tree and a large stone. I enter, bow, locate my man in the shadows, sit down across from him, and enter into the ancient give and take.

When we walk far enough, we hike clear out of twentieth-century North America into central India, 500 BCE. Seeking the closest possible contact with the trail, we contact our Dharma ancestors. Like us they diligently sought release from delusions separating the self and all things; like us they earnestly explored for Dharma gates admitting them to re-union. Confronting delusions that seem inexhaustible and gates that seem impossibly narrow, we follow the trail they blazed. Gratefully. The ways of getting lost in this wild tract are countless.

At the end of our morning's meditation, under a lightening sky, we say our bodhisattva vows, so brave and poignant in all this space: "Beings are numberless, I vow to enlighten them . . ." We shuffle to the dining area where the cooks have set out a pot of steaming water. I take my cup of tea up the hill to where the sun is just peeking over the horizon. If I have a favorite moment of the schedule, it's this, this edge between night and day, stillness and movement, silence and speech.

Shakyamuni himself, of course, wasn't alone in the forest. Without the help of hermits, the hospitality of villagers, and the guidance of the best teachers and religious traditions of his day, the palace-pampered prince would soon have perished in the jungle. From them he would have learned to avoid frostbite in the mountains and heat stroke in the desert, as well as to survive the mind's extremes.

We drift back from our various edges to the breakfast circle. In lieu of the wooden clappers we use in the meditation hall at home, two stones struck together begin the meal chant. By the time food is in my bowl I'm salivating: plain oats at such a time are better than pancakes! The serving of seconds and another striking of stones signal the transition from silence to conversation. "Anybody else hear that hooting last night? . . . That must have been David thrashing around in his sleep again. . . . Nahh, that was a screech owl." We're all in this together.

After his enlightenment, Buddha, having mastered these overlapping crafts—the practical ones of safeguarding the body and the spiritual ones of cultivating the mind—walked the byways of India instructing his followers, as they in turn instructed theirs. Buddhist pioneers journeying to China, traversing the cliffs and fording the streams between the two cultures, would have required the accumulated wisdom of their Indian predecessors. Bodhidharma's legendary "coming from the West" would not have happened without that early trailwork.

In China, Ch'an Buddhism established itself on the remotest peaks, requiring monks to travel on foot for months, from one craggy teacher to another. Later yet, as Buddhism travelled to Japan, it cross-fertilized with the indigenous nature tradition of Shintoism, producing the *yamabushi*, "those who linger in the mountains." The eighteenth-century haiku poets, deeply influenced by Zen, made lengthy pilgrimages to temples and sites of natural beauty, leaving us such travel notes as Matsuo Basho's *Narrow Road to the Far North*.

Our ancestors' foot travel, slow but sure, eventually reached North America. In the 1950s, "Dharma bums" Gary Snyder, Jack Kerouac, and Philip Whalen climbed the mountains of the West and hermitted in the fire lookouts. Poets Lew Welch shuttled back and forth from a backwoods shack to San Francisco streets, "letting it all come in," the leaping deer of Idaho along with the down-and-out shoeshiners of Mission Street. With few experienced guides, practice forms, or sangha available to them, these Dharma forefathers sometimes paid dearly for their adventures. Welch, at age forty-six, walked into the mountains with a shotgun, leaving behind a suicide note. Kerouac came to an equally premature end in fame, drugs, and alcohol.

Wash dishes, brush teeth, pack up gear, break camp. Voices, laughter. The first time out with these people I wondered if this was really a meditation retreat. Did high spirits have a place in the high mountains? Since then

I've certainly found it a trick—an enlivening one to be sure—to walk the line between intensity and indulgence.

We reassemble at the blast of the conch for morning meeting. How are we doing—feet, backs, shoulders, hearts? Do we need to slow down, or can we push a little more? Though our able trail leaders know the route, from previous scouting and from educated readings of the topographical map, only we know ourselves. They advise us, rather than direct. This is a tribe, the tenderfoot among us as valued as the veteran.

Crisscrossing the planet and the mind for over two millennia, our predecessors have left us a topographical map of the Great Wilderness. That wilderness can be found even within the confines of a meditation hall. Protected by temple walls and roofs, we still encounter our uncultivated bodies and minds and the wild nature of things in general. We're dealing with enough hazards without having to worry about *Giardia*-tainted drinking water, tick-borne Lyme disease, and rattlesnakes.

Having become acquainted with the Great Wilderness inside the temple, we may at some point be moved to step into the Great Wilderness outside. Is one environment larger than another, one practice better than another? Truth is truth, practice, practice. And yet . . . and yet . . . as we squat to relieve ourselves on open ground, alert to the blistering reds and glossy greens of poison oak, something ancient awakens in us that simply doesn't on a porcelain commode.

Trail meeting concluded, we turn to Dharma. We hear from Dogen, who encourages us to forget what we think we know about mountains and walking: "Mountains' walking is just like human walking. Do not doubt mountains' walking even though it does not look the same as human walking."

"Sounds good," one of us comments. "How do we do it?" Our leader reviews the practice of mountains' walking: "When walking, lower the eyes and unfocus," he says. "No need to sightsee. No need to send your vision out to the woodpecker in the top of a tree, the flower by the side of the trail, the companion up ahead. Let the feet go their own way. They'll find their own footing without the eyes. Walk like this, and the mountain flows through like river over stone."

Enough said. We help each other hoist our packs. The bell sounds and

*we set out, very slowly. After a few minutes we break into the hiking stride
we maintain until lunch. We've talked the talk. Now we walk the walk.*

Just as in temple practice it would be folly to rank the range of activities that make up its total life, so, too, in Mountains and Rivers practice.
It all hangs together: sitting on the ground, cooking over campfires, putting up and taking down tents, trail meetings, Dharma talk, the walking
itself. However, just as sitting meditation would be the heart of the temple experience, so walking meditation would be the heart of Mountains
and Rivers.

*Everyone in the group has a job: leading, following, purifying water, keeping time. Mine is lunch preparation. As the sun approaches high noon, I
hike out ahead, and by the time the group catches up I've set out cheese and
crackers on a stone lunch table. How simple food can be! Do I really need
the elaborate sandwiches I pack in my daily-life lunchbox?*

The further we walk, the more we tend to forget whose burden is
whose, who carries too much or too little, whose problem it is keeping
up the pace or slowing down. Single file on the trail, or fanning out cross-country, more and more we do so as an organism, less and less as individuals.

*In the afternoon we again hike silently, another two or three hours. We
don't put in more than five to seven miles in a day, but where are we going,
after all? The main thing is to give ourselves to the walking, while still
getting into camp early enough to set up tents, locate kitchen, dining area,
meditation circle, and interview space, and cook dinner. If there's still time
for stretching, conversation, wandering, swimming, or bathing, that's
gravy.*

The distinctions between us and our trail mates continue to blur.
We feel ourselves in company with the haiku poets of Japan, the Ch'an
monks of China, Bodhidharma coming from the West, and finally Shakyamuni himself. We walk more than just one mile in his shoes. We
sense—through the touch of feet to the path, the ache in the shoulders,

the in and out of the breath—what it took to bring him to the Bo Tree. We have in our own eyes the soft gaze by which he saw the morning star that provoked his enlightenment. "How wonderful!" Indeed, we concur with him: "Buddha-nature *does* pervade the whole universe!"

> *The conch calls us together, and again the bells and stones guide us through our meal. As in the morning, after the first serving of food there's time for talk, but talk tapers down as we prepare for the evening block of meditation. When I put my cushion down tonight, it's in a new place. Adapting itself to each new terrain, the sitting space is sometimes elliptical, sometimes ovoid, never a geometrically perfect circle.*
>
> *After the day's hike—movement lingering in my muscles, sun still radiating in my face, supper in my belly—I don't feel as edgy as in the morning. Still, by the last sitting I'm ready for sweet sleep. As I hunker down in my bag, letting myself slip into the nighttime wilderness, the coyotes start up their ragged yipping.*

"Buddha-nature pervades the whole universe," we say. No question that it pervades the meditation hall, the office building, the hospital, the school, the dinner table, just as much as it pervades the mountains and rivers. But the whole universe of the hall, the building, the school, the table will still be confined to the extent that these environments are sheltered from cold and heat, buffered from stones and gravel, protected from bugs. Even the shelter of the Bo Tree diminishes the scope of the sky. I follow a Buddha who is endlessly walking, completely footloose.

In Search of the Snow Leopard

PETER MATTHIESSEN

November 11

IN THE EAST, AT DARK, BRIGHT MARS APPEARS, and soon the full moon follows the sun's path, east to west across a blue-black sky. I am always restless in the time of the full moon, a common lunatic, and move about the frozen monastery, moon-watching. Rising over the White River, the moon illuminates the ghostly prayer flag blowing so softly on the roof of the still hut, and seems to kindle the stacked brushwood; on its altar stone my small clay Buddha stirs. The snow across the river glows, and the rocks and peaks, the serpentine black stream, the snows, sky, stars, the firmament—all ring like the bell of the universal Buddha. *Now!* Here is the secret! *Now!*

In hope of seeing the snow leopard, I have made a wind shelter and lookout on this mountain, just at snowline, that faces north over the Black Canyon all the way to the pale terraces below Samling. From here the Tsakang mountainsides across Black River are in view, and the cliff caves, too, and the slopes between ravines, so that most of the blue sheep in this region may been seen should they be set upon by wolf or leopard. Unlike the wolves, the leopard cannot eat everything at once, and may remain in the vicinity of its kill for several days. Therefore our best hope is to see the griffons gather, and the choughs and ravens, and the lammergeier.

The Himalayan griffon, buff and brown, is almost the size of the great lammergeier. Its graceful turns against the peaks inspire the Tibetans, who, like the vanished Aryans of the Vedas, revere the wind and sky. For Buddhist Tibetans, prayer flags and wind bells confide spiritual longings to the winds, and the red kites that dance on holidays over the old brown city of Kathmandu are of Tibetan origin as well. There is also a custom called "air burial" in which the body of the deceased is set out on a wild crag such as this one, to be rent and devoured by the wild beasts; when only the bones are left, these are broken and ground to powder, then mixed into lumps of dough, to be set out again for passing birds. Thus all is returned into the elements, death into life.

Against the faces of the canyon, shadows of griffons turn. Perhaps the Somdo raptors think that this queer lump on the landscape—the motionless form of a man in meditation—is the defunct celebrant in an air burial, for a golden eagle, plumage burnished a heraldic bronzy-black, draws near with its high peeping, and a lammergeier, approaching from behind, descends with a sudden rush of feathers, sweeping so close past my head that I feel the break of air. This whisper of the shroud gives me a start, and my sudden jump flares the dark bird, causing it to take four deep, slow strokes—the only movement of the wings that I was ever to observe in this great sailer that sweeps up and down the Himalayan canyons, the cold air ringing in its golden head.

Dark, light, dark: a raptor, scimitar-winged, under the sun peak—I know, I know. In such a light, one might hope to see the shadow of that bird upon the sky.

The ground whirls with its own energy, not in an alarming way but in a slow spiral, and at these altitudes, in this vast space and silence, that energy pours through me, joining my body with the sun until small silver breaths of cold, clear air, no longer mine, are lost in the mineral breathing of the mountain. A white down feather, sun-filled, dances before me on the wind: alighting nowhere, it balances on a shining thorn, goes spinning on. Between this white feather, sheep dung, light, and the fleeting aggregate of atoms that is "I," there is no particle of difference. There is a mountain opposite, but this "I" is opposite nothing, opposed to nothing.

I grow into these mountains like a moss. I am bewitched. The blinding snow peaks and the clarion air, the sound of earth and heaven in the silence, the requiem birds, the mythic beasts, the flags, great horns, and old carved stones, the rough-hewn Tartars in their braids and homespun boots, the silver ice in the black river, the Kang, the Crystal Mountain. Also, I love the common miracles—the murmur of my friends at evening, the clay fires of smudgy juniper, the coarse, dull food, the hardship and simplicity, the contentment of doing one thing at a time: when I take my blue tin cup into my hand, that is all I do. We have had no news of modern times since late September, and will have none until December, and gradually my mind has cleared itself, and wind and sun pour through my head, as through a bell. Though we talk little here, I am never lonely; I am returned into myself. Having got here at last, I do not wish to leave the Crystal Mountain. I am in pain about it, truly, so much so that I have to smile, or I might weep. I think of Deborah and how she would smile, too. In another life—this isn't what I know, but how I feel—these mountains were my home; there is a rising of forgotten knowledge, like a spring from hidden aquifers under the earth. To glimpse one's own nature is a kind of homegoing, to a place East of the Sun, West of the Moon—the homegoing that needs no home, like that waterfall on the upper Suli Gad that turns to mist before touching the earth and rises once again into the sky.

November 12

Yesterday a circumambulating wolf left a whole circle of tracks around the prayer wall across the river, at the foot of the trail that climbs around the mountains to Tsakang, and this morning, on the trail itself, there are prints of leopard. As if seeking protection, the blue sheep feed close by the hermitage, where I go with Jang-bu to call on the Lama of Shey.

When we arrive, the lama is inside chanting sutras, but his attendant sits outside, cutting and sorting their small store of potatoes; he is an aspirant monk, or *trapa*, whose clear gaze makes him look much younger than he is. His name is Takla, he is twenty-two years old, and he comes from the great north plain of Tibet.

On the sunny ledge, under the bright blue window of the gompa, we listen to the murmurs of the lama and contemplate the prospect of the snows. Soon the mountains stir, then shift and vibrate—how vital these rocks seem, against blue sky! If only they would fly apart, consume us in a fire of white light. But I am not ready, and resist, in fear of losing my death grip on the world, on all that provides the illusion of security. The same fear—of loss of control, of "insanity," far worse than the fear of death—can occur with the hallucinogenic drugs. Familiar things, losing the form assigned to them, begin to spin, and the center does not hold, because we search for it outside instead of in.

When the lama appears, he seems glad of our visit, though we lack the gift of a *kata*, or ceremonial white scarf, that is customary on such occasions. He is an imposing man with the long hawk nose and carved cheekbones of a Plains Indian. His skin is a dark reddish copper, his teeth are white, his long black hair is tied up in a braid, and he wears an old leather jacket with brass buttons, patched with burlap homespun of strange colors. When talking, he sits with legs crossed, barefoot, but puts on ancient laceless shoes when he moves around. In the doorway behind him hangs a wolf skin that he wears about his waist, indoors, to warm his back.

✻

The lama of the Crystal Monastery appears to be a very happy man, and yet I wonder how he feels about his isolation in the silences of Tsakang, which he has not left in eight years now and, because he is crippled, may never leave again. Since Jang-bu seems uncomfortable with the lama or with himself or perhaps with us, I tell him not to inquire on this point if it seems to him impertinent, but after a moment Jang-bu does so. And this holy man of great directness and simplicity, big white teeth shining, laughs out loud in an infectious way at Jang-bu's question. Indicating his twisted legs without a trace of self-pity or bitterness—they belong to all of us—he casts his arms wide to the sky and the snow mountains, the high sun and dancing sheep, and cries, "Of course I am happy here! It's wonderful! *Especially* when I have no choice!"

In its wholehearted acceptance of *what* is, this is just what Soen-roshi might have said: I feel as if he had struck me in the chest. I thank him, bow, go softly down the mountain. Butter tea and wind pictures, the Crystal Mountain, and blue sheep dancing on the snow—it's quite enough!

Have you seen the snow leopard?
No! Isn't that wonderful?

The Buddha Got Enlightened under a Tree

RICK FIELDS

A FEW YEARS AGO, I spent a week doing a retreat next to a stream at the foothills of the Sangre de Cristo Mountains in southern Colorado. The ground rules were fairly simple: retreatants were to live as close to "nature" as possible. Instead of sleeping in a tent, I slept either under the stars or under a tarp. I didn't build a fire, but ate bread, cheese, dried fruits, nuts. I drank water from the stream, and steeped tea in a bottle warmed by the sun. I never used a flashlight and left books, paper, and pen behind.

Like any other heat-seeking mammal, I followed the sun as it climbed the hillside, and by sunset I could look out across the broad valley which, millions of years ago, was the floor of a vast sea. During the mornings, I stayed in my sleeping bag until the sun reached the stream, and then I sat under one of the great pines, and practiced, watching my breath come and go like a gentle wind. It was during one of these morning sessions that it suddenly occurred to me that the Buddha got enlightened under a tree.

This may seem obvious, at least to people familiar with the story of the Buddha's life, but it nevertheless struck me as something of a revelation. All the Buddhist retreats I had attended in America had taken place inside—in polished black-and-white Japanese-style zendos, or rough-hewn reconverted "barndos," in luminously colored Tibetan temples, or in city lofts or generic Holiday Inn conference rooms, or in cabins and maybe tents. Of course, I had walked, sat, and laid down under trees, in various states of contemplative ease, but I had never—nor had any of my fellow Buddhists, so far as I knew—meditated under a tree for a sustained length of time, as the Buddha had done.

Of course, there were good reasons for this. Sitting under a tree or beneath an overhanging rocky ledge exposes us to the weather as well as to animals and insects. In the Buddha's own time, the forests of India contained tigers, rhinos, elephants, cobras, and scorpions. Nowadays, we seem to have reduced the dangerous to the merely distracting. We stay inside to avoid mosquitoes, flies, ants, spiders, stray dogs, and inquisitive neighbors.

Yet there is another perspective. The person who meditates outside for a few days may come to see dangers and distractions as messengers. Such messengers may arrive in surprising shapes. Midway through my retreat I found myself unable to crawl out of a particularly slippery and muddy hole of self-pity—until one morning a yellowjacket landed on my bare stomach, took a good bite, and flew off. Stung into awareness, self-pity and indulgence vanished. A small but crucial turning point, it worked just as well—if not better—than the "encouragement stick" wielded by watchful zendo monitors.

A little later, crossing the stream which divided our wilderness from the civilized amenities of base camp, I noticed a snake. Like the bee that had bitten me, it too was black with a yellowish stripe: a common Western garter snake, the field guides would say. But there was something a little uncommon, even strange about this particular snake. Poised upright in an elegant S-shaped curve, it didn't move at all, save for the flickering forked tongue, black as coal with two flame-red tips. We stared at each other. A field guide might have attributed its unwavering gaze to the fact that snakes have two sets of transparent scales covering their eyes, but the intensity of its perfect stillness and the S-shaped pose made me think of the mythical *naga*s, the serpentine Indian water spirits reputed to guard treasures hidden beneath the surface of lakes and rivers. So I bowed slowly, three times, forehead to the ground, and inhaled the pine resin of the earth. Still the snake did not move. The snake just looked not so much at me as through me, as if to say, "This is how to be, this is how to keep your meditation, in the world you are returning to."

These outdoor encounters—with the yellowjacket and snake—made me wonder about the Bodhi tree under which the Buddha had attained enlightenment. In the library, I discovered that the Bodhi or Bo tree as it was known was actually one of more than six hundred species of the Ficus or fig family; that its scientific name is *Ficus religiosa*, and that it was also known in India as the Pipal, Peepul, or Ashvata tree. L. H. Bailey's *The Standard Cyclopedia of Horticulture* refers to it as "the beautiful peepul tree of India," but H. F. MacMillan, late superintendent of the Royal Botanical Gardens, Ceylon, and author of *Tropical Planting and Gardening*, writes, "The tree is practically of no economic and little ornamental value." In any case, the bodhi tree was sacred to both Buddhists and

Hindus, who believed that the deity Vishnu was born beneath it. Consequently, MacMillan wrote, "Devout worshippers will not cut or injure the smallest seedling or branch of this tree."

The present Bodhi tree, which grows in the Indian village of Bodghaya on the spot where the Buddha attained enlightenment, is very probably a direct descendant of the original tree. The Buddhist emperor Ashoka paid homage to the tree in the tenth year of his reign, 259 BCE. According to one story, the emperor's ardent veneration of the tree inspired his jealous queen to have it cut down in the night. Ashoka prayed to the tree and bathed it in milk, and the tree sprang up again with in a few days. This time Ashoka built a ten-foot wall around it. Later in his reign, Ashoka sent a cutting of the tree to Ceylon, where it was planted with great pomp and ceremony in the capital city of Anuradhapura. This tree, according to Macmillan, is "supposedly the oldest historical tree known."

❊

With time, my curiosity grew into an obsession, and three years after my retreat in the Colorado mountains, I boarded an Air India jet for the two-day flight to Delhi; then took an overnight train to the market town of Gaya, in Bihar; and hired a *tempo*—a three-wheeled motor scooter—for the final journey to Bodhgaya.

The trip had taken three or four days, depending on whether you counted the day lost crossing the international dateline. The setting sun cast a dreamy orange glow over the open fields at the edge of town. I left my bag at the Burmese Vihar, showered, and walked through the market, past the open-air stalls selling incense, candles, and red and yellow flowers floating in shallow clay bowls, in through the outer gate past the ragged line of squatting beggars and urchins, and on through the inner gate to the temple complex itself. There were many trees, at least for this part of India, and a series of stone walkways and broad worn steps descending to the entrance of the Maha Bodhi Temple itself—180 feet tall, with buddhas and bodhisattvas carved into every niche.

The tree I was looking for was, in fact, totally obscured by the temple. I came upon it, in the course of my circumambulation, behind the temple in a sanctuary surrounded by a stone fence, six or seven feet high, which could be entered through an iron gate that was now padlocked shut for the night. The tree was shapely and well proportioned, with four limbs branching out from a smooth trunk which was wrapped, on that first evening, in gold and white brocade. As soon as I saw it, the temple itself seemed reduced to the status of the merely ornamental—nice enough, perhaps, but hardly necessary.

I returned as early as I could the next morning. I was not the first one there. Tibetan monks in their rough red robes were doing prostrations on shiny well-worn wooden boards pointed in the direction of the temple and tree, along with a scattering of Westerners dressed in sweatpants and T-shirts. Tibetans, Bhutanese, and Ladakhis wearing dusty *chuba*s spun prayer-wheels and fingered beads; Thais, Sinhalese, and Burmese laymen and laywomen walked in silent contemplation or animated conversation. Japanese in white shirts and dark trousers walked briskly and snapped photos.

The iron gate to the tree was open this time. Inside were twenty or so Burmese, men and women, wearing the white of pilgrimage. Three saffron-robed monks led the kneeling group in chanting the three refuges in Pali: "*Buddhanam saranam gochammi . . .*" The oblong stone marking the diamond seat where the Buddha had sat facing east, his back to the tree, was strewn with flower petals and shaded by delicate rice-paper parasols.

Over the next few days, I often joined pilgrims from around the world as they entered the little enclosure to pay homage and perform ceremonies. The Japanese, immaculate in black robes over snow-white kimonos, their freshly shaven heads glistening in the sun, chanted the *Heart Sutra*. Burmese, Thai, and Sinhalese chanted in Pali, Taiwanese in Chinese. Tibetans lit butter lamps and hung prayer flags.

One evening I sat next to a gray-clad Korean nun who sat on her knees, back straight, eyes downcast in rapt concentration. She stayed immobile all day and maybe all night too. The Indian caretaker locked and unlocked the gate to let various groups of pilgrims in as we went on sitting on the far side of the tree. The roots had broken through the circular concrete support, and were raising and breaking out of the confinement of the stone floor. The pale green long-stemmed heart-shaped leaves trembled in the slightest breeze.

Before the Buddha came here, he spent years wandering the forests and mountains of India. According to one legend, a *deva* (or goddess) had appeared to him while he was pursuing his ascetic practices in a nearby cave, which is now the site of a small Tibetan monastery. "This is not the place for a *Tathagata* [perfected one] to perfect supreme wisdom," the *deva* had said. "There is a Pipal tree fourteen or fifteen *li* from here, under which is a diamond throne. All the past buddhas seated on this throne have obtained true enlightenment, and so will those yet to come. Pray, then proceed to that spot." And so, the legend says, "The *deva*s going before, led the way and accompanied him to the Bodhi tree."

The Buddha seated himself beneath the tree on a mat of grass. When he defeated the forces of Mara, he called the earth to witness his accomplishment by touching it with his fingers. The moment he saw the morning star rise in the east, he woke to final enlightenment. None of these events, of course, could have happened to a buddha sitting inside a temple, no matter how grand.

The Buddha spent the weeks after his enlightenment outside as well. He walked back and forth along a course now marked by a raised platform, eighteen stone lotuses representing the flowers that sprang up under his feet. He went up the hill, where "he gazed unwinking at the Bodhi tree," as a sign now informs us, for seven days.

By the time he moved to the shore of Lake Mucalinda, six weeks after his enlightenment, the monsoon had started, and a great thunderstorm arose. My Rocky Mountain *naga* had appeared in the form of a garter snake, but the *naga* king that rose from the lake to shelter the Buddha was a seven-headed cobra. Today a larger-than-life statue in the center of the lake depicts the Buddha seated in meditation on the coils of the *naga* king, whose seven flared hoods shield him from the rains like seven parasols.

Years later, the Buddha's disciple Ananda asked the Buddha if a shrine could be built in the Jetavana monastery, so that people would have a place to make offerings during his absence. As recounted in the *Kalingabodhi-Jataka*, the Buddha replied that it was not proper to make a body-shrine until a buddha had entered nirvana, nor should anyone make a shrine containing an image, "because the connection depends on the imagination only."

"But," said the Buddha, "the great Bo tree used by the buddhas is fit for a shrine, be they alive or be they dead."

"Sir, while you are away on pilgrimage, the great monastery of Jetavana is without a visible symbol and the people have no place where they can show their reverence," Ananda said. "Shall I plant a seed of the great Bo tree before the gateway of Jetavana?"

"By all means do so, Ananda," the Buddha replied, "and that shall be as it were an abiding place for me."

As time went on, bodhi trees were planted all over India and Nepal. There is one now in the deer park in Sarnath, where Buddha first taught, transplanted from the tree that Emperor Ashoka first sent to Ceylon. There is another in Lumbini, the birthplace of the Buddha—a gnarled, twisty old tree set against the stark sky. When I saw it in that desolate place, I felt heartened, as if I had come across an old friend who was making the same pilgrimage as myself.

But we cannot be too literal, about either buddhas or trees. As the Indian scholar Dipak K. Barua tells us, "The bo tree was not Ashvata in all cases, the different buddhas having different trees." And since— according to the Buddha—we are all potential buddhas, any tree can be a bodhi tree. Which means, I think, that if we want to become buddhas we have to find our own trees. Buddhas and trees come together after all.

City Practice and Bush Practice

KUYA MINOGUE

W E HAVE JUST FINISHED our first two-week retreat at Amazenji, a Zen training center for women in British Columbia. During the first week, a hailstorm took down the tent zendo as we were sitting
in it, so we had to pitch it deeper in the woods where the trees provided
a windbreak. Mosquitoes and black flies then became a major challenge.
Mosquitoes prefer the woods because it's cooler there and the wind blows
less. *Bzzzzz. Bzzzzz. Bzzzzz. Lunch!* Sometimes they swarmed so thickly
that we could hardly see what we were doing through the mosquito-net
hats we wore as we worked. It became impossible to get into the zendo
with the traditional slow monk-walk. We took turns unzipping the tent
while the next person dove headfirst through the door into the zendo.

At first we tried not to kill mosquitoes as we sat, but they made zazen
impossible. Bare hands tenderly brushed the stinging Buddhas from eye,
ear, nose, tongue, and body, but we couldn't brush them from mind. After
a long discussion, we decided to kill the mosquitoes in the zendo before
we sat, so each sitting began with our own killing frenzy. Our judgments
about local ranchers, who were gunning for a cougar that had been killing
their sheep, faded. away. *Slap. Swipe. Squash.* Dharma talks turned to the
preciousness of life, and the tough decisions the precept against taking
life brings to us.

Morning temple clean-up included gathering all the mosquito
corpses and placing them on the altar in an empty incense bowl. At midday service, we performed our version of a Buddhist animal funeral for
the mosquitoes.

"A myriad of Buddhas have left their bodies. The universe trembles
slightly."

This is not a city practice.

❋

For two years I have lived in Tsay Keh, an isolated First Nations community in northern British Columbia. Thirty houses, one general store, one

school, and one tribal office make up the town. Bears, wolves, moose, foxes, and caribou are seen regularly in the village streets. A herd of wild horses comes through to graze. Until I went for a winter hike with Bessie, a woman who has not assimilated white ways, I thought I was living in the bush.

Bessie and I traveled for hours up a skidoo (snowmobile) trail, then stopped to make a small fire to heat our tea. Bessie looked out across the caribou tracks on the frozen lake, then up to the mountains on the far side.

"Oh, Kuya," she said, "this is so good." She sipped her tea and took a bite of the bannock (fried bread) she had just cooked on the fire. A full silence entered the space between us. "I sure hate them big cities."

It took me a minute to realize that she was talking about Tsay Keh, the village with thirty houses. What to me was "living in the bush" was a "big city" to Bessie. Astounding!

I'm writing this now from the Eugene Zendo, a temple in Eugene, Oregon, that I helped to establish a few years ago. To get here, I drove for hours in six-lane, bumper-to-bumper traffic. To me, this is a "big city."

In some ways, however, there is little difference between Tsay Keh and Eugene. Both serve as centers of commerce and communication. Both present machinery noise to the ear during zazen. In both places, alcoholism, drug addiction, and family violence produce immeasurable suffering. In both places, poverty, hunger, and environmental destruction provide rich fodder for engaged practice. And in both "big cities," refuge from greed, hate, and delusion is as close as the nearest zafu (sitting cushion)—whether that zafu is in a ten-by-twelve foot log cabin, or in a fully developed, inner-city Zen center. When the incense is lit, the meditation bell rung, and the body and mind settled, there is no city. There is no bush. There is only sitting.

When I left the Eugene Zendo three years ago, I didn't know I was leaving forever. Personal karma came up for me in a very strong way, and I went to the bush to sit. I fully intended to come back. But something about practicing in the bush grabbed me, and I ended up teaching for two winters in Tsay Keh to raise money to buy the seventy-six acres of hay fields and forest where Amazenji now sits. My practice is no longer a city practice.

*

Bush practice presents many challenges unknown in the city. When women inquire about coming for retreat, I write to tell them that we have mosquitoes, black flies, bears, wolves, moose, and lynx. I tell them we have no indoor plumbing, and that they must bring their own tent or camper. I tell them we have limited water, and that showers must be taken down the road at the local campground. I never hear from most city people again. But some brave Amazons come from the city to sit with mosquitoes in a place where they must remember to dispose of their blood rags in sealed plastic containers, to avoid attracting bears. They come from the city expecting the peace and quiet of nature, and are welcomed by screeching Canadian jays, by chattering squirrels who drop pine cones on the tent zendo, by moose cows crashing through the forest, by wolves howling at night.

They go back to the city stronger, and with a deeper understanding of how the concrete and tarmac separate them from the earth and from the messiness of life. They drive back to the city through miles of clear cuts, with a fuller appreciation of the animals who suffered as their homes were destroyed. They return home with a deeper appreciation of the comforts that city infrastructures offer: water that flows abundantly from the taps, light that comes with the flick of a switch. In the city there are no mosquitoes waiting for their bare bums in an outhouse, or landing on their hands as they hold the cosmic mudra. Practice in the city seems easier. Gratitude arises for what had been taken for granted. And a deeper understanding of the habitats that cities have destroyed becomes possible. Engaged practice around environmental issues becomes more immediate.

Bush practice is not for everyone. But neither is the city. Each place has its drawbacks for practice. Each place has its offerings. It's good to be able to finish this piece of writing and then fill a bathtub with hot water that comes through pipes from miles away. But I can hardly wait to get back to Amazenji for the next full-mon retreat. Sitting zazen inside a mosquito net, while the full moon rises behind the distant hills and wolves howl in the background, I find it hard to hold on to the delusion of separation. The interconnectedness I feel when the wolf's eerie cry climbs up my spine makes this planet seem more precious. The struggle to inject wisdom and generosity into nearby logging and mining operations becomes more pressing. I see more clearly the price the planet has paid to develop and maintain its cities.

Mall Mindfulness

ELIAS AMIDON

A FEW WEEKS AGO, I FOUND MYSELF STANDING in a ceremonial circle alongside twenty-five of my graduate students outside of a large suburban shopping mall. We had come there to partake in a "Mall Quest," a journey of discovery into a citadel of our culture. This was part of a six-day training in ecopsychology practices. We had spent the previous day in a beautiful natural setting in the foothills of the Rockies on a contemplative nature walk, a practice aimed at remembering one's connections with the natural world and experiencing elements of nature as a mirror: signs and symbols of your own life's journey that are reflected from the more-than-human world about you.

But I had decided to try something new this day—to contrast the grounded wisdom achieved through walking mindfully in *non-human-made nature* with the lessons revealed through walking mindfully in that temple of *human-made nature*: the shopping mall. I always do what I ask of my students—so, not ever having tried it, there I stood hand-in-hand invoking a meditative state in front of the doors to this familiar world. One of the students spoofed a mystical chant for the occasion:

Sacred Mother Mall,
Provider of All,
Give us what we need,
Satisfy our greed.

Then one by one we passed in silence and alone into the well-lit climate-controlled space. We were to walk in a similar manner as we had during the contemplative nature walk: slowly and attentively, allowing ourselves to be drawn by whatever attracted us, observing both our own physical and emotional reactions and whatever signs or symbols touched our consciousness. We were not allowed to buy or eat or speak unless we were spoken to.

As I entered the mall I felt an astounding difference from any other time I had been there. By maintaining mindfulness, the environment became psychedelic in its intensity. A thousand simultaneous messages flooded in: colors, images, words, sounds, smells, movement, everything beckoning for attention: "Buy me! Buy me!" Each storefront was bursting with abundance, the entire mall a cornucopia. I breathed calmly and witnessed this extraordinary onslaught. It was like entering a mythic underworld, an astral realm where beings wandered perpetually shopping for things to fill an unassuageable void within them. I cautioned myself not to judge, just to witness. It was difficult. I knew that every product in this vast sea of products had left a trail of disruption somewhere in the world: forests clearcut, exhaust smoke in the air, bulldozers flattening some creature's habitat, noise breaking a tranquil morning, oil sheen in the puddles. What were we doing? Is it really worth it? A hundred years ago in this spot, I would have been looking out on a tall-grass prairie running up to the foot of the mountains, there to join with the conifer forests. Antelope and buffalo would be wandering here.

I drifted into a "nature store"—there were posters of idyllic waterfalls and a mountain lion crouching on a rock. I was becoming numb. After a few minutes I found myself staring at a phosphorescent wall sticker for $6.99 entitled: "The Earth—It Glows in the Dark!" Sadness, a kind of aching poignancy, came over me. I began to notice how many products throughout the mall had pictures of wild nature on them—T-shirts with every animal imaginable, frogs as door stops, mugs with mountain scenes, stores filled with stuffed animals, sheets that were fields of daisies—merchandisers had focused on our unconscious and conscious longing for free nature and were packaging it in every conceivable form.

In another shop my eyes were drawn to an advertising blurb for cellular phones: "LIVE BEYOND LIMITS! GET MORE ROOM IN

YOUR LIFE FOR THE THINGS THAT MATTER MOST!" It happens to be one of my own teaching lines: "the things that matter most"—I often question students about what these things are for them. It is my attempt to distinguish between a high standard of living and high quality of life, but in this blurb the two are conflated: quantity IS quality. Is this the credo of the religion of consumerism—to live beyond limits? What in the name of the planet are we doing?

I was by that time in my Mall Quest nearly overwhelmed by the vacuity and presumption of my people. Yes, these *are* my people, I realized. They are not an abstract "they" somewhere else who I could blame. My own life and destiny is caught up in theirs, in their choices and impulses, and to varying extents, I partake in those choices and impulses. My heart was about to break. I asked for some guidance, some sign to show a way out of this Earth-destructive and self-destructive addiction we are caught in.

I wandered into a toy store—gaudy plastic dinosaurs and strange robot warriors greeted me—I kept wandering. Finally, toward the back, I stood in front of long shelves of boxes and jigsaw puzzles. My eyes scanned across them, and then stopped at the following quote written in small letters on a gaily colored puzzle of the Earth:

In the end we will conserve only what we love;
we will love only what we understand;
and we will understand only what we are taught.

Yes, that is the way. But if our elders are addicted to the trinkets of commercial culture—who will teach the young? As Annie Dillard writes, "There is no one but us."

Time was up and I made my way back to the mall entrance to rejoin the students. Most of them were deeply shaken by the experience. "What do we love?" I asked them. "What do we love?"

Garden Practice

WENDY JOHNSON

I

YEARS AGO, RICHARD BAKER ROSHI DESCRIBED the field of Zen practice as a "nonrepeating universe." Whenever I sow seeds, I remember these words. Every garden sown from seed is a world within a world, a complete mystery. And this winter, in particular, as I roll more than thirty-five varieties of wildland seed into little clay seed balls to resow fire-devastated land, the nonrepeating universe stirs to life inside each globe of clay.

Every January and February at Green Gulch Farm and Zen Center, we tend the wider watershed that stretches beyond the garden gate and links our garden to that mosaic of gardens that dot the curved horn of the California headlands. This year I've been packing "seed gardens" inside of protective balls of clay to help revegetate the fire-scoured wilderness north of us on Point Reyes peninsula.

Seed ball gardening is an elegantly simple and ruthlessly effective method of revegetation conceived by the natural farmer and teacher Masanobu Fukuoka Sensei, who has worked for almost fifty years restoring damaged and desiccated land. Anyone can do it. You simply mix together three parts seed, one part raw soil, and five parts dry red or brown clay powder and moisten the mix with one or two parts of water. Sterile soil will not do. Seed ball culture depends on the complex guilds of living mycorrhizae, or beneficial fungi that inhabit raw soil. These fungi live in symbiosis with the roots of sprouting seed plants, nourishing the host plant with food from the soil humus and from their own digestive proteins. Each seed plant is host to a particular mycorrhizae, and healthier plants abound where guilds of mycorrhizae are at work.

The seed we mix this winter—purple needle grass and nodding stipa, coyote bush and coastal stage, Chinese houses and owl's clover—was gathered in late summer, walking the ridges and lowland meadows of Redwood Creek and Gospel Flats. As I beat clouds of ripe, wildland seed into an old pillowcase, I was picky, careful not to gather the renegade weed species of Europe, the Scotch broom and foxtail barley. These non-native plants also cloak the headland bluffs, choking out the local vegetation and creating a fire hazard. When I remember, I carry a burlap sack and cut off the ripe seed-heads of these invaders so they will not reproduce.

Now in the short light of winter we work in a circle, in silence, a guild of friends making seed balls. Three-year-old Sabrina mixes seed with a sixty-year-old Zen monk. First, the ripe seeds are coated with dry soil from the bottom of an old compost pile. This raw soil is loaded with myccorhizae ready to go to work. Next we sift red clay dust over the mix and moisten the whole lot with water. Soon we are elbow-deep in seed and clay gumbo. When the mass coheres, we pinch off tiny pieces and roll them out between our hands into half-inch-diameter clay balls, stuffed with seed.

These clay seed balls are living models of entire ecosystems; shaped by human hands, they nevertheless carry the signature of their native habitat. In a few days we will fan out over the blackened flanks of Mount Vision, scattering seed. The clay balls will sleep on the earth until their protective shells grow soft with rain and threadlike roots burrow through into burned soil. Green blades will unfurl their flags overhead, heralding a nonrepeating universe mixed from a handful of dust.

2

In early summer, just when gardeners should be tying up the waving tentacles of Marmande tomatoes or pinching back the tips of imperial larkspur, I find myself once again at the periphery of the garden, sowing a fresh border of Good Bug Blend. This miracle mixture of herb, flower, and vegetable seeds is sown to attract beneficial insects to the garden. These "good bugs"—the golden chalcid and the minute pirate bug, the green lacewing and the big-eyed bug—are all natural pest control allies that keep the June garden clean of pernicious troublemakers. But lately I've been wondering what my role is in the cycle of predation and rebirth.

I used to be an organic gardener concentrating solely on plants, but these days I feel more like a frontier rancher herding hosts of visible and invisible beasts to the harvest table. This turning toward animals happened to me last winter, when I reluctantly fell under the spell of a scrawny pack rat rodent, the dusky-footed wood rat. In early January I joined 400 other gardening volunteers for a habitat restoration project in Muir Woods National Monument, just a few miles north of the Green Gulch garden. My assignment was to dig up a section of ancient forest floor in the pristine Bohemian Grove and to plant understory communities of tan oak, coffeeberry, and sword fern beneath the redwoods. "Why tan oak and sword fern?" I asked innocently. "To encourage wood rats to nest in the woods," answered the park ranger.

I confess that this business of planting elaborate gardens to lure wildlife to the land has always been a hot koan for me. Why should I waste precious gardening time growing acorns for pack rats? I know that a koan can be a vital instrument in the work of awakening, just as a pickax is an essential instrument for opening the ground. But even when I learned that *Neotoma fuscipes*, the dusky-footed wood rat, was the primary prey of the rare and endangered northern spotted owl, that totem guardian of old-growth forests, I still balked at planting habitat for crafty rodents.

Every summer at Green Gulch we spend tedious hours repairing our battered deer fence, setting gopher traps between the lines of dessert apples, paying our children two cents apiece for every snail they pluck out of the Chinese delphiniums, and fashioning circular collars out of old roofing paper to protect our tender-necked sweet pea plants. Instinctively, I stiffen whenever I see an insect at work in the garden. I'm sure that every chrysalis contains the tomato hornworm and never the beneficent chalcedon checkerspot. So it has been a real stretch for me to welcome wood rats and assassin bugs into my life.

How did it happen? The wood rat pushed me to the edge, and then I just moved over. The garden got bigger. Way bigger. I gave up struggling against the "great majority" and slowed down long enough to watch them. Whenever possible, I looked them in the eye. I breathed on cold honeybees, torpid in the frosty blue core of borage flowers, and watched them fire back to life. I laid down on the ground below the Poorman gooseberries when they were heavy with fruit and followed the Argentine ants rolling rotten berries home to their nest. I stopped running away from snakes. Instead of discriminating between the food grown for market and the crops that go to wood rats and good bugs, I began to plant a little bit more of both.

Gardening is consequential work. It has its haunting sweetness and it has its sting. For relief, I take the time to walk in Muir Woods, no matter how busy I am. High up in the broken-out redwood snags, spotted owl chicks begin to hatch out now, an event that coincides exactly with the summer birth of wood rat litters. I imagine the newborn wood rats curled deep in their sword fern nests. They are pink, almost blind, and strangely translucent. Later, I know that I have helped draw them to the woods when I see their tender bones poking at odd angles out of fresh owl scat voided on the floor of the forest.

3

These days I am obsessed with poop. Poop and rot. Walking the narrow trail that traverses the autumn headlands, I pause to break apart the dry scat of raccoon and gray fox to see what they've been dining on. In the garden I know the Steller's jays are robbing the raspberries by their loose splatter of red-seeded stool. And there's no better way to warm up in the morning than by shoveling hot horse manure into our vintage Apache pickup.

In autumn we build compost with a vengeance. Long windrows of twisted sunflower stalks, smashed pumpkins, and blackened vines of fingerling potatoes are stacked under blankets of hot manure. In a few days the piles begin to smoke with decay on the fringe of the garden. Rot rules the windswept land.

In nature's wheel of life, composting happens on the bottom of the cycle, where death's processes are turned back into life. Every biologically sound garden is built on the rhythm of the compost pile. What I love best about rot is that whatever we discard becomes a rare treasure, an uncontested source of fertility for the earth.

Anything that was once alive can be composted. Decay picks every bone clean. It happens fast. One autumn some years ago a young doe snapped her neck trying to jump the nine-foot-high deer fence that encloses our garden at Green Gulch Farm. Katagiri Roshi was with us then, leading a sesshin. "Shouldn't we put her out of her misery?" we asked him as we surrounded the wild-eyed doe. "Let's just sit with her," he answered. She died quickly, with a shudder of warm blood in her throat, encircled by patch-robed sitters. We laid her on the compost pile and covered her with dry stalks of bishop's weed and dyer's chamomile. On top of this we forked fresh horse manure and sealed the pile with a foot-deep bed of oat straw. In two months she was gone, broken down and incorporated into the life of the pile, digested by millions of microbes and absorbed the white mycelia of countless fungi.

Our culture honors the art of arranging flowers—why not the craft of arranging garbage? You can do it. Shit happens, compost happens. Begin by separating your waste. Keep a covered bucket for your organic matter. Include kitchen scraps, old hair, coffee grounds and filter papers, used tea bags, moist paper towels and napkins . . . you can even add unmendable clothing (it all breaks down in the compost pile). If you have land, it is best to build a pile 3′ × 3′ × 3′; if you have no land, you can make anaerobic compost in a ten-gallon bucket and present your houseplants with fine fertilizer in six months.

For a free-standing compost pile, arrange your garbage like this: First, a thick layer of carbon materials like fallen leaves, old straw, or woody plant prunings. Next, cover these dry materials with nitrogen-rich kitchen scraps and fresh garden weeds. Add animal manure if you have it. Keep building your pile in layers. Decomposer microorganisms need carbon for energy and nitrogen to build protein for their bodies. So arrange your garbage and feed your decomposers. A handful of compost contains more microorganisms than there are people on earth.

These mornings it is cold in the garden. At dawn we discover seven feral cats sleeping on top of the compost pile. It's warm up there. Temperatures upwards of 150° F are generated by decomposers rearranging our arranged garbage. The breakdown ball is in full swing. From the rankest dung heap at the edge of the garden, I catch a whiff of poetry, in this case Robert Aitken's:

> Little white maggots
> In fermenting night soil
> Steam with Buddhahood

CHOOSING WHAT TO EAT

❧

Buddha and the Beasts

HELEN TWORKOV

WESTERNERS WHO KNOW LITTLE of Buddhism often associate it with vegetarianism. Zen monks in Japan are mistakenly thought to subsist on a diet of nothing but brown rice. A book of "famous vegetarians" features an image of Shakyamuni Buddha on the cover, but it makes no mention of Adolf Hitler, despite his well-documented vegetarian eating habits. A closer look shows our assumptions about Buddhism and vegetarianism are not always correct.

Tibetans in exile are notorious for their love of Big Macs. Their general predilection for red meat is often explained by the agricultural limitations of their snow-capped country. Yet their Burmese neighbors to the south keep their monks well supplied with pork, which they believe to have been the last meal of Shakyamuni Buddha—never mind that tainted pig meat may have been the cause of his death.

As contemporary Buddhists apply the Dharma to such subjects as euthanasia, abortion, organ donation, or genetic engineering, the Dharma Wheel is energized by fresh investigations into "what the Buddha really taught." The need for reexamination enters the food debate most urgently because of the conditions associated with modern slaughterhouses. Their inhumane mechanization—along with the extravagant exploitation of land relegated to animal feed—has catalyzed a worldwide campaign against meat-eating. Boycotting the animal industry addresses spiritual considerations for some activists, but not for all. What characterizes this debate for Buddhists, however, is not its new dimensions, but its antiquity, for the controversy over what Buddhists ought to eat is as old as Buddhism itself.

The Buddhist menu differs from one culture to another—and usually includes fresh foods—but Buddhist history is filled with voices that opposed the accepted culinary customs of their time and place. Yet these voices need not go beyond the parameters of Buddhist teachings for their arguments, for Buddhism itself provides ample material for both sides of the debate. Moreover, it is the Buddhist teachings themselves, beginning with Shakyamuni Buddha, that have placed one's choice of food within a spiritual context.

While Buddhism is hardly unique in giving primacy to the sacredness of life, the inclusion of "all sentient beings" is so central to the Buddhist view that, contrary to Western religious traditions, the right to subjugate animals to human needs, even for survival, cannot be taken for granted. The first great vow—to save all beings—is a natural response to suffering, the first of the Four Noble Truths. The first precept, "Not to kill," is therefore something more than a moral injunction. Its implications are as broad and deep as all of Buddhism. For this reason, even the more erroneous assumption about Buddhism and vegetarianism reveals some core of truth.

The bodhisattva vow "to save all sentient beings" is compelling precisely because it cannot be honored in any literal way, nor apprehended with the intellect alone. If we don't kill cows, we kill carrots. If not carrots, then rice. Is the distinction between killing animals and vegetables borne of compassion, or of anthropocentrism? We have to eat, and those who choose meat are not necessarily "pro" killing. Even the Buddha's behavior was circumscribed. Politically, he may have gone as far as possible in rejecting the animal sacrifices common to the India of his day; forbidding meat altogether might have antagonized the ruling Brahmin priesthood in ways that might have stopped Buddhism dead in its tracks. How much of his response to food issues was informed by compassion for all living beings, and how much was mere diplomacy? We don't know. After 2,500 years we find ourselves with no easy answers.

As we consider anew the question of what to eat, the question gnaws at us. It makes us uncomfortable, pushes us further to investigate our ideas of self and other. One sentient being, alive, dead, raw, or cooked, can push us into the great mangle of living and dying and being born, where there is no ultimate safety and no pat response. What's eating us? Perhaps the question itself is the true legacy of the Buddha.

Vegetarianism as Practice
PHILIP GLASS

THE FAMILIAR ARGUMENTS IN FAVOR of a vegetarian diet are usually based on issues of either health, environment, ecology, or—from the Buddhist point of view—of compassion. Of these arguments, some are easier to dismiss than others. Take health, for example. The fact is that very few people (apart from South India where vegetarianism is part of the culture) have been able to maintain a pure vegetarian diet for any extended period of time. A vegetarian diet often results in various ailments and general weakness for even the most nutrition-conscious. It may be possible to give up red meat for long periods, making do with fish and chicken, but giving up animal products entirely invites health problems for most people. Because this is not generally admitted, people have a vague feeling of guilt about their diets. But if you look around, you will find very few true vegetarians. In fact, I caution anyone against attempting a purely vegetarian diet, or, at least, if you do, be aware of possible problems. And guilt has no place here. After all, how can you hope to work toward the benefit of other sentient beings if the way you are living makes you too weak or sick to do anything useful?

The question of compassion can be tricky also. After all, sentient beings are going to die anyway, and perhaps some of those deaths will serve the needs of others, proving to be beneficial in their way (or so the argument goes). Not to mention that I have yet to meet a Tibetan lama, from the lowest rank to the highest, who is a vegetarian.

Environmental/ecological arguments are somewhat more convincing, although, despite a proliferation of very intelligent books on this subject, it remains difficult to convince individuals that even an occasional omelet or hamburger can make much difference globally.

But there remains another approach to vegetarianism, specifically Buddhist in nature, which, for me, is the most persuasive. Here, I mean vegetarianism as an actual practice. You need physical stamina to undertake this, and, if you have it, count it as a blessing. In vegetarianism-as-practice we view all sentient beings—fish, birds, cows, bugs, etc.—as equal to ourselves. This becomes a practice to develop equanimity to *all* sentient beings (even the delicious ones). By not eating these other sentient-being life forms, we hope gradually to view them in a wholly different light—not as potential meals, snacks, and delicious flavors for our own appetites and pleasures, but as beings worthy of consideration equal to ourselves. This is a slow process: after being a vegetarian for thirty-five years I still occasionally catch myself regarding fish as food. But my own view has changed enough so that now I truly believe it possible to transform our habitual mental patterns through this practice and to arrive at a perception of fellow sentient beings that is in complete accord with a Mahayana Buddhist point of view.

Put simply, equanimity is a powerful opponent of the self-cherishing and self-grasping that are at the root cause of ignorance. According to the Four Noble Truths taught by Shakyamuni Buddha, this ignorance is the cause of suffering. Viewed in this way, we see the importance of equanimity in the Buddhist path and in our lives—how vegetarianism is proposed not on moral or ethical grounds (i.e., "you shouldn't eat meat because it is wrong"), but as a potentially powerful tool for our own spiritual development.

It may be possible to undertake this practice gradually. Done consciously, or as a method of self-transformation, perhaps a less than perfect vegetarian diet could still be beneficial—not in terms of health or environment, but beneficial toward awakening an equaniminous view of those sentient beings with whom we share, for a moment, this world system/universe.

This is my practice and this is my hope.

Compassion for All Beings

BODHIN KJOLHEDE

NOT LONG AGO A ZEN TEACHER, during the course of an introductory workshop, stated three times, vehemently, "Buddhism is not vegetarianism." He later argued that to be vegetarian is a kind of attachment. What are we to make of such assertions?

First of all, let us agree that Buddhism is not vegetarianism. Neither is it "virtue," "peace," or "wisdom," or any other word or concept. To identify it with anything at all is to reduce what in essence is limitless. In fact, Buddhism isn't even Buddhism.

But now let us leave the safe world of negation and consider living practice. How are we to understand the long tradition of abstaining from flesh foods in Buddhist temples in India and throughout the Mahayana countries of China, Korea, and, until recently, Japan? Were all those generations of abbots simply mired in a collective delusion? Those who suggest that vegetarianism can be dismissed as peripheral to the Buddha's teaching need to account for this practice that has endured over the centuries.

For inhabitants of polar regions, vegetarianism would indeed be attachment—and one that would cost them their lives. In Tibet, too, where little can be grown, meat is a practical necessity. And even in tropical underdeveloped countries where resources are meager and distribution limited, maintaining a vegetarian diet could become a disproportionate concern, demanding much of one's time, energy, and money.

But those of us living in modern, industrialized countries in North America, Europe, and Asia are blessed with a vast array of food choices. Most of us are able to obtain an abundance of nonflesh foods that can keep us robustly healthy our whole lives. With such a variety of nonanimal foods available, who would choose to support the slaughter mills and foster the misery involved in factory farming, by continuing to eat flesh? There are those who fear that without meat or fish their health would suffer (the irony!), others who may be unaware of how enormously the meat industry contributes to the misuse and waste of global resources.

But for most meat eaters, I suspect that the habit of eating animals is simply too pleasurable for them to stop. They know the reasons to give it up, but won't. What's more, rather than being honest with themselves, too many such people mask their true motivation with the pleasing fragrance of such Buddhist concepts as "nonattachment."

To go on eating animals while knowing it is unnecessary, then, is usually just attachment to one's selfish preferences. But vegetarianism can also be attachment. It depends on one's state of mind. After twenty-five years of refraining from eating meat, I no longer think of myself as "vegetarian" (though the label is still convenient to use in some circumstances). I just don't eat flesh foods. There is really nothing special about this, least of all any painful deprivation. My teacher Roshi Kapleau has always warned, "Don't give up meat; let meat give *you* up." When a diet, whether vegetarian or macrobiotic, becomes a dogma to which we cling and gives rise to self-righteousness and judgmentalism, it also becomes our bondage. But one can also get stuck in the notion of "freedom"—and that is an attachment that can cause vastly more harm to other sentient beings.

Can we maintain a nonmeat diet for reasons of compassion and still be free of attachment to it? In the *Platform Sutra*, the Chinese patriarch Hui Neng relates that after inheriting the Dharma from the Fifth Patriarch, he spent years in seclusion with a group of hunters. "At mealtimes," he tells us, "they cooked meat in the same pot with the vegetables. If I was asked to share, I replied, 'I will just pick the vegetables out of the meat.'" Was he, then, attached to vegetarianism? And if refraining from eating flesh foods is itself an "attachment," does it follow that refusing to give up flesh foods shows nonattachment?

It is sad to see how many American Buddhists are managing to find a self-satisfying accommodation to eating meat. Some airily cite the doctrine of emptiness, insisting that ultimately there is no killing and no sentient being being killed. Others find cover behind the excuse that taking life is the natural order of things and, after all, "the life of a carrot and that of a cow are equal." The truth is, though, that as humans we are endowed with discriminating minds that we can use to educate ourselves to the implications of our volitional acts and to choose those foods that minimize suffering to living beings.

Our aspiration in Mahayana Buddhism, inasmuch as we can speak of an aspiration, is to liberate our innate compassion and fulfill the bodhisattva vows. In the first of those vows, "All beings, without number, I vow to liberate," we commit our compassion to *all* beings, not just humans. Eschewing meat is one way to express that commitment to the welfare of other creatures. Once we leave habitual preferences behind and forgo nimble rationalizations, the issue of vegetarianism comes down to a question of need. If you *need* to eat flesh foods to sustain your life or, in extreme cases, your health, do so, and do so with awareness and gratitude. But if you don't, why contribute to unnecessary suffering?

Nets of Beads, Webs of Cells

GARY SNYDER

THE PRIMARY ETHICAL INJUNCTION OF BUDDHISM is known as the First Precept. It is against hurting and taking life, *ahimsa* in Sanskrit, glossed as meaning "cause no unnecessary harm." Not eating flesh is a common consequence of this precept in the Buddhist world, which has largely consisted of agrarian peoples. This has posed a thorny question for normally tolerant Buddhists in the matter of how to regard the spiritual life of people in those societies for whom eating fish or animals may well be a matter of economic necessity. My own home place is beyond the zone of adequate water and good gardening soil, so my family and I have grappled with this question, even as we kept up our lay Buddhist life.

I have plenty of neighbors for whom Buddhism is not even on the map. I know hunters and antihunters, usually decent people on both sides, and have tried to keep my mind open to both. As a student of hunting and gathering cultures, I've tried to get some insight into fundamental human psychology by looking at the millennia of human hunting and gathering experience. I have also killed a few animals, to be sure. On two occasions I put down deer that had been wounded by sport hunters and had wandered in that condition into our part of the forest. When I kept chickens, we maintained the flock, the ecology, and the economy by eating excess young roosters and, at the other end of the life cycle, by stewing an occasional elderly hen. In doing this I experienced one of the necessities of peasant life worldwide. They (and I) could not but run their flock this way, for anything else would be a luxury—that is to say, uneconomic.

Also my hens (unlike commercial hens who are tightly caged) got to run wild and scratch all day, had a big rooster boyfriend, and lived the vivid and sociable life of jungle fowl. They were occasionally taken away by bobcats, raccoons, wild dogs, and coyotes. Did I hate the bobcats and coyotes for this? Sometimes, taking sides with the chickens, I almost did. I even shot a bobcat that had been killing chickens once, a fact of which I am not proud. I probably could have come up with a different solution, and I now think that one must stand humbly aside and let the Great System go through its moves. I did quit keeping chickens, but that was because it was not practical. Happy loose flocks cannot compete with factory egg production, which reduces hens to machines (but protects them from bobcats). (On a deep level I do not think I can approve of the domestication of birds and animals; too much is taken out of their self-sufficient wild natures.)

As for venison, for many years several families in this area have carefully salvaged fresh roadkill deer rather than let flesh go to waste. (But then, letting it feed vultures or carrion beetles is no waste . . .) And by keeping a sharp eye on the roadside I have saved myself the quandary of whether to hunt or not to hunt deer. Fewer and fewer Californians are hunting. But in place of hunters we have a fine resurgent cougar population, and sometimes find their kills in the woods, not far from the house at that.

The public and private forests and grasslands of the western Sierra Nevada make up a sizable ecosystem marked by pines, oak, songbirds and owls, raccoons, deer, and such. The web of relationships in an ecosystem makes one think of the Hua-yen Buddhist image of Indra's net, where, as David Barnhill describes it, "the universe is considered to be a vast web of many-sided and highly polished jewels, each one acting as a multiple mirror. In one sense each jewel is a single entity. But when we look at a jewel, we see nothing but the reflections of other jewels, which themselves are reflections of other jewels, and so on in an endless system of mirroring. Thus in each jewel is the image of the entire net."

This perception of a "sacramentalized ecosystem" lies behind the ceremonies of compassion and gratitude in foraging cultures, where a special respect is paid to the spirits of the game. Wild-plant gathering and gardening also call for respectful attention to the lives of the plants; almost as much mindfulness is asked of the vegetarian as of the hunter.

The very distinction "vegetarian/nonvegetarian" is too simple. Some populations, especially in India and Southeast Asia, are deliberate Buddhist and Hindu vegetarians, but most of the rest of the people of the Third World are semivegetarians by default. They are grateful for a little fish or chicken when they can get it. When and where people can live by grains and vegetables alone and get adequate nutrition, it is to be applauded. But there are people of the high latitudes, of the grasslands and deserts and the mountains, who have always relied on much nonplant food. Most people of the world have always had to live by a mixed food economy. Shall Buddhists then consider them beyond the pale? Surely the Bodhisattva spirit does not allow us to reject the other cultures and food economies of the world out of hand. As for modern food production, although it is clear that the beef economy of the developed world is a wasteful luxury, it is doubtful that the Third World could easily get by without cows, chickens, pigs, sheep, and the life of the sea.

Americans, Australians, New Zealanders, and some Europeans are the largest per capita meat consumers of the world. In the developed world vegetarians are usually educated members of a privileged class. Most North American Buddhists have no real need to eat meat, so the choice is theirs. (We then need to study our dependence on fossil fuel agriculture, which produces vegetables and grains in a manner that degrades soil, air, and water and which endangers the health of underpaid immigrant laborers.)

But the real question is how to understand more deeply this First Precept. When Oda Sesso Roshi, my teacher at the Daitoku-ji monastery, came to the koan in the *Mumonkan*, "Nansen Kills a Cat," he chose not to sit in the high chair but sat on the tatami, on the same level as the *unsui* (monks). He said, "This is a case that can be easily misunderstood, and we in Japan have on some occasions perhaps abused it." At the time I thought he was referring to the apparent lack of resistance on the part of the Zen establishment to the emergence of Japanese militarism in the thirties, leading to World War II. Now I think that he was indicating that *anyone* in a discussion who raises the question of deliberately taking life should be sitting right on the floor. One cannot be too humble about this issue. As I listened to his formal Zen lecture back in 1961, I must confess I felt a certain righteousness, because I had been a lifelong pacifist (and on-and-off vegetarian) and thought I knew how to understand the precept. Not so easy.

I had also noticed that even some of the masters (let alone the monks) ate fish when away from the monastery. One time I was visiting at the temple of a roshi near Mount Fuji and asked him why it is that some priests and monks eat meat or fish. He responded heartily, "A Zen man should be able to eat dog shit and drink kerosene." My own teacher was a strict vegetarian. But he once said to me, "Just because I eat pure food, and some of the other priests do not, does not mean that I am superior to them. It is my own way of practice. Others have other ways. Each person must take the First Precept as a deep challenge, and find his own way through life with it."

In my natural curiosity I like to know where food has come from and who it was, plant or animal. (Okra is a member of the *Hibiscus* genus, originally from Africa! Tomatoes, tobacco, potatoes, and jimsonweed are all Solanaceae together, with those trumpet-shaped flowers. I love such facts.) My family and I say grace and do a little meditation on our food before meals, just as is done on a larger scale in *sesshin*, "meditation weeks," with the meal verses.

The First Precept goes beyond a concern just for organic life. Yet our stance in regard to food is a daily manifestation of our economics and ecology. Food is the field in which we daily explore our "harming" of the world. Clearly it will not do simply to stop at this point and declare that the world is pain and suffering and that we are all deluded. We are called instead to practice. In the course of our practice we will not transform reality, but we may transform ourselves. Guilt and self-blame are not the fruit of practice, but we might hope that a *larger view* is. The larger view is one that can acknowledge the simultaneous pain and beauty of this complexly interrelated world. This is what the image of Indra's net is for.

So far it has been the earlier subsistence cultures of the world, especially the hunters and gatherers, who have—paradoxically—most beautifully expressed their gratitude to the earth and its creatures. As Buddhists, we have something yet to learn on that score. Animals and plants live mutually on each other, and throughout nature there is a constant exchange of energy—a cycle of life-and-death affairs. Our type of universe is described in the sutras as a realm of *kama*, of biological desire and need, which drives everything. Everything that breathes is hungry. But not to flee such a world! Join in Indra's net!

None of what I have been saying is to be seen as a rationalization or justification for "breaking" the precept. As Ryo Imamura recently wrote, "in Buddhism there is no such thing as a 'just' war." If we were to find ourselves going against the precept in some drastic situation and killing or injuring someone else in (say) self-defense, we must not try to justify it. We can only say this was my decision, I regret that it happened, and I accept whatever results it may entail.

The precept is the Precept, and it stands as a guide, a measure, an ideal, and a koan. It cannot be a literal rule, as if it were one of the Ten Commandments. "Take no life" or "Commit no harm" is impossible to keep perfectly. The Jains of India tried to take *ahimsa* to its literal (not logical) conclusion, and the purest among them started an institution of starving themselves to death as a moral act. But this is violence against one's own body.

Every living thing impinges on every other living thing. Popular Darwinism, with its emphasis on survival of the fittest, has taken this to mean that nature is a cockpit of competitive bloodshed. "Nature red in tooth and claw," as the Europeans are fond of quoting. This view implicitly elevates human beings to a role of moral superiority over the rest of nature. More recently the science of ecology, with its demonstrations of coevolution, symbiosis, mutual aid and support, interrelationship, and interdependence throughout natural systems, has taught us modesty in regard to human specialness. It has also taught us that our understanding of what is and is not "harmful" within the realm of wild nature is so rudimentary that we should not even bother to take sides between predators and prey, between primary green producers and detritus-side fungi or parasites, or even between "life" and "death."

Thich Nhat Hanh once said at a gathering of Buddhist Peace Fellowship leaders at Green Gulch, a Zen farming community in northern California, that we should be grateful for any little appearance of *ahimsa* wherever it is found in this world. I believe he said that if one officer in a battle leads his troops with a bit more spirit of *ahimsa* than another, it is to be appreciated. It is my sense of it, then, that we must each find our own personal way to practice this precept, within quite a latitude of possibilities, understanding that there will be no complete purity and in any case not indulging in self-righteousness. It is truly our "existential koan." This is why I have glossed it, in the Mahayana spirit, as "commit no unnecessary harm."

One can wonder what the practice of *ahimsa* is like for the bobcat, in the bobcat Buddha-realm. As Dogen says, "dragons see water as a palace," and for bobcats, the forest is perhaps an elegant *jikido*, dining hall, in which they murmur *gatha*s of quiet appreciation to quail, sharing them (in mind) with demons and hungry ghosts. "You who study with Buddhas should not be limited to human views when you are studying water" (*Mountains and Waters Sutra*). And what world is it for quail? I only know this: at death, my death and suffering are my own, and I hope I will not blame my distress on the tiger (or cancer, or whatever) that has brought me down. Of the tiger I would simply hope to ask, "Please, no waste." And maybe growl along with her.

There is an old Zen story of a teacher finding a single discarded chopstick on the drain. He scolds the dishwasher monk, saying, "You have taken the life of this chopstick." This story is used to illustrate how deeply the First Precept reaches. We can look thus at a wasted chopstick and understand how it has been harmed. But then it should also be added, "You might even be killing a rain forest," as the use of disposable wood chopsticks—in staggering quantities—in Japan and America suggests.

Did the master know that next step? Probably not. Buddhist compassion for creatures sometimes meant purchasing and then ceremonially releasing caged pigeons and captured fish, the focus being on individual creatures. Individual lives are only part of the story. Even as the Buddhists were practicing vegetarianism and kindness to creatures, wild nature in China suffered significant species extinction and wholesale deforestation between the fifth and the fifteenth centuries CE. India too was vastly deforested well before modern times. Now, with insights from the ecological sciences, we know that we must think on a scale of a whole watershed, a natural system, a habitat. To save the life of a single parrot or monkey is truly admirable. But unless the forest is saved, they will all die.

The whole planet groans under the massive disregard of the precept of *ahimsa* by the highly organized societies and corporate economies of the world. Thousands of species of animals, and tens of thousands of species of plants, may become extinct in the next century. To nourish living beings we must not be content simply to have a virtuous diet. To save all beings, we must work tirelessly to maintain the integrity of these mandala-like places of habitat, and the people, creatures, and Buddhas who dwell in their palace-like spaces.

PART SIX

❋

CHALLENGES
in
BUDDHIST
THOUGHT
and
ACTION

A Buddhist philosopher works with the grain of history, respecting the actual situation: he has no grand designs, no inflexible ideologies, no particular set of instructions to peddle—only the principle of *upaya*, or "skillful means" that manifest wisdom in action.

—*William Ophuls*

INTRODUCTION

❊

E ARLY INTERPRETATIONS of Buddhist environmental views tended toward a romanticized version of human–nature relations. In contrast to the Western pattern of warfare against the natural world (blamed partly on religion), Buddhism has seemed to offer a more peaceful alternative. Upon closer examination, these generalizations are simplistic. Buddhist traditions espouse a wide range of approaches to nature, and the application of promising ideals to environmental problems has been uneven at best. Although core Buddhist principles call for a compassionate response to a relational world, that response has taken place (and failed to take place) in very different cultural and economic contexts. The initial enthusiasm for "green Buddhism" is now being tempered by the work of analysis and reflection in light of today's complex environmental issues.

The first three essays contemplate the history of Buddhism and environmentalism in the West. Peter Timmerman shows that spiritual encounters with nature served at times as a means of resistance to the cold rationalism of the Industrial Revolution. William Ophuls considers how a Buddhist politics might restrain the excesses of individualism and their deleterious environmental impact. Major tenets would include tolerance, simplicity, nonviolence, and service, which all seem to thrive in small-scale contexts. Bill Devall explores environmental activism from a deep ecology perspective, assessing how nonviolent action can lead to structural change.

When engaged Buddhist scholars look at present-day environmental issues, they encounter difficult moral terrain. Kenneth Kraft investigates "eco-karma" in the form of nuclear waste, wondering how Buddhism or any religion can deal meaningfully with deadly plutonium and its half-life of 25,000 years. Confronting the population explosion, Rita Gross identifies ego-inflating aspects of pronatalist arguments, as well as Buddhist resources for restraint in childbearing. In order to address the root causes of environmental destruction, contemporary Buddhist ethics will need to develop appropriate new concepts and new language.

How, then, to think about the future? Do we have the will and the ability to make wise decisions on behalf of coming generations? In the last essay, Zen teacher Robert Aitken shares his positive vision of Buddhist and kindred communities working together to create an alternative society, "forming networks of decent and dignified modes of life." Aitken expects increasing numbers of people to be drawn to collaboration on a small scale, where vital relations can be built from the ground up. A just and ecologically sane society would extend compassion not only to people, but also to plants, animals, and places.

Building on one another's work, committed thinkers are developing skillful means for creating a peaceful and sustainable future. In the process they are also laying the groundwork for the environmental branch of an emerging field, engaged Buddhist studies. Animal welfare, biotechnology, toxic waste, environmental justice—the challenges are daunting. How can Buddhist analysis, in dialogue with other viewpoints, shed light on critical ecological issues? This is a formidable eco-koan for the next millennium.

※

Western Buddhism and the Global Crisis

PETER TIMMERMAN

IN SEPTEMBER 1989, a special issue of the magazine *Scientific American* was published with the title "Managing the Planet." This is only one sign of a movement toward planetary management that is gathering force as the official strategy for handling the global environmental crisis. Within the next twenty years, unless we make substantial changes in our ways of doing and being, we will soon find ourselves on a planet managed according to the principles of bureaucratic rationality and economic growth which have been grinding themselves into the face of the earth for the past 150 years. The power of the human race is now great enough for us to do this. But our power is not yet—nor may it ever be—enough to sustain the results permanently. Our understanding of planetary ecology is so poor, our capacity for limiting our excesses is so limited, and our ability to stun nature into submission is so temporary that, sooner or later, earth is likely to shrug us off into the abyss, and go on about its business.

To find our own place and voice in addressing the crisis—as Westerners, environmentalists, and perhaps as Buddhists—at least three elements of our current situation need to be explored. This essay touches on aspects of each of these elements and is therefore divided roughly into three parts.

First of all, we need to consider how Buddhism was translated when it came to the West: what was the West looking for, and what did it find in Buddhism? This meeting of cultures set the stage for certain themes in the emerging Buddhist environmentalism of the late twentieth century.

So we begin by looking at the circumstances that awaited Buddhism at the time of its full-scale arrival in Europe and America in the nineteenth century.

Secondly, we need to have some understanding of the environmental movement and the forces—social, economic, political, and psychological—that have helped, and are helping, to shape it.

Thirdly, we need to investigate the resources offered by Buddhist thought and practice that can help Western environmentalists find new and effective ways of addressing the crisis.

Contrary to the popular view of Buddhism as a "refuge" from the world, to become a Buddhist today is definitely a political act. More specifically, it is a *geo*political act. If there is a basic premise of our global situation, it is that there is no escape from the world. Just as there is no longer an "away" to throw our waste, there is no longer an "away" to hide ourselves. The famous picture of the blue ball of earth hanging in black space has become linked with the idea that we must set certain limits on our activities. We are presented with something at once very old and very new: the connection of our daily activities to the sustaining of the vast, intricate, and amazing world around us. This connection is known and celebrated by many religious traditions as the sacredness of the ordinary.

ESCAPE AND INSCAPE

When Buddhism arrived in the West in the middle of the nineteenth century, Western culture had, in a sense, been preparing for it for some time. One hundred and fifty years earlier, the Western Enlightenment, spearheaded by the physical sciences, had begun its dissection of nature for the purpose of examining it and reassembling it according to human specifications. The ultimate goal was to free humanity from the constraints of nature. It was the birth of scientific rationalism, a world view that believed everything could be measured and explained according to observable physical laws. There were no miracles and no unseen spiritual forces. The fathers of the Enlightenment asserted that if there was a God, he was like "the good watchmaker." He had made a mechanically perfect world and then withdrawn to let it tick away of its own accord.

The rationalism and scientific investigations of the Enlightenment led directly to the Industrial Revolution and to the Romantic movement, which was a reaction against it. The Romantics rebelled against the increasingly mechanized, industrialized, rational world, which they saw as isolating individuals from society, from nature, and from their own inner power and creativity. They sought to regain the enchantment of a now dis-enchanted world. But although Romanticism was a reaction against many aspects of the Enlightenment, it had inherited a belief in the human individual as the measure of all things.

This was the Western scenario that Buddhism entered, one that was quite different from the Eastern societies in which it had developed. Not surprisingly, it was interpreted and misinterpreted in ways which have had a lasting effect on the Western understanding of Buddhism and on why Westerners turn to Buddhism. Perhaps the easiest way of describing what happened is to use an example.

In 1888, a year before he committed suicide, the painter Vincent Van Gogh, then in Arles in the south of France, painted a portrait of himself as a Japanese Buddhist monk, head shaved, eyes orientalized—as he himself wrote, "a simple worshiper of the eternal Buddha." Around his head, Van Gogh painted a halo of brushstrokes, reinforcing the powerful image of the artist as monk, faithful to the eternal in art. The painting has a claim to be the first piece of truly Western Buddhist art.

Only six years before he painted this stunning self-portrait, Van Gogh had been an apprentice Christian minister, preaching the Gospel among the poor miners of Belgium. He had failed at this career, offending various people by his waywardness and eccentric lifestyle (he insisted on living in even more extreme poverty than those to whom he preached), and he then turned toward art as a new kind of faith. He saw it at first as a new way of capturing the life and sincerity of the poor, and then as a way of capturing the eternal and infinite in the physical world around him. Like other radical painters of his day, Van Gogh was assisted in his efforts by the discovery of Japanese art (carried to the West, so the legend goes, through color woodcut prints used as packing paper around shipments), and he became wildly enthusiastic about all things Japanese. In a letter to a friend about how the world is to be comforted after the loss of Christianity, Van Gogh writes:

> If we study Japanese art, we see a man who is undoubtedly wise, philosophic, and intelligent, who spends his time doing what? In studying the distance between earth and the moon? No. In studying Bismarck's policy? No. He studies a blade of grass. But this blade leads him to draw every plant and then the seasons, the wide aspects of the countryside, then animals, then the human figure. Isn't it almost a true religion which these simple Japanese teach us, who live in nature as though they themselves were flowers?

For Van Gogh, the artist had become a kind of priest, devoted to showing in his art the divine shining through the world. Oriental ways of perceiving—including Buddhism—could be called upon as part of the attempt to see with a fresh eye, unblinkered by Western rationalism. When the artist used his clarity of vision, he transformed himself into a better and higher self. The idea of the artist as a new kind of priest, uniting art and spirituality, can be found elsewhere in this period among many artists, poets, musicians, and others. That is the main reason it is called the Romantic era. In many ways, it can be seen as a time when the erosion of Western faith in Christianity encouraged people to seek spiritual experience through new channels, including works of art and works of nature.

It is important to examine the attitudes of the Romantics more closely, since by a winding route Romanticism leads eventually to environmentalism—and especially that part of environmentalism that is most connected to spirituality.

As the "dis-enchantment of the world" continued, the Romantics found themselves operating on two fronts. On the one hand, they exalted individual genius for tapping into the infinite power of deeper consciousness to overcome the split between the self and the world. On the other hand, they searched for momentary visionary gleams in everyday life and unspoiled nature to reunite them with the world. According to this approach, the world in fact has its own sacred meaning that is waiting to be found by the patient or sensitive artist, rather than being a dead material world that has to have a new meaning imposed upon it by the creative imagination of a powerful genius.

One difficulty was that many Romantics were obviously more attracted to the first approach, which exalted their own role as generators of meaning and power in the world. This idea is immensely attractive, but it is also immensely dangerous. For one thing, it reinforces the individualism to which Western society is already prone, and for another, it suggests that the infinitely powerful individual is a good thing—a suggestion that has been taken up by people we revere (such as Shelley) and those we abhor (such as Hitler). It has also strongly influenced the images we use to form our personal ideal.

When Buddhism arrived in the West in the mid-nineteenth century, it was immediately interpreted according to the individualistic views of Romanticism, which was then at its peak. Buddhism was either mistaken for a kind of Hinduism in which the individual self eventually becomes part of an infinite Self, or it was seen as a world-denying religion in which the religious genius overcomes this dismal world by sheer will power. For the next century, these two alternatives governed what people in the West thought Buddhism was all about. This made it very difficult to understand the true nature of the challenge posed by Buddhism, in which the self, not the world, is the stumbling block.

But as well as looking to the individual as the source of all meaning, there remained the other Romantic approach of uncovering visionary gleams or what the poet Wordsworth called "spots of time," and the novelist James Joyce would later call "epiphanies." These are special moments of life when sudden profound meaningfulness radiates out from what appears to be ordinary experience. All we need is to be sensitive to the world so that we can tune in to them. This mystic materialism, to be found especially in nature, is exemplified by William Blake's famous phrase, "To see a world in a grain of sand, and a Heaven in a wild flower."

Through the course of the nineteenth century, writers such as the social critic John Ruskin and the poet Gerard Manley Hopkins developed a more intense exploration of what Hopkins called "inscapes"—the sacredness of natural things as they express themselves just by existing. There had already been a long tradition of seeing nature as the "second book of God." But what was new was the celebration of the pure thereness of things, the sheer graininess of rocks, trees, and other objects. If one could see this, one could escape into inscape.

Among the earliest environmentalists or naturalists who followed in the footsteps of the Romantics, we find many examples of sudden revelations of the spiritual in nature. Some of these revelations are strikingly similar to certain Buddhist enlightenment experiences. This similarity was not just accidental. For instance, the most famous American environmentalist, Henry David Thoreau, was a student of Indian religion, and was the first translator of part of the Buddhist *Lotus Sutra* into English. The second most famous early naturalist, John Muir, was a powerful spokesman for wilderness experience as a form of religious experience. In his 1911 book *My First Summer in the Sierra*, he writes:

> The snow on the high mountains is melting fast, and the streams are singing bankfull, swaying softly through the level meadows and bogs, quivering with sun spangles, swirling in pot-holes, resting in deep pools, leaping, shouting in wild, exulting energy over rough boulder dams, joyful, beautiful in all their forms. No Sierra landscape that I have ever seen holds anything truly dead or dull, or any trace of what in manufactories is called rubbish or waste; everything is perfectly clean and pure and full of divine lessons. . . . When we try to pick out anything by itself, we find it hitched to everything else in the universe.

Inspired by giant redwood trees, or sequoias, Muir declares:

> I wish I was so drunk and Sequoical that I could preach the green brown woods to all the juiceless world, descending from this divine wilderness like a John the Baptist eating Douglass squirrels and wild honey or wild anything, crying, Repent for the Kingdom of Sequois is at hand!

The original writings and experiences of Thoreau and Muir have become something of a bible for the spiritual side of environmentalism (at least the North American variety). Almost single-handedly they established in the popular imagination the idea of wilderness as a vehicle for personal mystical experience. This has developed into the widespread environmentalist belief that a deep, clear, witnessing of unhumanized nature is crucial to our human self-understanding.

THE RISE OF ENVIRONMENTALISM

Ensuring that there is wilderness in which to have such experiences has been a main theme throughout the rise of environmentalism. However, right from the start, there has been a fundamental tension in the environmental movement. One pole has emphasized the appropriate management or stewardship of nature and its resources. The other pole has emphasized the protection of nature from human encroachment. This first pole remains a human-centered environmentalism; the second is more eco-centric, or nature-centered. There has been a natural tendency for those interested in spiritual matters to gravitate towards the second of these two poles, and (at least until recently) to be primarily concerned with mystical identification with nature.

Because environmentalism from 1900 to 1960 was primarily concerned with the pole of management, the spiritual dimension of environmentalism more or less disappeared (or went underground). The history of environmentalism during this period was one in which two activities predominated. The first was the creation of parks and conservation areas to counterbalance rapid urbanization and provide people with recreational space. The second was the gradual creation of ecological science, which began to describe the weblike interdependence of natural communities. There were only occasional hints that there might be something less immediately practical and scientific at stake in this new kind of ecological understanding. For example, the ecologist Aldo Leopold in his *Sand County Almanac* (1949) spoke of the need for a "land ethic," that is, the extension of our human ethics to include the other species with whom we share the land and who support us.

It was only toward the end of this period (1945–1960), after the catastrophe of two world wars and the development of nuclear weapons, that certain philosophers began to be troubled by the implications of our new technological capacities. Two events in the early 1960s brought these concerns together with the first stirrings of an ecological consciousness.

These were the discovery of strontium 90 in mothers' milk after atmospheric nuclear testing, and the spread of the pesticide DDT through the environment, as revealed in Rachel Carson's *Silent Spring* (1963). Out of these events came a new picture of an earth where things were interconnected with other things by complex ecological cycles; and where something dumped in the water or air in one corner of the world might pop up thousands of miles away in something as pure and innocent as mothers' milk; and where man-made artifacts (atomic bombs and synthetically constructed chemicals like DDT) could affect the life-support system of our planet.

These events and the political events of the later 1960s helped generate the beginnings of the contemporary environmental movement. In the same period, various governments began to legislate against the most blatant local forms of pollution. The stage was then set for the appearance of left-wing, almost anarchic, Ecology and Green parties in Europe (and to a lesser extent in North America) and for the commitment of mainstream political parties to mild ecological reforms, up to and including sustainable development.

It is again noteworthy that during this period the contribution of religious thought or experience to environmentalism was practically nil. The exception was a flurry of accusations launched at the Christian church for its teaching of man's dominion over nature, which was blamed for the West's exploitation of nature. These accusations were straws in a slowly gathering wind that would eventually require religious communities to reevaluate their traditions.

As the 1980s wore on, it became more and more obvious that the series of local environmental crises were, in fact, symptoms of an emerging global environmental crisis. This was dramatically signaled by the news of the hole in the ozone layer discovered over the Antarctic, and the dire predictions of global warming that finally broke through into the public consciousness in 1988. It was at last recognized that we were at one of the great turning points of human history, and that decisions made (or avoided) by this generation would shape the ecological future of the earth.

Unfortunately, the response to this recognition has been slow, not just because of the reluctance of governments to move faster. For its part, the environmental movement has found it hard to make the transition from simple protest—saying "no"—to coherent political action—saying what to do. Part of the difficulty can be traced to the Romantic roots still visible in the movement. The side of Romanticism that glories in nature is obviously no problem for environmentalists; but the other side that promotes infinite individualism is now identified with many of the problems that infect modern life. For example, left-wing politics are full of Romantic images of the heroic freedom of the individual (or the society as one great heroic individual) breaking chains, knocking down barriers, and smashing limits. Meanwhile at the other end of the political spectrum, conservatives who should be interested in "conserving" have developed a form of free-market individualism that seems to dissolve all traditions in its path, including long-standing traditions of using nature sustainably. This has made it equally hard for conservatives to feel at home in the environmental movement.

These kinds of confusion have made it impossible to identify environmentalists as simply left or right and made the creation of a strong environmental political movement very complicated. For some environmentalists, the confusions and complications are signs that the environmental movement is still not truly grounded. This is one reason for the turn toward spiritual traditions as possible guides in finding that true ground.

Toward a Buddhist Environmentalism

If there is one essential task of environmentalism today, it is to create a new politics that can respond powerfully and adequately to the problems we face. It should be kept in mind that the major political parties of our time, of left, right, or center, were all created in the nineteenth century, out of the turmoil of the Industrial Revolution. They were based on the need to manage a growing, newly democratized population. Now, at the end of the twentieth century, the visions and theories upon which these parties were based are quite exhausted. We can see this in the widespread decline in party loyalty among voters, and the lack of ideological coherence in the policies of the parties.

What is needed is an original vision that addresses our current situation fully. It should provide a coherent framework of values and ideas based on a definition of a person which puts him or her in a broader context: how a person interacts with and affects (or ought to interact with and affect) other people, other species, and the environment generally. It should open up ways in which we can contribute, and are inspired to contribute, to our local and global community. Current political theories, based as they are on nineteenth-century experience, do not do this for us any more. We no longer live in a world of expanding frontiers, unlimited resources, and technological optimism. As a result, when we listen to our political leaders, there is an unreality about them. Their antiquated ideologies have little bearing on what we can see happening around us.

One of the most pressing issues is to reassess our popular model of the ideal person, which is a cheap copy of the Romantic ideal. What characterizes modern societies is that they are made up of mini-Van Goghs—that is, millions of citizens who are struggling for self-fulfillment and the fulfillment of their desires according to the ideas of infinite freedom, rebellion, and creativity. This role model, which destines us for frustration and neurosis, has been tied to an economic theory (also hammered out in the nineteenth century) which suggests that human beings are fundamentally self-interested creatures with an infinite capacity to consume, and that our deepest desires are expressed in the things we buy. It is therefore the role of modern society to monitor and manage the inevitable conflicts among greedy beings, and to use the market system to provide us with enough resources to satisfy as many of our desires as possible. The entire system is what could be called Industrial Romanticism, or: "how shopping became a way of life."

This immensely powerful vision, based on individualism and supported by the exploitation of natural resources, is the driving force of what we see happening all around us. What makes this dynamic especially dangerous is that it is not only unsustainable, but it is so entrenched in the modern understanding of freedom and self-fulfillment that it is almost irresistible. How can we deny people their right to self-fulfillment? Yet how can we survive on a planet of ten billion points of infinite greed?

It is at this dangerous point that the possibility of turning to Buddhism begins to make sense. If we have to completely rethink our way of life as the first step toward a new political vision, then perhaps we can use Buddhism to help us.

The most important construction of modern culture which Buddhism is well placed to analyze, assess, and perhaps dismantle is the Romanticized individual self fed by a mass of technology designed to reshape the physical world. Until now, the environmental movement has mostly focused on the results rather than the causes of this situation, e.g., the belching smokestack rather than the manipulation of desires that made certain objects seem essential to our personal well-being—and which made the smokestack happen in the first place. This misplaced focus is largely due to environmentalism's confused allegiance to the political visions of the last century.

Although Buddhism was associated with Western Romanticism, it leads toward a quite different vision. In common with native traditions and some of the other major world religions, Buddhist understanding is of a world in which personal fulfillment is found in interdependence and not independence, where the self is temporary and nonessential rather than the center of the universe; and where infinite spiritual development is possible within a physical existence that is understood and *accepted* as finite. While some of these themes echo familiar Western ideas, their implications are different and go completely against the grain of the current political options. In particular, by promoting a different vision of what it is to be a person, Buddhism undercuts the aggression driving today's society. Also, by giving a different—and positive—interpretation to the meaning of a life lived according to the limits and constraints of a Middle Way, Buddhism presents itself as a serious alternative basis for environmental thought and action.

I suggested above that to be a Buddhist today is a geopolitical act, for the obvious reason that every one of our acts now adds to or subtracts from the load of human affairs which burden the earth. It is also a geopolitical act because, given the continuing devotion to consumerism, one of the most radical acts we can perform in our society is to consume less, to sit quietly meditating in a room, or to try and think clearly about who we are trying to be. And finally, being a Buddhist is a geopolitical act because it provides us with a working space within which to stand back from our aggressive culture and consider the alternatives.

This working space, with its ways of carefully considering and meditating on what we do, is part of what can be called nonviolent thinking. It is likely to be one of the only strategies that will work against a system which is so aggressive in its pretentions to rationality, and which provokes irrational responses in those who are subjected to the working of its powerful machinery. Going to spiritual traditions for solutions to the global crisis will always appear to some people an irrational response—and given the current resurgence in religious fundamentalism, there are often good grounds for this accusation. Indeed, this was one of the great accusations of the Enlightenment thinkers. In 1753, the French philosopher Diderot wrote the following in his book *Thoughts on the Interpretation of Nature:*

> Having strayed into an immense forest during the night, I have only a small light to guide me. I come across a stranger who says to me: "My friend, blow out your candle in order the better to find your way." This stranger is the theologian.

Having ignored the stranger, the West took a different route over the last 200 years, and pushed back a lot of darkness that needed pushing back. Nevertheless, there remains a nagging suspicion that the end result of pushing back the darkness will not be finding our way out of the woods, but completely cutting down the forest to make room for a bright new tree museum.

Buddhism presents itself as a challenging alternative to Diderot's concerns, and to the aggressive ideas that have for so long shaped our thoughts and our actions. The following ancient Zen koan makes the challenge and the alternative explicit:

> Tokusan asked Ryutan about Zen far into the night. At last Ryutan said, "The night is late. You had better leave." Tokusan made his bows, lifted up the door curtain, and went out. He was confronted by darkness. Turning back to Ryutan, he said, "It is dark outside." Ryutan thereupon lit a candle and handed it to him. Tokusan was about to take it when Ryutan blew it out. At this, Tokusan was suddenly enlightened.*

---

*Zenkei Shibayama, *Zen Comments on the Mumonkan* (New York: Harper & Row, 1974), 207.

Notes for a Buddhist Politics

WILLIAM OPHULS

PROGRESS AS WE HAVE KNOWN IT has nearly reached its physical and psychological limits. Despite the remaining (and still sizable) areas of controversy, it is almost universally acknowledged that ever bigger and better ad infinitum is impossible and would be horrible even if it were possible. As a consequence, the quietly radical ideas of the British political economist E. F. Schumacher—epitomized by the title of his underground best seller, *Small Is Beautiful: Economics As If People Mattered*—have begun to attract respectful attention.

The essential spirit of Schumacher's thought is contained in the chapter entitled "Buddhist Economics." In it, following the Buddha, Schumacher maintains that the goal of economic life should be "Right Livelihood." That is, the economy must be designed to provide all members of society with a sufficiency of material well-being through livelihoods that are inherently satisfying, that do not harm others materially or spiritually, that involve the individual in service to his community, and that therefore contribute to the purification of character that is the goal of Buddhist life. To this end, says Schumacher, to the extent that they conflict with Right Livelihood, efficiency, rationality, and all the other materialist values of economic man that pervade modern industrial civilization must be resolutely rejected. A new economics characterized by ecological harmlessness and stewardship, by a refined simplicity of ends and means alike, and above all by a scrupulous regard for the quality of individual human lives must take its place. These can only be achieved if the scale of economic institutions and of technology is deliberately kept small. Thus, "Small Is Beautiful."

It is evident that such a "Buddhist economics" must necessarily go in tandem with a "Buddhist politics," for the unrestrained pursuit of individual material happiness upon which the essentially laissez-faire societies of the Western industrial nations are founded is incompatible with the goals of Buddhist economics. In effect, our political values are simply those of economic man transferred to the political sphere. To state the conclusion baldly, in politics as in economics, "small is beautiful": the scale of communal life must be reduced to more human (and, at the same time, more democratic) dimensions. Above all, however, political life must come to be based on some canon of public morality higher than the self-interest of the egotistical individual.

THE ALLEGED REALITY OF SELFISHNESS

The modern worldview says that man is fundamentally a selfish hedonist. Concerned only with the satisfaction of his own desires, he rationally pursues fame, profit, and position—which inevitably puts him in conflict with others. Since this is so, realism requires us to found our political and social institutions on the fact of human selfishness. Thus, we merely try to channel self-seeking behavior in benign directions—for example, by harnessing private advantage to public good or by pitting opposing interests against each other in the hope that their worst evils will cancel out and leave a residue of good. In fact, we take the position that progress will inevitably emerge out of such competitive striving. Thus, Adam Smith's famous "invisible hand" is indeed the paradigm of modern political economy: seeking *only* our own gain, we *inadvertently* benefit others and promote the commonweal. In this philosophy, controls on individual behavior to prevent direct and immediate personal harm to others are permitted—but any attempt to impose standards or values constitutes an unwarranted invasion of the individual's sacred right to pursue happiness *as he defines it*.

A Buddhist political philosopher would naturally join with other critics of this philosophy in noting that there is an inevitable tendency for the strong or callous to drive the weak or scrupulous to the wall—and, what is perhaps worse, to feel little remorse for doing so in a dog-eat-dog world. The Buddhist would also note that cultural life in such a system is bound to be debased: with no agreed standards and with so much profit to be gained from pandering to the desires of the multitude, the coarse will tend to drive the fine from the cultural marketplace (and tough luck for the sensitive few); worst of all, the impressionable young will be forced to breathe in, willy-nilly, the miasma of pornography and violence thus created, which sets up a vicious circle of corruption. In addition, the Buddhist would join ecologists and environmentalists in pointing out that a system founded on greed is no longer compatible with the physical realities of existence on the planet; if individuals and groups continue rationally to pursue material gratification without heed for the morrow, much less posterity, then the inevitable outcome of such an orgy of competitive overexploitation of the planet's resources will be the near-total devastation and depletion of the biosphere upon which life, especially the quality of life, ultimately depends.

However, for the Buddhist philosopher, the inherent callousness, moral depravity, and self-destructiveness of modern civilization are only secondary objections. The principal crime, in Buddhist eyes, is that we take selfishness and hedonism to be social facts—instead of the primordial problems that human beings are placed upon earth to solve. Thus, a vicious circle is set up in which the presumption of selfishness fosters behavior that reinforces the original presumption.

Buddhism does not, of course, deny the actuality of selfish behavior in the world, but it does not view this as a given to be regarded with complacency out of a misguided sense of realism. According to the Buddha, man's essential nature is good, but the conditions of life on earth foster a spiritual ignorance that almost always leads to the loss of his original goodness. If the ignorance that holds us all in thrall can be diluted—or, better yet, dissolved—then men will moderate or abandon their selfishness.

Spiritual ignorance is created in the following fashion: immaculately conceived, individuals are soon conditioned to think of themselves as separate entities or egos; this delusion of separateness leads them to believe that their interests are essentially opposed to those of others; thus, greed, hatred, and other defilements arise; worse, these defilements cause conflict and suffering that tend to reinforce the original delusion of a separateness that must at all costs be preserved and enhanced. The way to cut through this vicious circle of selfishness (called *samsara*) that we are all caught up in is the purification of character, not only in the economic sphere through the practice of Right Livelihood, but in all other spheres of life as well (as spelled out in the Noble Eightfold Path). When character has been purified, ignorance is seen through, and the selfish ego can no longer dominate one's life; *samsara* is cut off at its root; the innate wisdom and compassion that are the birthright of every human being are reborn; and one strives constantly thereafter to live in harmony with the Dharma, the moral law that governs the universe.

Although Buddhism, in common with other religions, enjoins the avoidance of evil and the doing of good upon its followers, it places primary emphasis on reeducating individuals to perceive the Dharma with their own hearts, for genuine liberation from selfishness and the suffering it causes is only to be found in total inner awareness, not in obedience to preceptual morality. The Buddhist philosopher is therefore interested in promoting psychological and social conditions that maximize individual opportunities for profound self-understanding and constructive self-development.

Conversely, things that tend to narcotize people or focus their attention on trivial externals—the widespread use of drugs, the hypnotic power of the mass media, the vast entertainment industry, and so on—would be regarded as profoundly undesirable. Indeed, a Buddhist would see our vaunted educational system, aptly dubbed "the Church of Reason" by Robert Pirsig, as the worst narcotic of all. With its exclusive dedication to instrumental rationality and its virtually total neglect of character training and psychophysical development, this system has become a barrier to self-knowledge and a prime cause of individual and social suffering. In Buddhist eyes, our civilization is all head and no heart; our view of reality and our sense of human possibilities are therefore seriously askew. By contrast, in a Buddhist polity, education would be predominantly experiential and aimed at the whole person. It would be carried out not in segregated educational factories, but by society as a whole (especially, of course, by the family), and the structure of society would have to permit and promote this kind of pervasive, lifelong apprenticeship.

THE PURSUIT OF DHARMA, NOT HAPPINESS

What, briefly, are the major tenets of a political philosophy founded on Dharma rather than the pursuit of happiness? The first principle of Buddhist politics is respectful tolerance. All beings and all authentic paths being spiritually equal, there is no basis for discrimination among them. Thus, a Buddhist must live and let live, without imposing anything on others—even Buddhism. This does not mean that one lapses into apathetic quietism. To the contrary, it is the duty of a Buddhist to persevere in promoting the worldly expression of the Dharma—but he must take care that, in doing so, he does not unleash further suffering. This requires him to work slowly, patiently, and carefully, scrupulously respecting the rights of others. Moreover, he must always remember that his primary duty is to bring about benign changes *in himself*; indeed, for a Buddhist this is the chief way in which society can be improved, because the good society can be created only from the bottom up, not from the top down. Accordingly, a Buddhist philosopher works with the grain of history, respecting the actual situation: he has no grand designs, no inflexible ideologies, no particular set of institutions to peddle—only the principle of *upaya*, or "skillful means" that manifest wisdom in action. The truth of the Dharma must be given concrete form according to the peculiar historical conditions prevailing in a given place at a given time. At one time these conditions may call for a monarchy, at another a democracy; at one place they may require a Buddhist culture, at another a Christian or even a so-called pagan culture. The important thing is the quality of individual human lives and the inner meaning of a culture, not structure and other externals.

Second, secular equality follows naturally from spiritual equality—but not necessarily egalitarianism, for people can be equal without being the same. There are natural differences between man and woman, and between man and man. To take cognizance of these differences and to reflect them *appropriately* in the social order (to the extent that historical conditions allow) fosters harmony and permits individuals to follow their own special vocation. By contrast, egalitarianism as we know it, which is too often fueled by envy, tends to reduce the social diversity that fosters genuine individuality, and at the same time throws people into conflict as everyone tries to climb to the top of the same pole. . . .

Third, given that egotism is the fundamental personal and social problem, the emphasis ought to be placed on duties instead of rights. A primary characteristic of the enlightened man is compassion; he lightens the load of others instead of aggrandizing himself. He is also gratefully aware of all the debts he owes to parents, teachers, and the like, and attempts generously to repay them by benefiting others in turn. One of the major paths toward self-purification is therefore the performance of loving service to one's community in whatever capacity one's talents and circumstances allow (with the spirit in which the service is performed, not the results achieved, being all-important). It just so happens that adherence to this principle of service tends also to create a better world for all, including the servitor. Conversely, a world composed primarily of miserly rat racers, dogs in the manger, and lookers-out-for-number-one is a world in which unbearable tension, pain, crime, and violence are inevitable.

A fourth principle of Buddhist politics is simplicity. The primary cause of suffering is desire, for this makes one constantly want and grasp things (as opposed to simply enjoying what one already has without being attached to having it or lusting after more). But wants are infinite, and even their constant fulfillment can never bring lasting satisfaction. A society in which wants are deliberately multiplied and in which this kind of happiness is pursued is therefore going to contain many frustrated and unhappy people—*no matter how successful their pursuit is.* The way to peace is spiritual poverty—not wanting to be better off than one already is materially, socially, even spiritually. A simple society without great extremes of rank, wealth, or knowledge is likelier to foster this spirit of tranquil nonattachment than one in which people are constantly made (often deliberately) to feel insecure, disadvantaged, or inadequate. In addition, as a byproduct, a simple society maximizes individual opportunities to participate meaningfully in social life and to be of direct service to others; it is therefore better suited to serve the cause of self-development. By contrast, to construct a society so complex and grandiose that it frustrates people's need to be creatively involved with the world puts individuals largely at the mercy of remote bureaucrats and arrogant experts or reduces political participation to a token vote.

Finally, an essential requirement of a Buddhist polity is nonviolence—and not just toward other humans, but also toward all the rest of creation. Perfect nonviolence is impossible. Humans cannot feed, clothe, or house themselves without doing some violence. But by taking heed, by being frugal, and by using or doing things with respect, we can minimize our violence and alleviate most of its harmful effects. To do as we now do, gouging the earth to gratify our demand for energy and materials that we then proceed to use wastefully to support a gluttonous standard of living and a monstrous military establishment, is to give full rein to violence. Then the ecological wasteland without mirrors the spiritual wasteland within. We need not go to the opposite extreme of self-abnegation either, for Buddhism is the Middle Way. Accordingly, the fulfillment of genuine needs and the enjoyment of natural pleasures that harm neither self nor others is legitimate, and these legitimate ends can be readily attained in a society that has eschewed violence for simplicity and frugality. Moreover, it is the spirit in which things are done, as much or more than the deed itself, that matters. . . .

WHY SMALL IS BEAUTIFUL

All the above principles are interrelated and mutually reinforcing. Thus, tolerance, equality, service, and simplicity all support nonviolence, and vice versa. However, more important, all of the above are in turn dependent on a critical social variable—the scale of institutions. Bigness leads to complexity, not simplicity. Complexity in turn leads to the necessity for rationalized bureaucratic rules and controls that frustrate or ignore the promptings of the human heart and that make people feel powerless and inadequate; it leads indirectly to inequality, quarrelsomeness, power struggles, and violence. In addition, problems that used to be solved with local initiative and ingenuity mushroom in size and become qualitatively different; citizens can no longer cope, and the call goes up for government to "do something."

Bigness also cuts down on individual opportunities for self-development; when every important decision is made "at the center," all but a few are denied meaningful participation in life. No matter how busy they are in executing policy or meeting the quota, people know deep down that they are working for "headquarters," not themselves. As a consequence, we cannot expect much in the way of civic virtue from the average person. . . . Democracy, which is supposed to *involve* the citizen in making the laws that are to govern him, becomes symbolic at best, fraudulent at worst. In short, even if smallness were not necessary to support Buddhist economics, it would be essential in its own right.

Naturally, smallness should not be made into a fetish. A critical mass is necessary for some undertakings, and there are genuine economies of scale in some areas. Thus, in accordance with the principle of *upaya*, a follower of the Middle Way would go about determining the appropriate size of social institutions pragmatically and with an open mind. Nevertheless, we can safely put aside the question of *how* much smaller would be beautiful for the moment, because it is overwhelmingly clear that in almost every area it would be *very* much smaller than at present.

This ought not to be a startling conclusion. Aristotle and Plato both pointed out the social and political perils of overdevelopment in the strongest possible terms, and later democratic and republican political theorists have unanimously reiterated their conclusion: only a relatively small, face-to-face society is capable of promoting and preserving a spirit of civic virtue, democratic or republican self-rule, and a general atmosphere conducive to the self-development of the citizen. Conversely, bigness and complexity invite tyranny and social unrest.

But then, just like the Buddhist political philosopher, these thinkers were primarily concerned with what kind of human being was produced by a particular set of political institutions. In other words, although usually lacking the distinctive spiritual aspirations of Buddhism, they also saw the purification of character as the goal of human life.

To many readers, all of the above must seem hopelessly utopian, doomed to founder on the rock of reality. However, it must never be forgotten that social reality is *created*. Different times and different places have had vastly different realities. The ancient Athenians, for example, despised the merely wealthy. The only way to earn their respect was by excellence in the service of the community; not surprisingly, most citizens devoted themselves to public service, not private acquisition. Our current reality of selfishness is largely the product of a self-fulfilling prophecy: people have believed the worldviews of Thomas Hobbes, Adam Smith, and their ilk into existence, and this actuality can be dissolved by a willed suspension of belief. To propose a radically different, but not inherently unworkable, set of values is therefore not utopian after all, but a highly practical—indeed, indispensable—prerequisite to meaningful social and political change. Indeed, no greater—or more successful—utopians than the founding fathers of the American republic ever walked the face of the earth, and what they did can be done again.

On the other hand, it is evident that all actual polities will necessarily fall well short of the Buddhist ideal. What matters is not perfection, but the basic value orientation of the polity. Decisions are now made according to whether they will make us more secure, richer, more powerful, better off than our neighbor, and so on. When they are instead made by asking whether simplicity and the other tenets of Buddhist politics will be enhanced or not, then we would be on the right path. Above all, anything that aggrandizes the power of government, so that it begins to look after us instead of helping us to look after ourselves, must be examined with deep suspicion, for this seems inevitably to lead to bigness and complexity.

Naturally, the Middle Way is not easy to tread, and merely reducing the size of communal institutions to the appropriate level will not banish evil from the world. But it would reduce the massiveness of the evil that could be done, and bring us back into the realm of personal evil, which we can understand and deal with.

Nor would smallness per se always guarantee freedom. However, the tyranny currently exercised over our lives by impersonal forces—the market, efficiency, technology, and the like—beyond any individual's ken, much less control, should not be overlooked.

The Search for Models

Unfortunately, there are no useful models of Buddhist politics that we can readily apply to our current historical circumstances. But Americans, and even many Europeans, will find most of its essential features in the thought of Thomas Jefferson. (Others, especially in the Third World, may prefer to follow Gandhi.) Perhaps it is time to pit Jefferson's vision of republican simplicity against Alexander Hamilton's rival vision of national power and commercial complexity once again—but this time decide in favor of Jefferson, now that we have learned the hard way the truth in his famous maxim, "That government is best that governs least."

Of course, to a Buddhist philosopher, Jefferson's vision, although firmly grounded in Christian ethics, lacks a certain spiritual depth. Perhaps the thought of Henry David Thoreau can repair some of this lack. *Walden*, the record of his symbolic critique of a society that had spurned Jefferson for Hamilton, is an extended sermon on the necessity of natural simplicity as the only way to avoid living the quietly desperate life of those weighed down by selfish striving for power, possessions, and position. Additional inspiration can be found in Thomas More's *Utopia*, still unexcelled as a description of a social order in which individuals are spontaneously obedient to moral law. Nor need the Christian tradition be neglected; indeed, Schumacher, who is not a Buddhist but a Catholic, has pointed out that the Four Cardinal Virtues of Christianity—*prudentia*, *justitia, fortitudo*, and *temperantia*—could serve as readily as Buddhist principles as the foundation for social and economic sanity. In short, Buddhist politics accords totally with the highest teachings in Western tradition. It could not be otherwise, for there is only one Dharma, however differently it is expressed by different cultures.

So it appears that small is indeed beautiful. Moreover, this would be true even if one rejected totally the spiritual goals of Buddhism or the other religions. Following the principles of Buddhist politics would lead toward a more pleasant, harmonious, and humane worldly existence, even without regard to ultimate spiritual consequences. So, now is not too soon to begin changing realities—starting, as always, with oneself.

Deep Ecology and Political Activism

BILL DEVALL

JOHN MUIR, CONSIDERED BY MANY HISTORIANS to be the
founder of the American conservation movement, came back from
lobbying politicians for conservation legislation one day in the first decade of this century and wrote with exasperation in his journal, "Politics
saps at the heart of righteousness."

No doubt many environmental activists since Muir's time have felt
similar exasperation and even desperation as they toiled on a political
campaign to end commercial hunting of whales, protect endangered spotted owls, or convince legislators to pass bills requiring recycling. Many
sensitive people give up hope and withdraw from political activism when
they consider the amount of violence and ignorance in our culture, the
drastic and negative impact of industrial civilization on the Earth, and the
rising species extinction-rate due to human impacts. Does the human
species have the will and the ability to make wise decisions for present
and future generations? Are most humans motivated only by narrow self-
interest, greed, and desire for power over other humans?

Other people, however, find renewed strength to work for social
transformation. These activists, many of them in quite humble economic
situations in their private lives, give voice to endangered sea turtles, dolphins, and ancient forests. Following in the tradition of John Muir, Aldo
Leopold, Rachel Carson, David Brower, Chico Mendez, Gandhi, Martin
Luther King, Jr., and Bob Brown, they realize that they will make, in
Gandhi's term, "Himalayan mistakes" in political games, but with clear
intent and an open heart they are drawn to the task at hand. What some
teachers call "heart-politics" involves the activist in open, honest, truthful
affirmation. Heart politics is dramatically different from cynical, back-
stabbing, power-grabbing, egotistical game playing, which many associate
with the mainly masculine game of politics as played in corporations,
public bureaucratic agencies, and in national and state legislatures.

These deeply motivated activists recognize that they are living in a
time of war—a great worldwide war against other species, against whole

bioregions, against indigenous peoples on every continent. The environmental movement, by the broadest definition, is the only political movement that provides a loyal opposition to the hegemony of capitalist and socialists economic development in the late twentieth century. By that I mean that so-called conservative and liberal political parties, such as Democrats and Republicans in the United States, have governed as coalition governments on major issues of economic growth, massive public works projects, and the approval of huge military budgets. Because supporters of the deep, long-range ecology movement are in opposition to the dominant paradigm and dominant political regimes, some of them will be branded as deviants, hunted down as criminals by agents of state security agencies, and even murdered. Some environmental groups will be infiltrated by secret agents. Some leaders will be corrupted by government agents. When environmental groups or particular individuals are seen as particularly irritating to state agencies, they will be labeled as "terrorists" or "extreme environmentalists." Attempts may be made to murder some environmental leaders in certain nations. The murder of Chico Mendez shows that what many in the United States call "environmental politics" involves us in age-old conflicts over the use of natural resources. The plot by the French secret service to bomb the Greenpeace vessel in Auckland harbor is an example of the lengths to which some government agencies will go to stop ecoactivists.

After a period of intense, full-time political work during which personal relationships, spiritual practice, and even physical health may be neglected, many people experience burnout. They find it physically and mentally impossible to continue. Yet they feel guilty if they are not working to protect rain forests, to stop the killing of whales, and to educate other people on the dangers of the increasing hole in the ozone, global warming, or destruction of ancient forests. Some people may be so wounded by periods of intense activism that they spend the rest of their lives engaged in physical and psychological healing.

From a deep ecology perspective, we are called to ask spiritual, psychological, and philosophical questions concerning our actions. Political action includes many activities besides power politics, political tactics, and political rhetoric. John Seed, an Australian supporter of deep ecology who, along with Joanna Macy, created the Council of All Beings as a way to introduce people to deep ecology perspectives, writes about his own experiences transcending anthropocentrism. "I became the rainforest, speaking for itself," he says.

Suzanne Head is a woman who has engaged in Buddhist practice for many years, been a leader in the rain forest protection movement, and has written with deep perception on topics relating to deep ecology. She posed the questions listed below concerning activism to scholars, teachers, and students who attended a conference on Humans in Nature held at The Naropa Institute in Boulder, Colorado, in May 1991.

These challenging questions provide a framework within which to discuss political activism from a deep ecology perspective. My commentary on each question reflects my current position. My position concerning some questions has changed over the years as I have reflected on my own political activism and the activities of some of my associates. My position may also change in the future. My commentaries are quite modest. Each reader is encouraged to reflect on these questions based on his or her experiences. Although based on ancient principles, the deep, long-range ecology movement is still a very young movement in contemporary civilization.

❖

Is it possible to work for change within the national and international arena and still maintain one's personal integrity and sacred outlook? Is it possible to gain national recognition and influence if one does not play the Washington, D.C., brand of politics? How much influence can one have if one doesn't?

In political circles in Washington, D. C., environmental groups are frequently seen as just another special interest group. From my deep ecology perspective, nature, Gaia, the Earth, whatever we call this planet we dwell upon, is in peril. When we speak for Gaia, for dolphins, for any nonhuman creatures on this planet or for the basic processes of ecosystems, of evolution, of life, we are not just another special interest group. Put the Earth first. That is a basic principle of all who love the planet that we dwell upon. We do not compromise on principles.

However, politics, as many have noted, does make for strange bedfellows. Grassroots coalitions focused on specific issues with as broad a range of support as possible can have positive effectiveness in Washington, D.C., politics. The civil rights movement demonstrated this point. Cooperation with any groups who put the Earth first can help further ecosophy. As we search for ecosophical solutions to problems, we can work with many different political parties, ethnic group organizations, unions, and consumer groups. There are, of course, honest disagreements concerning what tactics are most appropriate to a particular campaign. Principles, however, are never compromised.

In specific political campaigns, grassroots organizations and national environmental organizations are frequently in disagreement. This can provide healthy tension to the campaign, but it can also lead to a pervasive sense of distrust of national environmental leaders by grassroots activists. Grassroots leaders are frequently motivated by the suffering that they have experienced in their bioregion. Victims of toxic wastes and radioactive wastes, people who have witnessed the clearcutting of ancient forests, citizens who have seen the effects of massive housing subdivision projects on drained wetlands—these are the people who agitate for political solutions. Grassroots leaders see leaders of national, reform environmental groups making deals (with bureaucrats in federal agencies or with congressional committees) that compromise the principles for which they fought and that create more problems than they solve.

Grassroots groups, sometimes with the cooperation of public interest law firms, have gone to court to obtain decisions on corporate or government actions. Courts are expected to base their decisions on evidence and principles. Seeking court judgments to enforce provisions of the National Environmental Policy Act and the Endangered Species Act provides activists with an arena in which to state principles without compromise. If political regimes corrupt the courts or prohibit certain types of suits, as has happened frequently during the past decade in the United States, then environmentalists take protest to the streets, to log decks, to toxic waste sites to affirm their principles through civil disobedience.

It is now recognized that the environmental movement has helped to foster democratic decision-making over the past two decades. By insisting on more open discussion of issues, by redefining the agenda of politics, by refusing to play by the rules of the Washington, D.C., political game, supporters of the deep, long-range ecology movement have grown in influence and effectiveness.

Let me use an example from my own experience in which I clearly stated my principles and goals and opposed any compromise of those principles. Based on my understanding of the ecology of ancient forests of the Pacific Northwest and my understanding of the extent of clearcutting of ancient forests, as well as my strong emotional identification with the forests, my goal is to end logging in ancient forests on public and private lands. I cannot endorse any legislation that compromises this goal by stating that the timber industry can have a certain percentage of remaining ancient forests, and the environmentalists can have a certain percentage.

The polls indicate that most Americans support protection of ancient forests. The people therefore are with the grassroots campaign to end logging in ancient forests. I must oppose the politics of compromise.

From my deep ecology perspective, I must speak for the truth as I see it. Social transformation cannot occur based on lies. I must be like the Lorax in Dr. Seuss's book (1971) by that name: "I am the Lorax. I speak for the trees. I speak for the trees, for the trees have no tongues."

※

How effective can one be if one insists on maintaining purity? How effective can one be if one doesn't?

Effectiveness is a somewhat ambiguous term. To be effective in gaining passage for some legislation may give the impression that ecoactivists are winning the political game, but that act of legislation may be worse than the status quo. Activists must always ask, are we really changing the political game, or are we being used by major players in the game?

Effectiveness could be defined as effective in making clear statements based on our principles. Effectiveness could be to plant seeds of thought that may bear fruit in the far future. Rather than asking if I am effective, I ask, Am I being true to myself, to my principles?

Purity is also an ambiguous term. We are clear in our intentions, clear in our goals, clear in our principles. However, we may not fully comprehend the implications of our actions, and we may be deceived by politicians and by some leaders of environmental groups.

Supporters of deep ecology whom I know and admire are modest people. They are not engaged in political action to further their own egos or to achieve power for the sake of power. They are not professional politicians nor do they want to be professional politicians or bureaucrats. If purity means to avoid corruption, bribery, and gross manipulation of others to achieve a goal, then I would answer, yes. We must maintain our purity of what Arne Naess calls "ultimate norms." If purity means always using deep ecology-type of arguments, then I would say, no. What Arne Naess has called a "shallow" type of argumentation may be the most practical, honest, and effective type of argumentation in specific situations.

※

How can we go beyond the right-wing/left-wing dualism that is currently perceived in the deep ecology movement?

The statement by the German Green party is most relevant in answering this question. We are neither left nor right; we are in the vanguard. The old categories of left and right have less relevance in the age of ecology than in previous eras. The environmental movement cannot be coopted or infiltrated by the political agendas of leftist or rightist movements.

People coming from different ideological perspectives can agree on some social and economic issues. I can agree with anyone, be they leftists and or rightists, if they see the need for radical changes in society based on putting the Earth first. Social justice movements, peace movements, and reform ecology movements can share a vision of ecotopia based on deep ecology insights.

I consider myself a social ecologist. I have studied the social and economic reasons for our current dilemma. I have studied theories of bureaucracy and social class. I find great strength in arguments that identify imperialism and growth of state power as a cause of our problems. I also find great cogency in the arguments by feminists that patriarchy and androcentrism have contributed to the crisis of character and culture that we call the environmental crisis. I feel that I am a victim of the patriarchy. I also agree with those who study political economy and who argue that the logic of capitalism leads to environmental degradation. I can also agree with those who argue that bureaucracy has social costs and that privatization of some aspects of land can further the long-term environmental quality of the land, if the stewards of the land respect its integrity. Intellectuals in the deep, long-range ecology movement can debate and discuss these issues honestly.

However, when rhetoric replaces discussion and when social ecology is defined in a narrow, sectarian way, then divisiveness replaces discussion. A self-proclaimed anarchist who is a social ecologist theorist and who lives in New England provides a notorious example. This person rejects ecocentrism. He has repeatedly used ad hominem attacks in place of rational arguments. He has corrupted the discussion over the best strategy for family planning and lowering the birth rate and frequently makes rhetorical attacks, using distorted definitions for commonly used concepts.

Political revolution and liberal reform have been part of the vocabulary of social change movements in the West for over two centuries. Freedom, individualism, economic development, and "progress" have also been guiding myths of much modern political theory. However, we are now less free to hear the howl of the wolves, to explore deep identity with nonhumans, to be embedded in the cosmos. The deep, long-range ecology movement is a kind of resistance movement to the excesses of modern views of nature, excesses of progress and economic development that have led to massive state and private bureaucracies that dominate, domesticate, control, and destroy vast areas of the Earth. Many supporters of deep ecology like the slogan, "Resist much, obey little": that is, resist those who would dominate nature for narrow human goals; obey the laws of ecology.

Racism, sexism, the battle between the sexes, gender politics, the fight against heterosexism, social equality for different ethnic groups, social justice—all these are worthy, important movements. However, the deep, long-range ecology movement does put the Earth first.

Believers of either left or right political ideologies who support the deep, long-range ecology movement can agree that we want to enrich the experience of humans on Earth by helping humans realize their broad and deep identification with nature.

Believers of any political ideology as well as believers of various religions can affirm the integrity of the principle of preserving native biological diversity, wilderness, forests, and marine ecosystems.

Believers of any political ideology or religion who support the deep, long-range ecology movement can agree that humans are one modest species among many dwelling on this planet. Humans have no right to cause the extinction of other species nor to drastically alter the habitat of many species in all the ecosystems of the planet.

Believers of any political ideology who support putting the Earth first can encourage movements that affirm environmental quality in Third World nations, where such movements also tend to strengthen democracy, protect human rights, and encourage social equality between classes, genders, and ethnic groups.

✻

Is what we do as important as how we do it?

All actions will initiate reaction. How we engage in political activism is part of our practice. I have never met a supporter of deep ecology who had not embraced the norm of nonviolence. Of course, the history of environmental movements has been remarkably nonviolent in comparison to such social movements as the labor movement, social justice movements, and Marxist-leftist movements.

Political revolution is not part of the vocabulary of supporters of the deep, long-range ecology movement. Ecology subverts the narrow humanism and materialism of both the Left and Right and rejects both the myth of revolution and the myth of individual ego as supreme in the world, as well as the myth of the sanctity of private property rights. Nonviolence, of course, is interpreted differently in different cultural contexts. Nonviolence is not passive. A person acting from the principle of nonviolence can be very assertive, speak out for principles, engage in protest demonstrations, even engage in illegal actions of many kinds.

To be nonviolent does not mean that one has to be intimidated by threats of violence, or threats of legal action by corporations, or political regimes, or by bureaucrats for natural resources agencies such as the U.S. Forest Service, who are dedicated to resource exploitation and intensive management for the purpose of maximizing timber cutting in the short term. Supporters of deep, long-range ecology feel empowered to speak out for right livelihood (i.e., not doing harm), and for restoration of human-damaged lands.

We can also use human creations as our teachers. For example, Joanna Macy and her associates have established a Nuclear Guardianship Project as a further extension of the deep ecology perspective. Participants in this project use the poison fire of nuclear reactors as their teacher. In less than fifty years, some humans have displaced radioactive material and concentrated that material into bombs, nuclear reactors, and other products. The radioactivity of these products will decay over hundreds or thousands of years, depending on the type of radioactive particle. While these radioactive particles are decaying, they are a health hazard to humans and many other lifeforms. The Nuclear Guardianship Project places humans in league with beings of future generations. It is a network of citizens working to develop nuclear policies and practices that respect the power of the poison fire and reflect the responsibility of people in this generation to present and future life.

The statement of purpose of the project reads:

> To curtail rampant radioactive contamination the Project calls for a halt to the production and transportation of nuclear wastes, and for citizen involvement in the responsible care of the wastes produced to date. It promotes the guardianship of the wastes at their points of generation in monitored, retrievable storage facilities. And it develops educational programs to begin the training in technical knowledge and moral vigilance required to establish and maintain these Guardian Sites. The Project recognizes that radioactive wastes represent our most enduring legacy to future life on earth.

In sum, the practice and the process are as important as are the goals of political action.

*

How narrowly do we want to define political action? How broadly do we want to define political action?

I have a friend who rides his bicycle fifteen miles each way to work each day—rain or shine. He says his bike ride is his Zen practice. He is in pain some days from bike riding. But he continues to ride. He is an example to the rest of us who drive our vehicles each day to work. Is his action political? In a broad sense it is. The deliberate choice of lifestyle is a political action.

What we teach is a political action. When I teach theories of the ecology of ancient forests in my college classes at Humboldt State University, I am engaged in a political act. Ecology, as Paul Shepard (1969) noted nearly twenty-five years ago, is a subversive science. It is subversive to the reductionism of conventional science. It is subversive to the dominant social paradigm. In my bioregion of northwestern California, the timber industry uses the ideology of "natural resources conservation and development"—that is, very heavily managed forests, multiple-use forests, cloned trees, maximum yield, trees are for people, enhancing nature—these are the slogans used by those who want business as usual, who want humanistic, capitalist approaches to forest management.

Any statements of solidarity with the integrity of ancient forests are considered political statements. I have received death threats after letters to the editor defending the listing of northern spotted owls as a threatened species were published in local newspapers. Freedom of speech is at issue here. Any of our statements, any expression of ideas, even shopping at certain stores is considered a political action.

Political action defined broadly allows people to select the style of activism that suits their own life condition and temperament. If green lifestyles are not stated in political terms, then police, and many school teachers, will see them as deviant, criminal, or resulting from mental illness. In the county in which I dwell, for example, even the decision to shop in certain stores has been defined by pro-logging groups as "political." Some groups in my county have organized "Boycott Arcata" campaigns, because the city of Arcata has been seen as harboring pro-environmental people. Some businesses located in Arcata have supported the local environmental information center, but other business leaders have said that it hurts their business to have ecoactivists walking the streets of Arcata.

Whether we like it or not, our lifestyles, our opinions, the mode of transportation we choose, our decision to consume less—all these ideas and actions have already been politicized. When I tell some people I know that I wear old clothes rather than shop at the mall, I am condemned by these people as "hippie," antidevelopment, and anticapitalist. When I put a bumper sticker on my auto proclaiming "Save Ancient Forests," I could be a target for a sniper's bullet.

✳

Is it possible to work effectively with power and authority and to maintain integrity in social change work if one has not worked through one's early childhood conditioning and emotional wounds?

As adults we are all conditioned by our childhood experiences. Many of us were deprived of earth-bonding experiences as children. Millions of Americans will grow to adulthood without ever having had the opportunity to see a mountain lion, or a black bear, or an elk in wild habitat. As adults, we seek opportunities to heal our relationships with wild nature as well as with humanized landscapes, the scars of clearcut logging, mining, nuclear reactors, toxic waste dumps. Many people are isolated from human warmth and loving relationships and have low self-esteem. Social isolation and low self-esteem have been identified by social scientists as the two factors that contribute most to dysfunctional social relationships in adulthood.

Adults can transcend childhood trauma, can be courageous in the face of a hostile social environment, through creation of their lifestyle. Alfred Adler coined the term *lifestyle* in 1929 after he broke with his teacher, Freud. Adler saw the importance of insight and courage in the struggle to live life fully and well. He defined lifestyle as the sum of eccentricities, values, meaningful acts, passions, and knowledge. Lifestyle includes a person's vision of how to make peace in the wasteland that we call modern society.

Many groups and movements are available to help people heal childhood traumas and cultivate courageous lifestyles. These include primal therapy, which was pioneered by Arthur Janov, and the men's movement developed by Robert Bly and others, which encourages bonding between men, nonviolence, openness in relationships, acceptance of vulnerability, love, and companionship between men rather than domination.

Co-counseling, adult children of alcoholic groups, the twelve-step movement, personal growth workshops, and many groups focusing on co-dependency are examples of healing in our culture. Supporters of the deep, long-range ecology movement can participate in and encourage others to participate in such healing and bonding activities.

Thich Nhat Hanh, a Vietnamese Buddhist teacher, for example, offers meditation retreats for environmentalists that open the possibilities of sitting and walking meditation to men and women who lead hectic lives as political activists. Retreats offered by Joanna Macy and others that she has trained help adults move from despair and denial into empowerment.

Transpersonal psychology suggests that adults can be self-realizing beings who explore themselves as leaves on the tree of life. The Council of All Beings, developed by Joanna Macy and John Seed, provides a ritual for expressing our grief over the loss of many species and a way to empower people to speak for other beings with compassion and power. Some Christian groups have provided opportunities for their congregations to participate in a Council of All Beings.

The deep, long-range ecology movement has a powerful, affirmative message. We do not have to live our lives as victims of military-industrial oppression, victims of toxic wastes, victims of doublespeak by politicians and bureaucrats.

Bearing witness to our emotional wounds, our alienation from the rest of nature, we can move into healing relationships with a watershed, with our bioregion, with Gaia.

Supporters of deep ecology do not engage in political activism to advance the ego, to gain power for the sake of power over other persons, but to advance and affirm the myriad of beings, the integrity of our broad and deep self. When acting in roles of leadership, we must clarify our motivation and engage in what Gary Snyder (1980, 7) calls the "real work." Our sexual frustrations, our personal attractions or dislike of other people in our activist group, our need for ego advancement, as well as our

fears and fantasies must be watched, noted, and dealt with compassionately in order to maintain effective activism.

Chagdud Tulku Rinpoche (1991) wrote, while contemplating the
consequences of the war in the Persian Gulf, a statement that is wise and
clear:

> As we aspire to peace, now and in the future cycles of our existence,
> we cannot deny the possibility that each of us may be confronted
> with the need for wrathful intervention in order to prevent greater
> harm. May the spiritual training we undertake now allow us to
> enter such situations free from the delusions of the mind's poisons.
> May we act with spontaneous compassion to bring ultimate libera-
> tion to all alike, both victims and aggressors. (p. 13)

*

*How do we integrate our personal and collective shadows so that they do not
continue to darken the world?*

Understanding our own shadows requires courage and skill. We
need skillful teachers and therapists to guide us. Both teachers and therapists have a special responsibility in this time of global crisis to help their
students and clients integrate themselves so that they understand their
broad identification and put the Earth first.

We help the world when we help to heal ourselves, when our selves
are very broad and deep. Compassion and insight are brought forth from
our own suffering. When we seek to be healers of the world, we begin by
realizing that we are wounded healers. We have been damaged by our
experiences of suffering while living on this planet during this era.

We are also damaged by our socialization to American culture in the
late twentieth century. Our collective, cultural shadow includes our fear
of insecurity, our nationalistic desire to "win" at any cost, our desire to
be number one, our culturally induced desire to find new frontiers to
conquer.

Strenuous practice may be required to break our psyches of these
delusions. We must learn to practice on this planet, not on Mars. Supporters of the deep, long-range ecology movement are not much interested in terraforming Mars. Earth is and will continue to be our home.

As I stated at the beginning of this essay, questions concerning political activism can be addressed in many ways. Many types of activism are appropriate and complementary. Arne Naess, who coined the term *deep ecology*, says "the front is very long" (1991). In the midst of the worldwide war against nature, we are all victims and we are all potentially heroes.

The courageous stance, it seems to me, is to become a gentle ecowarrior or, in Buddhist terms, to become bodhisattva warriors. Perhaps we can speak for a few ancient forests, a few species that would otherwise have gone extinct without notice.

We help as much as we can, as much as we have energy to bear witness on this Earth—but the outcome of this war is not dependent on any one individual or group.

REFERENCES

Naess, A. 1991. Speech given at The Naropa Institute Conference, May 4, Boulder, Colo.

Chagdud. 1991. Bodhisattva warriors. In *Buddhist Peace Fellowship Newsletter*, Winter.

Seuss, D. 1971. *The lorax*. New York: Random House.

Shepard, P. and D. McKinley, eds. 1969. *The subversive science; essays toward the ecology of man* Boston: Houghton-Mifflin.

Snyder, G. *The real work: interviews and talks 1964-79*. Edited by W. Scott McLean. New York: New Directions.

Nuclear Ecology and Engaged Buddhism

KENNETH KRAFT

FIFTY-PLUS YEARS INTO THE NUCLEAR AGE, the disposition of nuclear waste has stymied industrial societies scientifically, technically, socially, politically, and ethically. Radioactive waste repels most people even as a subject for consideration, in part because the present formulations of the problem are stale, blocking both insight and action. We lack a fresh conceptual framework that incorporates the relevant resources and engages our imaginations. So I have been experimenting lately with the concept of *nuclear ecology*.[1]

As a field, nuclear ecology might serve to integrate the disparate disciplines and individual roles required for the long-term management of nuclear materials. Under the ecology rubric alone there are several subfields that pertain to nuclear materials but have never been consolidated in the service of nuclear-waste management. These include radiation ecology (also called radiobiology), applied ecology, industrial ecology, restoration ecology, and deep ecology. In recognition of the rights of future generations, a unified nuclear ecology should embody some vision of stewardship or guardianship, derived from secular or religious sources. Buddhism, with its "cosmic ecology"[2] and a range of other resources, may have something to contribute.

BUDDHIST RESPONSES TO NUCLEAR ISSUES

Buddhists have been sensitive to nuclear issues for several decades, especially in North America. Concern about radioactive waste was prefigured by varied expressions of opposition to nuclear weapons, including marches across the United States, sit-ins at the United Nations, demonstrations at the Nevada Nuclear Test Site, individual acts of civil disobedience, and participation in local watchdog groups. In 1974, poet Gary Snyder wrote in his Pulitzer Prize-winning book, *Turtle Island*, "No more kidding the public about nuclear waste disposal: it's impossible to do it safely."[3] Vietnamese Zen master Thich Nhat Hanh speaks of nuclear waste as "the most difficult kind of garbage" and a "bell of mindfulness."[4] The Dalai Lama's five-point peace plan for Tibet, first announced in 1987, has an explicit antinuclear plank: it calls for "the abandonment of China's use of Tibet for the production of nuclear weapons and dumping of nuclear waste."[5]

The most influential Buddhist thinker-activist in this area is Joanna Macy, author of the concept of nuclear guardianship. Macy's ideas and example have inspired many, including me. Rather than shrink in dread from nuclear waste, she argues, we must take responsibility for it. Macy cultivates an awareness of future beings, imagining that one of their urgent questions to us might be: "What have you done—or not done—to safeguard us from the toxic nuclear wastes you bequeathed to us?" She proposes the creation of guardian sites, former nuclear facilities where radioactive materials are monitored in a manner that reflects a widely shared moral commitment to the task. Such sites might also have religious dimensions, serving as places of pilgrimage, meditation, or rituals associated with stewardship. The Nuclear Guardianship Project, a group led by Macy, flourished from 1991 until 1994. In study groups and public workshops, participants experimented with futuristic ceremonies that expressed the vision of guardianship. Although the Nuclear Guardianship Project has not developed organizationally, some of its ideas have circulated as far as the Energy Department's Office of Environmental Management.[6]

Several American Buddhist communities have incorporated concern about nuclear issues into their religious practice. In 1995, the Green Gulch Zen Center, north of San Francisco—probably the most active in this regard—staged an evocative multimedia ceremony-and-performance to commemorate the fiftieth anniversary of the bombing of Hiroshima and Nagasaki. Members of a small Zen group in Oregon became so determined to do something about the "poison fire" of nuclear waste that they added a fifth vow to the traditional four vows of a bodhisattva:

Sentient beings are numberless; I'll do the best I can to save them
Desires are inexhaustible; I'll do the best I can to put an end to them.
The Dharmas are boundless; I'll do the best I can to master them.

The Poison Fire lasts forever; I'll do the best I can to contain it.
The Buddha way is unsurpassable; I'll do the best I can to attain it.[7]

In April 1994, about fifty American Buddhists commemorated Buddha's birthday at the Nevada Nuclear Test Site. The outdoor ceremony, created collaboratively the previous evening, included offerings at an altar, recitation of sutras, and circumambulation. One by one, participants expressed their concerns and their aspirations. A woman spoke tenderly of her stepfather, who as a young soldier had been forced to witness aboveground atomic tests. A college student stoutly declared, "I dedicate my life to working for the earth and all beings." Others placed handwritten messages on the altar, silently pinning scraps of paper under rocks. The possibility of nonviolent civil disobedience was an integral part of the event because the walking meditation led right up to a boundary guarded by men in uniform. Some of the walkers deliberately stepped over the line and were arrested. The ceremony concluded with the following invocation:

> All merit and virtue that may have arisen through our efforts here, we now respectfully turn over and dedicate to the healing of this beautiful sacred land and to all beings who have been injured or harmed by the weapons testing on this place, so that the children of this world may live in peace free from these profane weapons, and thus may have their chance to realize the Buddha's Way.[8]

If one were to select the term most often used to characterize Buddhist practice in the West today, it would be *mindfulness*. This is the case not only in Buddhist circles but also in the popular press. A recent article in *USA Today*, cleverly entitled "Buddhism: Religion of the Moment," called mindfulness "the heart of Buddhist meditation . . . the ability to live completely in the present, deeply aware and appreciative of life."[9] Such definitions are unobjectionable. However, in a nuclear or environmental context a practitioner may be prompted to ask: What is the scope of my mindfulness?

At times mindfulness involves complexities and challenges that cannot be reduced just to living in the present. Socially and environmentally concerned Buddhists recognize that they must attend to breadth as well as breath, and that their breath connects them to their breadth.[10] Authentic practice aims continuously to broaden and deepen the scope of mindfulness. In this spirit, Thich Nhat Hanh attempts to connect mindfulness with nuclear waste:

> The most difficult kind of garbage is nuclear waste. It doesn't need four hundred years to become a flower. It needs 250,000 years. Because we may soon make this earth into an impossible place for our children to live, it is very important to become mindful in our daily lives.
>
> Nuclear waste is a bell of mindfulness. Every time a nuclear bomb is made, nuclear waste is produced. There are vast amounts of this material, and it is growing every day. Many federal agencies and other governments are having great difficulty disposing of it. The storage and clean-up expense has become a great debt we are leaving to our children. More urgently, we are not informed about the extent of the problem—where the waste sites are and how dangerous it can be.[11]

Thich Nhat Hanh does not explain at greater length how mindfulness in daily life might apply to nuclear-waste problems. In this case, being mindful could entail research on local sources of energy and possible alternatives, efforts to alter one's own lifestyle and the lifestyles of others, broader political activism, and so on. The society-wide vigilance required to keep radioactive materials out of the biosphere now and in the future can also be seen as a kind of collective mindfulness.[12]

KARMA ISN'T WHAT IT USED TO BE

One way to assess nuclear waste from a Buddhist perspective would be to analyze certain issues in karmic terms. For example, what are the karmic implications of creating long-lived radioactive materials that put perhaps thousands of generations of descendants at risk? From a scholarly standpoint or a religious one, traditional understandings of karma do not readily accommodate problems of this nature. Are we talking about the karmic import for us, for our descendants, for the environment, or for all of those? At the very least, previous thinking about karma needs to be extended or adapted.

In Buddhism's long history, understandings of karma have varied considerably. Among contemporary Buddhists in the West, karma principally signifies the moral implications of action, with the sense that causation mysteriously operates in the realm of ethics as well as the realm of physics. A basic tenet of engaged Buddhism is that—whatever one's intentions—it is not possible to follow a spiritual path in a social or political or environmental vacuum. While practicing mindfulness in daily life, even while meditating in a meditation hall, one's actions and nonactions continue to have wider repercussions. Sometimes, to our dismay, we realize that we are reinforcing large systems based on privilege and ecological blindness.[13] There is no such thing as a karma-free zone.

It was not uncommon in Asia to use beliefs about karma to *evade* responsibility ("It's their karma to be poor—why should I try to help them?"). However, according to other interpretations, karma enjoins a radical degree of responsibility: even though we cannot possibly know all the causes and conditions that have led us to be who we are, we have to take responsibility for our past and our present anyway. Karma can be seen positively as a recognition of the interrelatedness of all beings and phenomena. The work of bodhisattvas and aspiring bodhisattvas takes place in this realm of relatedness.

In all Buddhist cultures the primary arena of karmically significant action has been the individual: one's present situation is supposed to be the fruit of one's past actions, and one's future will be similarly conditioned by one's current actions. Although Buddhism holds that the laws of moral causation operate over vast spans of time, in practice the significant effects of karma were usually thought to extend over a few lifetimes at most. The operation of karma was considered to be orderly and relatively comprehensible—otherwise, the karmic worldview would lose its persuasiveness. So bad things can happen to good people, and vice versa, without necessarily destroying one's faith in some kind of cosmic system of justice.

Current nuclear and environmental problems challenge these assumptions in several ways. Where Buddhism has focused on individual karma, now we also need better ethical analysis of collective behavior. How might notions of group karma be rendered in modern terms? Our understanding of institutional discrimination offers a parallel: even if individuals do not have the intention to discriminate, the institution as a whole may function prejudicially. In that sense, entire systems can have intentions. In the face of systemic problems, engaged Buddhists seek ways to act effectively in groups. Karma theory must also be able to account for the relation between individual and collective responsibility.

Where Buddhism has focused on the immediate future, now we also need ways to account for the effects of our actions over time spans of geologic proportions. (Plutonium remains toxic for 250,000 years, or about 100,000 generations.) And where Buddhism has focused on seemingly comprehensible laws of moral cause-and-effect, now we also need to confront the increased opacity of moral consequences in a nuclear, technological age.

Eco-karma

To illuminate the ethical dimensions of actions that affect the environment, a concept such as *eco-karma* may prove useful.[14] Today, we have a growing appreciation of the ways in which our past behavior has affected the biosphere, and of the ways in which our present behavior will shape the environment of the future. Einstein may have (inadvertently) enunciated a first law of eco-karma when he said, "Humanity will get the fate it deserves."[15]

As new terms are auditioned and defined, one of the tests will be their compatibility with prior Buddhist tradition. Initially, an expansion of karma in an ecological direction does not seem to conform very closely to Buddhism's past. Although Buddhists valued nature highly at different points in various cultures, one hesitates to call premodern Buddhism ecological in the present-day sense of that word. Cardinal virtues such as nonviolence and compassion were applied to individual animals but not to species or ecosystems. At the same time, other features of Buddhism could be cited to justify the invention of eco-karma. Animals, for instance, have been regarded as subject to the laws of karma. In comparison with

Western religious and intellectual history, that belief alone is a significant step away from anthropocentrism (human-centered thinking).

When one attempts to bring some of these considerations to bear on the specific problem of nuclear waste, the complexities intensify. Assigning agency, for instance, is no easy matter. To say that "we" are creating nuclear waste is accurate enough from a far-future perspective—most of us take full advantage of the opportunity to live a developed-world lifestyle, thereby exporting some of the true costs of privilege to distant places or distant generations. We take it for granted that we have abundant electricity twenty-four hours a day. Yet "we" can also be used too loosely. Before one makes blanket assertions about the karma of flicking a light switch, specific situations must sometimes be taken into account. Analysis of a particular region may reveal, for example, that the energy sources there are nearly or fully sustainable (wind power, solar power, and so on). It may also be necessary, on ethical grounds, to draw a distinction between an executive in the nuclear-power industry and, say, a homemaker who uses electricity drawn partially from nuclear sources.

Even if we recognize that nuclear waste puts untold future generations at risk, ethical scrutiny of that legacy depends on a host of factors, including the scientific and social nature of the risks themselves. As ethicist Kristen Shrader-Frechette notes, the magnitude of a risk is only one of the pertinent variables:

> Numerous other factors, in addition to mere magnitude, determine the acceptability of a risk: whether it is assumed voluntarily or imposed involuntarily; whether the effects are immediate or delayed; whether there are or are not alternatives to accepting the risk; whether the degree of risk is known or uncertain; whether exposure to it is essential to one's well-being or merely a luxury; whether it is encountered occupationally or nonoccupationally; whether it is an ordinary hazard or (like cancer) a "dread" one; whether it affects everyone or only sensitive people; whether the factor causing the risk will be used as intended or is likely to be misused; and whether the risk and its effects are reversible or irreversible.[16]

Such complexities may spur contemporary Buddhists to clarify distinctions between karmically significant factors and karmically insignificant factors.

Precisely when we need to take more responsibility for bigger and bigger things, our sense of responsibility is being eroded by powerful social forces. Public figures who try to broach the subject of accountability in moral terms, using available Western principles and language, are often accused of being too moralistic. The Buddhist tradition offers another way and another language. If today's engaged Buddhists manage to refine and enrich karma doctrine to suit current conditions, karma won't be what it used to be, but it may serve constructive purposes in unforeseen arenas.

CHALLENGES OF BUDDHIST-ENVIRONMENTALIST PRACTICE

Although Buddhist environmentalism is a recent development, several practical challenges can already be identified. Some of these are common to any environmental issue; others pertain especially to nuclear waste. Let's imagine a Generic American Buddhist Environmentalist and call him Gabe for short. Assume that Gabe has a deep-seated aspiration to come to enlightenment and an equally deep-seated aspiration to protect the earth. Such a person is likely to encounter a number of stumbling blocks on the Buddhist-environmentalist path, among them the following: discontinuities between traditional Buddhist teachings and contemporary realities; the need to clarify the priority of Dharma work or environmental work; difficulties that attend the creation of public-interest groups; and doubts about the efficacy of symbolic actions in response to ecological threats.

We have seen above that karma doctrine is one domain that reveals potential gaps between past teachings and present circumstances. For someone interested in nuclear-waste issues, the topic of waste offers another example of apparent discontinuity. In Zen, monks and other serious practitioners are not supposed to waste anything or treat anything as waste. The instructive stories are graphic: a novice is scolded for discarding a single chopstick; a monk runs alongside a mountain stream to retrieve a single piece of lettuce; Zen master Dogen uses only half a dipper of water to wash his face. "No waste" usually has two linked meanings in these contexts: "do not waste" and "do not perceive anything as waste."

A contemporary Zen master declared, "Roshi's words that originally there is no rubbish either in men or in things actually comprise the basic truth of Buddhism."[17]

These doctrines and practices are exemplary, and they seem applicable in a broad sense to nuclear waste. If we related to the earth and all living beings with the respect and oneness exhibited by a Dogen, we would probably not produce any nuclear waste in the first place. Or, if constructive purposes (for example, medical uses) unavoidably generated a limited amount of radioactive waste, our descendants would cheer if we were able to safeguard that waste with the intensity of the monk who chased the lettuce leaf downstream.

Yet these same examples also raise some questions. No premodern forms of waste were toxic in the ways that nuclear waste is. How might Zen teachings apply to toxic waste? Dealing with the waste produced by a monastery is one thing; dealing with the tens of thousands of tons of atomic waste generated by nuclear reactors and weapon plants is a problem on a different scale. While a monk may be able to retrieve a stray lettuce leaf before the rice is cooked, plutonium cannot be handled safely until 250,000 years have elapsed. We also notice a discrepancy between the focus on individual action in the Zen examples and the highly complex collective action required for the production and prospective containment of nuclear waste. Attempting to reconcile such gaps, engaged Buddhists seek new approaches that are transformative not only for the toxic waste but also for those who deal with it.

There are only twenty-four hours in a day, and at times an ecologically aware Buddhist must choose (however reluctantly) between one activity and another. If an apparent conflict arises between Dharma work and environmental work, what are the priorities of a Buddhist environmentalist? Imagine that Gabe, on a given day, has mindfully fulfilled family, job, and civic duties and then realizes that he has some free time. "Ah," he thinks to himself, "should I use this hour for some uninterrupted meditation, or should I use it to write my congressman to oppose the makeshift plans for a nuclear dump in our state?" You may alter the hypothetical conditions and substitute any inner-directed practice for meditation, but there will always be situations in which there is a choice between one course and another.

If a practitioner is meditating peacefully in her room, and suddenly outside the window she hears the screech of brakes, a loud thump, and a frantic scream, the proper course of action is obvious. At that moment, running to the scene *is* Buddhism. But when problems are more protracted and complex—as most environmental problems are—it is less clear when a situation calls for one to remain on the mat and when to leave it. Joanna Macy, questioned about the apparent discrepancy between Dharma practice and nuclear-related activism, emphatically replied, "This nuclear work *is* the Dharma. One of the aims of practice is to be able to transform our own actions. For those who are involved in this work, the 'poison fire' is a Dharma teacher."[18]

With regard to environmental problems in general and nuclear issues in particular, Buddhists have experienced difficulty translating the values and practices of Buddhism into meaningful public action, concrete policies, and enduring organizations. Of course, Buddhist environmentalists are not alone in this regard. Charlene Spretnak, an ecofeminist and a practitioner of *vipassana* meditation, asks:

> How can we induce people and institutions to think in terms of the long-range future, and not just in terms of their short-range selfish interest? How can we encourage people to develop their own visions of the future and move more effectively toward them? How can we judge whether new technologies are socially useful—and use those judgments to shape our society?[19]

If Gabe wants to work publicly to motivate leaders and citizens to do the right thing about nuclear waste, one of his first impulses may be to credit Buddhism as a source of inspiration—after all, he is a *Buddhist* environmentalist. But on second thought, he may decide that if he wants to reach mainstream America, a Buddhist label might be counterproductive, tending to confuse or alienate potential supporters. Ironically, it may be most skillful in today's public arena to take the "Buddhism" out of Buddhist environmentalism.

The Buddha's birthday ceremony at the Nevada Test Site, noted above, exemplifies another challenge of Buddhist-environmentalist practice. In the face of real environmental threats—in this case the hazards posed by nuclear weapons and nuclear waste—what is the significance of symbolic/ritual activities? And if rituals *are* among the appropriate responses, what relevance do traditional ritual forms have in contemporary contexts? Several of the participants in the Test Site ceremony wondered aloud if their vows, prostrations, and other gestures have any real impact on the terrible dangers they seek to address. For some, the discrepancies of scale seemed unsurmountable. For others, rituals addressing nuclear concerns would have a better claim to relevance in a society that handled nuclear matters responsibly. A third group recognized the severity of our nuclear plight yet reaffirmed the efficacy of ceremonial acts, even if such behavior appears futile to skeptics.

As Buddhists and others struggle to come to terms with nuclear waste, they find that their fears and hopes call out for vehicles of expression that go beyond what can be fashioned individually. The leader of a citizen watchdog group in Amarillo, Texas, where plutonium cores from former atom bombs are literally being stacked in bunkers, recently told me of two strong emotions that she experiences in tandem: joy that the stacked cores signify the end of the Cold War, and near-despair at the prospect of safeguarding all the plutonium that is accumulating in her community. We had just left the office of a high-ranking Energy Department official, and my friend was crying quietly as she spoke. Many of today's de facto nuclear guardians would be receptive to new rites of remembrance, innovative rituals of forgiveness, and ceremonies that connect present generations to future generations. Scholars of contemporary environmentalism have suggested that radical environmentalists are engaged in "a kind of ritualized guerrilla warfare over sacred space in America," a contest that pits the desire for consecration against the danger of desecration.[20] In that sense, the Buddhist activists at the Nevada Test Site may have been taking the initial steps in the creation of spiritually evocative nuclear rituals.

ECOLOGY KOANS

Members of the Zen group in Oregon expressed their sense of accountability for nuclear waste by modifying the four bodhisattva vows of

Mahayana Buddhism, as cited above. A more literal rendering of the first bodhisattva vow is: "All beings, without number, I vow to liberate." What does a vow to save all beings mean in a nuclear age? In what ways does it include those who have already been harmed by nuclear-weapon production and nuclear-power production, from Japanese atom-bomb casualties to Navaho uranium miners and Chernobyl children? In what ways does it include the countless future beings, human and nonhuman, who will suffer the prolonged effects of current military and energy policies?

In eighth-century India the Buddhist monk and poet Shantideva proclaimed:

> For as long as space endures
> And for as long as living beings remain,
> Until then may I too abide
> To dispel the misery of the world.[21]

When the current Dalai Lama alludes to Shantideva's stanza he says, "No matter how extensive space, or how extensive time, I will save all beings."[22] This pledge was challenging enough—to comprehend and to actualize—in a premodern age. Today, with an appreciation shaped by science of the immensity of space and time, we also have a newfound awareness of the extensiveness of beings and the extensiveness of the threats to those beings. Thus, to affirm the bodhisattva vow with nuclear realities in mind is to declare a willingness to accept responsibility for the fate of all the beings who will be exposed in the next 250,000 years and beyond to the wastes we have created in just the past fifty years.

Our rational minds tell us that saving all beings is a preposterously grandiose notion. Yet those who undertake to fulfill such an aspiration assert that the very incomprehensibility of the task pushes the mind to deeper and deeper levels, until it becomes possible to transcend constraints of time and space, saving or not saving. Anyone familiar with Zen koans will recognize that bodhisattva vows and comparable declarations have a koan-like quality. A koan, strictly speaking, is a distinctive type of Zen practice:

> A koan is a spiritual puzzle that cannot be solved by the intellect alone. Though conundrums and paradoxes are found in the secular

and sacred literature of many cultures, only in Zen have such formulations developed into an intensive method of religious training. What gives most koans their bite, their intellect-baiting hook, is some detail that defies conventional logic.[23]

A koan differs from a riddle in that the person attempting to solve it *becomes* something in the process. In a similar way, a bodhisattva vow consumes the devotee to the point where she realizes that she is part of the vow.

The ecological crisis itself has koanlike aspects. Nuclear waste is a good example: we have difficulty grasping the problem conceptually, and we flounder when it comes to practical action. There are no certifiably safe ways to contain radioactive materials, yet we do not even have the sense to stop producing them. There may be beneficial ways to engage the following questions as *ecology koans* (or *eco-koans*, if we can stand another neologism):

What is waste?

What is the scope of my mindfulness?

What is my/our responsibility for our environmental legacy? for our nuclear legacy?

What is a spiritually motivated environmentalist's first priority, spiritual work or environmental work?

When do we know that we have done all that can be done?

These questions may lack an "intellect-baiting hook" in the style of classic Zen koans, yet they can nonetheless be probed in the sustained, penetrating way that one probes a koan. The questioning itself is often more valuable than any "answers" that are produced. We may achieve a dependable understanding of these and other ecology koans only after we live with them, allow them to question us, and restrain our impulse to accept merely conceptual solutions.

Some of the classic koans and related texts also invite fresh interpretations in light of contemporary conditions. The ninth-century Ch'an master Nan-ch'uan was once asked, "When one realizes that *there is*, where should one go from there?" Nan-ch'uan replied, "One should go down the hill to become a buffalo in the village below."[24] If asked today, maybe Nan-ch'uan would say, "One should go to Nevada to become a nuclear guardian at Yucca Mountain." Here is another example:

> The priest Hsiang-yen said, "It is as though you were up in a tree, hanging from a branch with your teeth. Your hands and feet can't touch any branch. Someone appears beneath the tree and asks, 'What is the meaning of Bodhidharma's coming from the West?' If you do not answer, you evade your responsibility. If you do answer, you lose your life. What do you do?"[25]

The question "What is the meaning of Bodhidharma's coming from the West?" has the thrust of "What is the essential truth of Zen?" So the hapless protagonist must somehow demonstrate his Zen insight without opening his mouth and falling to his death.

Humanity's current predicament in relation to the earth resembles the predicament of the person hanging from the branch: beyond a certain point, action and nonaction are equally ineffective. Culture historian Thomas Berry seems to be elucidating a planetary version of Hsiang-yen's koan when he writes:

> By entering in to the control of the planet through our sciences and our technologies in these past two centuries, we have assumed responsibilities beyond anything that we are capable of carrying out with any assured success. But now that we have inserted ourselves so extensively into the functioning of the ecosystems of the earth, we cannot simply withdraw and leave the planet and all its life systems to themselves in coping with the poisoning and the other devastation that we have wrought.[26]

If, in the spirit of a bodhisattva vow, we truly embrace the larger responsibilities that we customarily push out of awareness, our lives will change dramatically. Indeed, we will lose our (former) lives. A man hanging from a tree by his teeth, humans inserted irrevocably into earth's ecosystems . . . "If you do not answer, you evade your responsibility. If you do answer, you lose your life." *What do you do?*

NOTES

1. I have not found any previous uses of "nuclear ecology" in Western-language sources, but I have learned of an institute in Moscow called (in translation) the Center for Nuclear Ecology and Energy Policy.

   Any expression has its drawbacks. Nuclear ecology sounds too benign if it is misinterpreted as casting dangerous nuclear realities only in a positive light. Admittedly, nuclear ecology would stretch the meaning(s) of ecology (i.e., nuclear materials are not recyclable the way other materials are). For practical purposes, limits must be defined; I would suggest, for example, that nuclear-disarmament and nonproliferation issues fall outside the scope of nuclear ecology.

2. Francis H. Cook, *Hua-yen Buddhism: The Jewel Net of Indra* (University Park: Pennsylvania State University Press, 1977), 2.

3. Gary Snyder, *Turtle Island* (New York: New Directions, 1974), 94.

4. Thich Nhat Hanh, "The Last Tree," in Allan Hunt Badiner, ed., *Dharma Gaia: A Harvest of Essays in Buddhism and Ecology* (Berkeley: Parallax Press, 1990), 220.

5. The Dalai Lama, "Five-Point Peace Plan for Tibet," in Petra K. Kelly, Gert Bastian, and Pat Aiello, eds., *The Anguish of Tibet* (Berkeley: Parallax Press, 1991), 288, 292. For connections between nuclear waste and Tibet's threatened Buddhist culture, see International Campaign for Tibet, *Nuclear Tibet: Nuclear Weapons and Nuclear Waste on the Tibetan Plateau* (Washington, D.C.: International Campaign for Tibet, 1993).

6. Joanna Macy, *World as Lover, World as Self* (Berkeley: Parallax Press, 1991), 220–237 and passim. See also Kenneth Kraft, "The Greening of Buddhist Practice," in Roger S. Gottlieb, ed., *This Sacred Earth: Religion, Nature, Environment* (New York: Routledge, 1996), 492–494.

7. "Buddhist Vows for Guardianship," in Nuclear Guardianship Project, *Nuclear Guardianship Forum* 1 (spring 1992):2.

8. Tenshin Reb Anderson, "Dedication for Buddha's Birthday at the Gate of the Nevada Nuclear Test Site," 10 April 1994.

9. "Buddhism: Religion of the Moment," *USA Weekend*, 15–17 September 1995.

10. For engaged Buddhists, some of the traditional injunctions of breath-focused meditation practice still have meaning with the added "d," as in "follow your breadth," or "become one with your breadth."

11. Nhat Hanh, "The Last Tree," 220.

12. A study of the "revenge effects" of technology calls for a kind of vigilance that bears resemblance to Buddhist mindfulness; see Edward Tenner, *Why Things Bite Back: Technology and the Revenge of Unintended Consequences* (New York: Alfred A. Knopf, 1996), 277.

13. On average, one American consumes as much of the world's limited resources as fifty citizens of India. Even if a conscientious American Buddhist cuts the average rate of consumption in half, there is still a significant disparity.

14. Here and elsewhere I am guilty of what Ian Harris has called "terminological revisionism." Yet Harris also suggests that redefinitions are "part of a seamless reflexive process inherent to the Buddhist tradition itself" (Ian Harris, "Buddhist Environmental Ethics and Detraditionalization: The Case of EcoBuddhism," *Religion* 25, no. 3 [July 1995]:201–202).

15. Quoted in Peter Weiss, "And Now, Abolition," *Bulletin of the Atomic Scientists* 52, no. 5 (September/October 1996):43.

16. K. S. Shrader-Frechette, "Ethics and Energy," in Tom Regan, ed., *Earthbound: New Introductory Essays in Environmental Ethics* (Philadelphia: Temple University Press, 1984), 121.

17. Morinaga Soko, "My Struggle to Become a Zen Monk," in Kenneth Kraft, ed., *Zen: Tradition and Transition* (New York: Grove Press, 1988), 17.

18. Personal conversation with Joanna Macy, 19 August 1992.

19. Charlene Spretnak, "Ten Key Values of the American Green Movement," in Roger S. Gottlieb, ed., *This Sacred Earth: Religion, Nature, Environment* (New York: Routledge, 1996), 536.

20. David Chidester and Edward T. Linenthal, eds., *American Sacred Space* (Bloomington: Indiana University Press, 1995), 21.

21. Stephen Batchelor, trans., *A Guide to the Bodhisattva's Way of Life* (Dharamsala: Library of Tibetan Works and Archives, 1979), 193.

22. Martin Wassell, producer, *Heart of Tibet: An Intimate Portrait of the Dalai Lama* (New York: Mystic Fire Video, 1991).

23. Kenneth Kraft, *Eloquent Zen: Daito and Early Japanese Zen* (Honolulu: University of Hawaii Press, 1992), 58.

24. John C. H. Wu, *The Golden Age of Zen* (New York: Doubleday, 1996), 96 (slightly edited).

25. Robert Aitken, trans., *The Gateless Barrier* (San Francisco: North Point Press, 1990), 38.

26. Brian Swimme and Thomas Berry, *The Universe Story: From the Primordial Flaring Forth to the Ecozoic Era* (San Francisco: Harper San Francisco, 1992), 252.

Population, Consumption, and the Environment

Rita M. Gross

THIS ESSAY APPLYING BASIC BUDDHIST TEACHINGS to questions regarding fertility control and resource utilization is written by a feminist academic scholar of religion, for whom Buddhism is the long-standing religion of choice. I bring to this essay the perspectives of both an insider trained in Buddhist thought and an outsider with allegiance to the cross-cultural comparative study of religion and broad knowledge of major religious traditions.

As is the case with all major traditions, conclusions relevant to the current situation cannot be quoted from the classic texts: rather, the *values* inherent in the tradition need to be applied to the current, unprecedented crises of overpopulation and excessive consumption that threaten to overwhelm the biosphere. In this essay, I will work to some extent as a Buddhist "constructive theologian," interpreting the tradition in ways that bring the inherited tradition into conversation with contemporary issues and needs.

DEFINING THE ISSUES

This essay addresses the interlocking issues of the environment, resource utilization, and population growth from a Buddhist point of view. Relating these concerns to one another, one can imagine three alternatives: a sufficiently small population living well on a stable, self-renewing resource base; an excessive population living in degraded conditions on an insufficient resource base; or the present pyramid of a few people living well and large numbers of people barely surviving. Obviously, only the first option contains merit. It should be clear that population is the only negotiable element in this complex. In other words, when we look at the three factors under discussion—the environment, population, and consumption—there are two non-negotiables and one negotiable. Fundamentally, it is not negotiable that the human species must live within the boundaries and limits of the biosphere. However it is done, there is no other choice, because there is no life apart from the biosphere. Morally, it is not negotiable that there be an equitable *(equitable,* not *equal)* distribution of resources among the world's people. These two non-negotiables leave population size as the negotiable factor in the equation. It is hard to question the proposition that a human population small enough for everyone to enjoy a decent standard of living without ruining the environment is necessary and desirable. Human beings cannot increase the size of the earth and can only increase its productivity to a limited extent, but we, as a species, *can* control population.

Religions often criticize excessive consumption yet encourage excessive reproduction. Though I will note the Buddhist values that encourage moderate consumption, I will discuss in depth the Buddhist values that encourage moderation and responsibility regarding reproduction, which are considerable. I emphasize these elements in Buddhism precisely because there has been so little discussion of religious arguments that favor restraining human fertility. The example of a major, long-standing world religion whose adherents lead satisfying lives without an overwhelming emphasis on individual procreation is certainly worth investigating. Buddhism can in no way be construed or interpreted as pronatalist in its basic values and orientations. The two religious ideas that are commonly invoked by most religions to justify pronatalist practices are not part of basic Buddhism. First, Buddhism does not require its members to reproduce as a religious duty. Second, most forms of Buddhism do not regard sexuality negatively, as an evil to be avoided unless linked with reproduction (though all forms of Buddhism do include standards for sexual ethics). Therefore, fertility control through contraception as well as abstinence is completely acceptable. The practices regarding fertility and reproduction that would flow from fundamental Buddhist values favor reproduction as a mature and deliberate choice rather than as an accident or a duty.

By contrast, pronatalism as an ideology seems to be rampant on the planet; those who even mildly suggest that unlimited reproduction is not an individual right and could well be destructive are often derided. Pronatalist ideology includes at least three major ideas, all of which are subject to question. First, pronatalists always regard a birth as a positive occasion, under any circumstances, even the most extreme. To suggest that reproduction under many circumstances is irresponsible and might merit censure rather than support makes one unpopular with pronatalists. Second, pronatalists claim that it is necessary to reproduce to be an adequate human being; those who choose to remain childless are seen as less adequate and suffer social and economic liabilities. Third, pronatalists regard reproduction as a private right not subject to public policy, even though they usually insist that the results of their reproduction are a public, even a global, responsibility. The tragedy of pronatalism is that although excessive populations could be cut quite quickly by voluntary means, lacking those, they probably will be cut by involuntary means involving great suffering—diseases, violence, and starvation. Therefore, it is critical to counter pronatalist religious doctrines, socialization, peer pressure, tax policies, sentiments, and values that may help create such suffering.

Before discussing Buddhist teachings as a resource for an ethic of moderation concerning both reproduction and consumption, it is important to acknowledge two controversial issues. First, because the Buddhist concept of all-pervasive interdependence makes sense to me, I believe that individual rights should not extend to the point that they threaten the supportive matrix of life—a point that has already been reached in both consumption and reproduction. Whatever a person's wealth or values that drive them to inappropriate levels of consumption or reproduction, it is hard to argue that they have the right to exercise those levels of consumption or reproduction without regard to their impact on the biosphere. The rhetoric of individual rights and freedoms certainly has cogency against an overly communal and authoritarian social system. But today, that rhetoric and stance threaten to overwhelm the need for restraint in order to protect communities and species.

Second, in the need to counter pronatalist ideologies and policies, I feel we have reached a point beyond relativism. Relativism regarding worldview is virtuous because diversity of worldviews is a valuable resource. On the other hand, relativism regarding basic ethical standards leads to intolerable results. Are we really willing to say of a culture in which women are treated like property or children are exploited that

"that's just their culture"? There would be no international human rights movement if people really believed that ethical standards are completely relative and arbitrary. Because their conduct gravely affects everyone's life, consumption and reproduction are ethical issues of the highest order. It is my position that we can no longer afford to let individuals who believe that they should produce many children do so, just as we no longer condone slavery, exploitation of children, or treating women as chattel. Even though certain long-standing and deeply held cultural and religious values are at stake, I feel pronatalism is an inappropriate ethical stance, given current conditions. Due to modern medicine, the death rate has been greatly reduced but not the birth rate; this has resulted in dangerous growth of populations who want to consume at higher standards than ever before. I believe religions need to adjust their recommendations regarding fertility to these realities.

WALKING THE MIDDLE PATH IN AN INTERDEPENDENT WORLD

One of the most basic teachings of Buddhism concerns interdependence (*pratitya-samutpada* in Sanskrit and *paticca-samuppada* in Pali), which is said to be one of the discoveries made by the Buddha during his enlightenment experience. From a Buddhist perspective, all beings are seen as interconnected with one another in a great web of interdependence rather than as isolated and independent entities. All-pervasive interdependence is part of the Buddhist understanding of the law of cause and effect, which governs all events in the world. Actions unleashed by one being have effects and repercussions throughout the entire cosmos. Therefore, decisions regarding fertility or consumption are not merely private decisions irrelevant to the larger world. Any baby born anywhere on the planet affects the entire interdependent world, as does any consumption of resources. It cannot be argued that either private wealth or low standards of material consumption negate this baby's impact on the universal web of interdependence, though the degree of impact may vary. Nor can it be argued that private desires for children outweigh the need to take into account the impact of such children on the interdependent cosmos, since the laws of cause and effect are not suspended in any case.

Similarly, utilization of resources anywhere has repercussions throughout the entire planetary system. Often, consumption of luxuries in one part of the world is directly related to poverty and suffering in other parts of the world. When this understanding of interdependence is linked with the scientific understanding of the planet as a finite lifeboat, it becomes clear that a Buddhist position would regard appropriate, human, and fair fertility control as a requirement. It is equally clear that a Buddhist position would regard ecologically unsound practices regarding reproduction or consumption as selfishly motivated disregard for the finite, interdependent cosmos.

The vision of cosmic interdependence frames the big picture regarding reproduction and consumption. This vision becomes more detailed when we look specifically at the human realm within the interdependent cosmos. On the one hand, Buddhist traditions value tremendously the good fortune of human rebirth; on the other hand, Buddhists see all sentient beings as fundamentally similar in their urge to avoid pain and to experience well-being. What relates beings to each other is seen as much more fundamental than what divides them into species. Two phrases, "precious human body," and "mother sentient beings," apply when discussing Buddhist views about the human place in the interdependent cosmos. The preciousness of human birth is in no way due to humans having rights over other forms of life, for a human being *was* and could again be another form of life. This web of interdependence is so intimately a web of relationship and shared experience that the traditional Tibetan Buddhist metaphor declares that all beings have at some time been our mothers and we theirs. Rather than feeling superior or assuming that humans have rights over other forms of life, it is said over and over that, since we know how much we do not want to be harmed or to suffer, and since all beings are our relatives, we should not harm them or cause them pain, as much as possible.

In some traditions, rebirth is not necessarily as a human being, depending upon merit and knowledge from previous lives. Among possible rebirths the human rebirth is considered by far the most fortunate and favorable, favored even over rebirth in the more pleasurable divine realms. Taken alone, that belief might seem to encourage unlimited reproduction. But when one understands *why* human birth is so highly regarded, it becomes clear that excessive human reproduction destroys the very conditions that make human rebirth so valued. Rebirth as a human being is valued because human beings, more than any other sentient beings, have the capacity for spiritual development that eventually brings the fulfillment and perfection of enlightenment. Though all beings are said to have the inherent potential for such realization, its achievement is fostered by certain causes and conditions and impeded by others. It is very helpful, even necessary, for that being to be in the proper environment and to have the proper nurturing, physically, emotionally, and spiritually. This is the fundamental reason why a situation of fewer people well taken care of is preferable to many people struggling to survive.

The conditions that make human life desirable and worthwhile are summed up in the Buddhist concept of the Middle Way. This is also discussed as right effort, not too much, not too little, not too tight, not too loose. To avoid extremes in all matters is core to Buddhist practice, learned by the Buddha before his enlightenment experience and as a necessary precondition to it. First he learned that a life of luxury is meaningless; then he had to learn that a life of poverty also leads nowhere. The Buddha concluded that, in order to become fully human, one needs to live in moderation, avoiding the extremes of too much indulgence and too much poverty or self-denial.

The Middle Way emphasizes that too much wealth or ease tends to promote complacency, satisfaction, and grasping for further wealth—all attitudes that are not helpful spiritually. Thus, this concept provides a cogent corrective for the rampant overconsumption that is so linked with overpopulation. However, the Middle Way also points to minimum material and psychological standards necessary for meaningful human life. Buddhism does not idealize poverty and suffering, or regard them as spiritual advantages. Those in dire poverty or grave danger and distress do not have the time or inclination to devote themselves to enlightenment and therefore are unable to benefit fully from their human rebirth.

Before Buddhist teachings can be effective, there must first be a foundation of material well-being and psychological security. One cannot practice meditation on an empty stomach, or create an enlightening environment in the midst of degradation, deprivation, or fear. This point dovetails well with the point made by those who advocate that curbing excessive population growth is much more possible if people have an adequate standard of living. It is by now well known that one of the most effective ways to cut population growth is to improve people's economic lives, that people who have some material wealth can see the cogency of limiting their fertility, whereas people who are already in deeply degraded circumstances do not.

The concepts of interdependence and the Middle Way provide sensible and obvious guidelines regarding fertility control and consumption. Clearly, excessive consumption violates the Middle Path. But so does too much self-denial. Likewise too much fertility for the earth to sustain its offspring, and for communities to provide adequate physical and emotional nurturing, would be a contradiction of the Middle Way. It is crucial that human population not grow beyond the capacity of a family, a community, or the earth to provide a life within the Middle Way to all its members.

THE MAHAYANA BODHISATTVA PATH AND MOTIVATIONS TO REPRODUCE

Many religions, including major Asian traditions with which Buddhism has coexisted, command perpetuation of one's family lineage as a religious obligation. For a Buddhist, having children is not a religious requirement. In the Buddhist vision, one does not need to reproduce biologically to fulfill one's responsibilities to the interdependent web of mother sentient beings, or to realize the most exalted possibilities of human life. The arguments in their traditional form elevate celibacy over the householder lifestyle, rather than childlessness over biological reproduction. Buddhist texts suggest that biological reproduction may interfere with helping the world or realizing one's highest potential. Since Buddhists are like other human beings, it is important to explore what inspires them to embrace religious ideas that do not require reproduction and to investigate Buddhist discussions of appropriate reproduction.

The command to perpetuate family lineage is quite strong in some cultural traditions and fuels pronatalist behaviors. Usually this command coexists with a complex of ideas and practices, including that everyone must marry and reproduce, that one is remiss in one's religious obligations if one does not have a male heir, and that women have few or no options or vocations beyond maternity. Traditions that insist one must reproduce biologically to fulfill one's obligations seldom include the corollary command to not reproduce *excessively*, which could bring the preferred behaviors back from an extreme into some variant of the Middle Way. In fact, such traditions more actively *dis*courage attempts to limit fertility, making people feel unworthy if they want to limit reproduction, even if they have already produced a family heir. From a Buddhist perspective, such concern with perpetuating family lineage can be seen as an extension of ego, of the self-centeredness that causes all suffering.

Even so, Buddhism has come in for major criticism from Asian neighbors for not requiring biological reproduction of its members. This criticism strikes me as very odd. I would reply with two points. First, to contribute that which is most valuable to the interdependent web of mother sentient beings is in no way dependent on biological reproduction. From the Buddhist point of view, pursuit of wisdom and compassion to the point of enlightenment is what satisfies our deepest longings because it speaks to our fundamental human nature. Many Buddhists, contrary to much popular thinking, both Asian and Western, do not live their preferred lifestyle of moderation, meditation, and contemplation out of a self-centered desire to avoid pain. Buddhists do not reject family lineage as an ultimate value in order to seek individual fulfillment instead. Rather, Buddhists claim that we can never find fulfillment through reproduction or consumption, no matter how popular these pursuits may be or how rigorously religious or social traditions may demand them. Instead, the teachings emphasize the need to realize our spiritual potential.

Buddhists could argue that perpetuating family lineage is less important than cultivating and perpetuating our universal human heritage and birthright—the tranquility and joy of enlightenment. Rather than seek self-perpetuation through biological reproduction, Buddhists are encouraged to arouse *bodhicitta*, the basic warmth and compassion inherent to all beings. Then, to use a traditional Tibetan Buddhist metaphor, having recognized that we are pregnant with Buddha-nature *(tathagata-garbha)*, we vow to develop on the bodhisattva's path of compassion pursuing universal liberation. Rather than regarding this choice as a personal loss, it is regarded as joyfully finding one's true purpose in a maze of confused wandering and self-perpetuation.

Given that *bodhicitta* is regarded as the basic inheritance and potential of all sentient beings, including all humans, rousing and nurturing *bodhicitta* in oneself and encouraging its development in sentient beings is fostering family lineage in its widest sense, beyond the boundaries of genetic family, tribe, nation, or even species. Usually translated "awakened heart-mind," my teacher sometimes translated *bodhicitta* as "enlightened gene," thus emphasizing *bodhicitta* both as one's most basic inherited trait and as one's heritage to the mother sentient beings. Who could worry about transmitting family genes when one can awaken, foster, and transmit the gene of enlightenment?

Second, finding one's life purpose in either consumption or reproduction can strengthen what Buddhists call "ego," the deeply rooted human tendency to be self-centered in ways that ultimately cause suffering. In contrast to rousing *bodhicitta*, the motivations for biological reproduction can sometimes be quite narrow and unenlightened. Driven by a desire for self-perpetuation, parents often try to produce carbon copies of themselves, rather than children who are allowed to find their own unique lifeways in the world. The suffering caused by such motivation frequently goes unnoticed and perpetuates itself from generation to generation. As someone reared by parents who wanted a child who would reproduce their values and lifestyle, I am quite well acquainted with the emotional difficulty for children conceived out of their parents' attachment to their agendas. In my experience, most of my middle-class friends think population control is a vital issue—for some other segment of the population. Their drive to reproduce as much as they want is unassailable. The defensiveness that wells up with the intimation that maybe they are motivated by desire for self-perpetuation rather than by bodhisattva practice, suggests that, indeed, my suspicions may be correct. My concerns are deepened further when such people endure extreme expense and go to extreme measures to conceive their own biological child rather than adopt one of the many children already present in the world. Some people simply are overwhelmed by religious, family, or tribal pressures to reproduce and do not even make a personal decision regarding reproduction.

Instead, they are driven by the collective ego of cultural conditioning which functions similarly to the individual ego. Like all forms of ego, collective ego also results in suffering.

Implicit in this call to recognize the negative underbelly of motivations to reproduce is the call to value and validate alternative nonreproductive lifestyles. One of the most powerful psychological weapons of pronatalism is intolerance of diverse lifestyles and denigration of those who are unconventional. A Buddhist could argue that people who are childless should not be ostracized and criticized but rather valued as people who can contribute immensely to the perpetuation of the lineage of enlightenment. As a woman who always realized that in order to contribute my talents to the mother sentient beings I would probably need to remain childless, I am certainly familiar with the prejudice against women who are childless by choice.

Of course, reproduction can be an appropriate arena of Buddhist practice, and much contemporary Buddhist feminist thought is exploring the parameters of reproduction as a Buddhist issue and practice. In my view, for reproduction to be a valid Buddhist choice, it must be motivated by Buddhist principles of egolessness, detachment, compassion, and bodhisattva practice, not by social and religious demands, conventional norms, compulsive desires, biological clocks, or ego-based desires to perpetuate oneself. I believe that such detached and compassionate motivations are possible though not necessarily synonymous with parenthood.

An enlightened being can see the interdependence of all beings and forgo the fiction of private choices that do not impinge on the rest of the matrix of life. One who practices enlightened compassion cherishes all beings, not merely one's family, tribe, nation, or species as worthy of one's care and concern. The great mass of suffering in the world would be dramatically decreased if the detached pursuit of the Middle Way more commonly guided people's choices regarding consumption and reproduction. According to the Buddhist vision of *bodhicitta* as inalienable enlightened gene, both inheritance from and heritage to the mother sentient beings, that which makes life fulfilling is developing compassion and being useful—not self-perpetuation, through either individual egotism or biological perpetuation of family, tribe, or nation. This compassion is not regarded as something one has a duty to develop but, rather, as one's inheritance, the discovery of which makes life worthwhile and joyful. Pronatalism as religious requirement or obligation conflicts with this membership in the lineage of enlightenment. Freed of pronatalist prejudice and valued for their contributions to the lineage of enlightenment, not their biological reproduction, human beings choosing to become parents could do so, and those who make other, equally important contributions to the mother sentient beings could also be celebrated and valued.

SEXUALITY AND REPRODUCTION: A VAJRAYANA PERSPECTIVE

The commandment to perpetuate the family lineage, combined with criticism of people who limit or forego biological reproduction, is certainly one of the major religious sources of pronatalism. The other is antisexual religious rhetoric, which is at least equally powerful and is quite common in many religions, including some forms of Buddhism. Key to this position is that sexual activity is seen as problematic, evil, or detrimental to one's spirituality. Guilt, fear, or mistrust surrounding sexual activity, grounded in religious rhetoric or rules, leads to several equations or symbolic linkages which foster the agenda of pronatalism. Regarding sexual experience as forbidden fruit generally does not foster mindful and responsible sexuality.

The first of the major equations supporting religious fear of sexuality is the linking of sexuality and reproduction. Some religions espouse the view that the major, if not the only, valid purpose of sexuality is reproduction. Sexual activity not in the service of reproduction is said to cause negative moral and spiritual consequences for people who engage in it. Nonreproductive sexual activities, such as masturbation, homoerotic activity, or heterosexual practices that would not result in pregnancy are discouraged or condemned. The effect of such views often aids the pronatalist agenda. Breaking the moral equation between sexual activity and reproduction is a most crucial task, for as long as nonreproductive sexuality is discouraged or condemned, high birth rates are likely to continue. When we compare human patterns of sexual behavior with those of most other animal species, the primary purpose of sexuality in human society seems to be communication and bonding. Unlike most other species, sexual activity between humans can and frequently does occur even when pregnancy is unlikely because a woman, though sexually active, is not fertile. These nonreproductive sexual experiences are actually crucial to bonding between human couples and thus to human society. In addition, sexuality is one of the most powerful methods of human communication. Reproduction is, in fact, far less crucial and far less frequently the outcome of sexual activity.

The view that sexuality should be inextricably linked with reproduction is closely tied with a second equation that also has pronatalist implications. When sex cannot be dissociated from fertility, and when women have no other valid and valued identity or cultural role than motherhood, most women will become mothers. A symbolic and literal identity between femaleness and motherhood is taken for granted. Not many years ago, everyone assumed a female deity would inevitably be a "Mothergoddess." I remember well that such platitudes were commonplace when I began my graduate study in the history of religions. However, this assumption has proven to be naïve and culture-bound. When one investigates the mythology and symbolism of the divine feminine free of prevailing cultural stereotypes, one discovers that divine females are many things in addition to, sometimes instead of, mothers. They are consorts, protectors, teachers, bringers of culture, patrons of the arts, sponsors of wealth. Nor in mythology is their involvement in other cultural activities dependent on their being nonsexual. In the Tibetan Buddhist tradition one meets many divine females who are quite active sexually but who are not mothers or whose fertility is not stressed. Clearly, such religious symbolism and mythology of sexually active but nonreproductive females would not promote pronatalism.

The third equation links nurturing with motherhood, a common stereotype in both traditional religion and popular culture and psychology. If nurturing is so narrowly defined, then those who want to nurture will see no other option than to become parents. The equation between nurturing and motherhood also fosters the prejudice against nonreproducers with the claim that they are selfish and nonnurturing. The most serious implication of this equation is its unfortunate limitation on the understanding of nurturing. If nurturing is associated so closely with motherhood, then other forms of caretaking are not recognized as nurturing and are not greatly encouraged, especially in men. The assumption that nurturing is the specialization, even the monopoly, of mothers, and therefore confined to women, is one of the most consequential legacies of patriarchal stereotyping. Because of the strength of this stereotype, it is often assumed that feminist women, who do not submit to patriarchal stereotypes, are not nurturing. The feminist critique, however, is not a critique of nurturing; it is a critique of the ways in which men are excused from nurturing and women are restricted to, and then punished for, nurturing within the limits of patriarchal gender roles. Feminism is not about restricting nurturing even further or discouraging it, but about recognizing the diversity of its forms and encouraging it in all members of society in such activities as teaching, healing, caring for the earth, or engaging in social action. From a Buddhist point of view, it is equally important that all humans, including men, be defined as nurturers and taught nurturing skills, rather than confining this activity to physical mothers.

Because some of the grounds for fear, mistrust, and guilt surrounding sexuality lie in religion, a religious view of sexuality is significant to this discussion of population, consumption, and the environment. A religious view of sexuality as sacred symbol and experience, relevant rather than detrimental to spiritual development, would broaden the range of options available to women. Vajrayana Buddhism—the last form of Indian Buddhism to develop, significant today in Tibet and becoming more significant in the West—includes just such a resource. For our purposes, it is crucial that discussions of Vajrayana Buddhism be disassociated from the titillating misrepresentations of "tantric sex" that actually stem from fear and guilt about sexuality.

Symbolism and practice of sacred sexuality, such as that found in Tibetan Vajrayana Buddhism, is radically unfamiliar to many religious traditions, including those most common among Westerners. In Vajrayana Buddhism, the paired virtues of wisdom and compassion are personified as female and male. Not only are they personified, they are painted and sculpted in sexual embrace to form the "yab-yum" icon. This icon is used as the basis for contemplative and meditative practices, such as visualizing oneself as the pair joined in embrace. Rather than being a private and perhaps guilt-ridden indulgence, in this religious context sexuality is openly portrayed as a symbol of the most profound religious truths and as contemplative exercise for developing one's innate enlightenment.

One of the most profound implications of this icon is the fact that the primary human relationship symbolizing the nature of reality is that of equal consorts, of male and female as joyous, fully cooperative partners. This contrasts sharply with the tendency to limit religious symbolism to parent-child relationships, whether of Father and Son or of Madonna and Child. It also contrasts strongly with the rejection of divine sexuality that has been such a problem in those same traditions. One cannot help but speculate that open celebration of sexuality as a sacred and profoundly communicative and transformative experience between divine partners would challenge significantly the pronatalist belief that sex without procreation is wrong.

In the Vajrayana Buddhist realm of human relations, this symbolism has led to the possibility of spiritual and dharmic consortship between women and men. (The question of whether nonhetereosexual dharmic relationships are also possible is more difficult to answer.) Such relationships are not conventional domestic arrangements or romantic projections and longings, but are about collegiality and mutual support on the path of spiritual discipline. Sexuality seems to be an element within, but not the basis of, such relationships. Though relatively esoteric, such relationships were, and still are, recognized and valued in late North Indian Vajrayana Buddhism, as well as in Tibetan Buddhism. Western Buddhists are just beginning to discover or recover this possibility of consortship as collegial relationship between fellow seekers of the way and as mode of understanding and communicating with the profound "otherness" of the phenomenal world. To value, valorize, and celebrate such relationships would profoundly undercut pronatalist biases regarding the place of sexuality in human life, as well as contribute greatly to the creation of sane, caring, egalitarian models of relationship between women and men.

Envisioning the Future

ROBERT AITKEN

"SMALL IS BEAUTIFUL," E. F. Schumacher said, but it was not merely size that concerned him. "Buddhist economics must be very different from the economics of modern materialism," he said. "The Buddhist sees the essence of civilization not in a multiplication of wants but in the purification of human character."[1]

Schumacher evokes the etymology of *civilization* as the process of civilizing, of becoming and making civil. Many neglect this ancient wisdom of words in their pursuit of acquisition and consumption, and those with some civility of mind find themselves caught in the dominant order by requirements of time and energy to feed their families. As the acquisitive system burgeons, its collapse is foreshadowed by epidemics, famine, war, and the despoliation of the earth and its forests, waters, and air.

I envision a growing crisis across the world as managers and their multinational systems continue to deplete finite human and natural resources. Great corporations, underwritten by equally great financial institutions, flush away the human habitat and the habitat of thousands of other species far more ruthlessly and on a far greater scale than the gold miners who once hosed down mountains in California. International consortia rule sovereign over all other political authority. Presidents and parliaments and the United Nations itself are delegated decision-making powers that simply carry out previously established agreements.

Citizens of goodwill everywhere despair of the political process. The old enthusiasm to turn out on election day has drastically waned. In the United States, commonly fewer than 50 percent of those eligible cast a ballot. It has become clear that political parties are ineffectual—whether Republican or Democrat, Conservative or Labor—and that practical alternatives must be found.

We can begin our task of developing such alternatives by meeting in informal groups within our larger sanghas to examine politics and economics from a Buddhist perspective. It will be apparent that traditional teachings of interdependence bring into direct question the rationale of accumulating wealth and of governing by hierarchical authority. What, then, is to be done?

Something, certainly. Our practice of the Brahma Viharas—kindliness, compassion, goodwill, and equanimity—would be meaningless if it excluded people, animals, and plants outside our formal sangha. Nothing in the teachings justifies us as a cult that ignores the world. We are not survivalists. On the contrary, it is clear that we're in it together with all beings.

The time has surely come when we speak out as Buddhists, with firm views of harmony as the Tao. I suggest that it is also time for us to take ourselves in hand. We ourselves can establish and engage in the very policies and programs of social and ecological protection and respect that we have heretofore so futilely demanded from authorities. This would be engaged Buddhism, where the sangha is not merely parallel to the forms of conventional society and not merely metaphysical in its universality.

This greater sangha is, moreover, not merely Buddhist. It is possible to identify an eclectic religious evolution that is already under way, one to which we can lend our energies. It can be traced to the beginning of this century, when Tolstoy, Ruskin, Thoreau, and the New Testament fertilized the *Bhagavad Gita* and other Indian texts in the mind and life of M. K. Gandhi. The Southern Buddhist leaders A. T. Ariyaratne and Sulak Sivaraksa and their followers in Sri Lanka and Thailand have adapted Gandhi's "Independence for the Masses" to their own national needs and established programs of self-help and community self-reliance that offer regenerative cells of fulfilling life within their materialist societies.[2]

Mahayana has lagged behind these developments in South and Southeast Asia. In the past, a few Far Eastern monks like Gyogi Bosatsu devoted themselves to good works, another few like Hakuin Zenji raised their voices to the lords of their provinces about the poverty of common people, and still others in Korea and China organized peasant rebellions, but today we do not see widespread movements in traditional Mahayana countries akin to the village self-help programs of Ariyaratne in Sri Lanka, or empowerment networks similar to those established by Sulak in Thailand.

"Self-help" is an inadequate translation of *swaraj*, the term Gandhi used to designate his program of personal and village independence. He was a great social thinker who identified profound human imperatives and natural social potentials. He discerned how significant changes arise from people themselves, rather than from efforts on the part of governments to fine-tune the system.

South Africa and Eastern Europe are two modern examples of change from the bottom up. Perceptions shift, the old notions cannot hold—and down come the state and its ideology. Similar changes are brewing, despite repressions, in Central America. In the United States, the economy appears to be holding up by force of habit and inertia in the face of unimaginable debt, while city governments break down and thousands of families sleep in makeshift shelters.

Not without protest. In the United States, the tireless voices of Ralph Nader, Noam Chomsky, Jerry Brown, and other cogent dissidents remind us and our legislators and judges that our so-called civilization is using up the world. Such spokespeople for conservation, social justice, and peace help to organize opposition to benighted powers and their policies and thus divert the most outrageous programs to less flagrant alternatives.

Like Ariyaratne and Sulak in their social contexts, we as Western Buddhists would also modify the activist role to reflect our culture as well as our spiritual heritage. But surely the dharmic fundamentals would remain.[3] Right Action is part of the Eightfold Path that begins and ends with Right Meditation. Formal practice could also involve study, reciting the ancient texts together, Dharma discussion, religious festivals, and sharing for mutual support.

In our workaday lives, practice would be less formal and could include farming and protecting forests. In the United States, some of our leading intellectuals cultivate the ground. The distinguished poet W. S. Merwin has through his own labor created an arboretum of native Hawaiian plants at his home on Maui. He is thus restoring an important aspect of Hawaiian culture, in gentle opposition to the monocultures of pineapple, sugar, and macadamia nut trees around him. Another progressive intellectual, Wendell Berry, author of some thirty books of poetry, essays, and fiction, is also a small farmer. Still another reformative intellectual and prominent essayist, Wes Jackson, conducts a successful institute for small farmers. Networking is an important feature of Jackson's teaching.

He follows the Amish adage that at least seven cooperating families must live near each other in order for their small individual farms to succeed.[4]

All such enterprise takes hard work and character practice. The two go together. Character, Schumacher says, "is formed primarily by a man's work. And work, properly conducted in conditions of human dignity and freedom, blesses ourselves and equally our products."[5] With dignity and freedom we can collaborate, labor together, on small farms and in cooperatives of all kinds—savings and loan societies, social agencies, clinics, galleries, theaters, markets, and schools—forming networks of decent and dignified modes of life alongside and even within the frames of conventional power. I visualize our humane network having more and more appeal as the power structure continues to fall apart.

This collaboration in networks of mutual aid would follow from our experience of *paticca-samuppada*, interdependent co-arising. All beings arise in systems of biological affinity, whether or not they are even "alive" in a narrow sense. We are born in a world in which all things nurture us. As we mature in our understanding of the Dhamma, we take responsibility for *paticca-samuppada* and continually divert our infantile expectations of being nurtured to an adult responsibility for nurturing others.

Buddhadasa Bhikkhu says:

> The entire cosmos is a cooperative. The sun, the moon, and the stars live together as a cooperative. The same is true for humans and animals, trees and soil. Our bodily parts function as a cooperative. When we realize that the world is a mutual, interdependent, cooperative enterprise, that human beings are all mutual friends in the process of birth, old age, suffering, and death, then we can build a noble, even heavenly environment. If our lives are not based in this truth, then we shall all perish.[6]

Returning to this original track is the path of individuation that transforms childish self-centeredness to mature views and conduct. With careful, constant discipline on the Eightfold Noble Path of the Dharma, greed becomes *dana*, exploitation becomes networking. The root-brain of the newborn becomes the compassionate, religious mind of the elder. Outwardly the elder does not differ from other members; her or his needs for food, clothing, shelter, medicine, sleep, and affection are the same as anyone else's. But the elder's smile is startlingly generous.

It is a smile that rises from the Buddha's own experience. *Paticca-samuppada* is not just a theory but the profound realization that I arise with all beings and all beings arise with me. I suffer with all beings; all beings suffer with me. The path to this fulfillment is long and sometimes hard; it involves restraint and disengagement from ordinary concerns. It is a path that advances over plateaus on its way, and it is important not to camp too long on any one plateau. That plateau is not yet your true home.

Dharmic society begins and prevails with individuals walking this path of compassionate understanding, discerning the noble option at each moment and allowing the other options to drop away. It is a society that looks familiar, with cash registers and merchandise, firefighters and police, theaters and festivals, but the inner flavor is completely different. Like a Chinese restaurant in Madras: the decor is familiar, but the curry is surprising.

In the United States of America, the notion of compassion as the touchstone of conduct and livelihood is discouraged by the culture. Yet here and there one can find Catholic Workers feeding the poor, religious builders creating housing for the homeless, traditional people returning to their old ways of agriculture.

Small is the watchword. Huge is ugly, as James Hillman has pointed out.[7] Huge welfare goes awry, huge housing projects become slums worse than the ones they replace, huge environmental organizations compromise their own principles in order to survive, huge sovereignty movements fall apart with internal dissension. The point is that huge *anything* collapses, including governments, banks, multinational corporations, and the global economy itself—because all things collapse. Small can be fluid, ready to change.

The problem is that the huge might not collapse until it brings everything else down with it. Time may not be on the side of the small. Our awareness of this unprecedented danger impels us to take stock and do what we can with our vision of a dharmic society.

The traditional sangha serves as a model for enterprise in this vision. A like-minded group of five can be a sangha. It can grow to a modest size, split into autonomous groups, and then network. As autonomous lay Buddhist associations, these little communities will not be sanghas in the traditional sense but will be inheritors of the name and of many of the original intentions. They will also be inheritors of the Base Community movements in Latin America and the Philippines—Catholic networks that are inspired by traditional religion and also by nineteenth-century anarchism.[8] Catholic Base Communities serve primarily as worship groups, study groups, moral support societies, and nuclei for social action. They can also form the staff and support structure of small enterprises.

The Catholic Base Community is grounded in Bible study and discussions. In these meetings, one realizes for oneself that God is an ally of those who would liberate the poor and oppressed. This is liberation theology of the heart and gut. It is an internal transformation that releases one's power to labor intimately with others to do God's work.[9]

The Buddhist counterpart of Bible study would be the contemplation and realization of *paticca-samuppada*, of the unity of such intellectual opposites as the one and the many found in Zen practice, and the interdependence presented in the sacred texts, such as the *Hua-yen ching*.[10] Without a literal God as an ally, one is thrown back on one's own resources to find the original track, and there one finds the ever-shifting universe with its recurrent metaphors of interbeing to be the constant ally.

There are other lessons from liberation theology. We learn that we need not quit our jobs to form autonomous lay sanghas. Most Base Communities in Latin America and the Philippines are simply groups that have weekly meetings. In Buddhist countries, co-workers in the same institution can come together for mutual aid and religious practice. In the largest American corporations, such as IBM, there will surely be a number of Buddhists who could form similar groups. Or we can organize cohousing arrangements that provide for the sharing of home maintenance, child care, and transportation and thus free up individuals for their turns at meditation, study, and social action. Buddhist Peace Fellowship chapters might consider how the Base Community design and ideal could help to define and enhance their purposes and programs.[11]

Thus it wouldn't be necessary for the people who work in corporations or government agencies to resign when they start to meet in Buddhist Base Communities. They can remain within their corporation or government agency and encourage the evolution and networking of communities, not necessarily Buddhist, among other corporations and agencies. Of course, the future is obscure, but I find myself relating to the mythology of the Industrial Workers of the World—that as the old forms collapse, the new networks can flourish.

Of course, the collapse, if any, is not going to happen tomorrow. We must not underestimate the staying power of capitalism. Moreover, the complex, dynamic process of networking cannot be put abruptly into place. In studying Mondragón, the prototype of large, dynamic cooperative enterprise in the three Basque counties of northern Spain, William and Kathleen Whyte counted more than a hundred worker cooperatives and supporting organizations with 19,500 workers in 1988. These are small—even tiny—enterprises, linked by very little more than simple goodwill and a profound sense of the common good. Together they form a vast complex of banking, industry, and education that evolved slowly, if steadily, from a single class for technical training set up in 1943.[12]

We must begin with our own training classes. Mondragón is worth our study, as are the worker-owned industries closer to home—for example, the plywood companies in the Pacific Northwest. In 1972 Carl Bellas studied twenty-one such companies whose inner structures consisted of motivated committees devoted to the many aspects of production and whose managers were responsible to a general assembly.[13]

In the course of our training classes, it is also essential that we examine the mechanism of the dominant economy. Usury and its engines have built our civilization. The word *usury* has an old meaning and a modern one. In the spirit of the old meaning of usury—lending money at interest—the banks of the world, large and small, have provided a way for masses of people for many generations across the world to own homes and to operate farms and businesses. In the spirit of the modern meaning of usury, however—the lending of money at *excessive* interest—a number of these banks have become gigantic, ultimately enabling corporations almost as huge to squeeze small farmers from their lands, small shopkeepers from their stores, and to burden homeowners with car and appliance payments and lifetime mortgages.

For over 1,800 years, the Catholic Church had a clear and consistent doctrine on the sin of usury in the old sense of simply lending money at interest. Nearly thirty official church documents were published over the centuries to condemn it.

Out of the other side of the Vatican, however, came an unspoken tolerance for usury so long as it was practiced by Jews. The church blossomed as the Medici family of bankers underwrote the Renaissance, but at the same time, pogroms were all but sanctioned. The moral integrity of the church was compromised. Finally, early in the nineteenth century, this kind of hypocrisy was abandoned—too late in some ways, for the seeds of the Holocaust had already been planted. Today the pope apologizes to the Jews, and even the Vatican has its bank.[14] Usury in both old and modern implications is standard operating procedure in contemporary world culture.

Like the Medicis, however, modern bankers can be philanthropic. In almost every city in the United States, bankers and their institutions are active in support of museums, symphony orchestras, clinics, and schools. Banks have almost the same social function as traditional Asian temples: looking after the poor and promoting cultural activities. This is genuine beneficence, and it is also very good public relations.

In the subdivisions of some American cities, such as the Westwood suburb of Los Angeles, the banks even look like temples. They are indeed the temples of our socioeconomic system. The banker's manner is friendly yet his interest in us is, on the bottom line, limited to the interest he extracts from us.

One of the banks in Hawaii has the motto "We say 'Yes' to you," meaning "We are eager for your money." Their motto is sung interminably on the radio and TV, and when it appears in newspapers and magazines we find ourselves humming the tune. Similar lightweight yet insidious persuasions are used with Third World governments for the construction of freeways and hydroelectric dams and administrative skyscrapers.

Governments and developers in the Third World are, in fact, the dupes of the World Bank and the International Monetary Fund (IMF):

> It is important to note that IMF programs are not designed to increase the welfare of the population. They are designed to bring the external payments account into balance. . . . The IMF is the

ultimate guardian of the interests of capitalists and bankers doing international business.[15]

These are observations of the economist Kari Polyani Levitt, quoted as the epigraph of a study entitled *Banking on Poverty*. The editor of this work concludes that policies of the IMF and the World Bank "make severe intrusions upon the sovereign responsibilities of many governments of the Third World. These policies not only often entail major additional cuts in the living standards of the poorest sectors of Third World societies but are also unlikely to produce the economic results claimed on their behalf."[16]

Grand apartment buildings along the Bay of Bombay show that the First World with its wealth and leisure is alive and well among the prosperous classes of the old Third World. The Third World with its poverty and disease flares up in cities and farms of the old First World. In *The Prosperous Few and the Restless Many*, Noam Chomsky writes:

> In 1971, Nixon dismantled the Bretton Woods system, thereby deregulating currencies.[17] That, and a number of other changes, tremendously expanded the amount of unregulated capital in the world and accelerated what's called the globalization of the economy.
>
> That's a fancy way of saying that you can export jobs to high-repression, low-wage areas.[18]

Factories in South Central Los Angeles moved to Eastern Europe, Mexico, and Indonesia, attracting workers from farms. Meantime, victims in South Central Los Angeles and other depressed areas of the United States, including desolate rural towns, turn in large numbers to crime and drugs to relieve their seemingly hopeless poverty. One million American citizens are currently in prison, with another two million or so on parole or probation. More than half of these have been convicted of drug-related offenses.[19] It's going to get worse. Just as the citizens of Germany elected Hitler chancellor in 1932, opening the door to fascism quite voluntarily, so the citizens of the United States have elected a Congress that seems bent on creating a permanent underclass, with prison expansion to provide much of its housing.

Is there no hope? If big banks, multinational corporations, and cooperating governments maintain their strategy to keep the few prosperous and the many in poverty, then where can small farmers and shopkeepers and managers of clinics and social agencies turn for the money they need to start up their enterprises and to meet emergencies? In the United States, government aid to small businesses and farms, like grants to clinics and social agencies, is being cut back. Such aid is meager or nonexistent in other parts of the world, with notable exceptions in northern Europe.

Revolving credit associations called *hui* in China, *kye* in Korea, and *tanamoshi* in Japan have for generations down to the present provided start-up money for farmers and owners of small businesses, as well as short-term loans for weddings, funerals, and tuition. In Siam there are rice banks and buffalo banks designed for sharing resources and production among the working poor.[20] The Grameen banks of Bangladesh are established for the poor by the poor. Shares are very tiny amounts, amounting to the equivalent of just a few dollars, but in quantity they are adequate for loans at very low interest to farmers and shopkeepers.[21]

Similar traditional cooperatives exist in most other cultures. Such associations are made up of like-minded relatives, friends, neighbors, coworkers, or alumnae. Arrangements for borrowing and repayment among these associations differ, even within the particular cultures.[22] In the United States, cooperatives have been set up outside the system, using scrip and labor credits—most notably, Ithaca Hours, involving 1,200 enterprises. The basic currency in the latter arrangement is equal to ten dollars, considered to be the hourly wage. It is guaranteed by the promise of work by members of the system.[23]

We can utilize such models and develop our own projects to fit our particular requirements and circumstances. We can stand on our own feet and help one another in systems that are designed to serve the many, rather than to aggrandize the wealth of the few.

Again, small is beautiful. Whereas large can be beautiful too, if it is a network of autonomous units, monolithic structures are problematic even when fueled by religious idealism. Islamic economists theorize about a national banking system that functions by investment rather than by a system of interest. However, they point out that such a structure can only work in a country where laws forbid lending at interest and where administrators follow up violations with prosecution.[24] So for those of us who do not dwell in certain Islamic countries that seek to take the Koran literally, such as Pakistan and some of the Gulf states, the macrocosmic concept of interest-free banking is probably not practical.

Of course, revolving credit associations have problems, as do all societies of human beings. There are defaults, but peer pressure among friends and relatives keep these to a minimum. The discipline of Dharma practice would further minimize such problems in a Buddhist loan society. The meetings could be structured with ritual and Dharma talks to remind the members that they are practicing the virtues of the Buddha Dharma and bringing *paticca-samuppada* into play in their workaday lives. They are practicing trust, for all beings are the Buddha, as Hakuin Zenji and countless other teachers remind us.[25] Surely only serious emergencies would occasion a delinquency, and contingency planning could allow for such situations.

Dharma practice could also play a role in the small Buddhist farm or business enterprise. In the 1970s, under the influence of Buddhists, the Honest Business movement arose in San Francisco. This was a network of small shops whose proprietors and assistants met from time to time to encourage one another. Their policy was to serve the public and to accept enough in return from their sales to support themselves, sustain their enterprises, and pay the rent. Their account books were on the sales counters, open to their customers.[26]

The movement itself did not survive, though progressive businesses here and there continue the practice of opening their account books to customers.[27] Apparently the Honest Business network was not well enough established to endure the change in culture from the New Age of the 1970s to the pervasive greed of the 1980s. I suspect there was not a critical mass in the total number of shops involved, and many of them might have been only marginal in their commercial appeal. Perhaps religious commitment was not particularly well rooted. Perhaps also there was not the urgency for alternatives that might be felt in the Third World—an urgency that will surely be felt in all worlds as the dominant system continues to use up natural resources.[28] In any case, we can probably learn from the Honest Business movement and avoid its mistakes.

In establishing small enterprises—including clinics and social agencies and their networks—it is again important not to be content with a plateau. The ordinary entrepreneur, motivated by the need to support a family and plan for tuition and retirement, scrutinizes every option and searches out every niche for possible gain. The manager of an Honest Business must be equally diligent, albeit motivated by service to the community as well as by the family's needs.

Those organizing to lobby for political and economic reforms must also be diligent in following through. The Base Communities throughout the archipelago that forms the Philippines brought down the despot Ferdinand Marcos, but the new society wasn't ready to fly and was put down at once. The plateau was not the peak, and euphoria gave way to feelings of betrayal. However, you can be sure that many of those little communities are still intact. Their members have learned from their immediate history and continue to struggle for justice.

A. J. Muste, the great Quaker organizer of the mid-twentieth century, is said to have remarked, "There is no way to peace; peace is the way." For our purposes, I would reword his pronouncement: "There is no way to a just society; our just societies are the way." Moreover, there is no plateau to rest on, only the inner rest we feel in our work and in our formal practice.

This inner rest is so important. In the short history of the United States, there are many accounts of utopian societies. Almost all of them are gone—some of them lasted only a few weeks. Looking closely, I think we can find that many of them fell apart because they were never firmly established as religious communities. They were content to organize before they were truly organized.

Families fall apart almost as readily as intentional communities these days, and Dharma practice can play a role in the household as well as in the sangha. As Sulak Sivaraksa has said, "When even one member of the household meditates, the entire family benefits."[29] Competition is channeled into the development of talents and skills; greed is channeled into the satisfaction of fulfillment in work. New things and new technology are used appropriately and are not allowed to divert time and energy from the path of individuation and compassion.

New things and new technology are very seductive. When I was a little boy, I lived for a time with my grandparents. These were the days before refrigerators, and we were too far from the city to obtain ice. So under an oak tree outside the kitchen door we had a cooler—a kind of cupboard made mostly of screen, covered with burlap that trailed into a pan of water. The burlap soaked up the water, and evaporation kept the contents of the cupboard cool, the milk fresh, and the butter firm. We didn't need a refrigerator. I can only assume that the reason my grandparents ultimately purchased one in later years was because they were persuaded by advertisements and by their friends.

We too can have coolers just outside the kitchen door or on the apartment veranda, saving the money the refrigerator would cost to help pay for the education of our children. Like our ancestors, we too can walk or take public transportation. We can come together like the Amish and build houses for one another. We can join with our friends and offer rites of passage to sons and daughters in their phase of experimenting and testing the limits of convention.

Our ancestors planned for their descendants; otherwise we might not be here. Our small lay Buddhist societies can provide a structure for Dharma practice, as well as precedent and flexible structures for our descendants to practice the Dharma in turn, for the next ten thousand years.

In formally sustaining the Dharma, we can also practice sustainable agriculture, sustainable tree farming, sustainable enterprise of all kinds. Our ancestors sustain us; we sustain our descendants. Our family members and fellow workers nurture us, and we nurture them—even as *dana* was circulated in ancient times.

Circulating the gift, the Buddhist monk traditionally offers the Dharma, as we offer him food, clothing, shelter, and medicine. But he also is a bachelor. Most of us cannot be itinerant mendicants. Yet as one who has left home, the monk challenges us to leave home as well—without leaving home. There are two meanings of "home" here. One could be the home of the family, but with the distractions that obscure the Dharma. The other may involve the family but is also the inner place of peace and rest, where devotion to the Buddha Way of selflessness and affection is paramount. The monks and their system of *dana* are, in fact, excellent metaphorical models for us. The gift is circulated, enhancing character and dignity with each round. Festivals to celebrate the rounds bring joy to the children and satisfaction to the elders.

I don't suggest that the practice of circulating the gift will be all sweetness and light. The practice would also involve dealing with mean-spirited imperatives, in oneself and in others. The Buddha and his elder leaders made entries in their code of *vinaya* (moral teachings) after instances of conduct that were viewed as inappropriate. Whether the Buddhist Base Community is simply a gathering of like-minded followers of the Dharma that meets for mutual support and study, whether it has organized to lobby for justice, or whether it conducts a business, manages a small farm, or operates a clinic, the guidelines must be clear. General agreements about what constitutes generous conduct and procedure will be valuable as references. Then, as seems appropriate, compassionate kinds of censure for departing from those standards could gradually be set into place. Guidelines should be set for conducting meetings, for carrying out the work, and for networking. There must be teaching, ritual, and sharing. All this comes with trial and error, with precedent as a guide but not a dictator.

Goodwill and perseverance can prevail. The rounds of circulating the gift are as long as ten thousand years, as brief as a moment. Each meeting of the little sangha can be a renewal of practice, each workday a renewal of practice, each encounter, each thought-flash. At each step of the way we remember that people, and indeed the many beings of the world, are more important than goods.

NOTES

1. E. F. Schumacher, *Small Is Beautiful: Economics As If People Mattered* (New York: Harper & Row, 1975), 55.
2. A. T. Ariyaratne, *Collected Works*, vol. 1 (Dehiwala, Sri Lanka: Sarvodia Research Institute, n.d.); Sulak Sivaraksa, *A Buddhist Vision for Renewing Society: Collected Articles by a Concerned Thai Intellectual* (Bangkok: Thai Watana Panich, 1981).
3. I originally used *Dhamma*, the Pali orthography, rather than *Dharma*, out of deference to my Theravada listeners.
4. Wes Jackson, *Altars of Unhewn Stone: Science and the Earth* (San Francisco: North Point Press, 1987), 126.
5. Schumacher, *Small Is Beautiful*, 55. A woman's work blesses us and equally our products as well! Schumacher wrote his words before male writers finally learned that the term "man" is not inclusive.

6. Donald K. Swearer, "Three Legacies of Bhikkhu Buddhadasa," in *The Quest for a New Society*, ed. by Sulak Sivaraksa (Thai Interreligious Commission for Development; Santi Pracha Dhamma Institute, 1994), 17. Cited from Buddhadasa Bhikkhu, *Buddhasasanik Kap Kan Anurak Thamachat (Buddhists and the Conservation of Nature)* (Bangkok: Komol Keemthong Foundation, 1990), 34.

7. James Hillman, "And Huge Is Ugly." Tenth Annual E. F. Schumacher Memorial Lecture, Bristol, England, November 1988.

8. Charles B. Maurer, *Call to Revolution: The Mystical Anarchism of Gustav Landauer* (Detroit: Wayne State University Press, 1972), 58–66. For Spanish origins and developments of the Grupo de Afinidad, see *The Anarchist Collectives: Workers' Self-Management in the Spanish Revolution 1936–1939*, ed. by Sam Dolgof (New York: Free Life Editions, 1974).

9. Mev Puleo, *The Struggle Is One: Voices and Visions of Liberation* (Albany: State University of New York, 1994), 14, 22, 25, 29.

10. Thomas Cleary, *Entry into the Inconceivable: An Introduction to Hua-yen Buddhism* (Honolulu: University of Hawaii Press, 1983), 7.

11. William Foote Whyte and Kathleen King Whyte, *Making Mondragon: The Growth and Dynamics of the Worker Cooperative Complex* (Ithaca, N.Y.: ILR Press, Cornell University, 1988), 3, 30. Other cooperatives worthy of study include the Transnational Information Exchange, which brings together trade unionists in the same industry across the world; the Innovation Centers, designed in Germany to help workers who must deal with new technologies; and Emilia Romagna in northern Italy, networks of independent industries that research and market products jointly. Jeremy Brecher, "Affairs of State," *The Nation* 260, no. 9 (6 March 1995): 321.

12. After presenting this paper, I learned about Tavivat Puntarigvivat's Ph.D. dissertation at Temple University, *Bhikkhu Buddhadasa's Dhammic Socialism in Dialogue with Latin American Liberation Theology* (Ann Arbor, University Microfilms, 1995).

13. Carl J. Bellas, *Industrial Democracy and the Worker-Owned Firm: A Study of Twenty-one Plywood Companies in the Pacific Northwest* (New York: Praeger Publishers, 1972).

14. Peter Stiehler, "The Greed of Usury Oppresses," *The Catholic Agitator* 24, no. 7 (November 1994): 5.

15. Jill Torrie, ed., *Banking on Poverty: The Global Impact of the IMF and World Bank* (Toronto: Between the Lines, 1983), n.p.

16. Torrie, *Banking on Poverty*, 14. See also Doug Bandow and Ian Vásquez, eds., *Perpetuating Poverty: The World Bank, the IMF, and the Developing World* (Washington, D.C.: Cato Institute, 1994), and Kevin Danaher,

Fifty Years Is Enough: The Case Against the World Bank and the IMF (Boston: South End Press, 1994).

17. The Bretton Woods system of international currency regulation was established at the United Nations Monetary and Financial Conference, representing forty-five countries, held at Bretton Woods, New Hampshire, in July 1944. The United States dollar was fixed to the price of gold and became the standard of value for all currencies.

18. Noam Chomsky, *The Prosperous Few and the Restless Many* (Berkeley: Odonian Press, 1993), 6.

19. Gore Vidal, "The Union of the State," *The Nation* 259, no. 22 (26 December 1994): 789.

20. I use *Siam* rather than *Thailand* to honor the position taken by progressive Buddhists in that country, who point out that the Thais are only one of their many ethnic peoples and that the new name was imposed by a Thai autocrat.

21. Abu N. M. Wahid, *The Grameen Bank: Poverty Relief in Bangladesh* (Boulder, Colo.: Westview Press, 1993).

22. See, for example, Ivan Light and Edna Bonacich, *Immigrant Entrepreneurs: Koreans in Los Angeles, 1965–1982* (Berkeley: University of California Press, 1988), 244.

23. Paul Glover, "Creating Economic Democracy with Locally Owned Currency," *Terrain*, December 1994, 10–11. See also "An Alternative to Cash: Beyond Banks or Barter," *New York Times*, 31 May 1993, p. 8, and "The Potential of Local Currency," by Susan Meeker Lowrey, *Z Magazine*, July-August 1995, 16–23.

24. Nejatullah Siddiqui, *Banking Without Interest* (Delhi: Markazi Maktaba Islami, 1979), x–xii.

25. Robert Aitken, *Encouraging Words: Zen Buddhist Teachings for Western Students* (San Francisco: Pantheon Press, 1993), 179.

26. Michael Phillips and Sallie Raspberry, *Honest Business: A Superior Strategy for Starting and Conducting Your Own Business* (New York: Random House, 1981).

27. Real Goods, for example, retailers of merchandise that helps to sustain the habitat. Address: 966 Mazzoni Street, Ukiah, CA 95482-0214. Catalog for March 1995, 37.

28. One does feel this urgency in the literature of Real Goods. Let us hope this remarkable company is a forerunner of others.

29. Sulak Sivaraksa, *A Buddhist Vision for Renewing Society*, 108.

*

PART SEVEN

Passages
for
Ceremonies
and
Daily
Practice

A monk asked Dong-shan, "Is there a practice for people to follow?"

Dong-shan answered, "When you become a real person, there is such a practice."

—*Zen dialogue*

INTRODUCTION

❊

EVERY STREAM OF BUDDHIST TRADITION has its own chants, meditations, rituals, and ceremonies. Only a few of these practice forms address the environment directly. Today, as Buddhism meets environmentalism in Asia and the West, teachers and students are creatively transposing old genres to meet new needs. A fresh "scriptural" collection is emerging, its full shape not yet revealed.

The first part of this section presents recent adaptations of traditional vows and *gatha*s, or practice verses. They offer ways to expand environmental awareness and cultivate mindfulness, especially in the midst of everyday activities such as eating or gardening. A meal verse by Thich Nhat Hanh serves as a succinct reminder:

> In this food,
> I see clearly the presence
> of the entire universe
> supporting my existence.

For Gary Snyder, a traditional Zen chant becomes a way of saying grace when receiving food. In a similar spirit, new versions of the bodhisattva vows and the ten guiding precepts extend the realm of ethical practice to animal and plant relations.

The next selections offer guided meditations on death, compassion, and mutual support—exercises pertinent to the challenges of the ecocrisis. Joanna Macy does not hesitate to turn respected methods of contemplation into tools for spiritual activists. "As part of our planetary heritage," she asserts, "they belong to us all." In a modern context, the Four Brahmaviharas or Great Abodes of the Buddha can reinvigorate intentions to help others and heal the world. Wendy Johnson uses the act of eating an apple to create an extended meditation on the interdependent web. The poem "Flowers" can be used to celebrate the beauty of impermanence even in death.

Both playful and serious, Gary Snyder has adapted the stately language of sutras to inspire environmental caring. Snyder's "Smokey the Bear Sutra," written in 1969, declares:

> Now those who recite this Sutra and then try to put it in practice
>   will accumulate merit as countless as the sands of Arizona and
>   Nevada,
> Will help save the planet Earth from total oil slick,
> Will enter the age of harmony of humans and nature,
> Will win the tender love and caresses of men, women, and beasts,
> Will always have ripe blackberries to eat and a sunny spot under a
>   pine tree to sit at,
> *And in the end will win highest perfect enlightenment.*

Robert Aitken vows "with all beings" to keep his practice simple and to live with restraint. Going from what is close at hand to the vast cosmic context, poet Nanao Sakaki offers a deep-space, deep-time perspective on loving the earth.

The passages assembled here, far from exhaustive, are simply a place to start. As Buddhists find fresh ways to practice in relation to the environment, the store of ecological Buddhist texts will expand and mature. One can sense the outlines of a new collection that draws from the rich spiritual resources of past tradition, preparing for a time when bountiful Dharma rain will again nourish a radiantly restored earth.

✳

The Four Bodhisattva Vows

Beings are numberless, I vow to save them.
Desires are inexhaustible, I vow to end them.
Dharmagates are boundless, I vow to enter them.
Buddha's way is unsurpassable, I vow to become it.

—San Francisco Zen Center

✳

All beings, without number, I vow to liberate.
Endless blind passions I vow to uproot.
Dharma gates, beyond measure, I vow to penetrate.
The Great Way of Buddha I vow to attain.

—Rochester Zen Center

✳

The many beings are numberless, I vow to save them.
Greed, hatred, and ignorance rise endlessly, I vow to
   abandon them.
Dharma-gates are countless, I vow to wake to them.
Buddha's way is unsurpassed, I vow to embody it fully.

—Diamond Sangha, Hawaii

A modern, ecological version of these vows has been written by
Allen Ginsberg, Gary Snyder, and Philip Whalen.

Sentient beings are numberless; I vow to save them.
Consuming desires are endless; I vow to stop them.
Bio-relations are intricate; I vow to honor them.
Nature's way is beautiful; I vow to become it.

Invocation for Earth Relief Ceremony

Rochester Zen Center

Tonight we have offered candles, incense, fruit, and tea,
Chanted sutras and *dharani*.
Whatever merit comes to us from these offerings
We now return to the Earth, sea, and sky.
May our air be left pure!
May our waters be clean!
May our Earth be restored!
May all beings attain Buddhahood!

Ecological Precepts

GREEN GULCH ZEN CENTER

Three Pure Precepts

I vow to refrain from all action that ignores interdependence.
This is our restraint.
I vow to make every effort to act with mindfulness.
This is our activity.
I vow to live for the benefit of all beings.
This is our intention.

Ten Guiding Precepts

Knowing how deeply our lives intertwine,
We vow to not kill.
Knowing how deeply our lives intertwine,
We vow to not take what is not given.
Knowing how deeply our lives intertwine,
We vow to not engage in abusive relationships.
Knowing how deeply our lives intertwine,
We vow to not speak falsely or deceptively.
Knowing how deeply our lives intertwine,
We vow to not harm self or others through poisonous thought
    or substance.
Knowing how deeply our lives intertwine,
We vow to not dwell on past errors.
Knowing how deeply our lives intertwine,
We vow to not speak of self separate from others.
Knowing how deeply our lives intertwine,
We vow to not possess any thing or form of life selfishly.
Knowing how deeply our lives intertwine,
We vow to not harbor ill will toward any plant, animal, or human
    being.
Knowing how deeply our lives intertwine,
We vow to not abuse the great truth of the Three Treasures.

Earth Verses

THICH NHAT HANH

(first step of the day)

The green Earth
is a miracle!
Walking in full awareness,
the wondrous Dharmakaya is revealed.

(turning on water)

Water flows from the high mountains.
Water runs deep in the Earth.
Miraculously, water comes to us
and sustains all life.

(washing hands)

Water flows over my hands.
May I use them skillfully
to preserve our precious planet.

(sweeping)

As I mindfully sweep the ground of enlightenment,
A tree of understanding springs from the Earth.

(walking)

The mind can go in a thousand directions.
But on this beautiful path, I walk in peace.
With each step, a gentle wind.
With each step, a flower.

(gardening)

Earth brings us into life and nourishes us.
Countless as the grains of sand

in the River Ganges,
all births and deaths are present in each breath.

(the watering garden)

Water and sun green these plants.
When the rain of compassion falls,
even the desert becomes an immense, green ocean.

(recycling)

Garbage becomes rose.
Rose becomes compost—
Everything is in transformation.
Even permanence is impermanent.

(watering plants)

Dear plant, do not think you are alone.
This stream of water comes from Earth and sky.
This water *is* the Earth.
We are together for countless lives.

(planting trees)

I entrust myself to Buddha;
Buddha entrusts himself to me.
I entrust myself to Earth;
Earth entrusts herself to me.

Meal Verses

THICH NHAT HANH

(blessing the meal)

This food is the gift of the whole universe—the earth, the sky, and
    much hard work.
May we live in a way that makes us worthy to receive it.
May we transform our unskillful states of mind, especially our greed.
May we take only foods that nourish us and prevent illness.
We accept this food so that we may realize the path of practice.

(filling the plate)

My plate, empty now,
will soon be filled
with precious food.

(seeing the full plate)

In this food,
I see clearly the presence
of the entire universe
supporting my existence.

(sitting down to eat)

Sitting here
is like sitting under the Bodhi tree.
My body is mindfulness itself,
entirely free from distraction.

(before the first bite)

Many beings are struggling for food today.
I pray that they all may have enough to eat.

(contemplating the food)

This plate of food,
so fragrant and appetizing,
also contains much suffering.

(the first four mouthfuls)

With the first taste, I promise to offer joy.
With the second, I promise to help relieve the suffering of others.
With the third, I promise to see others' joy as my own.
With the fourth, I promise to learn the way of nonattachment and
    equanimity.

(upon finishing the meal)

The plate is empty.
My hunger is satisfied.
I vow to live
for the benefit of all beings.

(holding a cup of tea)

This cup of tea in my two hands—
mindfulness is held uprightly!
My mind and body dwell
in the very here and now.

Grace

GARY SNYDER

THERE IS A VERSE CHANTED BY ZEN BUDDHISTS called the Four Great Vows. The first line goes: "Sentient beings are numberless, I vow to save them." *Shujo muhen seigando.* It's a bit daunting to announce this intention—aloud—to the universe daily. This vow stalked me for several years and finally pounced: I realized that I had vowed to let the sentient beings save *me.* In a similar way, the precept against taking life, against causing harm, doesn't stop in the negative. It is urging us to *give* life, to *undo* harm.

Those who attain some ultimate understanding of these things are called buddhas, which means "awakened ones." The word is connected to the English verb "to bud." I once wrote a little parable:

Who the Buddhas Are

All the beings of the universe are already realized. That is, with the exception of one or two beings. In those rare cases the cities, villages, meadows, and forests, with all their birds, flowers, animals, rivers, trees, and humans, that surround such a person, all collaborate to educate, serve, challenge, and instruct such a one, until that person also becomes a New Beginner Enlightened Being. Recently realized beings are enthusiastic to teach and train and start schools and practices. Being able to do this develops their confidence and insight up to the point that they are fully ready to join the seamless world of interdependent play. Such new enlightened beginners are called "buddhas" and they like to say things like "I am enlightened together with the whole universe" and so forth.

—*Boat in a Storm,* 1987

Good luck! one might say. The test of the pudding is in the *eating.* It narrows down to a look at the conduct that is entwined with food. At mealtime (seated on the floor in lines) the Zen monks chant:

Porridge is effective in ten ways
To aid the student of Zen
No limit to the good result
Consummating eternal happiness

and

Oh, all you demons and spirits
We now offer this food to you
May all of you everywhere
Share it with us together

and

We wash our bowls in this water
It has the flavor of ambrosial dew
We offer it to all demons and spirits
May all be filled and satisfied
Om makula sai svaha

And several other verses. These superstitious-sounding old ritual formulas are never mentioned in lectures, but they are at the heart of the teaching. Their import is older than Buddhism or any of the world religions. They are part of the first and last practice of the wild: *Grace*.

Everyone who ever lived took the lives of other animals, pulled plants, plucked fruit, and ate. Primary people have had their own ways of trying to understand the precept of nonharming. They knew that taking life required gratitude and care. There is no death that is not somebody's food, no life that is not somebody's death. Some would take this as a sign that the universe is fundamentally flawed. This leads to a disgust with self, with humanity, and with nature. Otherworldly philosophies end up doing more damage to the planet (and human psyches) than the pain and suffering that is in the existential conditions they seek to transcend.

The archaic religion is to kill god and eat him. Or her. The shimmering food-chain, the food-web, is the scary, beautiful condition of the biosphere. Subsistence people live without excuses. The blood is on your

own hands as you divide the liver from the gallbladder. You have watched
the color fade on the glimmer of the trout. A subsistence economy is a
sacramental economy because it has faced up to one of the critical problems of life and death: the taking of life for food. Contemporary people
do not need to hunt, many cannot even afford meat, and in the developed
world the variety of foods available to us makes the avoidance of meat an
easy choice. Forests in the tropics are cut to make pasture to raise beef
for the American market. Our distance from the source of our food enables us to be superficially more comfortable, and distinctly more ignorant.

Eating is a sacrament. The grace we say clears our hearts and guides
the children and welcomes the guest, all at the same time. We look at
eggs, apples, and stew. They are evidence of plenitude, excess, a great
reproductive exuberance. Millions of grains of grass seed that will become
rice or flour, millions of codfish fry that will never, and *must* never, grow
to maturity. Innumerable little seeds are sacrifices to the food chain. A
parsnip in the ground is a marvel of living chemistry, making sugars and
flavors from earth, air, water. And if we do eat meat it is the life, the
bounce, the swish, of a great alert being with keen ears and lovely eyes,
with four-square feet and a huge beating heart that we eat, let us not
deceive ourselves.

We too will be offerings—we are all edible. And if we are not devoured quickly, we are big enough (like the old down trees) to provide a
long slow meal to the smaller critters. Whale carcasses that sink several
miles deep in the ocean feed organisms in the dark for fifteen years. (It
seems to take about two thousand to exhaust the nutrients in a high civilization.)

At our house we say a Buddhist grace—

We venerate the Three Treasures [teachers, the wild, and friends]
And are thankful for this meal
The work of many people
And the sharing of other forms of life.

Anyone can use a grace from their own tradition (and really give it meaning)—or make up their own. Saying some sort of grace is never inappro-

priate, and speeches and announcements can be tacked onto it. It is a plain, ordinary, old-fashioned little thing to do that connects us with all our ancestors.

A monk asked Dong-shan, "Is there a practice for people to follow?" Dong-shan answered, "When you become a real person, there is such a practice."

Sarvamangalam, Good Luck to All.

Spiritual Exercises for Social Activists

JOANNA MACY

To HEAL OUR SOCIETY, our psyches must heal as well. Haunted by the desperate needs of our time and beset by more commitments than we can easily carry, we may wonder how to find the time and energy for spiritual disciplines. Few of us feel free to take to the cloister or the meditation cushion to seek personal transformation.

We do not need to withdraw from the world or spend long hours in solitary prayer or meditation to begin to wake up to the spiritual power within us. The activities and encounters of our daily lives can serve as the occasion for that kind of discovery. I would like to share five simple exercises that can help in this.

The exercises—on death, loving-kindness, compassion, mutual power, and mutual recognition—happen to be adapted from the Buddhist tradition. As part of our planetary heritage, they belong to us all. No belief system is necessary, only a readiness to attend to the immediacy of your own experience. They will be most useful if read slowly with a quiet mind (a few deep breaths will help), and if put directly into practice in the presence of others. If you read them aloud for others or put them on tape, allow several seconds when three dots (. . .) are marked, and when more are marked (. . . . . .), leave additional time, as appropriate.

MEDITATION ON DEATH

Most spiritual paths begin by recognizing the transiency of human life. Medieval Christians honored this in the mystery play of *Everyman*. Don Juan, the Yaqui sorcerer, taught that the enlightened warrior walks with death at his shoulder. To confront and accept the inevitability of our dying releases us from attachments and frees us to live boldly.

An initial meditation on the Buddhist path involves reflection on the twofold fact that "death is certain" and "the time of death is uncertain." In our world today, nuclear weaponry, serving in a sense as a spiritual teacher, does that meditation for us, for it tells us that we can die together at any moment, without warning. When we allow the reality of that possibility to become conscious, it is painful, but it also jolts us awake to life's vividness, its miraculous quality, heightening our awareness of the beauty and uniqueness of each object and each being.

As an occasional practice in daily life:

Look at the person you encounter (stranger or friend). Let the realization arise in you that this person lives on an endangered planet. He or she may die in a nuclear war, or from the poisons spreading through our world. Observe that face, unique, vulnerable . . . Those eyes still can see; they are not empty sockets . . . the skin is still intact . . . Become aware of your desire that this person be spared such suffering and horror, feel the strength of that desire . . . keep breathing . . . Also let the possibility arise in your consciousness that this may be the person you happen to be with when you die . . . that face the last you see . . . that hand the last you touch . . . it might reach out to help you then, to comfort, to give water . . . Open to the feelings for this person that surface in you with the awareness of this possibility . . . Open to the levels of caring and connection it reveals in you.

MEDITATION ON LOVING-KINDNESS

Loving-kindness, or *metta*, is the first of the four "Abodes of the Buddha," also known as the Brahmaviharas. Meditation to arouse and sustain loving-kindness is a staple of the Sarvodaya Shramadana Movement for community development in Sri Lanka, and is accorded minutes of silence at the outset of every meeting. Organizers and village workers find it useful in developing motivation for service and overcoming feelings of hostility or inadequacy in themselves and others.

I first received instruction in this meditation from a nun in the Tibetan Buddhist tradition. Here is a version that I have adapted for use in the West:

Close your eyes and begin to relax, exhaling to expel tension. Now center in on the normal flow of the breath, letting go of all extraneous thoughts as you passively watch the breathing-in and breathing-out. . . . . .

Now call to mind someone you love very dearly . . . in your mind's eye see the face of that beloved one . . . silently speak her or his name . . . Feel your love for this being, like a current of energy coming through you . . . Now let yourself experience how much you want this person to be free from fear, how intensely you desire that this person be released from greed and ill-will, from confusion and sorrow and the cause of suffering . . . That desire, in all its sincerity and strength, is *metta*, the great loving kindness . . . . . .

Continuing to feel that warm energy flow coming through the heart, see in your mind's eye those with whom you share your daily life, family members, close friends and colleagues, the people you live and work with . . . Let them appear now as in a circle around you. Behold them one by one, silently speaking their names . . . and direct to each in turn that same current of loving-kindness . . . Among these beings may be some with whom you are uncomfortable, in conflict, or tension. With those especially, experience your desire that each be free from fear, from hatred, free from greed and ignorance and the causes of suffering . . . . . .

Now allow to appear, in wider concentric circles, your relations and your acquaintances . . . Let the beam of loving-kindness play on them as well, pausing on the faces that appear randomly in your mind's eye. With them as well, experience how much you want their

freedom from greed, fear, hatred and confusion, how much you want
all beings to be happy . . . . . .

Beyond them, in concentric circles that are wider yet, appear
now all beings with whom you share this planet-time. Though you
have not met, your lives are interconnected in ways beyond knowing.
To these beings as well, direct the same powerful current of loving-
kindness. Experience your desire and your intention that each
awaken from fear and hatred, from greed and confusion . . . that all
beings be released from suffering . . . . . .

As in the ancient Buddhist meditation, we direct the loving-
kindness now to all the "hungry ghosts," the restless spirits that
roam in suffering, still prey to fear and confusion. May they find rest
. . . may they rest in the great loving-kindness and in the deep peace
it brings . . . . . .

By the power of our imagination, let us move out now beyond
our planet, out into the universe, into other solar systems, other gal-
axies, other Buddha-fields. The current of loving-kindness is not affected by physical distances, and we direct it now, as if aiming a beam
of light, to all centers of conscious life . . . And to all sentient beings
everywhere we direct our heartfelt wish that they, too, be free of fear
and greed, of hatred and confusion and the causes of suffering . . .
May all beings be happy . . . . . .

Now, as if from out there in the interstellar distances, we turn
and behold our own planet, our home . . . We see it suspended there
in the blackness of space, blue and white jewel planet turning in the
light of its sun. . . . . . Slowly we approach it, drawing nearer, nearer,
returning to this part of it, this region, this place . . . And as you
approach this place, let yourself see the being you know best of all
. . . the person it has been given you to *be* in this lifetime . . . You
know this person better than anyone else does, know its pain and its
hopes, know its need for love, know how hard it tries . . . Let the
face of this being, your own face, appear before you . . . Speak the
name you are called in love . . . And experience, with that same
strong energy-current of loving-kindness, how deeply you desire that
this being be free from fear, released from greed and hatred, liberated from ignorance and confusion and the causes of suffering . . .

The great loving-kindness linking you to all beings is now directed to your own self . . . know now the fullness of it.

BREATHING THROUGH

Basic to most spiritual traditions, as well as to the systems view of the world, is the recognition that we are not separate, isolated entities, but integral and organic parts of the vast web of life. As such, we are like neurons in a neural net, through which flow currents of awareness of what is happening to us, as a species and as a planet. In that context, the pain we feel for our world is a living testimony to our interconnectedness with it. If we deny this pain, we become like blocked and atrophied neurons, deprived of life's flow and weakening the larger body in which we take being. But if we let it move through us, we affirm our belonging; our collective awareness increases. We can open to the pain of the world in confidence that it can neither shatter nor isolate us, for we are not objects that can break. We are resilient patterns within a vaster web of knowing.

Because we have been conditioned to view ourselves as separate, competitive and thus fragile entities, it takes practice to relearn this kind of resilience. A good way to begin is by practicing simple openness, as in the exercise of "breathing through," adapted from an ancient Buddhist meditation for the development of compassion.

Closing your eyes, focus attention on your breathing. Don't try to breathe any special way, slow or long. Just watch the breathing as it happens in and out. Note the accompanying sensations at the nostrils or upper lip, in the chest or abdomen. Stay passive and alert, like a cat by a mouse hole . . . . . .

As you watch the breath, you note that it happens by itself, without your will, without your deciding each time to inhale or exhale . . . It's as though you're being breathed—being breathed by life . . . Just as everyone in this room, in this city, in this planet now, is being breathed, sustained in a vast, breathing web of life . . . . . .

Now visualize your breath as a stream or ribbon of air passing through you. See it flow up through your nose, down through your windpipe and into your lungs. Now from your lungs take it through your heart. Picture it flowing through your heart and out through an opening there to reconnect with the larger web of life. Let the breath-stream, as it passes through you, appear as one loop within that vast web, connecting you with it . . . . . .

Now open your awareness to the suffering that is present in the world. Drop for now all defenses and open to your knowledge of that suffering. Let it come as concretely as you can . . . concrete images of your fellow beings in pain and need, in fear and isolation, in prisons, hospitals, tenements, hunger camps . . . no need to strain for these images, they are present to you by virtue of our interexistence. Relax and just let them surface . . . the vast and countless hardships of our fellow humans, and of our animal brothers and sisters as well, as they swim the seas and fly the air of this ailing planet . . . Now breathe in the pain like dark granules on the stream of air, up through your nose, down through your trachea, lungs and heart, and out again into the world net . . . You are asked to do nothing for now, but let it pass through your heart . . . . . . Be sure that stream flows through and out again; don't hang on to the pain . . . surrender it for now to the healing resources of life's vast web . . . . . .

With Shantideva, the Buddhist saint, we can say, "Let all sorrows ripen in me." We help them ripen by passing them through our hearts . . . making good rich compost out of all that grief . . . so we can learn from it, enhancing our larger, collective knowing . . .

If no images or feelings arise and there is only blankness, gray and numb, breathe that through. The numbness itself is a very real part of our world . . .

And if what surfaces for you is not the pain of other beings so much as your own personal suffering, breathe that through, too. Your own anguish is an integral part of the grief of our world, and arises with it . . . . . .

Should you feel an ache in the chest, a pressure in the rib cage, as if the heart would break, that is all right. Your heart is not an object that can break . . . But if it were, they say the heart that breaks open can hold the whole universe. Your heart is that large. Trust it. Keep breathing . . . . . .

This guided meditation serves to introduce the process of breathing through, which, once familiar, becomes useful in daily life in the many situations that confront us with painful information. By breathing through the bad news, rather than bracing ourselves against it, we can let it strengthen our sense of belonging in the larger web of being. It helps us remain alert and open, whether reading the newspaper, receiving criticism, or simply being present to a person who suffers.

For activists working for peace, justice, and the environment—those dealing most directly with the griefs of our time—the practice helps prevent burnout. Reminding us of the collective nature of both our problems and our power, it offers a healing measure of humility. It can save us from self-righteousness. For when we can take in our world's pain, accepting it as the price of our caring, we let it inform our acts without needing to inflict it as a punishment on others who are, at the present moment, less involved.

The Great Ball of Merit

Compassion, which is grief in the grief of others, is but one side of the coin. The other side is joy in the joy of others—which in Buddhism is called *mudita*. To the extent that we allow ourselves to identify with the sufferings of other beings, we can identify with their strengths as well. This is very important for a sense of adequacy and resilience, because we face a time of great challenge that demands of us more commitment, endurance, and courage than we can dredge up out of our individual supply. We can learn to draw on the other neurons in the neural net, and view them in a grateful and celebratory fashion, as so much "money in the bank."

This practice is adapted from the "Meditation of Jubilation and Transformation," taught in a Buddhist text written two thousand years ago at the outset of the Mahayana tradition. You can find the original version in chapter six of the *Perfection of Wisdom in 8,000 Lines*. I find it very useful today in two forms. The one closer to the ancient practice is this:

Relax and close your eyes. Open your awareness to the fellow beings who share with you this planet-time . . . . in this town . . . in this country . . . and in other lands . . . . . . See their multitudes in your mind's eye . . . . . . Now let your awareness open wider yet, to encompass all beings who ever lived . . . of all races and creeds and walks of life, rich, poor, kings and beggars, saints and sinners . . . see the vast vistas of these fellow beings stretching into the distance, like successive mountain ranges . . . . . . Now consider the fact that in each of these innumerable lives some act of merit was performed. No matter how stunted or deprived the life, there was a gesture of generosity, a gift of love, an act of valor or self-sacrifice . . . on the battlefield or workplace, hospital or home . . . From these beings in their endless multitudes arose actions of courage, kindness, of teaching and healing. Let yourself see these manifold and immeasurable acts of merit . . . . . .

Now imagine you can sweep together these acts of merit . . . sweep them into a pile in front of you . . . use your hands . . . pile them up . . . pile them into a heap viewing it with gladness and gratitude . . . Now pat them into a ball. It is the Great Ball of Merit . . . hold it now and weigh it in your hands . . . rejoice in it, knowing that no act of goodness is ever lost. It remains ever and always a present resource . . . a means for the transformation of life . . . So now, with jubilation and gratitude, you turn that great ball . . . turn it over . . . over . . . into the healing of our world.

As we can learn from contemporary science and visualize in the holographic model of reality, our lives interpenetrate. In the fluid tapestry of space-time, there is at root no distinction between self and other. The acts and intentions of others are like seeds that can germinate and bear fruit through our own lives, as we take them into awareness and dedicate, or "turn over," that awareness to our own empowerment. Thoreau, Gandhi, Martin Luther King, Dorothy Day, and countless nameless heroes and heroines of our own day, all can be part of our Ball of Merit, from which we can draw inspiration and endurance. Other traditions feature notions similar to this, such as the "cloud of witnesses" of which St. Paul spoke, or the Treasury of Merit in the Catholic Church.

The second, more workaday, version of the Ball of Merit meditation helps us open to the powers in people around us. It is in direct contrast to the commonly accepted, patriarchal notion of power as something personally owned and exerted over others. The exercise prepares us to bring expectant attention to our encounters with other beings, to view them with fresh openness and curiosity as to how they can enhance our Ball of Merit. We can play this inner game with someone opposite us on the bus or across the bargaining table. It is especially useful when dealing with a person with whom we may be in conflict.

> What does this person add to my Great Ball of Merit? What gifts of intellect can enrich our common store? What reserves of stubborn endurance can she or he offer? What flights of fancy or powers of love lurk behind those eyes? What kindness or courage hides in those lips, what healing in those hands?

Then, as with the breathing through exercise, we open ourselves to the presence of these strengths, inhaling our awareness of them. As our awareness grows, we experience our gratitude for them and our capacity to partake.

Often we let our perceptions of the powers of others make us feel inadequate. Alongside an eloquent colleague, we can feel inarticulate; in the presence of an athlete, we can feel weak and clumsy; and we can come to resent both ourself and the other person. In the light of the Great Ball of Merit, however, the gifts and good fortunes of others appear not as competing challenges, but as resources we can honor and take pleasure in. We can learn to play detective, spying out treasures for the enhancement of life from even the unlikeliest material. Like air and sun and water, they form part of our common good.

In addition to releasing us from the mental cramp of envy, this spiritual practice offers two other rewards. One is pleasure in our own acuity, as our merit-detecting ability improves. The second is the response of others who, though ignorant of the game we are playing, sense something in our manner that invites them to disclose more of the person they can be.

LEARNING TO SEE EACH OTHER

This exercise is derived from the Buddhist practice of the Brahmaviharas, also known as the Four Abodes of the Buddha, which are loving-kindness, compassion, joy in the joy of others, and equanimity. Adapted for use in a social context, it helps us to see each other more truly and experience the depths of our interconnections.

In workshops, I offer this as a guided meditation, with participants sitting in pairs facing each other. At its close, I encourage them to proceed to use it, or any portion they like, as they go about the business of their daily lives. It is an excellent antidote to boredom, when our eye falls on another person, say on the subway, or waiting in the checkout line. It charges that idle moment with beauty and discovery. It also is useful when dealing with people whom we are tempted to dislike or disregard; it breaks open our accustomed ways of viewing them. When used like this, as a meditation-in-action, one does not, of course, gaze long and deeply into the other's eyes, as in the guided exercise. A seemingly casual glance is enough.

The guided, group form goes like this:

Sit in pairs. Face each other. Stay silent. Take a couple of deep breaths, centering yourself and exhaling tension . . . Look into each other's eyes . . . If you feel discomfort or an urge to laugh or look away, just note that embarrassment with patience and gentleness, and come back, when you can, to your partner's eyes. You may never see this person again: the opportunity to behold the uniqueness of this particular human being is given to you now . . . . . .

As you look into this person's eyes, let yourself become aware of the powers that are there . . . Open your awareness to the gifts and strengths and the potentialities in this being . . , Behind those eyes are unmeasured reserves of courage and intelligence . . . of patience, endurance, wit and wisdom . . . There are gifts there, of which this person her/himself is unaware . . . Consider what these powers could do for the healing of our planet, if they were to be believed and acted on . . . . As you consider that, let yourself become aware of your desire that this person be free from fear . . . Experience how much you want this being to be free from anger, free from greed, free from sorrow, and the causes of suffering . . . . . . Know that what you are now experiencing is the great loving-kindness . . . . . .

Now, as you look into those eyes, let yourself become aware of the pain that is there. There are sorrows accumulated in that life, as in all human lives, though you can only guess at them. There are disappointments and failures and losses and loneliness and abuse . . . there are hurts beyond the telling . . . Let yourself open to that pain, to hurts that this person may never have told another being . . . . . . You cannot fix that pain, but you can be with it. As you let yourself simply be with that suffering, know that what you are experiencing is the great compassion. It is very good for the healing of our world . . . . . .

As you look into the eyes of this person, consider how good it would be to work together . . . on a joint project, toward a common goal . . . What it could be like, taking risks together . . . conspiring together in zest and laughter . . . celebrating the successes, consoling each other over the setbacks, forgiving each other when you make mistakes . . . and simply being there for each other . . . . . . As you open to that possibility, what you open to is the great wealth: the pleasure in each other's powers, the joy in each other's joy . . . . . .

Lastly, let your awareness drop deep within you like a stone, sinking below the level of what words can express, to the deep web of relationship that underlies all experience. It is the web of life in which you have taken being, in which you are supported, and that interweaves us through all space and time . . . See the being before you as if seeing the face of one who, at another time, another place, was your lover or your enemy, your parent or your child . . . . . . And now you meet again on this brink of time . . . And you know your lives are as intricately interwoven as nerve cells in the mind of a great being . . . . . . Out of that vast net you cannot fall . . . no stupidity, or failure, or cowardice, can ever sever you from that living web. For that is what you are . . . . . . Rest in that knowing. Rest in the Great Peace . . . Out of it we can act, we can venture everything . . . and let

every encounter be a homecoming to our true nature . . . Indeed it
is so . . . . . .

In doing this exercise we realize that we do not have to be particularly noble or saintlike in order to wake up to the power of our connection
with other beings. In our time that simple awakening is the gift the Bomb
holds for us. For all its horror and stupidity, the Bomb, like the toxins we
spew into our world, is also the manifestation of an awesome spiritual
truth—the truth about the hell we create for ourselves when we cease to
learn how to love. Saints, mystics, and prophets throughout the ages saw
that law; now *all* can see it and none can escape its consequences. So we
are caught now in a narrow place where we realize that Moses, Lao-Tzu,
the Buddha, Jesus, and our own inner hearts were right all along; and we
are as scared and frantic as a cornered rat, and as dangerous. But if we let
it, that narrow cul-de-sac can turn into a birth canal, pressing and pushing
us through the darkness of pain, until we are delivered into . . . what?
Love seems too weak a word. It is, as Saint Paul said, "the glory to be
revealed in us." It stirs in us now.

For us to regard the Bomb (or the dying seas, the poisoned air) as a
monstrous injustice to us would suggest that we never took seriously the
injunction to love. Perhaps we thought all along that Gautama and Jesus
were kidding, or their teachings meant only for saints. But now we see,
as an awful revelation, that we are *all* called to be saints—not good necessarily, or pious, or devout—but saints in the sense of just loving each
other. One wonders what terrors this knowledge must hold that we fight
it so, and flee from it in such pain. Can it be that the Bomb, by which we
can extinguish all life, can tell us this? Can force us to face the terrors of
love? Can be the occasion of our birth?

In that possibility we take heart. Even in confusion and fear, with all
our fatigues and petty faults, we can let that awareness work in and
through our lives. Such simple exercises as those offered here can help us
do that, help us to begin to see ourselves and each other with fresh eyes.

Let me close with the same suggestion that closes our workshops. It
is a practice that is a corollary to the earlier death meditation, where we
recognize that the person we meet may die in a nuclear war. Look at the

next person you see. It may be lover, child, co-worker, bus driver, or your own face in the mirror. Regard him or her with the recognition that:

In this person are gifts for the healing of our world. In him/her are powers that can redound to the joy of all beings.

Apple Meditation

WENDY JOHNSON

TODAY THE APPLE TREES OF NORTHERN OREGON offer you their great treasure. The earth herself, laid bare by the hoe's curved fang, brings up the heavy apple harvest of summer's end. Take this Jonagold apple into your hand. Reclaim your true liberty and courage: in full mindfulness and happiness, hold the fruit of understanding and compassion. Let your intellect, your thinking mind, float away on the back of the afternoon clouds.

The apple tree calls you into the center of your garden, into your own body. Gather yourself. In the heat of the afternoon, lift up your breathing and walk in the cool of the garden. With every breath in, a cool breeze rises; with every breath out, coolness pervades the garden. In the center of your garden is a tree—some call it the tree of knowledge, knowledge of good and evil; some call it the tree of action and repose; come call it the tree of life. Come into the center of the garden and sit under this ancient tree.

The apple has flourished since the Neolithic era. Arising in southwestern Asia, in Turkestan and the Caucasian Mountains, the original apple was the wild Siberian crabapple. Charred remains of an apple have been found in prehistoric lake dwellings in Switzerland, evidence of the eastern migration of the apple more than one hundred thousand years ago. The apple is the oldest of the rose-family fruits, sharing a direct lineage with the pear and medlar, quince and hawthorn, and with many other Rosaceae ancestors, among them the wild sisters of woodlands and mountains—alpine strawberry, tart currant, and thorny gooseberry. A "pomme" fruit, all apples have a true core. In this heart of the rose fruit, the apple seeds are encased in a leathery envelope, protected as they grow in the center of the crisp, sweet flesh. If you cut an apple globe along the middle equator, each half of the fruit reveals a star pattern. Taste the stars that dwell at the core, seeds of our joy and compassion.

These seeds have carried the apple out into the world in the craw of raccoon or badger, dropped by jay or robin, spreading themselves across the world. Alexander the Great brought the domestic apple out of Persia to Greece, 400 years before the birth of Christ. The parent of the Jonagold apple you hold in your hand is a descendant of this migration. All dessert apples are grafted onto the roots of crabapples. This means that the choicest apples share a common lineage: strong, wild roots of the ancient ancestral crabapple with a recent variety grafted onto the roots for refined flavor. The particular rootstock of this semidwarf apple is called the Paradise Apple stock, "paradise" from the Sanskrit word for "small enclosed park or garden."

Even now, all about us, autumn is assembling. Lean back against your tree. Let your breathing join the breath of the tree. In autumn, roots plunge down into the raw mineral depths of the earth, and trees turn inward. Feel secure in your stem and in your core: turn inward, send your roots down, let your true taste ripen. This is the work of coming home. Sit down with others and work for deep, tap-rooting happiness and courage in our times.

The apple tree loosens her leaves; they spin down around you. All summer long these leaves have breathed in carbon dioxide from the wide sky, breathing to form the apple in your hand. We know that it takes thirty to forty breathing leaves to provide one beautiful piece of fruit. Leaves breathe as we breathe, giving back to the sky moisture drawn up by the roots of the apple. An apple tree in peak growth returns to the atmosphere fifteen tons of transpired water in one growing season. Now these leaves release their stem hold, drifting down around us to become black soil with the winter rains. Let your breathing rise and fall with the breath of the leaves.

Lift your apple and breathe in its perfume. Feel the smooth burnished gold skin of the fruit. Imagine the bees working the apple blossoms of spring, fumbling in the apple flowers to pollinate the fruit you hold today. The apple contains the bee: in her lifetime one honeybee produces a teaspoonful of honey, perhaps gathered from the orchards of these very fruits. Remember her work as you taste the sweetness of this fruit.

These apples were harvested from the fertile valleys of northeastern Oregon. They are watered from the Columbia River, the second-largest westward-flowing river on the North American continent. The source waters of the Columbia River are mountain springs and lakes high in the western Canadian Rockies. The headwaters flow through thick forests of fir and larch, hemlock and spruce. In these forests roam bear, bighorn sheep, moose, and timber wolves. They drink from the same waters that nourished your apple. Although there are more than fifty hydroelectric dams on the great Columbia River, this watershed is not entirely tamed. In the Columbia River Gorge where this fruit was gathered, tributary waterfalls such as Bridal Veil, Elowah, Multnomah, and Horsetail Falls plunge more than 200 feet to the river as it completes its 1,200-mile journey to the sea.

Who picked this fruit for market? Perhaps descendants of the native Chinook or Clackamas people, or heirs of the Tillamook or Multnomah nations. Take a moment to feel their hands in the fruit you hold. Feel their history: they are people of the salmon, great explorers and artisans of the Columbia River valleys. Or possibly the *compañeros* of the southland worked to bring us this fruit, for they also labor seasonally in northern Oregon. Taste their lives in the living apple in your hands.

And please taste your own life. Taste your choice to stand in the garden, to accept and eat the fruit of the tree of knowledge. Taste your commitment to the garden you stand in, the garden you love. Gather yourself around this fragrant apple, a fruit produced with love and awareness. Taste the work and life of countless beings in the flesh of this fruit, and take all the time in the world to savor the sweetness of this present moment.

Flowers

BUDDHIST TEMPLE OF CHICAGO

Such a solemn world of flowers!
Such a spectacle,
this rich world of the flowers!
All beings are living brightness
Fulfilled with brightness
on the earth, under the heavens.

There is no gap between matter and man,
between sentient and nonsentient being:
all are living, all are dancing—
slate and pebbles are whispering,
dust and trash are shouting,
trees and grasses speak, the land sings.

People are born out of the earth.
The world appears
in the pores of each one's skin.
Gods appear from all beings.
Unimaginable light shines out!
Out of one pore appear
ten thousand times
ten thousand universes.
At the very point of this moment
is a bursting forth of
the eternal Buddha.
One Buddha has the world, and
holds all universes. Each
universe holds ten thousand
times ten thousand
universes.

The world is a flower.
Gods are flowers.
Enlightened ones are flowers.
All phenomena are flowers.
Red flowers, white flowers, green
flowers, yellow flowers, black flowers,
all of the different kinds
of the colors of flowers,
all of the different kinds
of love's shining-forth.
Life unfolds from life
and returns into life.
Such an immense universe!
Oh many lives!
Flowers of gratitude, flowers of sorrow,
flowers of suffering, flowers of joy,
laughter's flowers, anger's flowers,
heaven's flowers, hell's flowers.
Each connected to the others
and each making the others grow.

When our real mind's eye
opens to this world of flowers,
all beings shine,
music echoes through mountains and oceans.
One's world becomes the world of
millions. The individual
becomes the human race.
All lives become the individual—
billions of mirrors
all reflecting each other.

There is no death and life,
there is no death, no life.
There is changing life,
there is unchanging life.

There is nirvana, there is samsara.
Clouds change into
multitudinous forms.
Water changes form as it wishes,
taking the shape of its container.
Flowers change color,
moment by moment.

Such a vivid world!
Such a bright you!
You were born out of these flowers,
you gave birth to these flowers.
You have no beginning and
no ending, you are bottomless and
limitless, even as also
infinitesimal dust.

You are the flower.
You become man and embrace
all women,
you become woman and embrace
all men.
You are love,
you are the flower.
All beings shine out of their uniqueness,
all melt into the oneness of colors.
You are one, you are many,
only one moment, only one
unique place, only the unique you.
Beside you there is nothing:
you dance, appearing in all.

Sitting in silence,
dancing in gratitude,
dancing like the huge waves,
moving like the white clouds,

you see you, you see the you
who sees you,
with gratitude you see,
with gratitude you are seen:
the world as you, you as you;
you as actor, you as audience;
you as subject, you as object.
You are free, you are not free.

From nowhere you came.
You go nowhere.
You stay nowhere.
You are nowhere attached.
You occupy everything,
you occupy nothing.
You are the becoming of
indescribable change.
You are love. You are the flower.

Verses for Environmental Practice

ROBERT AITKEN

Waking up in the morning
   I vow with all beings
to be ready for sparks of the Dharma
from flowers or children or birds.

      ❁

Sitting alone in zazen
   I vow with all beings
to remember I'm sitting together
with mountains, children, and bears.

❊

Looking up at the sky
    I vow with all beings
to remember this infinite ceiling
in every room of my life.

❊

When I stroll around in the city
    I vow with all beings
to notice how lichen and grasses
never give up in despair

❊

Watching a spider at work
    I vow with all beings
to cherish the web of the universe:
touch one point and everything moves.

❊

Preparing the garden for seeds
    I vow with all beings
to nurture the soil to be fertile
each spring for the next thousand years.

❊

When people praise me for something
    I vow with all beings
to return to my vegetable garden
and give credit where credit is due.

❊

With tropical forests in danger
   I vow with all beings
to raise hell with the people responsible
and slash my consumption of trees.

⁜

With resources scarcer and scarcer
   I vow with all beings
to consider the law of proportion:
my have is another's have-not.

⁜

Watching gardeners label their plants
   I vow with all beings
to practice the old horticulture
and let plants identify me.

⁜

Hearing the crickets at night
   I vow with all beings
to keep my practice as simple—
just over and over again.

⁜

Falling asleep at last
   I vow with all beings
to enjoy the dark and the silence
and rest in the vast unknown.

Smokey the Bear Sutra

GARY SNYDER

ONCE IN THE JURASSIC, ABOUT 150 MILLION YEARS AGO, the Great Sun Buddha in this corner of the Infinite Void gave a great Discourse to all the assembled elements and energies: to the standing beings, the walking beings, the flying beings, and the sitting beings— even the grasses. to the number of thirteen billion, each one born from a seed—assembled there: a Discourse concerning Enlightenment on the planet Earth.

"In some future time, there will be a continent called America. It will have great centers of power such as Pyramid Lake, Walden Pond, Mount Rainier, Big Sur, the Everglades, and so forth, and powerful nerves and channels such as the Columbia River, Mississippi River, and Grand Canyon. The human race in that era will get into troubles all over its head and practically wreck everything in spite of its own strong intelligent Buddha-nature.

"The twisting strata of the great mountains and the pulsings of great volcanoes are my love burning deep in the earth. My obstinate compassion is schist and basalt and granite, to be mountains, to bring down the rain. In that future American Era I shall enter a new form, to cure the world of loveless knowledge that seeks with blind hunger, and mindless rage eating food that will not fill it."

And he showed himself in his true form of

SMOKEY THE BEAR.

A handsome smokey-colored brown bear standing on his hind legs, showing that he is aroused and watchful.

Bearing in his right paw the Shovel that digs to the truth beneath appearances, cuts the roots of useless attachments, and flings damp sand on the fires of greed and war;

His left paw in the Mudra of Comradely Display—indicating that all creatures have the full right to live to their limits and that deer, rabbits, chipmunks, snakes, dandelions, and lizards all grow in the realm of the Dharma;

Wearing the blue work overalls symbolic of slaves and laborers, the countless people oppressed by a civilization that claims to save but only destroys;

Wearing the broad-brimmed hat of the West, symbolic of the forces that guard the Wilderness, which is the Natural State of the Dharma and the True Path of beings on earth—all true paths lead through mountains—

With a halo of smoke and flame behind, the forest fires of the kali yuga, fires caused by the stupidity of those who think things can be gained and lost whereas in truth all is contained vast and free in the Blue Sky and Green Earth of One Mind;

Round-bellied to show his kind nature and that the great Earth has food enough for everyone who loves her and trusts her;

Trampling underfoot wasteful freeways and needless suburbs; smashing the worms of capitalism and totalitarianism;

Indicating the Task: his followers, becoming free of cars, houses, canned food, universities, and shoes, master the Three Mysteries of their own Body, Speech, and Mind, and fearlessly chop down the rotten trees and prune out the sick limbs of this country America and then burn the leftover trash.

Wrathful but Calm, Austere but Comic, Smokey the Bear will illuminate those who would help him; but for those who would hinder or slander him,

HE WILL PUT THEM OUT.

Thus his great Mantra:

Namah samanta vajranam chanda maharoshana
Sphataya hum traka ham mam

"I DEDICATE MYSELF TO THE UNIVERSAL DIAMOND—BE THIS RAGING
   FURY DESTROYED"

And he will protect those who love woods and rivers, gods and animals, hoboes and madmen, prisoners and sick people, musicians, playful women, and hopeful children;

And if anyone is threatened by advertising, air pollution, or the police, they should chant SMOKEY THE BEAR'S WAR SPELL:

> DROWN THEIR BUTTS
>
> CRUSH THEIR BUTTS
>
> DROWN THEIR BUTTS
>
> CRUSH THEIR BUTTS

And SMOKEY THE BEAR will surely appear to put the enemy out with his vajra shovel.

> Now those who recite this Sutra and then try to put it in practice
>   will accumulate merit as countless as the sands of Arizona and
>   Nevada,
> Will help save the planet Earth from total oil slick,
> Will enter the age of harmony of humans and nature,
> Will win the tender love and caresses of men, women, and beasts,
> Will always have ripe blackberries to eat and a sunny spot under a
>   pine tree to sit at,

AND IN THE END WILL WIN HIGHEST PERFECT ENLIGHTENMENT.

Thus have we heard.

A Love Letter

Nanao Sakaki

Within a circle of one meter
You sit, pray and sing.

Within a shelter ten meters large
You sleep well, rain sounds a lullaby.

Within a field a hundred meters large
Raise rice and goats.

Within a valley a thousand meters large
Gather firewood, water, wild vegetables and Amanitas.

Within a forest ten kilometers large
Play with raccoons, hawks,
Poison snakes and butterflies.

Mountainous country Shinano
A hundred kilometers large
Where someone lives leisurely, they say.

Within a circle ten thousand kilometers large
Go to see the southern coral reef in summer
Or winter drifting ices in the sea of Okhotsk.

Within a circle ten thousand kilometers large
Walking somewhere on the earth.

Within a circle one hundred thousand kilometers large
Swimming in the sea of shooting stars.

Within a circle a million kilometers large
Upon the spaced-out yellow mustard blossoms
The moon in the east, the sun west.

Within a circle ten billion kilometers large
Pop far out of the solar system mandala.

Within a circle ten thousand light years large
The Galaxy full blooming in spring.

Within a circle one billion light years large
Andromeda is melting away into snowing cherry flowers.

Now within a circle ten billion light years large
All thoughts of time, space are burnt away
There again you sit, pray and sing
You sit, pray and sing.

CREDITS

❋

1. TEACHINGS FROM BUDDHIST TRADITIONS

"Dwelling in the Forest" is from Garma C. C. Chang, ed., *A Treasury of Mahayana Sutras: Selections from the Maharatnakuta Sutra* (University Park, Pa.: The Pennsylvania State University Press, 1983), pp. 300–304. Copyright © 1971 by The Pennsylvania State University Press. Reproduced by permission of the publisher.

"A Tree-Spirit Joins the Assembly of Monks" is from *Buddhist Legends*, pp. 98–99, translated from the original Pali text by Eugene Watson Burlingame © 1921 by the Harvard University Press. Reprinted by permission of Harvard University Press.

"Love for Animals" is from *Cullavagga* 2:72–73 © Pali Text Society. Reprinted by permission of the publisher.

"The Wishing Tree and The Noble Hare" are selections from *Jataka Tales: Birth Stories of the Buddha*, Ethel Beswick (London: John Murray [Publishers] Ltd, 1956), pp. 12–13, 37–40. Reprinted by permission of the publisher.

"Loving-kindness" is a translation of the *Metta Sutta* from *Lovingkindness: The Revolutionary Art of Happiness* by Sharon Salzberg, pp. vii–viii (Boston: Shambhala Publications, 1995). Reprinted by permission of the publisher.

"How Bodhisattvas Serve Sentient Beings" is from Garma C. C. Chang, *The Buddhist Teaching of Totality: The Philosophy of Hwa Yen Buddhism* (University Park, Pa.: The Pennsylvania State University Press, 1971), pp. 194–195. Copyright © 1971 by The Pennsylvania State University Press. Reproduced by permission of the publisher.

"The Bodhisattva Path" is composed of selections from *A Guide to the Bodhisattva's Way of Life*, translated by Stephen Batchelor (Dharamsala, India: Library of Tibetan Works and Archives, 1979), pp. 23–24, 25. Reprinted by permission of the publisher.

"The Hunter and the Deer" is from Garma C. C. Chang, *The Hundred*

Thousand Songs of Milarepa (Seacaucus, N.J.: University Books, 1977), vol. 1, pp. 275–281. Reprinted by arrangement with Carol Publishing Group.

"Dharma Rain" is from *The Lotus Sutra*, pp. 100–102, translated by Burton Watson © 1993 Columbia University Press. Reprinted with permission of the publisher.

"One Truth, Countless Teachings" is a section from *The Flower Ornament Scripture*, translated by Thomas Cleary, vol. 1, pp. 302–304, © 1984. Reprinted by arrangement with Shambhala Publications, Inc., 300 Massachusetts Avenue, Boston, MA 02115.

"At Home in the Mountains" is from the *Theragatha* 1062–71, translated by Andrew Olendzki in *Insight* (spring 1996), p. 37. Reprinted by permission of the translator.

"Cold Mountain Poems" are selections from *Cold Mountain*, translated by Burton Watson © 1970 Columbia University Press. Reprinted with permission of the publisher.

"Haiku in the Rain" are selections from *The Sound of Water*, translated by Sam Hamill © 1995. Reprinted by arrangement with Shambhala Publications, 300 Massachusetts Avenue, Boston, MA 02115.

"The Jewel Net of Indra" is from Thomas Cleary, *Entry into the Inconceivable: An Introduction to Hua-yen Buddhism* (Honolulu: University of Hawaii Press, 1983), pp. 66–68. Reprinted by permission of the publisher.

"The Coincidence of Opposites" is a version by Nelson Foster with assistance from Joan Iten Sutherland. Reprinted by permission of Nelson Foster and Jack Shoemaker from *The Roaring Stream: A New Zen Reader*, edited by Nelson Foster and Jack Shoemaker (Hopewell, N.J.: Ecco Press, 1996), pp. 42–43.

"Letter to the Island" is from Donald S. Lopez, Jr., *Buddhism in Practice* © 1995 by Princeton University Press, pp. 89–91. Reprinted by permission of Princeton University Press.

"Mountains and Waters Sutra" is from *Moon in a Dewdrop: Writings of Zen Master Dogen*, edited by Kazuaki Tanahashi, pp. 97–107 © 1985 by the San Francisco Zen Center. Reprinted by permission of North Point Press, a division of Farrar, Straus, and Giroux, LLC.

"Poetry of Daito" is from Kenneth Kraft, *Eloquent Zen: Daito and Early Japanese Zen* (Honolulu: University of Hawaii Press, 1992), pp. 186–189, 192. Reprinted by permission of the publisher.

2. Contemporary Interpretations of the Teachings

"The Sun My Heart" is reprinted from *Love in Action* (1993) by Thich Nhat Hanh, pp. 127–138, with permission of Parallax Press, Berkeley, California.

"Early Buddhist Attitudes toward Nature" was originally published as "The Buddhist Attitude towards Nature" by Lily de Silva in Klas Sandell, editor, *Buddhist Perspectives on the Ecocrisis*, Wheel Publication No. 346/348 (Kandy, Sri Lanka: Buddhist Publication Society, 1987), pp. 9–29. Excerpted and reprinted by permission of the publisher.

"Thoughts on the Jatakas" is reprinted from *The Path of Compassion: Writings on Socially Engaged Buddhism* (1985) edited by Fred Eppsteiner, pp. 97–102, with permission of Parallax Press, Berkeley, California.

"Enlightenment for Plants and Trees," originally published as "Sattva: Enlightenment for Plants and Trees," is reprinted from *Dharma Gaia: A Harvest of Essays in Buddhism and Ecology* (1990), pp. 136–144, edited by Allan Hunt Badiner, with permission of Parallax Press, Berkeley, California.

"Buddhism with a Small *b*" is reprinted from *Seeds of Peace: A Buddhist Vision for Renewing Society* (1992) by Sulak Sivaraksa, pp. 62–72, with permission of Parallax Press, Berkeley, California.

"Blue Mountains Constantly Walking" is from *The Practice of the Wild: Essays* by Gary Snyder, pp. 97–115. © 1990 by Gary Snyder. Reprinted by permission of North Point Press, a division of Farrar, Straus, and Giroux, LLC.

"River Seeing the River" by Abbot John Daido Loori in *Mountain Record* 14:3 (spring 1996), pp. 2–10. Reprinted by permission of the publisher.

"The Third Turning of the Wheel" is excerpted from an article by Joanna Macy originally published in *Inquiring Mind* 5:2 (winter 1989), pp. 1, 10–12. Reprinted by permission of *Inquiring Mind*, a *dana*-supported journal of the Vipassana community, P.O. Box 9999, Berkeley, CA 94709.

3. BUDDHISM IN THE WORLD

"Buddhist Solutions for the Twenty-first Century" is excerpted from a talk given to the World Parliament of Religions, Chicago, 1993, and published as "A Buddhist Solution for the Twenty-first Century" by P. A. Payutto in *Seeds of Peace* 10:2 (May–August 1994), pp. 35–39. Reprinted by permission of the publisher.

"The Religion of Consumerism" and "Development As If People Mattered" are reprinted from *Seeds of Peace: A Buddhist Vision for Renewing Society* (1992) by Sulak Sivaraksa, pp. 3–9, 44–54, with permission of Parallax Press, Berkeley, California.

"Thailand's Ecology Monks" was originally published as "Buddhist Natural Conservation in Thailand" by Pipob Udomittipong in *Seeds of Peace* 11:1 (January–April 1995), pp. 39–42. Reprinted by permission of the publisher.

"Tree Ordination in Thailand" is excerpted from "The Ordination of a Tree: The Buddhist Ecology Movement in Thailand" by Susan M. Darlington in *Ethnology* 37(1):1–15, winter 1998. Reprinted by permission of the publisher and author.

"Dhamma Walk around Songkhla Lake" is an unpublished manuscript © Santikaro Bhikkhu. Reproduced by permission of the author.

"Resisting the Yadana Pipeline" was originally published as "Kalayanami-tra's Action on the Yadana Gas Pipelines" by Parvel Gmuzdek in *Seeds of Peace* 13:3 (September–December 1997), pp. 23–26. Reprinted by permission of the publisher.

"The Agony of Tibet" is reprinted from *The Anguish of Tibet* (1991) edited by Petra K. Kelly, Gert Bastian, and Pat Aiello, pp. 207–216, with permission of Parallax Press, Berkeley, California.

"Make Tibet a Zone of Peace" is from *The Dalai Lama: A Policy of Kindness*, compiled and edited by Sidney Piburn (Ithaca, N.Y.: Snow Lion Publications, 1990), pp. 40–45. Reprinted by permission of the publisher.

4. ENVIRONMENTAL ACTIVISM AS BUDDHIST PRACTICE

"Responsibility and Social action" is reprinted with the permission of Scribner, a Division of Simon and Schuster, from *Awakening to Zen: The Teachings of Roshi Philip Kapleau*, edited by Polly Young-Eisendrath and Rafe Martin, pp. 94–98. © 1997 by Rochester Zen Center.

"Zen Work" was originally published as "On Zen Work" in *Turning Wheel* (winter 1997), pp. 13–15. Reprinted by permission of the author.

"Encouraging Words for Activists" is reprinted with permission from Jo-anna Macy © 1993 Joanna Macy. Originally published as "Schooling Our Inten-tion" by Joanna Macy in *Tricycle: The Buddhist Review* 3:2 (winter 1993), pp. 48–51.

"Practicing with Passion" was originally published as "A Passion for the Dharma" in *Turning Wheel* (fall 1991), pp. 19–20. Reprinted by permission of the author.

"Renunciation and Daring" is made up of selections from *Shambhala: Sacred Path of the Warrior* by Chögyam Trungpa (pp. 20–23, 42–46, 89–92) © 1988. Reprinted by arrangement with Shambhala Publications, Inc., 300 Massachusetts Avenue, Boston, MA 02115.

"Meeting the Dralas" was originally published in *Shambhala Sun* 4:4 (March 1996), pp. 29–32. Reprinted with permission of the author.

"What Can I Do?" was originally published in *Turning Wheel* (winter 1993), pp. 15–17. Reprinted by permission of the author.

"Universal Chainsaw, Universal Forest" was originally published in *Turning Wheel* (winter 1998), pp. 31–33. Reprinted by permission of the author.

"The Rainforest as Teacher" was originally published in *Inquiring Mind* 8:2 (spring 1992), pp. 1, 6–7. Reprinted by permission of the publisher.

"Guarding the Earth" was originally published in *Inquiring Mind* 7:2 (spring 1991), pp. 1, 4–5, 12. Reprinted by permission of the publisher.

5. HOME PRACTICE, WILD PRACTICE

"The Attentive Heart" © 1993 by Stephanie Kaza, *The Attentive Heart: Conversations with Trees*, pp. 157–165. Reprinted by permission of Ballantine Books, a Division of Random House, Inc.

"Meditating with Mountains and Rivers" was originally published in *Inquiring Mind* 13:1 (fall 1996), pp. 17–18. Reprinted by permission of the author.

"In Search of the Snow Leopard" is from *Nine-Headed Dragon River* by Peter Matthiessen, pp. 98–102 © 1985 by the Zen Community of New York. Reprinted by arrangement with Shambhala Publications, Inc., 300 Massachusetts Avenue, Boston, MA 02115.

"The Buddha Got Enlightened under a Tree" is reprinted with permission from Rick Fields © 1992 Rick Fields. This material originally appeared in *Tricycle: The Buddhist Review* 2:2 (winter 1992), pp. 52–54.

"City Practice and Bush Practice" was originally published in *Turning Wheel* (fall 1997), pp. 15–16. Reprinted by permission of the author.

"Mall Mindfulness" was originally published as "The Mall Quest" by Elias Amidon in *Earth Matters* 4:3 (fall 1997), pp. 1–3, a publication of the Northwest Earth Institute. Reprinted with permission of the author.

"Garden Practice" selections are reprinted with permission from Wendy Johnson © 1996 Wendy Johnson. This material originally appeared in *Tricycle: The Buddhist Review* 6:2 (winter 1996); p. 97, 5:4 (summer 1996), pp. 90–91; 6:1 (fall 1996), pp. 126–127 under these titles: "A Non-Repeating Universe," "Year of the Rat," "Breakdown Ball."

"Buddha and the Beasts" is reprinted with permission from Helen Tworkov © 1994 Helen Tworkov. This material originally appeared in *Tricycle: The Buddhist Review* 4:2 (winter 1994), p. 4.

"Vegetarianism as Practice" is reprinted with permission from Philip Glass

6. Challenges in Buddhist Thought and Action

7. Passages for Ceremonies and Daily Practice

"Invocation for Earth Relief Ceremony" was originally published as "Earth Relief Ceremony Eko." Reprinted by permission of Rochester Zen Center, Rochester, New York.

"Ecological Precepts" originally appeared in the *Buddhist Peace Fellowship Newsletter* (summer 1990), p. 33. Reprinted with permission of Wendy Johnson and Stephanie Kaza.

"Earth Verses" are from *Dharma Gaia: A Harvest of Essays in Buddhism and Ecology* (1990), pp. 195–196, under the original title of "Earth Gathas," edited by Allan Hunt Badiner and reprinted with permission of Parallax Press, Berkeley, California.

"Meal Verses" are reprinted from *Plum Village Chanting and Recitation Book* (1999) with permission of Parallax Press, Berkeley, California.

"Grace" is from "Survival and Sacrament" in *The Practice of the Wild* by Gary Snyder, pp. 182–185. © 1990 by Gary Snyder. Reprinted by permission of North Point Press, a divisionh of Farrar, Straus, and Giroux, LLC.

"Spiritual Exercises for Social Activists" is reprinted from *World As Lover, World As Self* (1991), by Joanna Macy, pp. 39–49, with permission of Parallax Press, Berkeley, California.

"Apple Meditation" is reprinted by permission from Wendy Johnson from an unpublished manuscript, October 1993 © Wendy Johnson.

"Flowers" is from the Buddhist Temple of Chicago service book, reprinted by permission of *Zen Bow* 4:3 (Fall 1982), pp. 13–14.

"Verses for Environmental Practice" is reprinted from *The Dragon Who Never Sleeps: Verses for Zen Buddhist Practice* (1992) by Robert Aitken with permission of Parallax Press, Berkeley, California.

"Smokey the Bear Sutra" is from *A Place in Space: Ethics, Aesthetics, and Watersheds* by Gary Snyder (Washington, D.C.: Counterpoint, 1995), pp. 25–28. Reprinted by permission of the publisher.

"Love Letter" © Nanao Sakaki 1987, is from *Break the Mirror* by Nanao Sakaki. Reprinted by permission of the author's agent, Gary Snyder.

CONTRIBUTORS

❊

ROBERT AITKEN, Zen teacher, is founder and retired director of the Diamond Sangha in Honolulu. He cofounded the Buddhist Peace Fellowship in 1978. He is the author of nine books, including *Taking the Path of Zen*, *Encouraging Words*, and *Original Dwelling Place*.

ELIAS AMIDON, a cofounder of the Institute of Deep Ecology, leads wilderness vision quests in the United States and Southeast Asia. He is the coeditor, with Elizabeth Roberts, of *Earth Prayers* and *Prayers for a Thousand Years*.

THE DALAI LAMA is the exiled religious and political leader of Tibet. In 1989 he was awarded the Nobel Peace Prize in recognition of his efforts to find nonviolent solutions to Tibet's plight. He is the author of numerous books, including *A Policy of Kindness* and *The Art of Happiness*.

SUSAN M. DARLINGTON is associate professor of anthropology and Asian studies at Hampshire College in Massachusetts. She is working on a book about the Buddhist ecology movement in Thailand.

LILY DE SILVA is professor of Buddhist studies at the University of Peradeniya in Sri Lanka. She is the author of *One Foot in the World* and other works.

BILL DEVALL, professor emeritus of sociology at Humbolt State University in Arcata, California, is active in the movement to defend old-growth redwood forests. He is the author of *Simple in Means, Rich in Ends* and the coauthor, with George Sessions, of *Deep Ecology*.

RICK FIELDS (1942–1999) was editor of *Yoga Journal* and *The Vajradhatu Sun*. His books include *How the Swans Came to the Lake*, *Instructions to the Cook* (with Bernard Glassman), and *Chop Wood, Carry Water* (with Peggy Taylor et al).

NORMAN FISCHER, Zen teacher, served as abbot of the Green Gulch Zen Center in California, from 1995 through 1999. He is the author of six books of poetry, including *Precisely the Point Being Made*.

PHILIP GLASS is a musical composer living in New York City. His 1976 opera *Einstein on the Beach* is a landmark of modern music-theatre, and his score for *Kundun*, a film about the Dalai Lama, was nominated for an Academy Award.

PARVEL GMUZDEK is a graduate student in environmental leadership at the Naropa Institute in Colorado. He spent a year in Thailand working with the Alternatives to Consumerism Network.

RITA M. GROSS is professor emeritus of comparative studies in religion at the University of Wisconsin, Eau Claire. She is the author of *Soaring and Settling*, *Buddhism after Patriarchy*, and *Feminism and Religion*.

JEREMY HAYWARD, a senior teacher of Shambhala International, lives in France. He is the author of *Perceiving Ordinary Magic*, *Sacred World*, and *Letters to Vanessa*.

WENDY JOHNSON is a teacher in the Order of Interbeing. She has lived at the Green Gulch Zen Center in California since 1975, working in organic horticulture and native plant propagation.

PHILIP KAPLEAU, Zen teacher, established the Rochester Zen Center in 1966 and served as abbot there for twenty years. His books include *Awakening to Zen*, *The Zen of Living and Dying*, and *The Three Pillars of Zen*.

STEPHANIE KAZA is associate professor of environmental studies at the University of Vermont. A former chair of the Buddhist Peace Fellowship board of directors, she is the author of *The Attentive Heart* and numerous articles on Buddhism and ecology.

BODHIN KJOLHEDE, Zen teacher, has been abbot of the Rochester Zen Center, Rochester, New York, since 1986. He has written essays and articles on Zen in America.

KENNETH KRAFT is chair of the department of Religious Studies at Lehigh University, Bethlehem, Pennsylvania. His books include *Eloquent Zen*, *The Wheel of Engaged Buddhism*, and several edited works on contemporary Buddhism.

WILLIAM LaFLEUR is professor of Japanese studies at the University of Pennsylvania. He is the author of *Liquid Life, The Karma of Words, Buddhism*, and other works.

JOHN DAIDO LOORI is abbot of Zen Mountain Monastery in New York State and director of the Mountains and Rivers Order. His books include *The Eight Gates of Zen, Two Arrows Meeting in Mid-Air*, and *The Heart of Being*.

JOANNA MACY is a scholar of Buddhism, general systems theory, and deep ecology. She creates and leads workshops for spiritually motivated activists. Her books include *World as Lover, World as Self* and *Coming Back to Life* (with Molly Young Brown).

RAFE MARTIN, a professional storyteller, lives in Rochester, New York. He is the author of *The Hungry Tigress* and numerous award-winning children's books.

PETER MATTHIESSEN, a writer, naturalist, and Zen teacher, lives in New York State. His nonfiction books include *In the Spirit of Crazy Horse* and *The Snow Leopard*, which won a National Book Award in 1979.

PATRICK McMAHON, formerly a school teacher in northern California, wrote the education column for *Turning Wheel*, the Buddhist Peace Fellowship journal, from 1991 to 1994.

KUYA MINOGUE is founder and resident teacher of Amazenji, a Zen training temple for women in northern British Columbia. During the winter she lives and works in Canadian aboriginal communities.

THICH NHAT HANH is a Zen teacher, poet, and peace advocate. After being exiled from Vietnam in 1966, he created Plum Village, a practice community in southwestern France. His many books include *Being Peace, The Miracle of Mindfulness*, and *Living Buddha, Living Christ*.

WILLIAM OPHULS, a former member of the U.S. Foreign Service, has taught political science at Northwestern University. He is the author of *Requiem for Modern Politics* and *Ecology and the Politics of Scarcity*.

VANYA PALMERS, of Lucerne, Switzerland, codirects a retreat center in the Austrian Alps. He has been active in the animal rights movement in Europe and the United States.

PRAYUDH PAYUTTO, a Thai scholar-monk, was awarded the UNESCO Prize for Peace Education in 1994. He is the author of *Buddhadhamma* and numerous works in Thai.

GALEN ROWELL, nature photographer, has published several books on wilderness sites around the world. He coauthored *My Tibet* with the Dalai Lama.

NANAO SAKAKI, of Japan, is a poet, naturalist, and environmental activist. He is the author of a collection of poems, *Break the Mirror*, and numerous works in Japanese.

SANTIKARO BHIKKHU, an American, was ordained a monk in Thailand in 1985. He is active in the International Network of Engaged Buddhists and has translated several works by the late teacher Buddhadasa.

JOHN SEED, of New South Wales, Australia, is director of the Rainforest Information Center and editor of *World Rainforest Report*. He is the coauthor, with Joanna Macy, et al, of *Thinking Like a Mountain*.

SULAK SIVARAKSA, of Thailand, is cofounder of the International Network of Engaged Buddhists. A Nobel Peace Prize nominee, he won the Right Livelihood Award in 1995. His many books include *Seeds of Peace*, *Global Healing*, and *A Buddhist Vision for Renewing Society*.

GARY SNYDER is founder of the Ring of Bone Zendo in the Sierra foothills of northern California. He received the Pulitzer Prize in 1975 for his poetry collection *Turtle Island*. His other works include *Earth House Hold*, *The Practice of the Wild*, and *Mountains and Rivers Without End*.

PETER TIMMERMAN, a research associate at the University of Toronto's Institute for Environmental Studies, is the author of reports on global warming and other environmental problems.

CHRISTOPHER TITMUSS, the spiritual director of Gaia House Trust in South Devon, England, leads meditation retreats worldwide. He is the author of *The Green Buddha*, *Light on Enlightenment*, and *An Awakened Life*.

CHÖGYAM TRUNGPA (1939–1987) was recognized as a *tulku* (incarnate descendant of a lama) at eighteen months of age. He fled Tibet in 1959. He is founder of Vajradhatu and the Naropa Institute, and the author of numerous books, including *Cutting Through Spiritual Materialism*.

HELEN TWORKOV, the author of *Zen in America*, founded *Tricycle: The Buddhist Review* in 1991 and has since served as editor-in-chief. She lives in New York City.

PIPOB UDOMITTIPONG, of Thailand, is an environmental activist. He has worked for the Thai Interreligious Commission for Development and other nongovernmental organizations.

ERIN VOLHEIM, a former student at the Green Gulch Zen Center in California, is a founding member of Ecosattva, a group of Buddhist environmental activists.

INDEX OF CONTRIBUTORS

✻